HOME-BASED SERVICES FOR HIGH-RISK YOUTH

Assessment, Wraparound Planning, and Service Delivery

By
Stacey M. Cornett, MSW, LCSW, IMH-E®(IV)

CRI
Civic Research Institute
4478 U.S. Route 27 • P.O. Box 585 • Kingston, NJ 08528

Library of Congress Cataloging in Publication Data
Home-Based Services for High-Risk Youth: Assessment,
Wraparound Planning, and Service Delivery/Stacey M. Cornett,
MSW, LCSW, IMH-E®(IV)

ISBN 978-1-887554-83-1

Library of Congress Control Number: 2010943237

To my family who carries me through all of life's challenges and rewards:
My husband, Nathan, who is my greatest love and support.
My children, Logan, Gabrielle, Heather, Josie, and Lanie, who have
shown me the true meaning of unconditional love.

Table of Contents

PART 1: THERAPEUTIC SERVICES FOR YOUTH WITH SERIOUS EMOTIONAL CHALLENGES AND THEIR FAMILIES

Chapter 1: Origin and Development of Home- and Community-Based Services

**Chapter 3: Aligning Home- and Community-Based Services
With Wraparound Principles**

PART 2: BUILDING AND SUPPORTING THE WORKFORCE

Chapter 4: Recruitment and Development of Staff

Chapter 6: Determining a Model for Service Provision

PART 3: ASSESSMENT OF YOUTH WITH SERIOUS EMOTIONAL CHALLENGES AND THE FAMILIES WHO SUPPORT THEM

Chapter 7: Assessment Principles and Components

Chapter 8: Assessing Caregivers' Strengths and Needs

Chapter 9: Assessing Infants, Toddlers, and Preschoolers Within the Context of Family and Community

Chapter 10: Assessing School-Age Children Within the Context of Family and Community

Chapter 11: Assessing the Transition-Age Youth Within the Context of Family and Community

Chapter 12: Assessing the Family

PART 4: SERVICE PLANNING AND IMPLEMENTATION OF THERAPEUTIC INTERVENTIONS

Chapter 13: Designing an Effective Service Plan

**Chapter 14: Developing Interventions to Support Caregivers
and Family Within the Home and Community**

Acknowledgements

I would first like to thank all of the families in southeastern Indiana who have taught me so much about the true meaning of home- and community-based services. Nothing could replace the valuable lessons that I have learned from them.

I would also like to recognize the positive support and guidance that Joseph D. Stephens has given me. As the executive director of Community Mental Health Center in Lawrenceburg, Indiana, for the past twenty-two years, I have seen firsthand the importance of a true leader who has the gift of a vision that reflects an understanding of what recovery truly means. His constant support and belief in the value of home- and community-based services has been to the good fortune of the families of southeastern Indiana.

I also want to thank Dr. Joseph Cresci for his mentorship in developing an appreciation for the complexities related to serving youth and families. The constant reminder of the power of the attachment relationship has led me to a strong appreciation of the value of a relationship-based practitioner.

Foreword

It is a distinct pleasure for me to write the foreword for this important book. The child-serving system has been evolving consistently over the past several decades beginning with the introduction of the system of care philosophy. And though principles of this approach have stood the test of time, we now know a great deal about the process of effective implementation. This book is a practical treatise on how to implement and manage high-quality, effective home- and community-based services for children, youth, and families. Such a broad-based but practice-focused guide can be enormously helpful to agency and program directors, planners, administrators, and clinicians.

Program managers are always faced with the challenge of creating uniform individuality. Programs have rules and regulations that emphasize uniformity but that make the program less sensitive to individual differences. In this book, designing programs and interventions based on the needs and strengths of the individual youth and family is emphasized while respecting the need for program thinking. This is a valuable contribution to the evolution of our system to actually achieve the vision of youth- and family-driven systems that do not devalue the simultaneous contributions of family and youth and professionals to an effective service system.

By organizing the book developmentally, Stacey Cornett makes the content more accessible to people whose work focuses on a specific stage without losing the reality that planning for developmental transitions can be as important as addressing needs within any given period of development. While infants develop into toddlers, toddlers to children, children to youth, and youth to adults, the years from birth to age 18 remain a unique period of life. The chapter on working with infants and toddlers particularly builds from Stacey's expertise. However, the school-age and transition-to-adult chapters also provide valuable concepts and strategies for program and system planners and managers. Further, the book's focus on caregivers as a critical component of the child- and family-serving system is something that is often missing in books on child and youth mental health.

The writing style is testimony to the author's personality. For those who do not know her, Stacey Cornett is a smart, experienced, passionate professional who is also down to earth and quite practical. She is a no-nonsense clinician and administrator who has maintained both her integrity and sense of humor. These traits shine through the pages of this text making it a very accessible reading experience. Jargon and the sometimes overproduced sentence structures of more academic texts simply are not a part of this experience. Valuable content presented in a straightforward and clear style draw from Stacey's Midwestern roots. I believe you will find this text a very informative read. I also believe it will find a place on your bookshelf where you will periodically pull it back down to reread when faced with questions about designing, implementing, and managing home- and community-based services for children and youth. I certainly applaud Stacey on this excellent work. I believe that you will too.

—John S. Lyons, Ph.D.
Endowed Chair of Child &
Youth Mental Health
University of Ottawa
Children's Hospital of Eastern Ontario
September 2010

Introduction

I still remember the first family home that I visited. I remember seeing the creek that separated the road and the house on top of the hill. I had to be in the right place, as there were no other houses for miles. I sat in the car for a few moments collecting my thoughts about how I would help this family to "get along and manage behavior," as my supervisor had instructed me to do. As I found my way across the creek, I had no idea the impact that this experience would have on me. I have thought about this family many times over the years. I remember the overwhelming feelings this family evoked in me—the worry, the joy, and the sense of wonder about how to best support family members in their journey. Little did I know that they were there to show me. As I left the home nearly two years later, with a little girl walking alongside me, the power of her words stunned me as I drove away: "Thank you for helping my Momma like me."

As I drove down the road, I came to the conclusion that I knew two things to be true about the time I spent with this family. First, upon meeting the family members, I had no idea what I could possibly do to help a situation that seemed overwhelming and untenable. The only thing I could do was to keep showing up. Surprisingly, that strategy was later referenced in a comment by the mother: "I really didn't think you'd keep showing back up." Second, the true change came from the family's own bravery in facing a multitude of challenges. The only thing I had to offer this family was myself. The relationship that we developed trumped any magical "clinical strategy" or knowledge that I could have possibly pulled out of my hat. If there was an "expert hat" that I was wearing, I certainly lost it the moment my hair got tangled in the fly strip that hung in the doorway. I am certain that at that moment, the second time I came, the mother decided that she would give me a try. We made eye contact and laughed till our sides ached. No expert "diagnosis" or lecture on child development could have replaced the value of that moment.

Those of us who are given the privilege of meeting with families in their own homes must never forget the awesome opportunities for growth that this offers both us and the families we serve. If there is a third idea that I am certain about, it is the fact that this family, as well as many others, would simply not be empowered in the same way within an office setting. We do not do home visits simply because it is easier for families not to have to drive to the office. We do them because we know the power of this type of intervention. It certainly is not easy work. It takes a special mindset that respects families for who they are and the possibilities for change rather than focusing on the deficits. It takes special radar to hone in on unique strengths and capabilities. It means being a guide that offers hope. My hope is that this book will serve as a guide to the many home visitors that recognize the importance of these principles or want to consider a new way of thinking. And in learning from the words of the mother, who taught me so much, it is important to remember the value in "just showing back up."

Around the country, more and more programs are being developed to address the needs of youth with serious emotional challenges. The emphasis on providing home- and community-based services is apparent. We are in an age when the field of child mental health is being recognized as a critical need in addressing the needs of youth and families in an effort to invest in the future. The field has evolved in a manner that represents the principles and value base that have many ties and parallels to those established in the fields of early intervention as well as adult mental health services. The emphasis on strength-based services is one such example of this trend. The book is divided into four parts. Part 1, "Therapeutic Services for Youth With Serious Emotional Challenges and Their Families," begins with an overview of the origin and development of home- and community-based services. This review demonstrates the rich history of this intervention and the many areas that have been preserved, as well as modified, to take us to our present-day practices. An understanding of the way in which practice evolved has great merit. This part also offers the reader a common understanding of what the term "serious emotional disturbance" refers to in relation to children and how these issues are often manifested, often changing significantly as a child develops. It is critical to have a strong understanding of who we are trying to help. Last, this part provides the very important understanding of the theoretical underpinnings of empowerment, wraparound principles, and a recovery/resiliency orientation. If the field is going to work as a whole to improve the services to this underserved population, a common value base is crucial.

Part 2, "Building and Supporting the Workforce," offers essential and practical information regarding hiring, developing, and maintaining staff to support our youth. It has been my experience that the staffs who work best within these programs are unique and exhibit characteristics that are very important. This work can be challenging, and the staff "fit" in a program must be strongly evaluated. Unfortunately, our universities are not yet as effective as they could be in arming potential employees with the skill set and philosophical base that is needed to effectively meet the needs of families. Many newly graduated staff members have strong feelings about being "the expert," or they believe they are "wasting their education" on the services that are described in this book. Sadly, this is a huge misconception that supervisors must be aware of, and they must counter this by developing effective training programs. Strong clinical, administrative, and reflective supervision is required if we are to train staff members in an alternate way of thinking. Supervisors will benefit greatly from the information presented in Chapter 6, which offers guidance on the various types of models that can be utilized in a program. The important element to consider in this context is the strong need to understand the needs of the families being served, the cultural of the community, and the staffing issues/considerations in making this important decision.

Part 3, "Assessment of Youth With Serious Emotional Challenges and the Families Who Support Them," emphasizes the importance of a comprehensive, strength-based, family-driven, youth-guided, and culturally competent assessment. As there are distinct differences in the assessment needs of the youth that may be served in a particular program, this part devotes separate chapters to young children, school-age youth, and transition-age youth. The power of a good assessment cannot be overestimated. It is this information that should inform the service planning process to ensure that the services provided are related to client needs and preferences.

Finally, Part 4, "Service Planning and Implementation of Therapeutic Interventions," provides a plethora of information related to the concrete day-to-day tasks that must be performed by a practitioner in a home- and community-based program. It begins with an overview of important components to include in the service planning process. Many practitioners are accustomed to designing a plan in isolation from the family and then filing it away in a chart. The approach presented here very much suggests the contrary and fully supports the thinking that a plan should be a "living, breathing document," as a very smart woman once told me. The designing of nontraditional and specific interventions is also underscored in this part. Practitioners often feel frustrated with a sense of not knowing what to do once they arrive in a home. Many practitioners have told me that families often present with many crises, and it is overwhelming to develop a plan and stay on track. This is a common issue and can best be assisted by engaging the family members in a plan that makes sense to them, having the plan serve as a guide, and developing excellent crisis plans. Crisis planning along with transition planning are critical tasks in this process. This area is often overlooked; it is my hope that the book will support ways to prioritize these tasks. Sample forms and facilitation processes are offered. The wraparound process has been demonstrated, both in the research as well as in my personal experience, to be a valuable service to families of youth with serious mental health challenges. It often is the *only* thing that works for families. When one has the good fortune to work where home- and community-based services are a part of a wraparound process, it is critical to clearly understand how the principles that should be followed are manifested in the work that must be done. Commitment to this process has been my passion. I truly believe that families must experience services in this manner if the benefits are to be achieved. This is by no means an easy process, but it is definitely one that can make a difference. As practitioners continually challenge themselves to develop their skills and understanding in this area, they must embrace the concept of life-long learning. Perhaps, the most important way in which this can happen is the alliance with our most precious partners, the families. This book, I hope, fully supports the ways in which that can occur.

—Stacey M. Cornett

About the Author

Stacey M. Cornett, MSW, LCSW, IMH-E®(IV), is the director of Intensive Youth Services/Co-Project Director/Clinical Director of Systems of Care at the Community Mental Health Center in Lawrenceburg, Indiana. In this position, Ms. Cornett is responsible for the development and administration of intensive home- and community-based services and a system of care initiative for youth ages 0-22. She has served as a consultant to the state of Indiana in the development of the Indiana Comprehensive Child and Adolescent Needs and Strengths Assessment, birth to 5 version (CANS). In addition, she worked with the Allegheny County, Pennsylvania, early childhood system of care initiative to develop an early childhood version of the CANS. Ms. Cornett serves as the co-chair of the Indiana Association of Infant and Toddler Mental Health and has a governor appointment to the Indiana Mental Health Commission. She serves as a consultant to various early childhood and mental health programs, and frequently provides trainings around the country. She received her master's degree in social work from Saint Louis University in 1988 and completed a clinical traineeship with Michael Trout in infant parent psychotherapy in 1999.

Part 1

Therapeutic Services for Youth With Serious Emotional Challenges and Their Families

Chapter 1

Origin and Development of Home- and Community-Based Services

History is an angel falling backward into the future.

—Laurie Anderson

Those who cannot remember the past are destined to repeat it.

—George Santayana

INTRODUCTION

History shows us that the door has continually been opened to a friend, community member, or practitioner offering various types of support. Regardless of the motive, type of support, or frequency of the visits, there are common themes one can reflect on and learn from. As practitioners seek to learn about the current thinking and strategies associated with home- and community-based support, it is helpful to reflect on lessons from the past.

HISTORICAL PERSPECTIVES

The concept of caring for others in their homes has been documented as far back as biblical times. Mary visited Elizabeth when she heard of her pregnancy with John the Baptist to offer her congratulations and support. In Matthew 8:5-13, Jesus goes to the home of a centurion to heal his servant. While these examples demonstrate the goodwill of friends and community members, later in history, religious groups began to take a leadership role in ensuring that the needy were cared for, often in their home environments. Literature describes how sick, homeless, poor, or distressed individuals sought refuge or support from the churches and clergy in their communities. This was considered part of the mission of the churches and a way they fulfilled their duty of providing charitable works to others (Donahue, 1985). Priests, nuns, and clergy were made welcome in the homes of the needy as they assisted in meeting both physical and emotional needs. As there was no social welfare system, monastic orders would offer food, clothing, and shelter to those in need (Fink, 1942).

As the cities became larger and poverty became more of a social problem, governments enacted laws to develop a method to contain what was considered a "moral flaw." In England, one of the first efforts was the Act for the Relief of the

Poor in 1597. It reflected this mentality and made it the government's responsibility to monitor assistance to the poor. With this act, a position known as an Overseer of the Poor was created to manage charitable giving. Later, the Elizabethan Poor Law of 1601 in England was put into effect, and it became the basis for future developments in colonial America. Assistance could be given in the form of what was termed "indoor" or "outdoor" relief. Indoor relief was given in almshouses, and outdoor relief was offered in the homes of those in need. Outdoor relief was the most common form, as the cost of building almshouses and institutions was costly and prohibitive. By 1662, the Settlement Act in England was passed in an attempt to develop residency requirements for recipients. Individual "parishes" were formed with the task of caring for their own (Fink, 1942). The general sentiment regarding assisting the poor was to make the process of seeking assistance as undesirable as possible. Again, poverty was considered a moral flaw that needed correction (Barker, 1995).

The Elizabethan poor laws attempted to use government to control the effects of "pauperism"; over a century later, charitable organizations in two German cities developed a coalition that influenced the way the poor were treated. A central bureau that was advised by an executive board of five councilmen was established to supervise all charitable giving and services. This system became known as the Hamburg-Elberfeld system, named after the two German cities in which it originated. The Hamburg-Elberfeld system affected English thinking, and the first charity organization society was formed in London. The negative and sometimes even criminal treatment of the poor, which had been the earlier mindset, was modified with this approach. Home visitors investigated the needs of the poor and coordinated efforts to mitigate the causes of the poverty. This system had a strong influence on how early initiatives within the United States developed (Fink, 1942).

Early Developments in the United States

The Industrial Revolution of the late nineteenth century ushered in new challenges and concerns for the American people. Urbanization and rapid development brought along issues related to poverty, overcrowding, and health that could not be overlooked. These difficult issues were not supported by a public welfare, a public health, or an unemployment insurance program that could serve to control the deleterious effects. In an effort to address this situation, the National Conference of Charities was developed under the auspices of the American Social Science Association. In 1879, it separated from the American Social Science Association and became known as the National Conference of Charities and Correction. This organization was comprised of mostly volunteers with the mission of coordinating the humanitarian efforts related to social problems. The organization was formed by representatives in Massachusetts, Connecticut, New York, and Wisconsin (Goldstein, 1973). The split from the American Social Science Association was significant in that it underscored a philosophical belief that serving the needy should be less about the science of why and more about the practical and pragmatic concerns of how (Bruno, 1957).

Friendly Visitors. The first charity organization society in the United States was formed in Buffalo, New York, in 1877 under the influence of Reverend S. H. Gurteen. Its primary function was to organize local charities not to provide relief (Fink, 1942). The impetus for this was the belief that charitable giving was unorganized and therefore wasteful. Because of this widespread belief, and the strong impact that the depression of the 1870s had on families, many more charity organization societies were formed. By 1892, charity organization societies existed in ninety-two communities (Goldstein, 1973). The strategy for organizing giving included forming groups of paid agents and volunteers to sponsor and subsidize an office. Paid agents visited homes to investigate their needs and present this information to prominent society members in what was termed a "conference." Once the conference took place, "friendly visitors" were commissioned to visit the homes to form ongoing relationships with the families. An emphasis was placed on the value of personal contact needed to change the lives of families (Haynes & White, 1999). Friendly visitors typically were women volunteers from the upper classes who considered their work as good deeds for people who were beneath them (Hancock & Pelton, 1989). The job of the friendly visitors was to assist the families in resolving the issues that were causing their financial strain. Beder (1998) declared that "friendly visiting, as articulated through the efforts of the Charity Organization Societies, planted the tradition of the home visit firmly in the profession of social work" (p. 515).

Settlement Houses. While the friendly visitors focused on individual families, another movement was beginning in the late 1890s that strove to impact the community at large. Settlement houses, which originated in London, emphasized the importance of empowering communities rather than individual families alone. The emphasis on impacting a community's ability to provide for its own was broader than the focus of the charitable organization societies' attempts to assist individual families alone. The mission of the Settlement House Movement was to improve the living conditions of the poor. This occurred by practitioners "settling" among the poor, sharing the lives and cultures of the poor in order to truly understand and impact the needs of the community. Settlement houses, in which practitioners resided, were typically developed in areas where immigrants or the urban poor resided (Roberts, Wasik, Castro, & Ramey, 1991). They were typically staffed by residents who believed that living and working within the community put them in touch with the true needs of the community. This also allowed for interaction and direct contact between the social classes (Murdach, 2007). Some practitioners assisted in this mission without living on the premises, but they emphasized bringing about changes in the areas of recreation, education, and living conditions in the communities in which they served. As social action and advocacy were their focus, practitioners taught the communities to clean their environments, and they rallied for child labor laws, educational change, and child welfare laws. One of the most famous settlement houses was the Hull House, developed in 1899 by Jane Addams and Ellen Gates Starr (Addams, 1910).

Visiting Teachers. Developing out of the Settlement House Movement was the emergence of visiting teachers to meet the educational needs of youth. In 1906, Mary Marot, a settlement house practitioner, became the first visiting teacher. Her role was to promote compulsory education laws and meet the academic needs of youth in the community. This was accomplished by meeting with children in the school setting as well as the home environment. Understanding the influences of the home and community on the children regarding their academic development was the primary goal. Families with youth who were struggling would receive support in meeting the needs of the youth, and this resulted in more youth remaining in school (Bhavnagri & Krolikowski, 2000).

General Principles of Early Movements

The charitable organization societies, settlement houses, and visiting teachers are all examples of home- and community-based services that have significantly influenced current home visiting practices. Each movement had similarities as well as differences that are important to understand in order to grasp the significance of each. The themes that are no longer relevant today and the practices and beliefs that remain are all instructive in understanding current practice.

The Charity Organization Society Movement was developed in response to the need to help the impoverished and needy. A strong emphasis was placed on people taking personal responsibility for improving their situations, which was determined to be best developed by the use of friendly home visitors. This was a time of mass immigration, and often the families who were being served had newly arrived in the United States and were in need of guidance and support. The movement believed that a voluntary method was preferable to government intervention, which would take away the relationship component that needed to occur (Haynes & White, 1999). Although a relationship component was valued, there was a definite hierarchy whereby the person served was not equal to the friendly home visitor. The underlying belief that was reflected in the movement's practice, as well as its writing, was that the needy were to blame for their own plight and needed the positive influence of friendly home visitors. This judgment and mentality was described by Fink as "victims of their own vices and failings" (Fink, 1942, p. 24). The home visitors believed that their education, life experiences, cultural orientation, social status, and intelligence made them superior to those they were serving, and therefore the visitors were capable of instituting change (Weiss, 1993). Helping and almsgiving was ultimately thought of as a problem-solving process that attended to the deficits of the poor (Early & GlenMaye, 2000). The visitors would lead the way in developing the "answers" to the problems and deficits of the poor. The goal of the movement was to merge the upper and lower classes, through exposure and guidance, and to erase the need for almsgiving. Mary Richmond was one of the first to discuss home visiting in her book *Friendly Visiting Among the Poor: A Handbook for Charity Workers* 1899). Mary Richmond placed strong emphasis on what she considered a method to merge science with philosophy. The strategy of investigating, educating, monitoring, and then seeking cooperation with each family was emphasized (Haynes & White, 1999). In the investigation process, Mary Richmond concerned herself with understanding the needs of the individual family as well as the community influences. Through the home-visiting process, practitioners sought to take into account the surroundings of the home. This enabled them to best understand the impacts on the individual family. All of these areas were examined and considered in Mary Richmond's recommendations to the family. The investigation would eventually lead to a "diagnosis," which became the basis of interventions (Beder, 1998). She sought to identify extended family supports and social networks that were available to help in each situation as well (Murdach, 2007).

The Settlement House Movement represented a change from a focus on individual needs to a focus on community needs. Additionally, when individual families were in need, the perceived source of blame shifted from the individual family to the community. The community was considered responsible for supporting its members and providing for the needy. Settlement house practitioners saw almsgiving as undermining the overall mission of improving societal conditions. Instead of focusing on charity as a means to an end, the development of skills to impact one's community and take action was emphasized (Haynes & White, 1999). Jane Addams, one of the most influential practitioners associated with the Settlement House Movement, felt strongly that friendly home visitors did not have the correct perspective. Addams advocated for practitioners to engage and work alongside families in a supportive manner (Murdach, 2007). Although, the settlement practitioners strove to impact the lives of the disadvantaged, they did not see their goal as only assisting the needy. The settlement practitioners believed all members of society were in need of societal change and should be impacted by the Settlement House Movement.

While the concept of visiting teachers began in 1906, by 1921, visiting teachers were utilized in fifteen states, primarily impacting children in socially or economically deprived regions. The driving principle fueling this movement was the important impact early intervention had in promoting success (Hancock & Pelton, 1989). The philosophy of this movement was also represented in the notion that overall positive development in children is needed to promote academic success. This was attempted by forming a relationship with the entire family to best understand its unique needs. Additionally, the interventions of the earliest pioneers in this field sought to improve the entire neighborhood's ability to meet the needs of youth (Bhavnagri & Krolikowski, 2000).

Twentieth Century Developments and Governmental Influences

The early 1900s brought about changes in the way the American government considered the needs of children and families. In 1899, the first consideration of the differences between youth and adult offenders was demonstrated in the establishment of juvenile courts (Wells, 1995). In 1909, the first White House Conference on Children established a system in which mothers, who were seeking "pensions" or financial support, would use the juvenile court system as a mechanism to secure financial aid. The goal was to eliminate children being removed from homes in which poverty was impacting their well-being. The population of focus was typically mothers with dependent children. Practitioners would complete home visits to determine appropriateness and eligibility. While, this system served to help mothers and children, there was a great deal of judgment involved, and many were denied on what was considered "moral" grounds (Hancock & Pelton, 1989). These changes supported continued developments in the provision of services to families.

The work of the juvenile court system as well as of visiting teachers was built on the Child Guidance Clinic Movement. which began in early 1922. The first demonstration of the child guidance clinic was in 1922 in St. Louis, Missouri. It was operated by a psychiatrist, a social worker, and a psychologist. Children with behavioral difficulties in the community, home, and school were referred, and recommendations were made regarding needed services. The project was later expanded to Virginia, Minnesota, Texas, California, Ohio, and Pennsylvania. The benefits of community services following this project emphasized the concept of helping youth within their natural environments, as this was where the most impact could be made (Fink, 1955). Because of this movement, the notion that academic success is rooted in overall emotional stability became a foundational concept that continues to influence the educational system today (Dreyer, 1976).

In the period between the 1920s and the 1950s, the most common approach was largely supported by the thinking that the individual was more important to focus on than the family unit. The influence of Sigmund Freud also resulted in a heavy emphasis on the office setting being used to analyze individuals. Writings and research in this period supported this notion as well, and the profession of social work reflected it in its practices. Beginning in the late 1940s, however, the importance of the family slowly began to emerge again as a theme (Pecora, Reed-Ashcraft, & Kirk, 2001).

In the 1950s, the development of the Family-Centered Project of St. Paul, Minnesota, was occurring, and, by 1954, the project identified itself as working with multiproblem families within their homes and the community (Wells, 1995; Pecora et al., 2001). The methodology was cutting edge in the sense that it primarily considered the feelings, attitudes, and beliefs of families in providing interventions to assist them within the homes and community. The project considered the family as partners in the overall mission to improve family functioning. The project coordinated needs, referred resources, and supported the family as a whole. Although, the project saw promising results, it did not have quite enough influence to continue the momentum of this methodology until the 1970s (Wells, 1995). Despite, the gap in time between the beginning of the Family-Centered Project and the developments in the 1970s related to the Family Preservation Movement, the influence of the project on developing family-centered practice was great.

In the 1960s, two particularly significant influences on home visiting occurred. The first represented a paradigm shift that emphasized the family, rather than the practitioner, as being of primary importance to special needs children. Additionally, what primarily represented the paradigm shift, was the emergence of the concept that caregivers can and should be responsible to care for their special needs children. The need and desire for institutional placement was therefore significantly reduced. No more were caregivers seen as the source of their children's problems, but rather they were the key to maintaining the children within the community (Roberts et al., 1991). The second significant influence was the separation of financial and supportive assistance within the home-visiting domain. Public welfare practitioners were no longer obligated to go to homes to evaluate and enroll those in need of assistance (Hancock & Pelton, 1989). This represented a major change in the feelings associated with both asking for and receiving governmental financial assistance. Moving into the 1970s, society witnessed an emergence of many family support programs, such as the Homebuilders Program, in part because of the philosophy and supportive conditions that could better empower families.

Reflected in legislation that was passed in the 1980s and into the present was the ever-strengthening notion that families are important, capable, and integral to the care of special needs youth. One such example is the Adoption Assistance and Child Welfare Act of 1980 (Public Law No. 96-272). This law acknowledged the poor state of foster care and the strong need to keep families intact (Beder, 1998; Pecora et al., 2001). Another strong reflection of family-centered principles and the focus on supporting families was the federal Education of the Handicapped Acts Amendments, Part H (Public Law No. 99-457), which emphasized the benefits of families having strong impacts on the choices regarding their children's services and the need to offer such services in the natural environment (Allen & Tracy, 2008).

Perhaps the single greatest influence on the emergence of family-centered services for youth with serious emotional challenges has been the book *Unclaimed Children* (Knitzer, 1982). Knitzer's contention that two thirds of all youth with serious emotional needs were not getting the services they needed ultimately resulted in the development of the Child and Adolescent Service System Program (CASSP) in 1984. This program focused and continues to focus on assisting states in meeting the needs of youth with serious emotional challenges (Stroul & Friedman, 1986; see Figure 1.1 for the historical time line of the significant events discussed in this chapter).

Figure 1.1
Time Line of Significant Events Related to
Home- and Community-Based Services

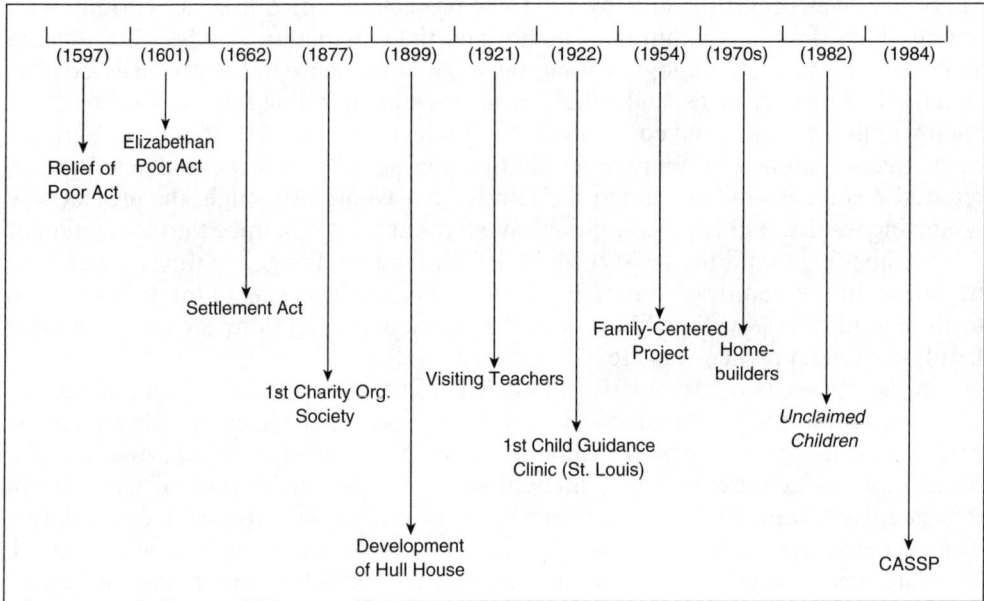

Convergence of Now and Then

There is no doubt that history has played a vital role in the current philosophy behind and provision of home-based services to youth with emotional and behavioral challenges. Although, home-based services have evolved, it should be emphasized that what remains is representative of what worked in the past, as well as what did not, in supporting youth and families. Originally, the well-intentioned home visitors helping the needy set themselves apart from those they served and imposed their values and judgments in the process. The notion of identifying strengths and fostering resiliency was not initially appreciated or supported. Most of the time, problems and deficits were what were identified and focused on. Efforts were put in place to "correct" a problem, even when a family did not identify it as such. Strength-based services, on the other hand, strive to make the overall situation more positive by putting the focus on what is going right for the family. This may, in turn, mitigate the effects that problem areas have on a family. When problems need to be focused on, the strategies are drawn from the youth and family's natural abilities. All areas of a youth's and family's lives are considered connected and possibly in need of support. More recent advancements related to home-based services reflect the gradual shift from expert to family-driven services (see Figure 1.2). No longer is it considered best practice to determine needs, services, and the time of termination solely based on the practitioner's opinion. As history has already demonstrated, the benefits of change, as well as research and evaluation to guide this process, are critical in order to avoid complacency and continue working toward what is pertinent and relevant for the youth and families in need.

Figure 1.2
Evolution of Family-Driven Perspective

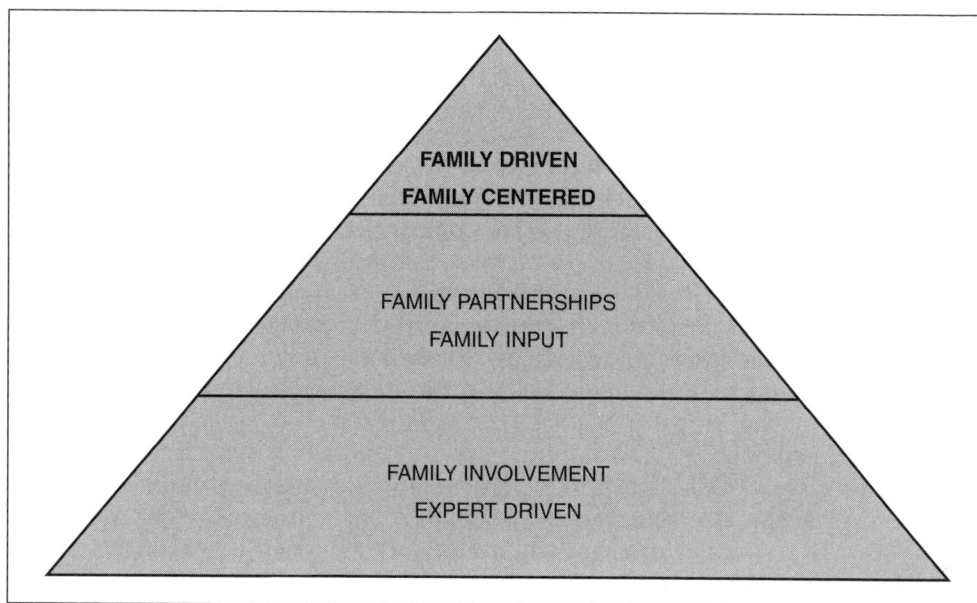

FAMILY DRIVEN
FAMILY CENTERED

FAMILY PARTNERSHIPS
FAMILY INPUT

FAMILY INVOLVEMENT
EXPERT DRIVEN

THEORETICAL FOUNDATIONS FOR CURRENT PERSPECTIVES

Systems Theory

Bertalanffy, a biologist by profession, is known for his work on systems theory. In his publication, *General System Theory* (Bertalanffy (1968), generalized, in terms of an organizational philosophy, the effects of individual parts on a whole. These concepts were later further developed and applied to families by other theorists. The notion that the family is a collective whole consisting of individuals who are interdependent on one another is a primary concept (Wasik & Bryant, 2001). The core belief—that the family is a unit—heavily influenced the development of family therapy as well as the field of family empowerment. The family is thought of much like a mobile: when one item moves, the others move along with it. To fully understand the influence of family systems theory on working with families, six guiding principles have been identified. Minuchin (1985, pp. 289-291) describes these principles as follows:

1. *Any system is an organized whole, and elements within the system are necessarily interdependent.* This major tenet is at the core of system theory. Individuals, no matter their status or hierarchy in the family, can only be fully understood from within the context of their family. What affects one family member will necessarily affect the others. This is true for both good and bad patterns of interaction, and movement away from established patterns will always have consequences. This is one of the most influential and well-known principles of systems theory that helps form a theoretical foundation for family-centered home-based services.

2. *Patterns in a system are circular rather than linear.* Within the systems theory way of understanding relationships, it is overly simplistic to assume that cause and effect is linear. Rather, to understand the effects of "A on B," it is more helpful to imagine a spiral-type diagram. Patterns of interaction have multiple effects, and there is no one way to affect the system. When considering where and how to intervene to affect change, there are multiple points of entry—with possibly different end results, depending on which one is chosen.

3. *Systems have homeostatic features that maintain the stability of their patterns.* The family is no different than any other system in that it develops specific patterns and ways of functioning. When someone or something attempts to make changes within the system, all members are acutely aware, and mechanisms are in place to bring the system back to what it is accustom to. This occurrence is predictable for both good and difficult changes, validating the fact that all changes have consequences. For example, this principle assists in the understanding of why children may seem to sabotage a caregiver's attempts to discontinue drinking alcohol. The children in this scenario are reacting to the disruption of the equilibrium within the family system. This change, however good it may seem, is therefore unfamiliar and often frightening. This understanding also helps home-based practitioners to consider the concept of "resistance" from a different framework. Working from this perspective allows for interventions to be considered from a family viewpoint and to be supported by all members of the system.

4. *Evolution and change are inherent in open systems.* While family systems strive for homeostasis, all systems must come to the point of change in order to survive or better the members at some point. Within a family system, these changes may be forced on the family when transitions, membership, or tragedies occur. Despite the overall anxiety that this may evoke, change will occur and the system will work until new patterns of interaction and homeostasis occur. When this occurs, whether it be alone or with the help of a practitioner, several tasks must occur. First, the family must come to the point of accepting the need for change. Additionally, it is important that the family take stock of the resources that are available to it as a system or that surround it. This helps assist both the transition to another state as well as in managing the anxiety associated with change. This is especially critical to consider when families of youth with serious emotional and behavioral challenges are facing stressors and change. The final task is to consolidate new patterns into familiar routines that begin to be considered homeostasis for the family.

5. *Complex systems are composed of subsystems.* Systems theory purports the belief that within any one system, there are unique subsystems that function as part of the larger system. Within a family system, this may include the caregiver subsystem, various caregiver-child subsystems, sibling-sibling subsystems, and extended family subsystems. It is important to understand how the family operates within the smaller units as well as the larger system.

6. *The subsystems within a larger system are separated by boundaries, and interactions across boundaries are governed by implicit rules and patterns.* The characteristics, rules, and boundaries of each subsystem are often different, yet usually are understood by all family members. It is important to recognize

that this knowledge, explicit or implicit, although understood by members may not be easily communicated or explained. Thus, practitioners must pay close attention to patterns of interaction in an attempt to understand the complex dynamics of the larger and smaller systems. Common difficulties for families may include lack of clear boundaries between the subsystems or inconsistent attention to these boundaries, depending on various factors or stressors.

The strong influence of systems theory in family-centered services cannot be disputed, and it is essential that practitioners in the field understand it. Stroul (1988) finds systems theory to be the essential foundation for home-based services. The core beliefs and practices that represent family-centered home-based services all reflect a systems theory understanding. Although, in the opinions of some practitioners, focus on individuals may be "easier" and behavior may change in some situations, true change for high-risk youth can only happen within the context of the family.

Ecological Theory

In 1866, Ernst Haeckel, a German biologist, was the first to use the term "ecology." He discussed ecology in terms of the relationship between an organism and the surrounding outer world. Previously, it was the norm to study individuals separate from their natural environments. This concept was furthered by many others (e.g., Darwin, Turnbull, Germain, and Bronfenbrenner). Germain (1973) began discussing casework practice in the context of how individuals relate to their broader environment (Wise, 2005). Bronfenbrenner (1979) proposes that individuals exist first within a family and then within a series of increasingly more complex environments. These environments include neighborhoods, communities, schools, churches, and institutions. It is critical to understand first the family system and then understand the other influences within the broader context of the community. No individual is isolated to only interacting within a family, and therefore the other influences and interactions must be examined. Each environment—school, church, or systems such as juvenile justice or child welfare—has its own culture, which includes rules, values, beliefs, and traditions. Wise (2005) advocates for a "person with environment" way of thinking, which supports the notion that an individual is interacting actively with his/her environment. The "person in environment" way of thinking suggests a more passive interaction. Within an ecological framework, practice is "directed toward improving the transactions between people and environments in order to enhance adaptive capacities and improve environments for all who function within them" (Germain, 1979, p. 8).

Home-based services are most effective when an "ecological family systems" orientation is employed. This respects not only the complex interplay of family relationships but includes the broader community environment. The interaction with peers, schools, social support networks, community agencies, and institutions are all thought about and supported (Stroul, 1988). Ecological theory therefore provides a framework for practitioners to ensure that interventions go beyond the family and influence the broader context of community (Wasik & Bryant, 2001).

When working from an ecological perspective, interventions are chosen that will impact individuals within their environments. Interventionists may chose to assist the family in developing an understanding of relevant systems in order to improve its ability to obtain what is needed from that system. For example, a practitioner may assist the family in developing knowledge regarding school rules and policies, as well as the culture of the school, when the practitioner is facilitating a relationship between caregivers and the school their child attends. When this is done, it may be more likely that caregivers can effectively communicate concerns and, thus, eventually see positive results for the child. This perspective also values understanding and building relationships from the viewpoint of competence rather than focusing on deficits. Practitioners are seen as empowering families in a way that facilitates environments to support them (Cox, 1992). In addition to building an understanding of formal systems that are available within communities, practitioners following this perspective seek to develop the use of natural supports. This allows for better support of the family without heavily relying on paid or professional caregivers. When this has occurred to the family's satisfaction, the ultimate goal of empowering family members to maintain the ability to function ideally within the family and community becomes the focus.

In later works, Bronfenbrenner further develops the concepts of ecological theory to describe the importance of family members responding to transitions and events across the life span (Bronfenbrenner, 1995, as cited in Wasik & Bryant, 2001). It is critical to attend to the interdependence of all family members when these situations occur. As family members interact with other systems, such as schools or residential treatment centers, the effects of the transition are relevant for all members. Interventions that appreciate and incorporate this dynamic are more likely to be effective and long lasting.

In an effort to best understand the needs of high-risk youth and families, the ecological family systems perspective is ideal. The influence of ecological theory blends the benefits of a humanistic perspective, focuses on strengths and competence, and uses environments to support coping (Cox, 1992). No child or family operates in a vacuum. The numerous studies on resiliency reflect the importance of building a strong sense of belonging to a community and social supports within that community. This perspective supports this research and provides the impetus for home-based practitioners to consider the individual, family, and broader community when working with families to design plans for change.

Family Empowerment Theory

Empowerment theory as a philosophical construct first influenced the home-based services work in the context of early intervention for those with developmental disabilities. It later became a basis for family preservation work. Empowerment theory has been influenced by the work of Mary Richmond during the settlement house era (see "General Principles of Early Movements"), in which practitioners valued improving families by developing capacity for change. The theory has only in the past few decades been more commonly associated with services that focus on youth with mental health challenges.

Empowerment has been identified by Staples (1990) as "the ongoing capacity of individuals or groups to act on their own behalf to achieve a greater measure of control over their lives and destinies" (p. 30).

The areas in which it is important to gain control are within the interpersonal and social environments in which youth and families interact. When considering these areas in a youth's life, empowerment for families may be reflected within the family, service system, and community interactions. Within the immediate family, there is a need to develop coping strategies for the behavioral and emotional struggles that may occur within the home. Families must also develop the ability to access, guide, and evaluate needed services for their youth. Within the community, families demonstrate empowerment when they are able to impact how well the community meets the needs of youth with challenges (Koren, DeChillo, & Friesen, 1992). Therefore, empowerment is not just an individual construct that promotes the development of skills, esteem, or capacities in those that are struggling. Empowerment includes individual development, with an emphasis on the expansion of group competencies, and action within the social and environmental conditions that are in need of change (Kemp, Whitaker, & Tracy, 1997). Families who experience obstacles at the individual, system, and community level have often been forced to find strategies to overcome barriers that have been opposed by others, often with little understanding of what is needed. To see improvement, not only is an improved sense of self needed but knowledge of social barriers and the development of resources and strategies to institute change (Lee, 1996).

Carl Dunst and his colleagues (Dunst, Trivette, & Deal, 1994) identified three guiding principles related to empowerment as a philosophy:

1. All people have existing strengths and capabilities as well as the capacity to become more competent.

2. The failure of a person to display competence is not due to deficits within a person but rather the failure of social systems to provide or create opportunities for competencies to be displayed or acquired.

3. In situations where existing capabilities need to be strengthened or new competencies need to be learned, they are best learned through experiences that lead people to make self-attributions about their capabilities to influence important life events. (p. 15)

GUIDING PRINCIPLES FOR SERVING YOUTH WITHIN THE HOME AND COMMUNITY

Empowerment theory, systems theory, and ecological theory are all represented in the delivery of family-centered home-based services, which are often used to support the wraparound process. Family-centered home-based services encompass a range of therapeutic interventions that include skill development, crisis management, counseling/therapy, advocacy, linkage to resources, case management, and education. Although there are numerous models, most of them have characteristics that they hold in common.

- Caseloads are small, usually no more than ten to twelve families per clinician to ensure that the proper attention and intensity of services are provided. Additionally, the relationship established between practitioner and family is highly valued, and therefore the caseload size must support this process. The ultimate goal of empowering the family occurs through the development of this relationship. Although one practitioner may serve as the primary clinician to the family, back-up supports are provided often on a twenty-four hour basis.

- The emphasis is on provision of services within the home. Natural supports, extended family, as well as community supports, are best understood and utilized when practitioners are present and available within the home setting.

- Perhaps most importantly, there is strong emphasis on having the caregivers remain "in charge" of their family's needs for nurturing and support (Pecora et al., 2001).

Family-centered home-based services supporting the wraparound process have a common value base that is demonstrated in their delivery, as described in the following paragraphs.

Interventions Are Focused on Entire Family

Youth with emotional challenges are no different than youth without emotional challenges in the sense that they function within the context of a family. The family, however defined by the youth, be it biological or not, is perhaps the greatest influence on youth. The family has the ability to support, empower, maximize potential, or sabotage a youth with special needs. When a youth is struggling with emotional or behavioral issues, it is therefore essential to consider the strengths and needs of all members of the family.

By supporting all members of the family, the overall functioning of the family is enhanced. For children, the extent to which their families are able to feel supported by their communities and others has proven to be a key indicator of family adaptation to life stressors (Greeff, Vansteenwegen, & Ide, 2006). Focusing on the family ultimately improves the lives of the youth because resilience in youth is reflected by their personal strengths—family strengths as well as support from their environment (Werner & Smith, 2001).

Educating family members on emotional and behavioral challenges also improves relationships and promotes a greater understanding of what a youth may need from the family. When emotional and behavioral challenges occur, the family is in a better position to support the youth in need and not inadvertently impede potential progress.

The concept of family resiliency, which was researched and further developed in the 1990s (Matthews & Johnson, 1997; McCubbin, McCubbin, & Thompson, 1993), supports this notion. Additionally, key elements of family resiliency have been described as positive family beliefs about the future, positive family values, effective communication and problem solving, adaptability, and emotionally close relationships (Walsh, 1998). When family resiliency occurs, the skills, abilities, and strategies for accepting life's challenges are present and available to offset potential negative effects of trauma. Families are better able to accept challenges and support their members when specific characteristics are present or developed. These characteristics include mutual interest in one another, ability to meet others' emotional needs, good communication, role clarification, adaptability, ability to seek social support, and ability to seek help from immediate family members (Enns, Reddon, & McDonald, 1999). As discussed in the publication, *Family Resiliency: Building Strengths to Meet Life's Challenges* (n.d.), an individual's success in such areas as school, relationships, and jobs is positively correlated with supportive caregiver and sibling relationships. Interventions are best designed with the mindset that what enhances the functioning of one member potentially enhances the functioning of all members. Home-based services, when operating from a family focus, support the family in becoming the change agent for the child (Stroul, 1988).

Interventions Are Individualized to Meet Unique Needs of Each Family

Most individuals respond more positively to discussions that are relevant to their experiences and situations. Many people describe having automatic filters for information that is not meaningful or valued. No family is exactly like another. Each family's strengths and challenges may be similar but, even so, the underlying causes, history, and nuances of the particular family are not. As home-based services have evolved, it is rare to find a program that denies the importance of developing individualized interventions. The deficit model, which is deemphasized more now than in the past, more readily supports looking at universal strategies to address a problem area. When the family's wishes and needs are understood from their unique perspective, the agreed-upon interventions will have more relevance. Discussing how direct service supports as part of a wraparound process should function, Penrod (2008) states, "Direct support services are individualized to the strengths and culture of the child and family rather than delivered as a scripted or pre-packaged set of service" (p.2). The process of mutually setting goals that are reflective of what the family wants to focus on and what it sees as underlying the challenges, leads to individualized services and interventions. This has been found to be a critical factor in ensuring that specific needs of families are met (Green, Johnson, & Rodgers, 1999).

Individualization is also reflected in the frequency, duration, and type of services provided to the family. The frequency of services should vary according to the needs and wishes of the family and not be predetermined by such things as diagnosis or program demands. The duration of services should also be a mutually determined and carefully planned according to the progress of the family. Although there may be a host of interventions that are appropriate for home-based services, the specificity of how the interventions occur, and in what manner, should always be unique. Individualization will naturally occur within all of the above areas when commitment to discovering and respecting the family's values, beliefs, and internal workings is prioritized.

Interventions Are Developed From a Strength-Based Perspective

The strength-based perspective is rooted in a belief system that all youth and families have the desire as well as the capacity to function effectively despite serious emotional and behavioral challenges. It is not merely a hope that the family with professional support can prevent the need for residential treatment, but rather a core belief that this is possible. Services are seen as partnerships that assist the families in reaching this potential. From this perspective, there is not a standard trajectory that occurs for all youth with certain diagnoses, risk factors, or family circumstances. Rather, past or current challenges are recognized, but they are not as important as the possibilities that exist in future situations. Change is possible, expected, and is reinforced by discovering success (De Civita, 2006). Laursen (2000) describes a strength-based approach as one that "encourages us to support and reinforce child and family functioning rather than focus on individual or family deficits, and it places the helping practitioners in the role of partner rather than expert." (p. 1). Caregivers also are seen as wanting positive outcomes for their youth as well as their family as a whole.

Although the strength-based perspective believes that families have the capacity to support all youth, it does not mean that needs are overlooked. This is a common misconception and criticism of a strength-based perspective. Needs are approached from a nonblaming, nonjudgmental perspective that looks at all contributing factors. Some needs must be prioritized, although the needs are often diminished by enhancing other areas of functioning within the youth and family. The interventions that are identified draw from the unique positive traits, characteristics, and capacities of the youth and family (Laursen, 2000). While some needs may never completely be resolved, this approach seeks to minimize the impact on the family, recognizing that a deficit model often misses opportunities for growth.

An important reflection of the fundamental belief system of a strength-based practitioner is the language and communication style that is used. People are not described as having a disorder, a deficit, or a label. The use of words, such as "challenges" or "obstacles," implies a belief that issues can be overcome. That is, instead of saying, for example, "a disordered child," the strength-based practitioner might say "a child with behavioral challenges." Additionally, the past is put in perspective, and a future orientation is demonstrated by more references to the future than the past. While careful attention to language occurs with this perspective, the message is even stronger when nonverbal communication is in sync with the content of what is said.

Services Are Commissioned Through a Child and Family Team

Many youth with serious emotional and behavioral challenges have unique needs related to service planning. Many youth are involved with multiple systems; therefore the need to coordinate care is often significant. Families and youth may have experienced services that have not met their needs. Service plans may have lacked specificity in such areas as the type, duration, and frequency of interventions. Additionally, the services families were offered in the past may not have been appreciative of their strengths and the presence of natural supports. When practitioners are given the opportunity to assist a youth and family in need, it is critical to instill hope and confidence that change can occur. A Child and Family Team (CFT) has the capacity as well as the expectation to address all of the above areas. A CFT is a group of people determined by the youth and family to have the capacity to develop, implement, and monitor a service plan that reflects the specialized needs of the youth and family (Vandenberg, Bruns, & Burchard, 2003). Home-based services may be designed and monitored through a CFT that is part of a formal wraparound process as well as an informal team that strives for the same goals (Penrod, 2008). When home-based services are part of a formal wraparound process, the CFT relates the needs to the home-based practitioners, and discussion takes place regarding how specifically services can be offered. The CFT may choose to accept services with the practitioner or determine that services are not a good fit. CFTs may choose to complete the needs and strengths assessment within the team or allow the home-based services practitioner to further assess the youth and family and discuss options at a later CFT meeting.

Interventions Are Designed in Appreciation of Family's Culture and Values

It is most probably safe to say that all mental health practitioners have at their core a desire to help the families they serve. Interestingly, no matter how strong this desire is, or how effective the interventions may seem, success is mostly contingent on how families judge the practitioner's ability to "see" their uniqueness; interventions should be designed with this in mind. Whether this uniqueness is thought of in the more obvious categories, such as ethnicity, or the more subtle variations of individuals, families, or child temperament, it is important all the same. Cultural sensitivity is often spoken of as something that one either has or does not have. Rather, cultural sensitivity should be thought of as how deep one's awareness and understanding of it is. The U.S. Census Bureau (2001) found that as of the 2000 census, of the 106 million people identified, 35 percent were people of color. The country is becoming more and more diverse, and respect and understanding for the differences that this creates is imperative. Families who seek help are first and foremost looking to be understood and supported. The relationship develops between families and practitioners, and it will fail miserably if respect and understanding does not occur. The ability to support families must take into account their values, beliefs, and customs in a way that does not merely categorize families but instills a true understanding. Cultural understanding is never fully achieved; rather, it is a process that supports the notion that practitioners are aware of the magnitude of what is not known and are open to learning through partnering with those that do.

Interventions Occur When Family Is in Need and at the Level of Frequency Needed

Families experiencing multiple challenges are in need of stability and hope for the future. They often participate in formal outpatient services that may not provide the level of support that is needed. Families and youth, as well as the literature (Gomby, Larson, Lewit, & Behrman (1993), reflect that interventions are most meaningful and productive when they occur at the time the family is in need. Discussing general concepts related to structure, discipline, or calming strategies, for instance, within an office setting does not have the same relevance or meaning as when these concepts are practiced in a "here and now" environment. Most families understand these concepts and have capacities to institute change, if coaching and support is given to build on their capacities as the problems are occurring. Often, the dynamics and subtle interactional patterns that are reinforcing struggles within a home environment are not able to be expressed by individuals within a family to even get to the root of what could make things better. It is more productive to "see" the struggles as they are occurring in order to impact the situation in a more comprehensive manner. Bringing out the capacities rather than focusing on the deficits is also much easier within the home environment because, as the family demonstrates needs, it is also displaying capacities. Both of these dynamics are not fully understood when families try to give words to situations that have occurred in the past while in an outpatient setting. Programs that provide home-based services strive to be available to families during their time of need, not during the time that is convenient for the practitioner. If the family is struggling during morning or evening routines, the practitioner is there to intervene and support the family. In this way of thinking, the family's needs are the priority; the program hours should be flexible to support this. Programs assure the family that twenty-four hour crisis intervention is available, often within the home environment. Families who are desperate for change need this level of support to experience stability and change.

Goal Is to Keep Youth in the Community

The strong emphasis on keeping youth in their home communities is reflected in family-centered home-based services. There are numerous reasons why this is beneficial to both youth and families. The highly valued relationship between caregivers and their youth is not to be ignored. No one can replace the value of this relationship nor influence youth more than their caregivers. Additionally, when youth are supported within their homes and communities, there is less challenge in coping with issues related to transitioning back from a residential to a community setting. Youth often are exposed to new behaviors and have developed coping strategies that are related to the confines of the residential setting. Adjusting to the reality of family and community life is often extremely challenging. The separation issues alone are paramount for both the youth and families.

Serving Youth and Family in the Natural Environment Is Critical

In a family-centered home-based services approach, there are many reasons why serving the youth within the home is critical. Although practical issues for the family, such as transportation and child care, may indeed be ameliorated through use of a home-based approach, these are not the primary reasons why the family benefits. Families may experience a deeper level of commitment on the part of the practitioner when the effort and value is placed on being present and available within the home environment. It may seem more meaningful to the family to have the practitioner be available to assist the family as issues occur.

Youth and families who come for help within an office setting are asked to explain their challenges verbally within the confines of the office. Although there may be opportunities for the family to display communication patterns, alliances, and the hierarchy of the family, the clinic setting may not foster the most accurate understanding of this. What the family cannot re-create completely in the office is how the sequence of events link to comments, associations, and reactions in both the youth and caregivers who are best understood as they occur in the natural setting. In addition, the family cannot communicate what it is not consciously aware of.

> *Example:* Rebecca is the 25-year-old mother of Shane, a 6-year-old boy, who is struggling academically. In the office, Rebecca explains, "I'm doing the best I can to help him when he comes home from school, but he won't work with me." She further states that the teacher is being "mean and uncaring." She has a difficult time explaining what is occurring beyond this.

> The home-based practitioner agrees to be at the home during the time that Shane comes off the bus to observe what occurs. Shane runs from the bus eager to share a paper about an upcoming field trip. Rebecca refuses to look

at the paper, saying, "Show me the agenda first and then do your home-work." Shane has an obvious look of disappointment and worry. As Rebecca opens the agenda, she immediately tenses and reads in a loud and annoyed manner, "Shane was unable to find his homework assignment for today, this can't continue, although I will allow him to bring it in tomorrow." Rebecca states to the interventionist, "See how his teacher is being; this reminds me of how things were when I was a kid." Shane interjects, "My teacher said I can turn it in tomorrow, Mom." This angers Mom further, and she contin-ues with a story about how she remembers her teachers embarrassing her in front of others.

Although the issue for Rebecca, in the example above, could have surfaced within an office setting, the scenario illustrates how the issue was seen in a different way when observed within the home. Rebecca's feelings about her past experiences appear to be getting in the way of her clearly seeing Shane's situation and creating problem-solving strategies to assist him. Her reactions appear to worry Shane and possibly hinder him from focusing on homework.

Despite practitioners' best efforts to engage families in the office setting, it may be difficult to overcome the anxiety that some family members may experience. Family members are often left with the impression that they are "performing," to some degree, to alleviate blame being placed on them, and they have difficulty containing their anxi-ety. What may be described and observed in the office may look different within the home environment, where caregivers and their children feel comfortable. Their reac-tions and behaviors may demonstrate themselves naturally as caregivers are speaking with the practitioners, for example, where a home situation triggers overwhelming feelings that cannot be contained.

Example: Bill and Ashley are the caregivers of two children, Will, age 10, and Annie, age 12. As the family meets with the office-based practitioner, the issue that is presented is that Annie is often angry, withdrawn, and prefers to stay in her room. She is described as being "slow in school" and "difficult to talk to." Will, who has been silent the entire session, is described as having no difficul-ties at home or school, and the caregivers believe that the focus of treatment should be working individually with Annie. Annie, when asked what she feels about this, merely shrugs her shoulders and states, "Whatever."

Upon arriving at the home, the practitioner is greeted by both caregivers, and Annie and Will are in the kitchen finishing their homework. The caregivers and the practitioner sit down in the living room area adjacent to the kitchen and discuss how the past week has gone. The youth are directed to finish what they are working on and join the meeting. The practitioner overhears Will tell-ing Annie, "Well since she's not going to be here all night you better just quit right now." As the caregivers hear this comment as well, Bill replies, "Annie, he's right, just come over." Ashley further states, "Will's much better at doing his homework than Annie."

The practitioner in this example has been given the opportunity to see the family dynamics in an entirely different light than was available in the office visit. A work-ing premise would likely be that Annie, although challenged academically, may well be feeling unsupported by her caregivers. Furthermore, her brother's reaction and comment is likely to be hurtful and damaging to her self-esteem. It becomes clear that this family can use some support in looking at the issue from a holistic and family perspective.

PHASES OF SERVICE DELIVERY

When considering the tasks and work that face both families and practitioners, it is helpful to divide the service delivery process into stages. In doing so, the overwhelming nature of what needs to occur becomes more manageable. Each stage is distinct and unique in and of itself. There are specific tasks and stages of development embedded into each service stage. While the stages build upon the previous stages' successes as well as failures, there may be some blending at all levels. Some of the tasks may need to be revisited, or the stages may manifest in different forms. Although there are generic tasks to accomplish within each stage of service delivery, the uniqueness and individualization for both families and service providers is never abandoned.

Orientation

The orientation stage of service delivery may well be the most important stage on a number of levels. This stage may best exemplify the adage, "first impressions count." Many families who request assistance have preconceived notions regarding the provision of services. They may have previously experienced care that left them feeling judged and perhaps less capable of caring for their youth. Some practitioners express that this may indeed be the most challenging and stressful stage of service delivery due to the need to "convince" families that they are safe, capable, and in a position to mutually assess and determine what services will be offered.

Benefits to Family and Youth. There are numerous benefits to the youth and family from participating in a supportive and educative orientation process. The first, and perhaps most obvious, benefit is that the family is fully empowered to make an informed decision regarding the appropriateness of what a program has to offer related to its own particular needs. In an orientation process that fully supports the family, service provision should not be assumed until the family "hires" the practitioner or program. The family should be invited to consider making the decision for "hiring" at the pace it feels comfortable with. If the family appears ambivalent, it is not appropriate to push for a decision. Rather, the family should be given an opportunity to take the time that is needed. The family should be encouraged to make contact with the practitioner when it has decided how it would like to proceed, without feeling that it has disappointed the practitioner by not deciding immediately (Carrilio, 2007). Encouraging this process sets the tone from the beginning that the family is fully capable and valued in taking the lead in guiding service delivery.

Another key benefit to families that should occur during the orientation phase is the instillation of hope. Families are often desperate for practitioners who can demonstrate a true understanding of their needs *and* deliver services that will result in change. Presenting a rationale for why youth with emotional challenges and their families may benefit from home- and community-based care is critical. Most families have previously received some type of help and wonder why they should expect something different than what has occurred before. The key concept that best communicates a reason to feel hopeful is that family-centered home-based services supporting a wraparound process take a "whatever it takes" position regarding services (Dunst et al., 1994). There is a strong commitment to thinking broadly and "out of the box," and traditional and standard procedures do not always apply. To feel a sense of hope, which is so critically important, the families must feel understood and believe that strategies can occur to keep all youth safely within their own homes and communities.

Last, and perhaps most importantly, is the experience of forming a relationship with the practitioner prior to the assessment process. The family and youth deserve to first feel comfortable and fully informed regarding the process for service provision. The relationship becomes the vehicle in which this may occur. The orientation process is a foundation for the therapeutic relationship and allows for the beginning of a therapeutic bond to develop. Sharing sensitive information with another is often challenging, and separating the orientation from the initiation of the assessment strengthens the likelihood of the assessment process supporting the development of a service plan that meets the needs of the family. Table 1.1 highlights the goals families experience with an orientation process.

Characteristics of Orientation. In keeping with the concepts highlighted above (see "Benefits to Family and Youth"), the orientation process includes information sharing, relationship building, and determining the needed steps for beginning services or referring the family to other options. As indicated by Wasik and Bryant (2001), the first visit should include rapport building, becoming acquainted, sharing the program goals and procedures, clarifying the practitioner and family's role, identifying the family and youth's expectations, and scheduling a next visit. This information and experience best occurs in a face-to-face encounter. Often, the family is phoned ahead of time to schedule the visit and asked to choose whether to meet in the home or at the office. Although there may be pros and cons to either environment, unless there are safety concerns, the family should be allowed to make this determination. The visit should be scheduled to meet the needs of the family, that is, all members should be available, and the appropriate amount of time should be allotted to complete the orientation. The family may have questions that should not be hurried or left unanswered.

The information that the family needs should be overviewed verbally and then provided in written form. To avoid overwhelming the family, the overview should just highlight the main points. The values and principles of family-centered home-based services should be shared and explained briefly; an example that illustrates the point is helpful. The program's mission, vision, eligibility criteria, and procedures for ending services should be overviewed as well. The phases of service delivery will be of more interest to the family, as its concerns about what the program may offer will be answered in this discussion. When describing the types and intensity of services, terms, such as "skill building" or "case management," should be described and illustrated by examples. The processes of assessment, crisis planning, service planning, and transition planning should all be described.

Families often are concerned with logistical issues. The financing of services and procedures for securing financing are of primary concern. Families need to know how to communicate if financial problems occur during treatment. Fully informing

Table 1.1
Goals of Orientation

- Inform youth and family of the meaning of services to aid them in their decision regarding potential involvement.
- Instill a sense of hope that change and recovery are possible.
- Lay foundation for positive relationship.
- Leave family and youth with an understanding of the importance of their full partnership and lead in designing services.

the family regarding the fees and anticipated coverage is critical. Also, there is a need to share what can and should be done if services do not meet expectations. All accredited programs should have a grievance procedure that is clearly shared. Both youth and families need reassurance that complete confidentiality will be kept. This process should be set out in writing as well.

Many families are already familiar with the concept of consumer rights and responsibilities. This, again, empowers the family and youth to feel more trusting and in control of the therapeutic experience. While programs may be mandated by accreditation entities or other requirements, there are a variety of ways in which clients' rights are articulated. Typically, rights include such areas as the following:

- The right to confidentiality;

- The right to be treated with respect;

- The right to make decisions regarding treatment;

- The right to appropriate and quality treatment;

- The right to know fees and billing procedures;

- The right to end treatment or modify treatment;

- The right to access or review records;

- The right to not be discriminated against; and

- The right to be treated by qualified staff who adhere to a professional code of ethics.

When discussing the family and youth's responsibilities, the following should be considered:

1. Families may be unable or unwilling to adhere to certain responsibilities, and therefore what will occur if problems arise in a particular area should be discussed. For example, keeping appointments or participation in services are areas that may be problematic for stressed families; usually provisions for dealing with these areas can be made.

2. The responsibilities should be presented in a manner that appreciates a family's culture and level of distress.

Following are typical examples of client responsibilities:

- Families and youth should participate in sharing needed information to complete the assessment.

- Families and youth should provide current billing and insurance information.

- Families and youth should follow the plan of care or request a change when needed.

- Families and youth should know the name of their practitioner and share with other practitioners when needed.

- Families and youth should keep or change appointments when necessary.

- Families and youth should fully participate in the development of service, crisis, and transition plans by making determinations based on their needs and preferences.

Table 1.2 may be useful to help a family understand the practitioner's versus the family's role in service provision.

Assessment

The process of assessment begins after the family has completed the orientation process. Assessment should be introduced to families and youth in a manner that exemplifies the collaborative nature of this process. Assessment may be threatening to some because it brings up feelings of being judged or evaluated. A careful introduction to this process, which highlights the family-driven, youth-guided, and culturally competent nature of the assessment, will be helpful in managing potential anxiety.

Function of Assessment. Assessment is a process of determining the strengths and needs of the family, which provides the basis for service planning. A strength-based assessment looks at all areas of a youth's and family's lives that may be impacting the youth's functioning. The assessment uncovers the positive ways in which the family as a whole interacts, the individual strengths of the family members, and the successes the family experiences in interacting with other's outside of the family (Sandau-Beckler, 2001). It is essential that this happens in a way that is respectful of the culture of the family so that the information accurately reflects the family and youth's needs and strengths.

Ongoing Nature of Assessment. A strong assessment that fully supports the development of a plan is the product of a therapeutic relationship. Although the therapeutic relationship begins in the orientation phase, it should always be considered as something that is ever changing and evolving. Often, families do not initially feel comfortable sharing issues, although later they may easily discuss the issues. This does not demonstrate a failure in the therapeutic alliance; it may simply be overwhelming for some families to discuss certain issues until a level of comfort has been developed. Additionally, the development of trust takes time to occur. Because of this, as well as the likelihood that unconscious processes will

Table 1.2
Role of Family and Practitioners

- **Practitioner:** Support the development of a family vision.
- **Family:** Express to practitioner its preferences and wishes for the family.
- **Practitioner:** Offer service delivery options.
- **Family:** Determine how services will best work for family.
- **Practitioner:** Guide family through the service delivery phases.
- **Family:** Inform practitioner of what success will look like in each stage of service delivery.
- **Practitioner:** Provide services in a respectful manner under the direction of the family.
- **Family:** Provide honest feedback regarding how services are working for the family.

be demonstrated in actions, assessment never stops. Figure 1.3 depicts the ongoing nature of assessment.

Planning

Designing a Plan for Change. When families and youth are seen from a deficit perspective, the offered services are often matched to the deficit and not to the individual family. Families who have youth with significant mental health challenges often have experienced practitioners who develop a plan with this mentality. The distinct difference for families who receive services from a family-centered perspective is that there is a commitment to change that is exemplified in the philosophy. Practitioners have the mindset that services should be flexible and modified as needed. The plan should be dynamic and useful. Changes in the intensity, duration, type, and location of interventions occur as often as needed, not only at scheduled reviews. Practitioners also redefine their roles to respond to a full range of family needs due to the understanding that what affects one affects all (Tracy, 2001). In concert with these unique perspectives is the overall strategy to utilize the best of what youth, families, and the community have to offer to build resiliency and facilitate recovery.

Committing to Plan. In the development of a service plan, the family and youth are the ones who have the most influence in the choices that are made. The commitment to the plan can therefore be much stronger when this occurs. To fully commit to the plan, it is also crucial that all members involved in the planning are mutually invested. This may be manifested in a common focus of change. If caregivers have a different agenda than the youth, change is potentially sabotaged. This is often the case, especially when behavior in the youth reflects caregivers' issues. The caregivers may want the behavior to change, while youth has invested in exposing the true issues with the caregivers through the behavior. In a study investigating the frequency of visits in community-based services, agreement on treatment goals independently predicted the number of visits. It was postulated that agreement represented stronger motivation for treatment as well as better overall family functioning (Brookman-Frazee, Haine, Gabayan, & Garland, 2008).

Even when choice in interventions occurs, the family, youth, or both may have varying degrees of commitment to the plan. This could be due to a lack of belief that change is possible or a fear of what may occur if change does occur. There are true

Figure 1.3
Ongoing Nature of Assessment

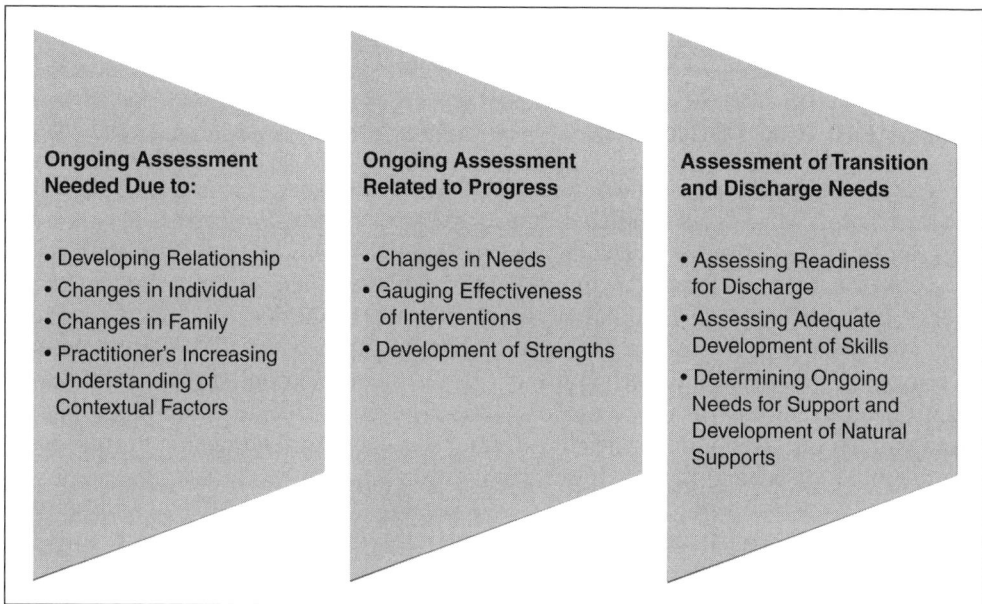

Ongoing Assessment Needed Due to:

- Developing Relationship
- Changes in Individual
- Changes in Family
- Practitioner's Increasing Understanding of Contextual Factors

Ongoing Assessment Related to Progress

- Changes in Needs
- Gauging Effectiveness of Interventions
- Development of Strengths

Assessment of Transition and Discharge Needs

- Assessing Readiness for Discharge
- Assessing Adequate Development of Skills
- Determining Ongoing Needs for Support and Development of Natural Supports

benefits to identifying issues related to commitment to the plan in that if the issues can be resolved, change is more likely to occur. It is unlikely that, at all stages, the same level of commitment is present, although careful attention to barriers in this process usually produces good results.

Utilizing Therapeutic Interventions. The therapeutic interventions are all strategies, conventional and sometimes not so conventional, that are utilized to support the family in meeting its identified goals. The interventions are typically implemented by the practitioners, although the family, youth, natural supports, or community supports may sometimes be assigned roles in working on the prioritized needs. Interventions are designed by the family and may include all types of interactions that support therapeutic change. The practitioner may assist the family in developing skills through many different types of interactions, which often includes taking part with the family in their everyday routines and activities.

Implementing the Plan. The plan is seen as a road map in getting a youth and family to their desired destination. The family identifies goals, which articulate its vision; objectives, which are markers in progress along the way; and interventions, which make the progress occur. The youth and family make the choices regarding when the plan will be implemented, how frequently and what interventions will occur, and what will determine when the plan is successful.

Evaluating and Reevaluating the Plan. The use of the plan is a process that is continually evaluated and reevaluated. It is not an event that occurs with little meaning and connection to what actually occurs on a regular basis in the home and when visits occur. Within any process is the reality that a number of factors can potentially change what is occurring or what needs to occur. If the service plan is being used correctly, this will also be reflected in the service delivery. The plan should be reflected on and updated when factors indicate that the process is no longer relevant to the needs.

Transition and Follow-Up

Transition at the Onset. At the beginning of service delivery, it is helpful to consider with the family what would indicate that services are no longer needed. This is often referred to as the "miracle question" and assists the family in articulating a vision. A vision for how the family members's lives will be when services are no longer needed is something that should always remain a part of the service delivery process. This guides the process and helps to keep the focus on recovery. There are a number of transition activities that can begin with engagement and continue until the family identifies its readiness for the transition phase. These activities include preparing the family and youth for no longer needing formal services and feeling able to fully manage potential crises, and the needs of their family.

Importance of Transition. Transition is an important phase of service delivery. This phase recognizes the accomplishments, strengths, and progress that the family has experienced. It simultaneously gives the family a chance to absorb the effects of these changes and prepare for sustaining them. The family in this stage is developing greater independence from the formal services that have been provided and relying and strengthening its informal networks of support. The family is seeing the practitioner less often and "practicing" the skills it has developed. The family, when it does see its practitioner, is spending less time actively learning new skills and more time reviewing its progress and focusing on preparation for discharge. The practitioner must spend time in this stage attending to his/her own feelings related to discharge, as the family is likely to also be experiencing its own ambivalence related to discharge. This phase must not be rushed, as the power of a successful transition to recovery is significant.

Function of Follow-Up After Discharge. As part of the transition plan that is developed with the family, it will be important to plan for follow-up. In the past, some practitioners have been taught that "termination" means that the relationship between the practitioner and family is discontinued. From the perspective of a family empowerment paradigm, this activity is considered important to preserve. Follow-up leaves the door open for supporting the family in the future to sustain its progress or even consider needed changes in its recovery plan. When following up with the youth and family, it is important to ask how this can best occur. Input from the youth and family should be sought both in regards to how this should best occur and at the time of follow-up.

CONCLUSION

The history of concern for families in need has evolved throughout time. The way in which families have been assisted in the past has elements that have been maintained as well as drastically changed. The basis for home- and community-based services has been substantiated through a number of different initiatives and areas of focus related to youth and families. An understanding of how the various theoretical underpinnings of home- and community-based services has also been discussed to strengthen the understanding of how these theories currently inform and guide service provision. The various phases of service delivery each hold important elements and tasks that, when woven together, produce an experience that supports recovery for youth and families who struggle with mental health challenges.

References

Addams, J. (1910). *Twenty years at Hull House.* New York: Macmillan.

Allen, S. F., & Tracy, E. M. (2008). Developing student knowledge and skills for home-based social work practice. *Journal of Social Work Education, 44*, 125-143.

Barker, R. L. (1995). *The Social Work Dictionary* (3rd ed.). Washington, DC: NASW Press.

Beder, J. (1998). The home visit, revisited. Families in society. *Journal of Contemporary Human Services, 79*, 514-522.

Bertalanffy, L. von (1968). *General system theory.* New York: Braziller.

Bhavnagri, N. P., & Krolikowski, S. (2000). Home-community visits during an era of reform (1870-1920). *Early Childhood Research and Practice, 2*(1), 1-39. Retrieved May 26, 2009, from http://ecrp.uiuc.edu/v2n1/bhavnagri.html

Bronfenbrenner, U. (1979). *The ecology of human development. Experiments by nature and design.* Cambridge, MA: Harvard University Press.

Bronfenbrenner, U. (1995). Developmental ecology through space and time: A future perspective. In P. Moen, G. H. Elder, Jr., & K. Luscher (Eds.), *Examining lives in context: Perspectives on the ecology of human development* (pp. 619-647). Washington, DC: American Psychological Association.

Brookman-Frazee, L., Haine, R. A., Gabayan, E. N., & Garland, A. F. (2008). Predicting frequency of treatment visits in community-based youth psychotherapy. *Psychological Services, 5*, 126-138.

Bruno, F. J. (1957). *Trends in social work practice: 1874-1956.* New York: Columbia University Press.

Carrilio, T. E. (2007). *Home-visiting strategies: A case-management guide for caregivers.* Columbia: University of South Carolina Press.

Cox, C. (1992). Expanding social work's role in home care: An ecological perspective. *Social Work 37*, 179-183.

De Civita, M. (2006, Winter). Strength-based efforts for promoting recovery from psychological harm. *Reclaiming Children & Youth, 14*, 241-244.

Donahue, M. P. (1985). *Nursing, the finest art: An illustrated history.* St. Louis, MO: CV Mosby.

Dreyer, B. (1976, January). The mental hygiene movement: Institutional response to individual concern the early years of the Philadelphia Child Guidance Clinic. *American Journal of Public Health, 66*, 85-91.

Dunst, C. J. & Trivette, C. M., & Deal, A. G. (1994). *Supporting & strengthening families: Methods, strategies and practices.* Cambridge, MA: Brookline Books.

Early, T. J., & GlenMaye, L. F. (2000). Valuing families: Social work practice with families from a strengths perspective. *Social Work, 45,* 118-130.

Enns, R., Reddon, J., & McDonald, L. (1999). Indications of resilience among family members of people admitted to a psychiatric facility. *Psychiatric Rehabilitation Journal, 23,* 127-135.

Family resiliency: Building strengths to meet life's challenges. (n.d.). Retrieved June 8, 2009, from http://www.extension.iastate.edu/Publications/EDC53.pdf

Fink, A. (1942). *The field of social work.* New York: Henry Holt.

Fink, A. (1955). *The field of social work* (3rd ed.). New York: Henry Holt.

Germain, C. B. (1973). An ecological perspective in casework practice. *Social Casework, 54,* 323-330.

Germain, C. B. (1979). Ecology and social work. In C. B. Germain (Ed.), *Social work practice: People and environments: An ecological perspective* (pp. 1-22). New York: Columbia University Press.

Goldstein, H. (1973). *Social work practice: A unitary approach.* Columbia: University of South Carolina Press.

Gomby, D., Larson, C. S., Lewit, E. M., & Behrman, R. E. (1993). Home visiting: Analysis and recommendations. *Future of Children, 3,* 6-22.

Greeff, A. P., Vansteenwegen, A., & Ide, M. (2006). Resiliency in families with a member with a psychological disorder. *American Journal of Family Therapy, 34,* 285-300.

Green, B., Johnson, S., & Rodgers, A. (1999). Understanding patterns of service delivery and participation in community-based family support programs. *Children's Services: Social Policy, Research & Practice, 2,* 1-22.

Hancock, B. L., & Pelton, L. H. (1989). Home visits: History and functions. *Social Casework, 70,* 21-27.

Haynes, D. T., & White, B. W. (1999). Will the "real" social work please stand up? A call to stand for professional unity. *Social Work, 44,* 385-391.

Kemp, S., Whittaker, J, & Tracy, E. (1997). Person-environment practice: The social ecology of interpersonal helping. New York: Aldine De Gruyter.

Knitzer, J. (1982). *Unclaimed children: The failure of public responsibility to children and adolescents in need of mental health services.* Washington, DC: Children's Defense Fund.

Koren, P. E., DeChillo, N., & Friesen, B. J. (1992). Measuring empowerment in families whose children have emotional disabilities: A brief questionnaire. *Rehabilitation Psychology, 37,* 305-321.

Laursen, E. K. (2000). Strength-based practice with children in trouble. *Reclaiming Children and Youth: Journal of Strength-Based Interventions, 9,* 70-75.

Lee, J. A. B. (1996). The empowerment approach to social work practice. In F. J. Turner (Ed.), *Social work treatment: Interlocking theoretical approaches* (4th ed., pp. 218-249). New York: Free Press.

Matthews, W., & Johnson, C. (1997). Strengthening diverse and dysfunctional families via family resiliency education. Presentation at the annual meeting of the American Association of Family and Consumer Sciences, Washington, DC.

McCubbin, H. I., McCubbin, M. A., & Thompson, A. I. (1993). Resiliency in families: The role of family schema and appraisal in family adaptation to crisis. In T. H. Brubaker (Ed.), *Family relations: Challenges for the future* (pp. 153-177). Beverly Hills, CA: Sage.

Minuchin, P. (1985). Families and individual development. Provocation from the field of family therapy. *Child Development, 56,* 289-302.

Murdach, A. D. (2007). Situational approaches to direct practice: Origin, decline and re-emergence. *Social Work, 52,* 211-218.

Pecora, P. J., Reed-Ashcraft, K., & Kirk, R. S. (2001). Family-centered services: A typology, brief history, and overview of current program implementation and evaluation challenges. In E. Walton, P. Sandau-Beckler, & M. Mannes (Eds.), *Balancing family-centered services and child well-being: Exploring issues in policy, practice, theory, and research* (pp. 1-33). New York: Columbia University Press.

Penrod, T. (2008). Direct support services in wraparound. In E. J. Bruns & J. S. Walker (Eds.), *The resource guide to wraparound.* Portland, OR: National Wraparound Initiative, Research and Training Center for Family Support and Children's Mental Health.

Richmond, M. E. (1899). *Friendly visiting among the poor: A handbook for charity workers.* New York: Macmillan.

Roberts, R. N., Wasik, B. H., Casto, G., & Ramey, C. T. (1991). Family support in the home: Programs, policy, and social change. *American Psychologist, 46,* 131–137.

Sandau-Beckler, P. (2001). Family-centered assessment and goal setting. In E. Walton, P. Sandau-Beckler, & M. Mannes (Eds.), *Balancing family-centered services and child well-being: Exploring issues in policy, practice, theory, and research* (pp. 93-127). New York: Columbia University Press.

Staples, L. H. (1990). Powerful idea about empowerment. *Administration in Social Work, 14,* 29-42.

Stroul, B. A. (1988). *Home-based services. Volume I. Series on community-based services for children and adolescents who are severely emotionally disturbed.* Washington, DC: Georgetown University Child Development Center.

Stroul, B. A., & Friedman, R. M. (1986). A system of care for children and youth with severe emotional disturbances. (Rev. ed.). Washington, DC: Georgetown University Child Development Center, CASSP Technical Assistance Center.

Tracy, E. M. (2001). Interventions: Hard and soft services. In E. Walton, P. Sandau-Beckler, & M. Mannes (Eds.), *Balancing family-centered services and child well-being: Exploring issues in policy, practice, theory, and research* (pp. 155-178). New York: Columbia University Press.

U.S. Census Bureau. (2001, May). *Profiles of general demographic characteristics: 2000 census of population and housing.* Retrieved February 1, 2009, from http://www.census.gov/prod/cen2000/dp1/2kh00.pdf

Vandenberg, J., Bruns, E., & Burchard, J. (2003). History of the wrap-around process. *Focal Point: A National Bulletin on Family Support and Children's Mental Health: Quality and Fidelity in Wraparound, 17*(2), 4-7.

Walsh, F. (1998). *Strengthening family resilience.* New York: Guilford.

Wasik, B. H., & Bryant, D. M. (2001). *Home visiting: Procedures for helping families* (2nd ed.). Newbury Park, CA: Sage.

Weiss, H. B. (1993). Home visits: Necessary but not sufficient. *Future of Children, 3,* 113-128.

Wells, K. (1995). Family preservation services in context: Origins, practices, and current issues. In I. M. Schwartz & P. AuClaire (Eds.), *Home-Based services for troubled children.* (pp. 1-28). Lincoln: University of Nebraska Press.

Werner, E. E., & Smith, R. S. (2001). *Journeys from childhood to midlife: Risk, resilience, and recovery.* Ithaca, NY: Cornell University Press.

Wise, J. B. (2005). *Empowerment practice with families in distress.* New York: Columbia University Press.

Chapter 2

Youth and Families Supported by Home- and Community-Based Services

One of the most valuable things we can do to heal one another is listen to each other's stories.

—Rebecca Falls

I see their souls, and I hold them in my hands, and because I love them they weigh nothing.

—Pearl Bailey

INTRODUCTION

Our society has long accepted the existence of physical and developmental concerns in children of all ages. Families typically feel comfortable discussing such issues with friends and family members, and seeking professional help when needed. Sadly, the same recognition and acceptance of mental health concerns in children has not been achieved. Families describe multiple layers of stigma that occur when mental health concerns are recognized in children. Just as adults struggling with mental health issues experience judgment and unnecessary discrimination, children are exposed to the same experiences. Additionally, caregivers often feel a strong sense of blame and criticism related to their child's struggles. Because of this, there are millions of families who suffer unnecessarily. This chapter reviews the range and prevalence of mental health issues that are seen in children of all ages. It describes how mental health issues manifest differently across the developmental spectrum and how this necessitates different services and supports for the various developmental stages.

DEFINITION OF YOUTH WITH SERIOUS EMOTIONAL CHALLENGES

Since the 1980s, there has been considerable concern in this country for the mental health needs of youth. In 1980, Congress passed the Mental Health Systems Act (Public Law No. 96-398), which reorganized the community mental health system, and later, in 1984, a national program for youth was developed. The Child and Adolescent Service System Program (CASSP) was developed through funding from the National Institute of Mental Health. Its focus was to respond to the needs of children and adolescents with mental health concerns. On July 10, 1992, the Alcohol, Drug Abuse, and Mental Health Administration Reorganization Act (ADAMHA Reorganization Act; Public Law No. 102-321) was enacted. This law created the Substance Abuse and Mental Health Services Administration (SAMHSA), and the Center for Mental Health Services (CMHS), which was to function as part of SAMHSA. CMHS was established to regulate and coordinate federal efforts in the prevention and treatment of mental illnesses. Additionally, CMHS was to seek and disseminate research and knowledge related to mental health and best practices in the treatment of disorders. CASSP also became part of CMHS in 1992 (Lourie, Katz-Levy, DeCarolis, & Quilan, 1996).

The ADAMHA Reorganization Act defined serious emotional disturbance as follows:

Children with a serious emotional disturbance are persons from birth up to age 18, who currently or at any time during the past year, have had a diagnosable mental, behavioral, or emotional disorder of sufficient duration to meet diagnostic criteria specified within DSM-III-R, that resulted in functional impairment which substantially interferes with or limits the child's role or functioning in family, school, or community activities. . . . Functional impairment is defined as difficulties that substantially interfere with or limit a child or adolescent from achieving or maintaining one or more developmentally appropriate social, behavioral, cognitive, communicative or adaptive skills. Functional impairments of episodic, recurrent, and continuous duration are included unless they are temporary and expected responses to stressful events in their environments. Children who would have met functional impairment criteria during the referenced year without the benefit of treatment or other support services are included. (Substance Abuse and Mental Health Service Administration, 1993, p. 29425)

This definition served to standardize the classification of youth with serious emotional disturbances so that funding and evaluation of programs could be more clearly linked to a specific population. This also gave the federal government a way to ensure that prevalence and incidence reports for the population of youth determined as seriously emotionally disturbed was accurate.

NEED FOR ACTION

Prevalence

Jane Knitzer claimed in her 1982 report for the Children's Defense Fund, *Unclaimed Children: The Failure of Public Responsibility to Children and Adolescents in Need of Mental Health Services,* that there were approximately three million children with serious mental health concerns. Of the three million children, she believed that two thirds were not getting the services and supports they needed. According to the 1999 report by the U.S. surgeon general, nearly 21 percent of U.S children between the ages of 9 and 17 had a mental or substance abuse disorder, which resulted in at least minimum impairment in functioning. Of the same youth, when the requirement for impairment in functioning was significant, the percentage was approximately 11 percent. Youth who had extreme functional impairment were estimated at 5 percent. The most common disorders were anxiety disorders, mood disorders, disruptive behavior disorders, attention deficit hyperactivity disorder (ADHD), and substance use disorders (U.S. Department of Health and Human Services, 1999).

In 1998, Costello, Messer, Bird, Cohen, and Reinherz conducted a study to determine prevalence rates of serious emotional disturbance in youth ages 4 to 18. Youth represented five different areas of the United States including Boston, upstate New York, Pittsburgh, North Carolina, and Puerto Rico. Youth were also representative of Hispanic, American Indian, African American, and white non-Hispanic ethnicities. Median percentage prevalence rates were reported as 14.5 percent of youth experiencing anxiety disorder, 8.3 percent experiencing conduct/oppositional defiant disorder, 3.3 percent experiencing ADHD, and 3.1 percent experiencing depressive disorder. There were no significant differences related to ethnicity, although low socioeconomic status was the strongest correlate of serious emotional disturbance.

Although there are fewer prevalence studies for young children, there have been reports that indicate that mental health concerns are present. Prevalence rates of serious behavior concerns in children between 2 and 3 years of age have been studied, and the majority of estimates falls between 10 and 15 percent (per researchers cited in Carter, Briggs-Gowan, & Davis, 2004). Additionally, caregiver and pediatrician reports for 1- and 2-year-olds showed a 10 percent prevalence of emotional and behavioral problems (Jenkins, Bax, & Hart, 1980). As well, Brauner and Stephens (2006) reported prevalence rates of mental health concerns in 0- to 5-year-olds to be between

9.5 and 14 percent. Although, most mental health specialists would agree that the *Diagnostic and Statistical Manual of Mental Disorders,* fourth edition, text revision (*DSM-IV-TR*; American Psychiatric Association, 2000) does not adequately reflect the clinical manifestations of the very young, there have been studies to determine diagnostic patterns. In a recently published study in which a cohort of 796 4-year-old children was studied, the most prevalent disorders diagnosed were oppositional defiant disorder (ODD) and ADHD. Youth with comorbid disorders were present at the rate of 6.3 percent (Lavigne, LeBailly, Hopkins, Gouze, & Binns, 2009; see Table 2.1).

Specialty Populations

Youth in Child Welfare System. Youth in the foster care system are of special concern. Being removed from caregivers and placed in an unfamiliar setting can only be considered a traumatic event. Several research studies have confirmed the high rate of mental health issues for children in the foster care system. Clausen, Landsverk, Ganger, Chadwick, and Litrownik (1998) report that their research not only confirms this notion but suggests the assumption that mental health needs exist for youth in foster care. The identification of what mental health issues need to be addressed, so that the most relevant and appropriate treatment can occur, is of concern. Overall, there is a strong need for comprehensive and thorough mental health screening for youth in foster care. But access to high-quality services is problematic (Pecora, Jensen, Romaelli, Jackson, & Ortiz, 2009).

One of the most common mental health issues that youth in the foster care system experience is traumatic stress. Child traumatic stress is defined as "a psychological reaction that some children have to a traumatic experience" (National Child Traumatic Stress Network, 2001, p. 3). The symptoms of child traumatic stress may include mood disturbances; changes in behavior; difficulties in school, home, or the community; difficulty eating or sleeping; and withdrawal. These symptoms are often persistent and affect a child's daily life in a variety of ways. Young children are at particularly high risk for trauma reactions when in the foster care system in part due to the tremendous strain that separation from primary caregivers creates. Additionally, young children in foster care, who have witnessed domestic violence or have experienced the failure of being protected, often experience significant disruptions in the development and maintenance of a healthy attachment pattern. School-age children's and adolescent's trauma reactions have been studied for more than twenty years, and research clearly shows that they can and do experience the full range of posttraumatic stress reactions that are seen in adults (National Child Traumatic Stress Network, 2001). Children that experience violence and traumatic stress are also affected neurobiologically; their physical health, cognitive functioning, and emotional and behavioral regulation can be negatively affected (DeBellis, 2001). Home- and community-based services can be beneficial to youth who have experienced trauma because development of coping skills and resiliency can be supported within the environments they are most comfortable. Home- and community-based services provide opportunites to understand youth's unique responses and coping strategies, and can often be best understood in these environments; they also present opportunities to educate and support the caregivers and adults who are present in the youth's lives.

Youth in Juvenile Justice System. Youth who are involved with the juvenile justice system often meet the criteria for serious emotional disturbance and are in dire need

Table 2.1
Characteristics of Youth With Serious Emotional Disturbances

Most Common Diagnosis in 9- to 17-Year-Olds
• Anxiety disorders • Mood disorders • Disruptive behavior disorders • Attention deficit hyperactivity disorder • Substance use disorders
Prevalence Rates of Emotional and Behavioral Problems in 0-5 Year Olds
• 9.5 percent to 14 percent (Brauner & Stephens, 2006) • Co-morbidity rate of 6.3 percent (Lavigne et al., 2009)

Source: U.S. Department of Health and Human Services (1999); Brauner & Stephens (2006); Lavigne et al. (2009). *Adapted by Permission from Indiana Association of Infant and Toddler Mental Health (IAITMH). © 2007.*

of mental health services. ODD and conduct disorder, which both have criteria that put youth at risk for legal involvement, are two of the most commonly diagnosed mental health conditions in youth with serious emotional disturbances (U.S. Department of Health and Human Services, 1999). In a study of youth in juvenile detention, nearly two thirds of males and nearly three quarters of females met diagnostic criteria for one or more mental health disorders. Substance use disorders were present in nearly half of both males and females, and nearly 40 percent of both males and females met the criteria for disruptive behavior disorders. Depression was also ranked highly, especially in females. The study believes that the actual prevalence rate of detained youth with mental health conditions is likely to be much higher due to research design issues and underreporting of symptoms and impairments (Teplin, Abram, McClelland, Dulcan, & Mericle, 2002).

The juvenile justice system is often the door by which youth enter the "system" and become known to child services agencies as high risk and in need of assistance. It is imperative that youth are treated holistically and that issues are not ignored. First-time offenders or those engaging in illegal behaviors that have not yet been arrested need to be considered for mental health concerns. Often, the timely and comprehensive treatment of mental health concerns can prevent detention and incarceration. Sadly, this has not been the experience of many youth and families.

Caregivers often do not know where to turn. In 2001, there were approximately 12,700 cases of youth placed in the custody of child welfare and juvenile justice solely based on the fact that they needed to access mental health services. Nearly 9,000 of these youth were placed in the juvenile justice system for delinquency issues that were directly related to emotional disorders (U.S. General Accounting Office, 2003). Of greatest concern is youth being placed in adult institutions. In these circumstances, youth are 500 percent more likely to be sexually assaulted, 200 percent more likely to be beaten by staff, and 50 percent more likely to be attacked by other inmates with a weapon (American Civil Liberties Union, 1996). It is likely that exposure to these types of traumas will not only exacerbate but create additional mental health concerns that can persist for years to come. Despite many people's contention that these types of experiences are isolated and overexaggerated, these and worse conditions have been documented and reported. The American Civil Liberties Union of Eastern Missouri

(ACLU-EM) investigated the St. Louis Justice Center and the Medium Security Institute (CJC/MSI) in 2007 because of allegations of civil liberties' violations and physical abuse. Findings in this investigation included, but were not limited to, inmate assaults provoked by correctional officers, sexual misconduct, medical neglect, systemic cover up of incidents, situations in which inmates were stripped naked and subjected to temperature extremes, and negligence resulting in death (Hudson, 2009). With this reality, attention must be paid to the mental health needs of youth in juvenile justice settings; gross negligence is suggested on the part of mental health practitioners who do otherwise.

Risks and Consequences of Inaction

Young children who experience mental health challenges often continue to be symptomatic for as long as one to two years beyond the time that the impairment is recognized (Mathieson & Sanson, 2000; Lavigne et al., 1996). This underscores the notion that mental health challenges in young children are not transient and do persist. What occurs as a result of these mental health difficulties is equally of concern. Disturbances that may have been at a mild level are often compounded and present with more serious consequences to a youth's functioning. It is also important to consider that the benefits of intervening early are great. One consideration is the likelihood that early developmental problems, especially ones that persist, are linked to later incompetence and challenges (Houck, 1999). When this occurs, caregivers may become less confident in their caregiving abilities, and their sense of efficacy may be diminished (Carter et al., 2004). This may, in turn begin to impact the caregiver-child relationship in a way that may have persistent and damaging consequences for relationship capacities throughout a child's lifetime. There are often serious consequences for youth, especially very young children, who experience ongoing and chronic states of anxiety and stress. This experience often creates a persistent state of hyperarousal and fear that leaves a youngster preoccupied and unable to reap the benefits of stimulation that would typically promote all areas of development. A child can be especially compromised socially, emotionally, and cognitively, despite the fact that all areas of development are likely to be influenced negatively by this experience (Perry, 1996). When these issues are minimized or overlooked entirely, there are also consequences clearly related to later school performance. Last, emotional well-being and social emotional development have long been considered the foundation for early learning, and numerous federal and state initiatives exist to support this (Shonkoff, Phillips, & Board on Children, Youth, and Families (États-Unis), Committee on Integrating the Science of Early Childhood Development, 2000).

As youth grow older, there continue to be serious consequences when intervention does not occur. Youth who endure years of suffering often experience challenges in school, both academically and behaviorally. Strained relationships with both adults and peers may result and reinforce youth's beliefs that they are unworthy and to blame for the mental health issues they are attempting to manage. Because untreated mental health disorders tend to become more severe, the additional stressors and attitudes only make treatment and outcomes less desirable in the future (Koppelman, George Washington University, & National Health Policy Forum, 2004). Statistically, youth diagnosed with mental, emotional, and behavioral disorders are more likely to use alcohol and drugs. This occurs both because they may be biologically vulnerable to substance abuse/dependence and also because they use substances to mitigate the effects of anxiety and depression. More than half of those with a mental health disorder that is chronic and persistent also have a substance use disorder. This is especially true for 15- to 24-year-olds who have the highest rates of this (U.S. Department of Health and Human Services, 1999). When stress and depression go for long periods without intervention, serious consequences can and do occur for all ages but especially for teens and young adults. The third leading cause of death among teens and young adults is suicide (Centers for Disease Control and Prevention, 2007). In addition to these effects, policy makers focus on prevention efforts in this arena due to the strong link between mental health issues and medical issues as well as juvenile justice problems (U.S. Department of Health and Human Services, 1999).

THE YOUNGEST AND MOST VULNERABLE

Evaluating Mental Health Needs in Infants, Toddlers, and Preschoolers

The most common and overwhelming effect of mental health challenges in infants, toddlers, and preschoolers is slowed, regressed, or stalemated development (Beitchman, Wilson, Brownlie, Walters, & Lancee, 1996; Irwin, Carter, & Briggs-Gowan, 2002). The areas of development include cognitive, social-emotional, speech and language, self-help, and motor. When a person of any age experiences stress or trauma, it is common to experience regression in some form. The effects of this on a youngster is more pronounced and notable. This is partially due to the fact that a young child's development is still in process, and success in one area is often dependent on success in another area. When development is not consolidated, the effects of a mental health condition are more dramatic and profound.

When considering emotional and behavioral conditions in young children, the *DSM-IV-TR*, which is used for diagnostic purposes, is considered by most infant mental health specialists to be narrow and inappropriate. There are several reasons for this. The first pertains to the fact that symptoms of disorders in the *DSM IV-TR* often represent normal behavior patterns for young children. An example is tantrums, which are part of the criteria for ODD. Another area of concern refers to the rapid changes in young children's development in terms of emotional and behavioral expressions. This creates challenges in applying time frames to meet the criteria for chronicity of disturbance. Also, young children are limited in their verbal and abstract thinking skills, and this prevents them from meeting criteria in some disorders, for example, depression, in which verbal expression of distress is needed. Alternative signs of distress that characterize young children are not seen in the *DSM IV-TR*. Last, the importance of young children's relationships and home environments is not fully appreciated in the *DSM-IV-TR* (Evangelista & McLellan, 2004).

The *Diagnostic Classification: 0-3R (Revised)* (*DC 0-3 R*) was created by the national organization, Zero to Three, which is dedicated to promoting knowledge regarding the 0-3 population. The *DC 0-3 R,* in contrast to the *DSM IV-TR,* attempts to accurately reflect mental health conditions in young children by appreciating the importance of relationships and offering developmentally based conceptualizations resulting in an alternate yet similar classification system. Categories of disorders include, but are not limited to, posttraumatic stress disorder and deprivation maltreatment disorder; disorders of affect; anxiety disorders of infancy and early childhood; depression of infancy and early childhood; disorders of relating and communicating; regulatory disorders of sensory processing; and adjustment disorders. The five axis system includes the following: Axis I: Primary Diagnosis; Axis II: Relationship Disorder Classification System; Axis III: Medical and Developmental Disorders and Conditions; Axis IV: Psychosocial Stressors; and Axis V: Functional Emotional Development (Zero to Three, 1994).

Posttraumatic stress disorder refers to either a single or chronic stressful event and more accurately reflects how young children express trauma. Disorders of affect and adjustment disorders conceptually are similar to the *DSM IV-TR* but have alternate duration and symptom descriptions. Regulatory disorders represent difficulty in regulating physiological, sensory, attentional, motor, or affective processes, coupled with a distinct behavioral response. Disorders of relating and communicating describe difficulty processing the same types of experiences but also have problems related to communication and relating to others (Evangelista & McLellan, 2004).

The Indiana Association of Infant and Toddler Mental Health (IAITMH) has written a crosswalk that relates the *DSM-IV-TR* diagnosis to the *DC 0-3 R* diagnosis (see Exhibit 2.1).

Development of Strength and Resiliency

Resiliency is described as the ability to cope with adversity and recover from setbacks (Ginsburg & Jablow, 2006). Without this capacity, young children will be limited in their ability to focus adequately on development. The main consideration in developing strengths in young children, which will facilitate the development of resiliency, is to support their primary caregivers. This support includes providing the caregivers with the needed tools to do their jobs sufficiently. When support is in place, caregivers can fully focus on nurturing the children in the manner that is needed. The key is often the development of important relationships outside of the family for both the caregivers and the children as they mature. Relationships outside of the family refer to the presence of supportive adults in the children's lives and resources within the community that are available and used by the children (Fraser, Kirby, & Smokowski, 2004). Caregivers with supportive others in their lives can use the power of the attachment relationship and the understanding of their children's temperaments to foster resiliency.

When considering the importance of fostering strengths within an individual child, there is nothing that has more of an impact and is more far reaching than attachment security. Numerous infant mental health specialists have emphasized how the infant-caregiver relationship is the vehicle for development and overall positive well-being. Several longitudinal studies have demonstrated significant benefits for children as development unfolds and throughout their lives. The multiple benefits that have been demonstrated include overall increased competence in such areas as self-esteem; independence and autonomy; resilience in the face of adversity; ability to manage feelings and impulses; long-term friendships; relationships with caregivers and authority figures; prosocial coping skills; trust, intimacy, and affection; positive belief system about self, family, and society; empathy, compassion, and conscience development; behavior performance; academic success; and overall health (Greenberg, Cicchetti, & Cummings, 1990; Hughes, 1997; Keck & Kupecky, 1995; Levy & Orlans, 1998; Ranson & Urichuk, 2008). Although it is easy to grasp how a secure attachment affects social-emotional competence, the influence on cognitive development and overall health are more difficult to comprehend. Schore (2001) reports findings that attachment security promotes brain growth and development, and improved cognitive functioning in such areas as object permanence, symbolic play, and problem solving. Additionally, children who are confident that their caregivers will meet their needs are able to focus on exploration and learning. Ranson and Urichuk (2008) report that strong attachment relationships buffer the effects of the stress hormone cortisol and support better overall health. The condition known as "failure to thrive" is also related to attachment security. Failure to thrive infants are two times as likely to exhibit anxious or disorganized attachment patterns than their securely attached counterparts (Ward, Lee, & Lipper, 2000). With this overwhelming evidence of the benefits of attachment security, interventionists should be prioritizing strategies to promote positive attachment.

Another important area to pay attention to when fostering strengths in young children is temperament. The Kauai Longitudinal Study, completed by Werner and Smith (1992), followed a cohort of 505 individuals for nearly forty years. The impact of biological factors, psychosocial risk factors, adverse life events, and protective factors were studied. Two areas, related to constitution, health, and temperament characteristics, impacted resilient children to the greatest degree (Werner & Smith, 1992).

Thomas, Chess, and Birch (1968) determined nine temperament characteristics that can be used to describe the way in which behaviors are displayed. These characteristics are as follows: sensory threshold, activity level, intensity, rhythmicity, adaptability, mood, approach/withdrawal, persistence, and distractibility. All of the characteristics are seen as having a range of manifestations that tend to make up an individual's life-long style of interaction. One pattern of temperament that emerged from this research was characterized as "easy temperament." This pattern was described as regularity in bodily functions, positive mood, high adaptability, positive approach to others, and mild intensity in reactions. These children developed regular sleep and feeding schedules, reacted positively to strangers, smiled and laughed often, and coped well with transitions and new experiences. All of these characteristics tended to afford them more positive interactions with siblings, peers, adult caregivers, and authority figures. In contrast, characteristics that tended to be problematic for children included low adaptability to transitions, high intensity of reactions, low level of persistence, and negative mood. Although temperament characteristics should not necessarily be considered indicative of a disorder, some characteristics are associated with challenges and mental health disorders. Several researchers have determined that temperament traits that are referred to as "difficult," such as slow adaptability, withdrawal, negative mood, high intensity, excessive persistence, and excessive distractibility, were associated with behavioral disorders (Thomas et al., 1968; Earls, 1981; Kolvin, Nicol, Garside, Day, & Tweedle, 1982). In terms of mental health issues, there is evidence that youth with high sensitivity and withdrawal are at risk of developing anxiety disorders (Aron, 2002; Kagan, Snidman, Arcus, & Reznick, 1994). Youth can be supported in developing effective coping skills especially when their natural reactions and behaviors cause difficulties for both the youth and others. With the significance and breadth of temperament research assisting practitioners in conceptualizing the protective nature that an easy temperament can offer, strategies to promote this should be taught, supported, and reinforced.

In an effort to assist young children, from a strength-based perspective, building capacity and strengths in the caregivers are crucial. One of the greatest areas in which to build strengths is in caregiver resources. This includes social, financial, and other types of resources. Caregivers who are struggling to meet the family's basic needs for

Table 2.2
Characteristics of Extended Family Support

Types of Extended Family Support	Indicators of Support Being of Benefit to Caregivers
Social Support/Socialization	Provides support that is enjoyable and meaningful to the caregivers
Provision of Services	Support is wanted and/or requested
Advice or Information	Support builds caregivers' competence
Emotional Support	Support is in line with caregivers' values and decisions
Role Models	Support complements caregiver-child relationship

survival arc often too preoccupied to meet a young child's emotional and other needs. Caregivers who have a network of friends, family, and community supports are well armed to face stressful situations in the future and keep a strong focus on the caregiving needs of their child (see Table 2.2).

As young children begin to experience social connections to adults (e.g., teachers and community members), it is helpful to ensure that these interactions are as supportive and positive as possible (see Table 2.3). Caregivers who have been assisted in understanding their children's needs and strengths should be empowered to advocate and support their children as they broaden their social experiences. The balance of understanding and supporting a child's individual personality profile, while meeting the needs of a group of children, is a daunting task for most teachers. This is more likely to occur if caregivers are able to develop positive relationships with teachers. Education, consultation, and support for identified teachers and other supportive adults should always be considered a priority for home- and community-based practitioners working with young children.

Unique Characteristics of Services to Infants, Toddlers, and Preschoolers

A young child's developmental capacities have definite implications for the way in which services should be delivered. As the most important element in service provision for young children is strengthening the caregiver-child relationship, creating a situation in which this is most likely to occur is crucial. A child under the age of 3 is typically developing the ability to keep a relationship in mind and remember the associated feelings that this relationship evokes. Object constancy refers to the ability to maintain a sense of a relationship even when the person is away or when the relationship is challenged with disappointments. A child who is able to do this can tolerate separations, feel comforted by thinking about the person he/she is separated from, and maintain positive feelings even when disappointments occur (Mahler, Pine, & Bergman, 1975). Before this ability is firmly established, reunifications are stressful and challenging due to the children not being able to fully remember the experience of being in a relationship with the person they have been separated from.

Table 2.3
Characteristics of Supportive Adult/Youth Relationships

- The child and supportive adult spend time together in activities that are pleasurable to the child.
- The child and supportive adult describe routines and traditions specific to their relationship.
- The child and supportive adult describe appropriate roles and boundaries within their relationship.
- The child is able to accept direction, structure, support, and affection from the adult; if challenges are present in this area, they are not inconsistent with reactions in other relationships and may reflect mental health or overall relationship challenges.
- The child's experiences with the supportive adult do not contradict rules, values, or expectations that adult considers important.
- The child's experiences with extended family members are consistent and predictable.

Although mental health practitioners must always remember the importance of supporting developing relationships between caregivers and child, they too must be able to establish a relationship with the child. If home visits occur too far apart, the ability to maintain the momentum and gains that the services have to offer is significantly minimized. It will feel as if the work must begin over and over. Additionally, it will be difficult for the child to become comfortable with the practitioner if visits are too far apart. This same challenge exists for caregivers who may be experiencing issues with their young child. Many adults need careful attention to the experience of developing a relationship, as their own early childhood experiences may have been less than ideal. Practitioners must take opportunities to facilitate strong relationships with the caregivers, as this will facilitate the caregivers' abilities to do build strong relationships with their child. While there must be a relationship between the practitioner and the child, and the practitioner and the caregivers, the practitioner must remember that his/her role is to support the relationship between the caregivers and the child. Keeping in mind the strengths of each, perspectives, and what each one brings to the relationship is often a challenging task.

Since development is not static, it is not uncommon for issues to appear to resolve quickly or to become overshadowed by different concerns. It is often stressful and difficult to accept that a young child is experiencing challenges. Caregivers often feel blamed and eager to see progress. Issues can manifest differently than what was initially identified. When this occurs, it may be a challenge for caregivers to continue with services and transition in a way that is well planned.

Caregivers of young children must be given a wide range of services in appreciation of the multiple challenges and expectations that they face. As development is usually affected by mental health challenges, the importance of education and support in understanding the range of what should be expected and how to enhance development is needed. The education that is needed should not occur until a cultural discovery has occurred that can serve to inform the practitioner of how the individual family functions from a cultural perspective. Development and mental health are always woven together. Additionally, supporting caregivers in getting their own needs met is necessary to optimize conditions so that attention to the child's needs is able to occur. Teaching skills that are needed to manage behavior, support development, and regulate emotion are also vital when working with young children.

SCHOOL-AGE YOUTH

Manifestations of Mental Health Needs in School-Age Youth

School-age youth present with mental health challenges in a variety of ways. Their development is more consolidated than younger children (see "The Youngest and Most Vulnerable"), so the impact and presence of developmental issues is less noticeable. School-age youth are typically focused on forming and maintaining relationships with their peers; developing relationships and interests separate from their families; and growing emotionally, cognitively, and physically. When mood disorders occur, it is common to see difficulties in these areas. Relationships with peers can be strained, distant, or even nonexistent, as depression alters a youth's perception and ability to cope with this task of middle childhood. Relationships with authority figures may be strained, and this is most often seen within the school environment. Outside interests and community activities may have stopped or be challenging for a youth to maintain. It may appear that a youth is withdrawing from others. As caregivers are often the ones to identify mental health challenges, behavior is usually identified as altered. Disruptive behavior disorders are frequently identified as the source of concern even when underlying depression or anxiety may be contributing to the issues. Friedman, Katash, and Duchnowski (1996), after synthesizing the results of six studies, identified youth with serious emotional disturbances to have problems in the life domains of school, community, and family relationships. Although there were many diagnoses, the most common were disruptive behavior disorders and mood disorders (Friedman et al., 1996).

It is believed by many mental health practitioners that the experience of trauma is prevalent in youth and that many youth are treated for other mental health conditions when trauma is the underlying cause. Many school-age youth have experienced both acute and chronic traumatic situations. Symptoms may include depression, behavioral concerns, risky behaviors, problems maintaining relationships, anxiety, and difficulty eating and sleeping. In a sample of youth served in system of care communities from 2002 to 2004, 75 percent had experienced at least one indicator of trauma or a posttraumatic stress disorder, and the youth who had experienced trauma were significantly more likely to have suicidal ideation or self-injury (U.S. Department of Health and Human Services, Substance Abuse and Mental Health Services Administration, Center for Mental Health Services, 2007). Trauma is of great concern and should always be considered in the presence of behavioral and emotional concerns.

Development of Strength and Resiliency

A long-lasting and impactful protective factor to strive for is the presence of a supportive adult or mentor outside of the family. This has been shown in numerous longitudinal and other research studies to be a common denominator in youth who cope well with adversity (Brooks, 1994; Grizenko & Pawliuk, 1994; Werner, 1993). Although, there is nothing more powerful than the caregiver-child relationship, when caregivers are stressed or compromised in their functioning, having another adult to support the youth is of great value. These relationships also serve to assist the youth in experiencing relationships outside of the families and strengthen their ability to trust and relate to others. Related to this protective factor is the strong benefit in strengthening community ties and activities. Youth who are active in their communities and feel connected and safe within their communities have more protection against adversity than those who do not.

Educational achievement is a strength that should be fostered in the individual youth. Although, youth may have challenges in this area, experiencing a school environment that maximizes youth's abilities to learn and have positive educational experiences is extremely beneficial to youth both while they are younger and into the future. Similarly, fostering problem-solving skills has far-reaching effects for youth. This can occur through skill-development activities and experiences in which success is reinforced and praised. Another skill to be fostered is sociability with both peers and adults (Thomlison, 2004).

Formation of a Network Within the Community

Mental Health: A Report of the Surgeon General (U.S. Department of Health and Human Services, 1999) states that mental health programs for youth with serious emotional disturbances are most effective when they work in connection with established and accepted community supports. Families usually first seek help from friends, family and community members, and from nontraditional sources prior to seeking professional help. Programs should work in tandem with one another, being aware of each other's missions and resources. This is especially true for minorities who often feel even more stigmatized than the majority culture. This point highlights the strong need to create strong communities that optimize youth's potential.

Youth with serious emotional disturbances are challenged in making use of the supports within their communities for a number of reasons. As disruptive behavior disorders and ADHD are commonly diagnosed conditions, the symptoms and issues associated with these conditions make interactions with peers, adults, family, and authority figures challenging. Children with these disorders frequently argue with adults, defy authority, blame others for their mistakes, and test limits (Weiner, 1997). This makes supervision of activities, such as participation on sports teams or clubs, difficult. Coaches and adults often ask that youth with these types of challenges be removed from their charge. Caregivers are often embarrassed by their child's behavior and may choose not to allow him/her to participate in these activities, despite adults willing to work with their child. Youth with mood disorders or traumatic experiences may be so overwhelmed with symptoms that engagement with others, interest in activities, and the ability to cope with stressors is so diminished that they withdraw and isolate themselves.

Due to the significant benefit use of community supports and interaction within a community has for youth with serious emotional disturbances, practitioners and community members alike must make concerted efforts to make this happen. Practitioners can support communities by consulting with community programs on what is most needed for youth to remain engaged in community activities. Additionally, practitioners can help address barriers such as financial concerns. Family members can make needs known and support their youth in attempting and sustaining activities.

TRANSITION-AGE YOUTH

Manifestation of Mental Health Needs in Transition-Age Youth

Transition-age youth are identified as 14- to 22-year-olds who are attempting to successfully transition from their caregivers' support and care to their own. Our society has seen distinct changes in the age of transition, as it has become more acceptable and the norm to transition at a later age. Often, a youth is closer to 30 years of age before successful transition occurs. When youth with serious emotional disturbances enter this stage of development, there are common challenges and issues. Many times, youth have struggled with family relationships prior to this phase, further complicating the challenge of becoming independent. Further, relationships with peers may be tentative. Mental health issues are frequently manifested as difficulty completing high school, maintaining jobs, finding housing, and maintaining stability in functioning. These issues are particularly troublesome when youth at age 18 are forced to transition from the public mental health system into the adult system, which often leaves them without a means to pay for services (Davis & Sondheimer, 2005).

Many youth between the ages of 17 and 25 struggle with substance abuse, anxiety disorders, and depressive disorders (Davis &Vander Stoep, 1997). All of these issues can make integration into the community, separation from family, and self-reliance challenging. Many youth with substance abuse issues experience legal problems that further complicate their mental health functioning. Despite the fact that youth may have a primary diagnosis, at least half of all adolescents who meet criteria for one psychiatric disorder also meet criteria for two or more disorders (Cohen et al., 1993). A number of these youth have been served in institutional settings, and unfortunately this makes transition even more challenging. A study conducted by Embry, Vander Stoep, Evens, Ryan, and Pollack (2000) determined that adolescents with mental health issues, who are discharged from an inpatient facility, are at significant risk for becoming homeless.

Development of Strength and Resiliency

Shifting to a recovery orientation for young adults with mental health challenges is something that does not come naturally. This is, for many, a paradigm shift that has not been introduced as a concept by practitioners or family members to the young adults who are reaching independence. Recovery does not mean that a person will not experience symptoms or need mental health services. It does mean that a person can successfully manage symptoms, setbacks, stigma, and even traumas. All of these things can happen with the support of others, and recovery will look different for different individuals (Rapp & Goscha, 2006). In discussing this notion, Ridgway (2001), described recovery as a process in which the following occur:

- Reawakening of hope after despair;
- Breaking through denial and achieving understanding and acceptance;
- Moving from withdrawal to engagement and active participation in life;
- Active coping rather than passive adjustment;

- No longer viewing oneself as primarily a person with a psychiatric disorder and reclaiming a positive sense of self; and

- Moving from alienation to a sense of meaning and purpose.

When young adults accept and truly believe in a recovery orientation, they possess possibly the greatest strength and protective factor; without this, change would not be possible.

While a recovery orientation is one that lays the foundation for empowerment and success, additional resiliency characteristics have been identified that can be helpful to young adults. Insight, creativity, independence, relationship skills, humor, morality, and initiative are characteristics that develop from adversity, which support a person's ability to overcome future challenges (Wolin & Wolin, 1993). These characteristics are not ones that are magically obtained but ones that can be fostered and developed. Services, both traditional and nontraditional, should find ways to support and develop these characteristics.

Unique Service Needs of Transition-Age Youth

As youth move from being under the guardianship of their caregivers to the ability to make decisions for themselves, a number of new experiences occur for them. Many youth did not participate in the decision to begin mental health services, nor do they have the same perception of needs that their caregivers may have had. Youth may also have a limited understanding of the type of mental health condition they are experiencing and therefore have a limited capacity to predict and monitor symptoms. When youth begin to make decisions, empowerment in these areas is important. How this occurs will need to be individualized, as many youth will not embrace lecturing or typical educational strategies. The strengths and needs, priorities and preferences all will need to be addressed through a relationship with a practitioner who is respectful of the youth's past experiences, cultural influences, and current environment.

While most youth experience a desire for employment and housing, these are by far not the only needs that young adults with mental health challenges typically experience. Many programs that serve this age group have predominantly focused on these two issues. Data from a study of youth receiving services in a system of care funded between 1997 and 2000 strongly suggested that transition-age youth did not receive the level of independent living and transition services that were needed for them to adequately move toward independence (U.S. Department of Health and Human Services, Substance Abuse and Mental Health Services Administration, Center for Mental Health Services, 2006). One model that is emerging as an evidence-based practice, the Transition to Independence Process (TIP) system, includes these areas as well as others. The process includes the following:

- Teaching community-relevant skills;

- Encouragement for completion of secondary education;

- Exposure to community-life experiences;

- Movement into postschool employment, educational opportunities, living situations, and community life;

- Removal of barriers between the child and adult serving systems; and

- Respect for the self-determination of young people (Clark, Deschenes, & Jones, 2000).

This type of service array will adequately meet the needs of young adults with emotional and behavioral concerns in a way that appreciates the youth culture and transition issues.

FAMILY CHARACTERISTICS

Caregiver Needs

Caregivers of children with serious emotional disturbances have a number of concerns and struggles related to meeting the needs of those children. A primary concern is the caregivers' abilities to work outside of the home. Caregivers may need flexible hours to attend meetings and appointments as well as the ability to accept calls at work related to the status of their children. Additionally, caregivers may be distracted by stressors or family issues that may negatively affect their job performances. Various studies have verified that caregivers' participation in the workforce is negatively affected by having children with disabilities. When caregivers, especially single mothers, do work, they may choose part-time positions and are overall less likely to work at all outside of the home (Powers, 2001, 2003; Porterfield, 2002). Almost half of the caregivers of children with behavioral and emotional problems were reported by Rosenzweig and Huffstutter (2004) to have chosen to quit their jobs at some point in the past to care for their children. Appropriate child care may be difficult to find, especially when youth have emotional and behavioral concerns. This is also problematic for caregivers, especially caregivers of young children, in attempting to maintain employment.

Another issue that makes employment challenging for caregivers of seriously emotionally disturbed youth is stigma. Rosenzweig, Brennan, and Malasch (2009) discuss the concept of courtesy stigmatization in relationship to the workplace. Courtesy stigmatization is defined in this article as "reflecting the prejudices, negative judgments, and discrimination extended to others, particularly partners, family members, and close friends who are caring for, or significantly connected to, an individual with a mental health disorder" (p. 29). Four types of stigmatization were identified through reviewing focus group transcripts of caregivers who were interviewed. The four types of stigmatization were identified as direct, indirect, perceived, and internalized. Despite the reality of all types of stigmatization, some employed caregivers, although not most, may choose to disclose to employers their status as caregivers of children with special needs. Considerations that impact this decision include culture of the workplace, perceptions regarding formal and informal lines of support, the type of job, and possibilities related to flexible hours and time off (Rosenzweig et al., 2009).

Sibling Needs

The needs of siblings of youth with serious emotional disturbances may be overlooked or minimized. Typically, siblings experience an increased amount of stress and decreased attention for caregivers due to the demands of their special needs siblings. Findings in a study conducted by Kilmer, Cook, Taylor, Kane, and Clark (2008), indicate that siblings of youth with serious emotional disturbances were exposed to high levels of adversity and show variability in behavioral and emotional strengths as well as needs. This supports the 1999 *Surgeon General's Report*, which recommends shifting focus from solely the identified client to the community, cultural, and family context (U.S. Department of Health and Human Services, 1999). In terms of strengths, siblings in the Kilmer et al. study (2008) had above-average to superior levels of personal strengths, scoring highest as a group on affective strengths. As seen in past resiliency studies, a family environment that was rated as cohesive, nurturing, and having positive support networks was protective for all youth. Research related to youth experiences with aggressive siblings indicates that youth were more likely to experience academic and behavior problems and aggressive interactions with their sibling than the compared group. Additionally, youth experienced later social and psychological problems when exposed to aggression in their sibling (Aguilar, O'Brien, August, Aoun, & Hektner, 2001). Due to the paucity of research specifically related to siblings of youth with serious emotional disturbances, it is helpful to consider related research of siblings of youth with physical or mental disabilities. Siblings of children with disabilities have been identified as experiencing higher levels of anxiety and depression, irritability, withdrawal, aggression as well as increased prosocial behaviors (Summers, White, & Summers, 1994). Additional positive characteristics have been identified as greater compassion, helpfulness, maturity, and empathy (Janus & Goldberg, 1995; Sargent et al., 1995). This research calls attention to both the risks of ignoring siblings as well as the opportunities to maximize and build on strengths that can potentially improve overall family functioning.

CONCLUSION

Youth with serious emotional disturbances experience a wide range of disorders and symptoms that are unique to each individual. The age of onset, duration, intensity, individual and family characteristics, culture of the family, and developmental stage of the youth all influence the way in which needs are manifested. The extent and severity of functional impairment is also a determinant of the above variables and reflects the uniqueness of the youth and the environment in which they function. The effects of serious emotional disturbances are not isolated to the youth but influence the functioning of siblings and caregivers as well. Early intervention that is coordinated, community based, strengths based, and culturally competent is needed to support the youth in reaching recovery.

References

Aguilar, B., O'Brien, K. M., August G. J., Aoun, S. L., & Hektner, J. M. (2001). Relationship quality of aggressive children and their siblings: A multiinformant, multimeasure investigation. *Journal of Abnormal Child Psychology, 29*, 479-489.

American Civil Liberties Union. (1996). *ACLU fact sheet on the juvenile justice system.* Retrieved on November 9, 2009, from http://aclu.org/racial-justice_drug-law-reform_immigrants-rights_womens-rights/aclu-fact-sheet-juvenile-justice-syst

American Psychiatric Association. (2000). *Diagnostic and statistical manual of mental disorders* (4th ed., text rev.). Washington, DC: Author.

Aron, E. N. (2002). *The highly sensitive child: Helping our children thrive when the world overwhelms them.* New York: Broadway Books.

Beitchman, J. H., Wilson, B., Brownlie, E. B., Walters, H., & Lancee, W. (1996). Long term consistency in speech/language profiles: I. Developmental and academic outcomes. *Journal of American Academy of Child and Adolescent Psychiatry, 35,* 804-814.

Brauner, B. C., & Stephens, C. B. (2006). Estimating the prevalence of early childhood serious emotional/behavioral disorders: Challenges and recommendations. *Public Health Reports, 121,* 303-310.

Brooks, R. B. (1994). Children at risk: Fostering resilience and hope. *American Journal of Orthopsychiatry, 64,* 545-553.

Carter, A. S., Briggs-Gowan, M., & Davis, N. (2004). Assessment of young children's social-emotional development and psychopathology: Recent advances and recommendations for practice. *Journal of child Psychology and Psychiatry, 45,*109-134.

Centers for Disease Control and Prevention. (2007). *Suicide trends among youths and young adults aged 10-24 Years—United States, 1990-2004.* Retrieved June 15, 2010, from http://www.cdc.gov/mmwr/preview/mmwrhtml/mm5635a2.htm

Clark, H. B., Deschenes, N., & Jones, J. (2000). A framework for the development and operation of a transition system. In Hewitt B. Clark & Maryann Davis (Eds.), *Transition to adulthood: A resource for assisting young people with emotional or behavioral difficulties.* (pp. 29-51) Baltimore: Paul H. Brookes Publishing.

Clausen, J., Landsverk, J., Ganger, W., Chadwick, D., & Litrownik, A. (1998). Mental health problems of children in foster care. *Journal of Child & Family Studies, 7,* 283-296.

Cohen, P., Cohen, J., Kasen, S., Velez, C., Hartmark, C., Johnson, J., et al. (1993). An epidemiological study of disorders in late childhod and adolescence-I. Age- and gender-specific prevalence. *Journal of Child Psychology and Psychiatry and Allied Disciplines, 34,* 851-867.

Costello, E. J., Messer, S. C., Bird, H. R., Cohen, P., & Reinherz, H. (1998). The prevalence of serious emotional disturbance: A re-analysis of community studies. *Journal of Child & Family Studies, 7,* 411-432.

Davis, M., & Sondheimer, D. (2005). Child mental health systems'efforts to support youth in transition to adulthood. *Journal of Behavioral Health Services and Research, 32,* 27-42.

Davis, M., & Vander Stoep, A. (1997). The transition to adulthood for youth who have serious emotional disturbance: Developmental transition and young adult outcomes. *Journal of Mental Health Administration, 24,* 400-427.

DeBellis, M. (2001). Developmental traumatology: The psychobiological development of maltreated children and its implications for research, treatment, and policy. *Development and Psychopathology, 13,* 539-564.

Earls, F. (1981). Temperament characteristics and behavior problems in three-year-old children. *Journal of Nervous and Mental Diseases, 169,* 367-373.

Embry, L. E., Vander Stoep, A., Evens, C., Ryan, K. D., & Pollack, A. (2000). Risk factors for homelessness in adolescents released from psychiatric residential treatment. *Journal of the American Academy of Child and Adolescent Psychiatry, 39,* 1293-1299.

Evangelista, N., & McLellan, M. J. (2004). The Zero to Three diagnostic system: A framework for considering emotional and behavioral problems in young children. *School Psychology Review, 33,* 159-173.

Fraser, M. W., Kirby, L. D., & Smokowski, P. R. (2004). Risk and resilience in childhood. In Mark W. Fraser (Ed.), *Risk and resilience in childhood: An ecological perspective.* Washington DC: NASW Press.

Friedman, R. M., Katash, K., & Duchnowski, A. J. (1996). The population of concern: Defining the issues. In B. A. Stroul (Ed.), Children's mental health: Creating systems of care in a changing society (pp. 69-96). Baltimore: Paul H. Brookes Publishing.

Ginsburg, K. R., & Jablow, M. M. (2006). *A parent's guide to building resilience in children and teens: Giving your child roots and wings.* Elk Grove Village, IL: American Academy of Pediatrics.

Greenberg, M. T., Cicchetti, D., & Cummings, E. M. (1990). *Attachment in the preschool years: theory, research and intervention.* Chicago: University of Chicago Press.

Grizenko, N., & Pawliuk, N. (1994). Risk and protective factors for disruptive behavior disorders in children. *American Journal of Orthopsychiatry, 64,* 534-544.

Houck, G. M. (1999). The measurement of child characteristics from infancy to toddlerhood: Temperament, developmental competence, self-concept, and social competence. *Issues in Comprehensive Pediatric Nursing, 22,* 101-127.

Hudson, R. (2009). *Suffering in silence: Human rights abuses in St. Louis correctional centers.* Retrieved September 17, 2009, from http://www.acluem.org/downloads/ACLUSufferingSummary.pdf

Hughes, D. (1997). *Facilitating developmental attachment: The road to emotional recovery and behavioral change in foster and adoptive children.* Northvale, NJ: Jason Aronson.

Irwin, J. R., Carter, A. S., & Briggs-Gowan, M. J. (2002). The social-emotional development of "late-talking" toddlers. *Journal of American Academy of Child and Adolescent Psychiatry, 41,* 1324-1332.

Janus, M., & Goldberg, S. (1995). Sibling empathy and behavioral adjustment of children with chronic illness. *Child: Care, Health and Development, 21,* 321-331.

Jenkins, S., Bax, M., & Hart, H. (1980). Behavior problems in preschool children. *Journal of Child Psychology and Psychiatry, 21,* 5-17.

Kagan, J., Snidman, N., Arcus, D., & Reznick, J. S. (1994). *Galen's prophecy: Temperament in human nature.* New York: Basic Books.

Keck, G., & Kupecky, R. (1995). *Adopting the hurt child: Hope for families with special needs kids.* Colorado Springs, CO: Piñon Press.

Kilmer, R., Cook, J., Taylor, C., Kane, S., & Clark, L. (2008). Siblings of children with severe emotional disturbances: Risks, resources, and adaptation. *American Journal of Orthopsychiatry, 78*(1), 1-10.

Knitzer, J. (1982). *Unclaimed children: The failure of public responsibility to children and adolescents in need of mental health services.* Washington, DC: Children's Defense Fund.

Kolvin, I., Nicol, A. R., Garside, R. F., Day, K. A., & Tweedle, E. G. (1982). Temperamental patterns in aggressive boys. In R. Porter & G. M. Collins (Eds.), *Temperamental difficulties in infants and young children* (pp. 252-268). London: Pitman.

Koppelman, J., George Washington University, & National Health Policy Forum. (2004). *Children with mental disorders: Making sense of their needs and the systems that help them.* Washington, DC: National Health Policy Forum.

Lavigne, J. V., Gibbons, R. D., Christoffel, K. K., Arend, R., Rosenbaum, D., Binns, H., et al. (1996). Prevalence rates and correlates of psychiatric disorders among preschool children. *Journal of American Academy of Child and Adolescent Psychiatry, 35,* 204-214.

Lavigne, J. V., LeBailly, S. A., Hopkins, J., Gouze, K. R., & Binns, H. J. (2009). The prevalence of ADHD, ODD, depression, and anxiety in a community sample of 4-year-olds. *Journal of Clinical Child and Adolescent Psychology, 38,* 315-328.

Levy, T., & Orlans, M. (1998). *Attachment, trauma, and healing: Understanding and treating attachment disorder in children and families.* Washington, DC: Child Welfare League of America Press.

Lourie, I. S., Katz-Levy, J., DeCarolis, G., & Quilan, W. A. (1996). The Role of federal government. In B. Stroul (Ed.), *Children's mental health: Creating systems of care in a changing society* (pp. 99-114). Baltimore: Paul H. Brookes Publishing.

Mahler, M. S., Pine, F., & Bergman, A. (1975). *The psychological birth of the human infant.* New York: Basic Books.

Mathiesen, K. S., & Sanson, A. (2000). Dimensions of early childhood behavior problems: Stability and predictors of change from 18-30 months. *Journal of Abnormal Child Psychology, 28,* 15-31.

National Child Traumatic Stress Network. (2001). *Understanding child traumatic stress.* Retrieved November 9, 2009, from http://www.nctsn.org

Pecora, P. J., Jensen, P. S., Romanelli, L. H., Jackson, L. J., & Ortiz, A. (2009). Mental health services for children placed in foster care: An overview of current challenges. *Child Welfare, 88,* 5-26.

Perry, B. D. (1996). *Violence and childhood trauma: Understanding and responding to the effects of violence on young children.* Cleveland, OH: Gund Foundation.

Powers, E. T. (2001). New estimates of the impact of child disability on maternal employment. *American Economic Review, 91,* 135-139.

Powers, E. T. (2003). Children's health and maternal work activity: Estimates under alternative disability definitions. *Journal of Human Resources, 38,* 522-556.

Porterfield, S. L. (2002). Work choices of mothers in families with disabilities. *Journal of Marriage and Family, 64,* 972-981.

Ranson, K., & Urichuk, L. (2008). The effect of parent-child attachment relationships on child biopsychosocial outcomes: A review. *Early Child Development & Care, 178,* 129-152.

Rapp, C., & Goscha, R. J. (2006). *The strengths model: Case management with people with psychiatric disabilities* (2nd ed.). New York: Oxford University Press.

Ridgway, P. (2001). Re-storying psychiatric disability: Learning from first person narrative accounts of recovery. *Psychiatric Rehabilitation Journal, 24,* 335-343.

Rosenzweig, J. M., Brennan, E. M., & Malasch, A. M. (2009). Breaking the silence: Parents' experiences of courtesy stigmatization in the workplace. *Focal Point: Research, Policy, & Practice in Children's Mental Health, 23*(1), 29-31.

Rosenzweig, J. M., & Huffstutter, K. J. (2004). Disclosure and reciprocity: On the job strategies for taking care of business . . . and family. *Focal Point: A National Bulletin on Family Support and Children's Mental Health, 18*(1), 4-7.

Sargent, J. R., Sahler, O. J., Roghmann, K. J., Mulhern, R. K., Barbarian, O. A., Carpenter, P. J., et al. (1995). Sibling adaptation to childhood cancer collaborative study: Siblings' perceptions of the cancer experience. *Journal of Pediatric Psychology, 20,* 151-164.

Schore, A. N. (2001). Effects of a secure attachment relationship on right brain development, affect regulation, and infant mental health. *Infant Mental Health Journal, 22,* 7-66.

Shonkoff, J. P., Phillips, D., & Board on Children, Youth, and Families (États-Unis), Committee on Integrating the Science of Early Childhood Development (Eds.). (2000). *From neurons to neighborhoods: The science of early childhood development.* Washington, DC: National Academy Press.

Substance Abuse and Mental Health Service Administration, 58 Fed. Reg. 29,422 (May 20, 1993).

Summers, C. R., White, K. R., & Summers, M. (1994). Siblings of children with a disability: A review and analysis of the empirical literature. *Journal of Social Behavior and Personality, 9,* 169-184.

Teplin, L. A., Abram, K. M., McClelland, G. M., Dulcan, M. K., & Mericle, A. A. (2002). Psychiatric disorders in youth in juvenile detention. *Archives of General Psychiatry, 59,* 1113-1143.

Thomas, A., Chess, S., & Birch, H. (1968). *Temperament and behavior disorders in children.* New York: New York University Press.

Thomlison, B. (2004). Child maltreatment: A risk and protective factor perspective. In Mark. W. Fraser (Ed.), *Risk and resilience in childhood: An ecological perspective* (2nd ed., pp. 89-131). Washington, DC: NASW Press.

U.S. Department of Health and Human Services. (1999). *Mental health: A report of the surgeon general.* Rockville, MD: U.S. Department of Health and Human Services, Substance Abuse and Mental Health Services Administration, Center for Mental Health Services, National Institute of Health, National Institute of Mental Health.

U.S. Department of Health and Human Services, Substance Abuse and Mental Health Services Administration, Center for Mental Health Services. (2006). *EvalBrief: Systems of care: Transition-age youth receiving services in systems of care, 7*(6), 1-4.

U.S. Department of Health and Human Services, Substance Abuse and Mental Health Services Administration, Center for Mental Health Services. (2007). *EvalBrief: Systems of care: Characteristics of children in systems of care who have experienced trauma, 8*(7), 1-4.

U.S. General Accounting Office (2003). *Child welfare and juvenile justice: Federal agencies could play a stronger role in helping states reduce the number of children placed solely to obtain mental health services.* Retrieved November 9, 2009, from http://www.gao.gov/new. items/d03397.pdf

Ward, M. J., Lee, S. S., & Lipper, E. G. (2000). Failure-to-thrive is associated with disorganized infant-mother attachment and unresolved maternal attachment. *Infant Mental Health Journal, 21*, 428-442.

Weiner, J. M. (1997). Oppositional defiant disorder. In J. M. Weiner (Ed.), *Textbook of child and adolescent psychiatry* (2nd ed., pp. 459-463). Washington, DC: American Psychiatric Press.

Werner, E. E. (1993). Risk, resilience, and recovery: Perspectives from the Kauai longitudinal study. *Development and Psychopathology, 5*, 503-515.

Werner, E. E., & Smith, R. S. (1992). *Overcoming the odds: High risk children from birth to adulthood.* Ithaca, NY: Cornell University Press.

Wolin, S. J., & Wolin, S. (1993). *The resilient self: How survivors of troubled families rise above adversity.* New York: Villard Books.

Zero to Three (1994). *Diagnostic classification of mental health and developmental disorders in infancy and early childhood.* Washington, DC: Author.

Exhibit 2.1
**Indiana Association for Infant and Toddler Mental Health *DC 0-3 R*
Crosswalk to DSM and ICD Systems**

Although the benefits of early identification and treatment of developmental and behavioral problems are well known, it has only been in the last decade that significant efforts to describe and categorize disorders specific to infancy and early childhood were begun. The first major effort was the *Diagnostic Classification of Mental Health and Developmental Disorders of Infancy and Early Childhood,* published in 1994 with a revision in 2005 (*DC 0-3 R*). The *DC 0-3 R* was designed to provide a systematic and developmentally informed approach to classifying both mental health and developmental disorders that present in early childhood. The *DC 0-3 R* was intended to complement more familiar systems, including the American Psychiatric Association's *Diagnostic and Statistical Manuals.* However, the *DC 0-3 R* expands some DSM classifications to allow clinicians to describe areas commonly in need of attention in early childhood, including problems with sleep and feeding, and includes descriptions of areas of clinical concern that are not addressed in the DSM at all, such as regulation disorders and caregiver-child relationship disturbances. The *DC 0-3 R* is also congruent with the 2001-2002 Research Diagnostic Criteria: Preschool Age (RDC: PA), a downward extension of some DSM categories completed by a task force supported by the American Academy of Child and Adolescent Psychiatry .

DC 0-3 R diagnoses provide valuable descriptions of the kinds of behavior patterns and challenges identified by parents and other caregivers of very young children. However, these diagnostic codes cannot, in most cases, be used for billing purposes. To address this gap in practice, several states have developed crosswalks to bridge between the descriptive *DC 0-3 R* diagnosis and a billable code. These crosswalks typically connect a *DC 0-3 R* diagnosis with an equivalent DSM or ICD code. *DC 0-3* crosswalks have been successfully used in some states, such as Maine, Florida, and California, for several years.

The Indiana Association for Infant and Toddler Mental Health's Infant Mental Health Task force (IMH Task Force) has developed a crosswalk specific to the needs of Indiana mental health professionals. The intention of the Indiana Crosswalk is to (1) encourage awareness of and dialogue about mental health and relationship concerns in infancy and early childhood; (2) introduce Indiana mental health professionals to *DC 0-3 R*; and (3) provide a means to use *DC 0-3 R* categories and concepts while maintaining acceptable billing practices.

The Indiana Crosswalk process included IMH Task Force members from various disciplines, including social work, psychology, speech and language pathology, and medicine, among others. The members met over a period of 4 months to discuss each diagnosis and axis in *DC 0-3 R*, review other state's crosswalks, and carefully compare *DC 0-3 R*, DSM, and ICD diagnostic criteria. The resulting Indiana Crosswalk is intended as a guide to clinical practice.

(Continued)

Adapted with permission from Indiana Association of Infant and Toddler Mental Health (IAITM). © 2007.
Note: DSM refers to the *Diagnostic and Statistical Manual of Mental Disorders.* ICD refers to the *International Classification of Diseases.*

Exhibit 2.1 *(Continued)*
AXIS I: CLINICAL DISORDERS

DC 0-3 R Code & Classification		*DSM-IV-TR* Code & Classification		*ICD-9-CM*	
100: Posttraumatic Stress Disorder					
100	Posttraumatic Stress Disorder	309.81	Posttraumatic Stress Disorder	309.81	Posttraumatic Stress Disorder
150	Deprivation/ maltreatment disorder	313.89	Reactive Attachment Disorder	313.89	Other mixed emotional disturbances of childhood and adolescence
200: Disorders of Affect					
210	Prolonged Bereavement/ Grief Reaction	V62.80	Bereavement	309.0	Adjustment Disorder with Depressed Mood
	296.2	Major Depressive Disorder, Single Episode	309.1	Prolonged depressive reaction	
220: Anxiety Disorders of Infancy and Early Childhood					
221	Separation Anxiety Disorder	309.21	Separation Anxiety Disorder	309.21	Separation Anxiety Disorder
222	Specific Phobia	300.29	Specific Phobia	300.29	Other isolated or specific phobia
223	Social Anxiety	300.23	Social Phobia	300.23	Social Phobia
224	Generalized Anxiety Disorder	300.02	Generalized Anxiety Disorder	300.02	Generalized Anxiety Disorder
225	Anxiety Disorder NOS	300.00	Anxiety Disorder NOS	300.00	Anxiety State, unspecified
230: Depression of Infancy and Early Childhood					
231	Type I: Major Depression	296.2	Major Depressive Disorder, Single Episode	296.2	Major Depressive Disorder, Single Episode
	296.3	Major Depression, Recurrent	296.3	Major Depression, Recurrent	
	309.0	Adjustment disorder with depressed mood			
	309.1	Prolonged depressive reaction			

(Continued)

Exhibit 2.1 *(Continued)*

DC 0-3 R Code & Classification		*DSM-IV-TR* Code & Classification		*ICD-9-CM*	
232	Type II: Depressive Disorder, NOS	311	Depressive Disorder, NOS	311	Depressive Disorder not elsewhere classified
	313.1	Misery and unhappiness Disorder			
240	Mixed Disorder of Emotional Expressiveness	296.90	Mood Disorder, NOS	296.90	Other and unspecified mood disorder
	313.9	Unspecified emotional disturbance of childhood			
300: Adjustment Disorder					
300	Adjustment Disorder	309.0	Adjustment Disorder with Depressed Mood	309.0	Adjustment Disorder with Depressed Mood
	309.24	Adjustment Disorder with Anxiety	309.24	Adjustment Disorder with Anxiety	
	309.28	Adjustment Disorder with Mixed Anxiety and Depressed Mood	309.28	Adjustment Disorder with Mixed Anxiety and Depressed Mood	
	309.3	Adjustment Disorder with Disturbance of Conduct	309.3	Adjustment Disorder with Disturbance of Conduct	
	309.4	Adjustment Disorder with Mixed Disturbance of Emotions and Conduct	309.4	Adjustment Disorder with Mixed Disturbance of Emotions and Conduct	
	309.9	Unspecified Adjustment Disorder	309.9	Unspecified Adjustment Reaction	
400: Regulation Disorders					
411	Hypersensitive:				
Fearful and Cautious	309.0	Adjustment Disorder with Depressed Mood	309.0	Adjustment Disorder with Depressed Mood	

(Continued)

Exhibit 2.1 *(Continued)*

DC 0-3 R Code & Classification		DSM-IV-TR Code & Classification		ICD-9-CM	
	309.24	Adjustment Disorder with Anxiety	309.24	Adjustment Disorder with Anxiety	
	309.28	Adjustment Disorder with Mixed Anxiety and Depressed Mood	309.28	Adjustment Disorder with Mixed Anxiety and Depressed Mood	
	309.9	Unspecified Adjustment Disorder	309.9	Unspecified Adjustment Reaction	
	300.00	Anxiety Disorder NOS	300.00	Anxiety State, unspecified	
	300.02	Generalized Anxiety Disorder	300.02	Generalized Anxiety Disorder	
	313.00	Overanxious Disorder			
412	Hypersensitive:				
Negative/Defiant	309.0	Adjustment Disorder with Depressed Mood	309.0	Adjustment Disorder with Depressed Mood	
	309.24	Adjustment Disorder with Anxiety	309.24	Adjustment Disorder with Anxiety	
	309.28	Adjustment Disorder with Mixed Anxiety and Depressed Mood	309.28	Adjustment Disorder with Mixed Anxiety and Depressed Mood	
	309.3	Adjustment Disorder with Disturbance of Conduct	309.3	Adjustment Disorder with Disturbance of Conduct	
	309.4	Adjustment Disorder with Mixed Disturbance of Emotions and Conduct	309.4	Adjustment Disorder with Mixed Disturbance of Emotions and Conduct	
	309.9	Unspecified Adjustment Disorder	309.9	Unspecified Adjustment Reaction	
	312.9	Disruptive Behavior Disorder, NOS	312.9	Unspecified Disturbance of Conduct	

(Continued)

Exhibit 2.1 *(Continued)*

DC 0-3 R Code & Classification		DSM-IV-TR Code & Classification		ICD-9-CM	
420	Hyposensitive/ underresponsive	309.9	Unspecified Adjustment Disorder	309.9	Unspecified Adjustment Reaction
	313.20	Sensitivity, shyness, and social withdraw			
430	Sensory Stimulation Seeking/ Impulsive	309.3	Adjustment Disorder with Disturbance of Conduct	309.3	Adjustment Disorder with Disturbance of Conduct
	309.4	Adjustment Disorder with Mixed Disturbance of Emotions and Conduct	309.4	Adjustment Disorder with Mixed Disturbance of Emotions and Conduct	
	312.9	Disruptive Behavior Disorder, NOS	312.9	Unspecified disturbance of conduct	
	312.3	Impulse Control Disorder	312.3	Impulse Control Disorder, unspecified	
500: Sleep Onset Disorder					
510	Sleep Onset Disorder	307.45	Circadian Rhythm Sleep Disorder	307.45	Circadian Rhythm Sleep Disorder of nonorganic origin
520	Night-Waking Disorder	307.45	Circadian Rhythm Sleep Disorder	307.45	Circadian Rhythm Sleep Disorder of nonorganic origin
	307.46	Sleep Terror Disorder	307.46	Sleep Arousal Disorder	
	307.47	Nightmare Disorder Parasomnia, NOS	307.47	Other dysfunction of sleep stages or arousal from sleep	
600: Feeding Behavior Disorder					
601	Feeding Disorder of State Regulation	307.59	Eating Disorder of Infancy, NOS	307.59	Eating disorder, other
	307.50	Eating disorder, unspecified			

(Continued)

Exhibit 2.1 *(Continued)*

DC 0-3 R Code & Classification		DSM-IV-TR Code & Classification		ICD-9-CM	
602	Feeding Disorder of Caregiver-Infant Reciprocity	307.59	Eating Disorder of Infancy, NOS	307.59	Eating disorder, other
		307.50	Eating disorder, unspecified		
603	Infantile Anorexia	307.59	Eating Disorder of Infancy, NOS	307.59	Eating disorder, other
		307.50	Eating disorder, unspecified		
604	Sensory Food Aversions	307.59	Eating Disorder of Infancy, NOS	307.59	Eating disorder, other
		307.50	Eating disorder, unspecified		
605	Feeding Disorder Associated with Concurrent Medical Condition	309.0	Adjustment Disorder with Depressed Mood	309.0	Adjustment Disorder with Depressed Mood
		309.24	Adjustment Disorder with Anxiety	309.24	Adjustment Disorder with Anxiety
		309.28	Adjustment Disorder with Mixed Anxiety and Depressed Mood	309.28	Adjustment Disorder with Mixed Anxiety and Depressed Mood
		309.3	Adjustment Disorder with Disturbance of Conduct	309.3	Adjustment Disorder with Disturbance of Conduct
		309.4	Adjustment Disorder with Mixed Disturbance of Emotions and Conduct	309.4	Adjustment Disorder with Mixed Disturbance of Emotions and Conduct
		309.9	Unspecified Adjustment Disorder	309.9	Unspecified Adjustment Reaction

(Continued)

Exhibit 2.1 *(Continued)*

DC 0-3 R Code & Classification		DSM-IV-TR Code & Classification		ICD-9-CM	
606	Feeding Disorder Associated with Insults to the Gastrointestinal Tract	309.0	Adjustment Disorder with Depressed Mood	309.0	Adjustment Disorder with Depressed Mood
	309.24	Adjustment Disorder with Anxiety	309.24	Adjustment Disorder with Anxiety	
	309.28	Adjustment Disorder with Mixed Anxiety and Depressed Mood	309.28	Adjustment Disorder with Mixed Anxiety and Depressed Mood	
	309.3	Adjustment Disorder with Disturbance of Conduct	309.3	Adjustment Disorder with Disturbance of Conduct	
	309.4	Adjustment Disorder with Mixed Disturbance of Emotions and Conduct	309.4	Adjustment Disorder with Mixed Disturbance of Emotions and Conduct	
	309.9	Unspecified Adjustment Disorder	309.9	Unspecified Adjustment Reaction	
700: Disorders of Relating and Communicating					
710	Multisystem Developmental Disorder	299	Autistic Disorder	299	Autistic Disorder
	299.9	Pervasive Developmental Disorder, NOS	299.9	Unspecified Pervasive Developmental Disorder	
	315.9	Unspecified delay in development			
	313.9	Disorder of Infancy, Childhood, or Adolescence, NOS			

(Continued)

Exhibit 2.1 *(Continued)*

AXIS II: RELATIONSHIP CLASSIFICATION

The IAITMH endorses and encourages the use of *the Parent-Infant Relationship Global Assessment Scale (PIR-GAS)* and the *Relationship Problems Checklist* found beginning on page 43 of the DC 0-3 R.

N/A	Overinvolved Underinvolved Anxious/Tense Angry/Hostile	V61.20	Parent-child Relational Problem	V61.20	Parent-child problems
				313.3	Relationship problems
	Verbally Abusive Physically Abusive Sexually Abusive	V61.21	Neglect Physical Abuse of Child Sexual Abuse of Child	V61.21	Counseling for victim of child abuse
				V61.22	Counseling for perpetrator of parental child abuse

AXIS III: MEDICAL AND DEVELOPMENTAL DISORDERS AND CONDITIONS

AXIS IV: PSYCHSOCIAL STRESSORS

The IAITMH endorses and encourages the use of the *Psychosocial and Environmental Stressor Checklist*, found on page 56 of the DC 0-3 R.

AXIS V: EMOTIONAL AND ENVIRONMENTAL STRESORS CHECKLIST

Capacities for Emotional and Social Functioning Rating Scale

(Continued)

Exhibit 2.1   *(Continued)*

Axis I Notes:

Depressive Disorders:

The committee advises users to consider Deprivation/Maltreatment Disorder if neglect, abuse, or parent depression is present as per page 17 in the *DC 0-3 R*.

For Mixed Disorder of Emotional Expressiveness, we considered and rejected using Cyclothymia. We do not want to encourage consideration of bipolar disorders at this age range, given the current state of knowledge.

Regulation Disorders:

The committee discourages the use of Oppositional Defiant Disorder in this age range. It is felt that the core cognitive capacity needed to act purposefully or intentionally to anger another person is not present in children this age. It was also noted that difficult behavior can occur when young children are overwhelmed, and it is important to avoid attributing intentionality in this situation.

Feeding Disorder:
When coding any Feeding Disorder with associated medical conditions (605 and 606) remember to code medical disorder on Axis III for *DC 0-3 R* and for *DSM-IV-TR*.

Axis II Notes:
Use of these terms describing relationship quality from the *RPCL* is recommended when *PIRGAS* score is less than 40. Clinicians are advised to consider both Axis II patterns and other Axis I diagnoses before considering Deprivation/Maltreatment Disorder or RAD, although both can be present in one dyad. RAD is very rare, but relationship problems that can be a focus of treatment appear to be more common.

Axis V Notes:

We strongly suggest that clinicians use a method or tool of their preference to assess a child's social and emotional skills as well as behaviors that suggest the presence of atypical behavior/ psychopathology. Some examples to consider in addition to the CESFRS are the Infant Toddler Social Emotional Assessment, the Child Behavior Checklist (1½ to 3) and in the future the DECA. In addition, screening tools such as the Ages and Stages Questionnaires: Social Emotional and curriculum based tools such as the HELP can be helpful in gathering information about a child's functioning.

Questions and comments about this document can be directed to Angela Tomlin, Ph.D.(atomlin@iupui.edu).

Chapter 3

Aligning Home- and Community-Based Services With Wraparound Principles

We may be personally defeated, but our principles never.
—William Lloyd Garrison

INTRODUCTION

People may spend much of their lives determining the principles by which they wish to live. Culture, life experience, family values, beliefs, and relationships all play a role in this determination. Therefore, the investment in thoughtful consideration and adoption of a set of personal principles becomes a "barometer" of success. As long as actions are in alignment with principles, people usually feel good about what they are doing.

New as well as experienced practitioners should have the ability to operate from a set of principles. By operating from a set of principles, practitioners have a shared vision of what is valued and important. It is the basis of a key strategy that is used in determining appropriate procedures, strategies, and even motives for service delivery. The strategy is simple and one that most will find intuitively by asking the question, "how does this fit with the principles?"

Knowledge is a beautiful thing. When a concept is understood, it can then be shared with others. The ongoing pursuit of developing skills in the work of helping families and how this is achieved may never end, but having the "theory of why" assures a guided path to discovery. This chapter serves to offer a foundation on what services to youth with emotional and behavioral challenges and their families should measure up against. The list of ten principles that are shared and discussed will support the work and help to ensure a quality experience for youth and families.

HISTORY AND DEVELOPMENT OF WRAPAROUND PROCESS

While the federal government clearly focused attention on children's mental health through the development of the Child and Adolescent Service System Program (CASSP; See Chapter 1 in this volume), several initiatives were occurring to define the way in which individual youth and families should experience services and supports. In the 1980s, Lenore Behar, a researcher on children's mental health, began using the term "wraparound" to describe a comprehensive array of community-based services for youth and families (Behar, 1986). The state of North Carolina, in response to a lawsuit, developed home- and community-based services to prevent institutionalization of youth. In 1985, Alaska sought consultation from Karl Dennis, a pioneer in the field of wraparound services. Karl Dennis led the program *Kaleidoscope,* which provided unconditional, individualized care to youth as an alternative to institutional placement. Alaska, through this consultation and implementation of a wraparound approach, was able to return nearly all of the institutionally placed youth to their home communities. In the 1990s, several pioneers (e.g., John Vandenberg, Karl Dennis, Ira Lourie, John and Sarah Burchard, and Robert Friedman) continued efforts in furthering the field of wraparound services through national conferences, writings, and gatherings. By 1998, several researchers, practitioners, and family members met to define the core components of the wraparound model. This led to a list of ten elements that are considered the foundation of the process (Vandenberg, Bruns, & Burchard, 2008).

While the history of wraparound services has its own identity and development, it would be incorrect to assume that other movements did not influence the wraparound principles. Empowerment theory (see Chapter 1 in this volume) and the approaches that support it, such as family-centered home-based services, fit nicely within the wraparound process. Many of the same concepts are emphasized. The methods related to family-centered home-based services give direction on the how services should occur, and the wraparound process refers to the coordination of such services and supports. The principles and methods related to family-centered services compliment and support the wraparound process.

DEFINING WRAPAROUND PROCESS

While there were many in the 1990s who used the term "wraparound" when describing their service provisions to families, a common definition was sought in

1998, along with the naming of the elements. The definition agreed upon became, "Wraparound is a philosophy of care that includes a definable planning process involving the child and family that results in a unique set of community services and natural supports individualized for that child and family to achieve a positive set of outcomes" (Goldman, 1999, p. 28). This process is meant to allow the system of care philosophy to be experienced at the service delivery level. Therefore, the relationship of system of care philosophy and wraparound process is just like the relationship of empowerment theory and family-centered home-based services (see Chapter 1 in this volume), all of which are complimentary and synergistic.

DESCRIBING WRAPAROUND PRINCIPLES

Family Voice and Choice

Family voice and choice refer to the strong value placed on the perspective of the family and youth being heard and represented throughout all phases of service delivery. The goal is to ensure that an individualized plan reflects the family values and preferences. This value reflects the importance of the relationships and bonds that family members have with one another. The family typically has far more impact than any other person or group of persons on a youth and is equally impacted by the youth. Thus, the family has a motivation and unique investment in facilitating success for the youth (Bruns et al., 2004).

Within the service delivery process, family voice should be reflected in all aspects of the care and the choices made in the interventions that fulfill the individualized service plan. Families and youth should have choices in the types of interventions they receive, how long the interventions should take place, at what frequency, when, and in what environment. Family voice respects the fact that these decisions are best made by the family and youth, as they know how their family will respond and under what conditions. The family should be given full opportunity to explore its needs with the guidance of a service provider. The process of thoughtful analysis and strong consideration of options should be facilitated and not rushed by the practitioner. With family voice and choice being a guiding principle, no two families should receive the same service plan.

In 2003, *Achieving the Promise: Transforming Mental Health Care in America* was produced by the President's New Freedom Commission on Mental Health. In this report, six goals were identified that would manifest a transformed mental health system. Goal two was "mental health care is consumer and family driven" (President's New Freedom Commission on Mental Health, 2003, p. 5). The report indicated that "consumers, along with service providers, will actively participate in designing and developing the systems of care in which they are involved. . . . Consumers needs and preferences will drive the types and mix of services provided, considering the gender, age, language, development and culture of consumers" (President's New Freedom Commission on Mental Health, 2003, p. 8). This became the impetus for strengthening the concept of "family focused," which is related to families having decision-making power regarding their treatments. When considering this core principle of systems of care, which seeks to transform the child-serving community at large, family voice and choice is a parallel concept, which occurs at the individual service delivery level.

Following the 2003 publication *Achieving the Promise: Transforming Mental Health Care in America,* the federal Center for Mental Health Services (CMHS) of the Substance Abuse and Mental Health Services Administration (SAMHSA) joined forces with the Federation of Families for Children's Mental Health to define the concept of family-driven care. As a result, a working definition and set of guiding principles were developed. The working definition of family-driven care is as follows:

> Family-driven care means families have a primary decision making role in the care of their own children as well as the policies and procedures governing care for all children in their community, state, tribe, territory and nation. This includes:
>
> 1. Choosing supports, services and providers
>
> 2. Setting goals
>
> 3. Designing and implementing programs
>
> 4. Monitoring outcomes
>
> 5. Partnering in funding decisions
>
> 6. Determining the effectiveness of all efforts to promote the mental health and well being of children and youth.

The guiding principles of family-driven care include:

1. Families and youth are given accurate, understandable, and complete information necessary to set goals and to make choices for improved planning for individual children and their families.

2. Families and youth, providers and administrators embrace the concept of sharing decision-making and responsibility for outcomes with providers.

3. Families and youth are organized to collectively use their knowledge and skills as a force for system transformation.

4. Families and family-run organizations engage in peer support activities to reduce isolation, gather and disseminate accurate information, and strengthen the family voice.

5. Families and family-run organizations provide directions for decisions that impact funding for services, treatments, and supports.

6. Providers take the initiative to change practice from provider driven to family driven.

7. Administrators allocate staff, training, support, and resources to make family-driven practice work at the point where services and supports are delivered to children, youth, and families.

8. Community attitude change efforts focus on removing barriers and discrimination created by stigma.

9. Communities embrace, value, and celebrate the diverse cultures of their children, youth, and families.

Everyone who connects with children, youth, and families continually advances their own cultural and linguistic responsiveness as the population served changes. (Osher, Penn, & Spencer, 2008, pp. 250-251)

Team Based

At the core of the wraparound process is the wraparound team, which is referred to as the Child and Family Team (CFT). This team functions to ensure that services and supports are identified, determined, and coordinated to best meet the needs of the youth and family. This principle underscores the value of using a team to mutually invest and take ownership of supporting the youth and family in whatever way possible. The team works as a group, with caregivers and youth making the ultimate decisions. Decisions are best made as an entire team to develop coordinated efforts that can keep the focus on what needs to be done. The team consists of the youth, family members, informal supports, and formal supports. All members of the team are chosen by the family and youth (Bruns et al., 2004). An example of the composition of a typical team may include natural supports (e.g., friends, neighbors, extended family), community members (e.g., ministers, librarians), service providers (e.g., home-based practitioners, psychiatrists), and school staff (see Figure 3.1). If there is involvement in multiple youth-serving systems, representatives from such systems as juvenile justice, child welfare, special education, early intervention, or vocational programs may be asked to join. The main concept that is emphasized is that anyone who touches the life of a youth and family in a way that can be supportive may be influential in making decisions to implement and coordinate supports. The composition of the team is most successful when it does not consist primarily of paid practitioners and represents supports that can help in an ongoing way. The team is facilitated by a staff member, commonly known as a wraparound facilitator. This person ensures that all members of the team are oriented to the process and abide by mutually determined rules and procedures. It is critical that the facilitator ensures that all CFT members understand the values and principles, and that they are manifested in the interactions with the family and youth. The facilitator keeps the caregivers' and youth's wishes at the forefront so that their needs and preferences are always honored.

Collaborative

The CFT functions in a collaborative manner so that all team members work together synergistically to meet the needs of the youth and family. The CFT decides as a whole who will intervene and exactly how this will occur. The wraparound plan reflects the principle of collaboration in that contributions of all members are represented and coordinated, demonstrating the team's commitment to the family (Bruns et al., 2004).

Natural Supports

Natural supports refer to the network of family, friends, and community members that families use to assist them with needs or support (see Table 3.1). If a natural

Figure 3.1
Typical Wraparound Team

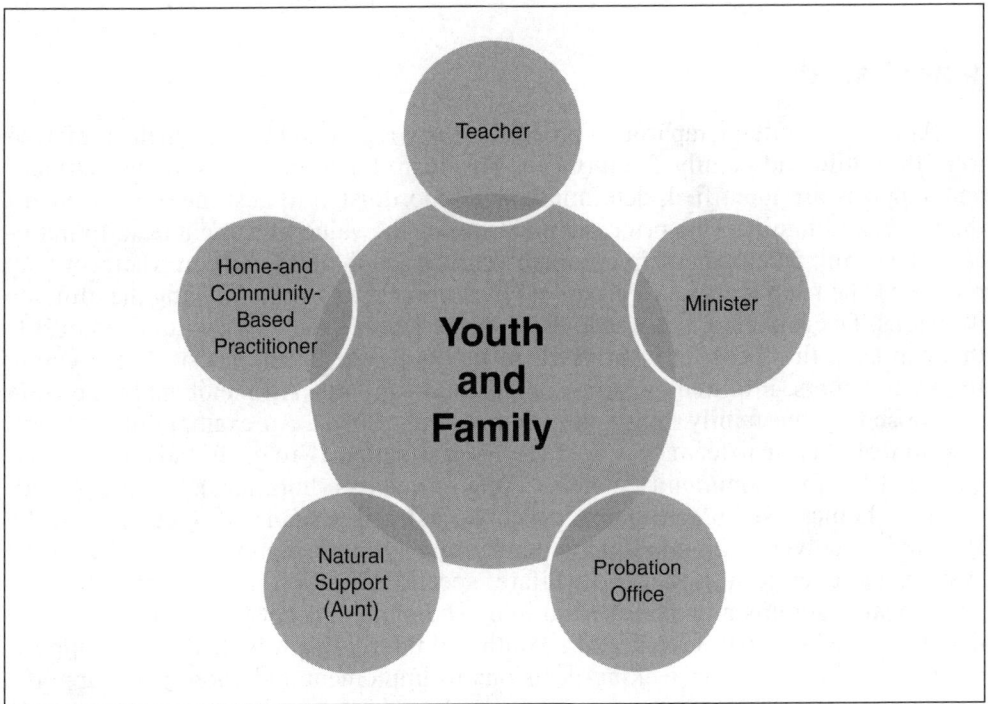

support also happen to be a practitioner, his/her role with the family is not blended, and the role is voluntary, unpaid, and developed through the relationship with the family. The support that is offered may be on a regular basis, ongoing basis, periodic basis, or only when in crisis. Often, these relationships have been in place for long periods of time and reflect the culture of the family in terms of its traditions, values, and beliefs. Some supports are valuable to the family as a whole; some supports are especially helpful to one member of the family. Youth may have a unique set of supports that can reflect their perspectives, and value is seen in relationships that focus primarily on youth as individuals. The wraparound process strongly recognizes the importance of utilizing, supporting, and promoting the use of natural supports while services are being offered as well as when they are terminated. While there is value in formal services, it is recognized that families truly rely on and need a strong network of support that is not dependent on a system, agency, or paid practitioner. The CFT members actively strive to have a majority of the team consist of natural supports, especially toward the end of services. The wraparound plan should consist of interventions and supports that are carried out by natural supports (Bruns et al., 2004). Often, a family has such a high level of need for support that it may have worn out the use of natural supports. A facilitator needs to find ways to develop strategies to restore relationships that may have been severed and find ways to ensure supports are not overtaxed (Walker, Bruns, & Penn, 2008).

Table 3.1
Types of Natural Supports

Extended Family	Big Brother/Big Sister
Friends	Neighbors
Peers	Church Members

Community Based

Community-based supports refer to the strong benefit of maintaining youth's connections to their home communities at all costs. This value emphasizes the strong benefit of promoting stability in relationships and living situations for youth. Integration in the community for both youth and families is highly valued and seen as protective (Walker, 2008). In the past, many youth with serious emotional challenges were often placed in institutions away from families and communities. This resulted in additional issues related to the trauma of being separated from their caregivers. Reunification issues often reflected the significance of this trauma, as youth endured adjustment issues related to restoring relationships with siblings and caregivers. Shifting from institutional schedules and routines to the reality of family life is extremely difficult. While there is a role for acute hospitalization or residential treatment at times, the risks and benefits should always be carefully considered. The safety of the youth should become the primary factor when this is being considered.

To fully appreciate this value, service providers must also understand the strong value of services being offered in natural environments. This includes the home, school, and community of the person being served. Most individuals with significant emotional and behavioral challenges find significant benefit in supports being relevant to their environment and offered in the "here and now." When practitioners are in youth's homes and community settings when challenges occur, the interventions are more relevant, and therefore the skills are more easily transferred to related challenges. A youth can gain enormous benefit from learning ways to control his/her anger when playing basketball with peers at a local park. If supports are provided at the park to facilitate this growth, a youth can then begin to see his/her community as a comfortable place in which to interact and benefit from the peer connections that are made. Office settings, while helpful in some situations, cannot offer this type of support. Additionally, when practitioners interact within home and community settings with the youth and families they serve, they are learning first hand the culture, traditions, and nuances that are relevant to a family. Youth and families experience an overall higher level of satisfaction and better outcomes when services are truly community based.

Culturally Competent

Cultural competency refers to the wraparound process "demonstrating respect for and building on the values, preferences, beliefs, culture, and identity of the child/youth and family, and their community" (Bruns, Walker, & National Wraparound Initiative Advisory Group, 2008, p. 7). Cultural competency is an ongoing process of engaging in the development and integration of cultural knowledge. This includes continual self-assessment and reflection on personal perceptions and influences related to various cultures. "Culture" as a term defines more than race or ethnicity. It encompasses beliefs, values, and practices (Matarese, McGinnis, & Mora, 2005). A few examples of cultures that are less frequently considered are the rural and youth culture. A lack of cultural competence can contribute to stigma and lessens the likelihood that supports are relevant and potentially successful. All activities of the wraparound process, including such activities as assessment, crisis planning, service planning, and transition planning, can only be effective when an understanding of the cultural influences of a family and its community are present. Culture influences the way in which youth and their caregivers evaluate development and adaptive behaviors, parent, interact within their families, express distress, and explain mental illness (Pumariega, 2003). When services are culturally competent, the determination of strengths and needs is seen through a filter of culture. This guides how needs are prioritized and interventions are determined. Interventions will only be successful if they appreciate the culture of the family and reflect what the family identifies as meaningful to it. This value recognizes the importance of having a strong cultural identity and being allowed and encouraged to verbalize this identity. Cultural identity has a tremendous influence on the way in which a person communicates and is socialized. Promoting understanding and accepting an individual's cultural identity supports clarity of values. Having clarity of values significantly helps youth and families. Clarity of values serves as the major component of the personality that helps maintain a sense of self and a positive self-esteem (Gudykunst, Lee, Nishida, & Ogawa, 2004).

Individualized

Prior to the wraparound principles, it was not uncommon for youth with serious emotional and behavioral concerns to receive services that were "canned" and in no way unique to the individual. There was a preponderance of programs that promoted categorical service models, which left little room for individualization. Additionally, there was no appreciation for the concept that needs should be met in a variety of ways through including nontraditional, natural, and community supports. There were single solutions for complex problems that often ignored what the family truly needed (Malysiak, 1997).

When services are truly individualized, there is no duplication of service plans or a "one size fits all" mentality. Individualized services occur by careful attention to procedures associated with the wraparound principles such as defining and prioritizing goals, using the team to exchange information, and soliciting feedback from youth and families. When family and youth are at the center of this process, determining focus and choosing the time, location, frequency, and types of interventions, individualization will occur (Walker & Schutte, 2004). The mission of the CFT is realized by placing value on flexibility, creativity, and collaboration. If these qualities are present in the process, a service plan that is meaningful and potentially effective for the family will be created. Not only does this value represent what should occur at the individual service delivery level but what should occur at the larger systems level (Walker & Schutte, 2005). When commitment to this principle occurs at all levels, families will experience a much higher likelihood of recovery.

Strengths Based

The value of a strength-based orientation is consistent with empowerment theory (see Chapter 1 in this volume), which has significantly influenced the wraparound approach. Empowerment theory focuses on identifying capabilities and environmental influences as opposed to cataloging risk factors and blaming victims. It promotes using individual strengths and competencies, natural helping systems, and proactive behaviors to foster change. It takes the focus from illness to wellness, and deficits to competence (Perkins & Zimmerman, 1995). A strength-based orientation believes that all individuals have resources, knowledge, skills, and competencies. When working with youth and families, this value emphasizes that all families, no matter how challenging their needs may be, have the capacity for growth and change (Early & GlenMaye, 2000). The wraparound principles achieve outcomes by using and increasing youth's and families' psychological assets, interpersonal assets, skills, and knowledge. This same strategy is applied to all members of the CFT, as everyone's unique talents are utilized to benefit the youth and family (Bruns et al., 2008). During the initial phase of the wraparound process, the wraparound facilitator, youth, and family engage in a strengths discovery. This process uncovers the present and past strengths of all family members. Strengths are identified in all major life domains to best understand how they can be utilized in specific ways (Rotto, McIntyre, & Serkin, 2008). The process of focusing on strengths does not end with the strengths discovery but remains as a guiding principle for intervention throughout the entire wraparound process. This experience supports the youth's and families' abilities to continue this focus into recovery.

Persistence

The wraparound approach believes in youth and families, and exemplifies this in an ongoing commitment to do whatever it takes to promote change. There are no terms or conditions for continued services, and termination occurs only when the CFT agrees that it is appropriate. Families and youth may have felt blamed, rejected, and ignored when difficulties arose. The wraparound approach attempts to see setbacks as opportunities and believes that families do not fail, but the plans that have been designed do. In this case, the service plan does not reflect the true needs, priorities, and appropriate interventions that can promote growth. There may not be an appropriate mix of natural, community, and formal supports. Often, families are told that services are not available to support their youth. The unconditional value does not use the absence of service options to give up on addressing needs. The most effective plans are creative, flexible, and use natural supports to address lack of formal services. This value also challenges practitioners to "think outside of the box" and not remain complacent when traditional ways of doing things do not work.

Outcome Based

Youth and families have seen many instances of failure and ineffective strategies. In a wraparound approach, it is vital to answer the question, "how will we know when we are successful?" This holds everyone on the team accountable for following through with interventions and focusing on measurable indicators of successes. The service plan will break down goals into reachable steps that allow the youth and the entire team to experience small successes along the way to recovery. Outcome monitoring keeps the focus on regularly assessing the effectiveness of the plan and not allowing for an ineffective plan to hold up progress. It also allows for evaluation data to validate the effectiveness of the wraparound approach and further develop the approach as needed (Bruns et al., 2008).

ENSURING THE VOICES OF YOUTH ARE HEARD

A strong value on the voices of families has always been an integral part of empowerment and the wraparound process. Collaboration with families has been demonstrated to have multiple benefits. These include improving the likelihood that services will be culturally competent, meaningful, and strengths based (Cheney & Osher, 1997). When family input is genuinely sought and valued, the road is paved for a true understanding of how services can be uniquely tailored to represent the family's culture, insights into its strengths and needs, and preferences for how services would best meet their needs. Due to the increasingly strong understanding of how the investment of youth must be present, there has been an evolution nationally to distinctly empower the voice of the youth. At the individual service delivery level, when youth are under the jurisdiction of their caregivers, there may be a disconnection between what the youth identify and prioritize as needs and what the caregivers do. This situation should be addressed, as mutual investment strongly increases the odds that the intervention plan will be successful. Although safety must always be paramount, there is much to be gained by allowing a youth to try an alternative intervention or focus. Skillful planning can be employed to integrate the preferences of the caregivers and youth into a plan that can be mutually beneficial and reevaluated on a regular basis. When youth experience opportunities to be heard, participate in planning, and engage in problem solving with a team, resiliency characteristics are being fostered. Research has demonstrated repeatedly that youth who experience a sense of purpose, respect, and an orientation to the future have an increased ability to cope with adversity (Benard & Educational Resources Information Center (U.S.), 1991; Linetsky, 2000).

Supporting the youth voice should occur at both the practice and policy levels. At the service level, including youth's perspectives in the assessment and planning process, and working toward a unified perspective with caregivers and youth are always beneficial. At the systems level, finding opportunities to have youth directly involved in the processes of planning and evaluating programs is valuable. As programs develop, committees that represent the tasks of planning and evaluating should include both youth and family representation. Additionally, youth focus groups can be convened to specifically hear what youth have to say. Choi (2000) explains that proponents of the youth development movement point out that practitioners working with youth have an obligation to promote opportunities for youth to

- Experience social support and caring relationships from adults as well as peers;
- Have input into decision making;
- Develop leadership roles;
- Become involved in the larger community to strengthen investment in their communities; and
- Expose youth to a wide variety of learning experiences within their communities.

All of these experiences are supported when youth are specifically engaged in planning at both the individual and system level.

INFUSING THE PRINCIPLES INTO THE DELIVERY OF HOME- AND COMMUNITY-BASED SERVICES

Adhering to the wraparound principles and values that empowerment theory (see Chapter 1 in this volume) has to offer is not an accidental occurrence. The wraparound process must be thoughtful, highly invested in, and reflected at all levels. The staff who ensure that this occurs must truly believe in the principles and reflect them on a regular basis in their activities and discussions. Policies that are developed should reflect the wraparound principles and be valued and understood by all levels of an organization or program. If programs evolve from a different value base, all policies should be reviewed to ensure that they are consistent with the newly adopted principles. Staff should be selected and hired based on their understanding and agreement with the wraparound principles. Minimally, potential staff should have an understanding that they are expected to reflect the principles in their service delivery. Assessing incompatibility in this area should be a part of the hiring process as well. Supervision and training should reflect the principles and be followed on a regular basis. Finally, a quality assurance process should be built into programs to evaluate alliance with values and principles.

CONCLUSION

A strong value base and commitment to a belief system is a necessary part of the service delivery process at all levels. The wraparound principles that have been presented in this chapter have considerable value for both practitioners and families. Practitioners who adhere to the principles will naturally support a process that has been shown to bring about positive outcomes. Families who experience the values inherent in the wraparound process learn skills that will continue to assist their youth long into recovery. Families can be supported to use the values as a guide for future interactions in which decisions and supports must be made to assist their youth. As families develop this expectation for how services will be delivered across all systems, they can work along with practitioners to transform how youth with mental health challenges are supported.

References

Behar, L. B. (1986). A state model for child mental health services: The North Carolina experience. *Children Today, 15,* 16-22.

Benard, B., & Educational Resources Information Center (U.S.). (1991). *Fostering resiliency in kids: Protective factors in the family, school, and community.* Portland, OR: Western Center for Drug-Free Schools and Communities, Far West Laboratory.

Bruns, E. J., Walker, J. S., Adams, J., Miles, P., Osher, T. W., Rast, J., et al. (2004). *Ten principles of the wraparound process.* Portland, OR: National Wraparound Initiative, Research and Training Center for Family Support and Children's Mental Health, Portland State University.

Bruns, E. J., Walker, J. S., & National Wraparound Intitiative Advisory Group. (2008). Ten principles of the wraparound process. In E. J. Bruns & J. S. Walker (Eds.), *The resource guide to wraparound.* Portland, OR: National Wraparound Initiative, Research and Training Center for Family Support and Children's Mental Health, Portland State University.

Cheney, D., & Osher, T. (1997). Collaborate with families. *Journal of Emotional & Behavioral Disorders, 5,* 36-40.

Choi, J. (2000). Valuing the voice of our young people. *Focal Point: A National Bulletin on Family Support and Children's Mental Health, 14*(2), 9-10.

Early, T. J., & GlenMaye, L. F. (2000). Valuing families: Social work practice with families from a strengths perspective. *Social Work, 45,* 118-130.

Goldman, S. K. (1999). The conceptual framework for wraparound: Definition, values, essential elements, and requirements for practice. In B. J. Burns & S. K. Goldman (Eds.), *Systems of care: Promising practices in children's mental health, 1998 series, vol. IV. Practices in wraparound for children with severe emotional disorders and their families* (pp. 27-34). Washington, DC: Center for Effective Collaboration and Practice, American Institutes for Research.

Gudykunst, W. B., Lee, C. M., Nishida, T., & Ogawa, N. (2004). Theorizing about intercultural communication: An introduction. In W. B. Gudykunst (Ed.), *Theorizing about intercultural communication* (pp. 3-33). Thousand Oaks, CA: Sage Publications.

Linetsky, M. (2000). Youth development: Putting theory into practice. *Focal Point: A National Bulletin on Family Support and Children's Mental Health, 14*(2), 11-14.

Malysiak, R. (1997). Exploring the theory and paradigm base for wraparound. *Journal of Child & Family Studies, 6,* 399-408.

Matarese, M., McGinnis, L., & Mora, M., (2005). *Youth involvement in systems of care: A guide to empowerment.* Washington, DC: Technical Assistance Partnerships Publications.

Osher, T., Penn, M., & Spencer, S. A. (2008.) Partnerships with families for family-driven systems of care. In B. A. Stroul & G. Blau (Eds.), *The system of care handbook: Transforming mental health services for children, youth and families* (pp. 249-273). Baltimore: Paul H. Brookes Publishing.

Perkins, D. D., & Zimmerman, M. A. (1995). Empowerment theory, research, and application. *American Journal of Community Psychology, 23,* 569-579.

President's New Freedom Commission on Mental Health. (2003). *Achieving the promise: Tranforming mental health care in America. Final report* (DHHS Publication No. SMA-03-3832). Rockville, MD: Author.

Pumariega, A. J. (2003). Cultural competence in a systems of care for children's mental health. In A. J. Pumariega & N. C. Winters (Eds.), *The handbook of child and adolescent systems of care: The new community psychiatry* (pp. 82-107). New York: Jossey-Bass.

Rotto, K., McIntyre, J. S., & Serkin, C. (2008). Strenth-based, individualized services in systems of care. In B. A. Stroul & G. Blau (Eds.), *The system of care handbook: Transforming mental health services for children, youth and families* (pp. 401-435). Baltimore: Paul H. Brookes Publishing.

Vandenberg, J., Bruns, E. J., & Burchard, J. (2008). History of the wraparound process. In E. J. Bruns & J. S. Walker (Eds.), *The resource guide to wraparound.* Portland, OR: National Wraparound Initiative, Research and Training Center for Family Support and Children's Mental Health, Portland State University.

Walker, J. S. (2008). *How and why does wraparound work: A theory of change.* Portland, OR: National Wraparound Initiative, Portland State University.

Walker, J. S., Bruns, E. J., & Penn, M. (2008). Individualized services in systems of care: The wraparound process. In B. A. Stroul & G. Blau (Eds.), *The system of care handbook:*

Transforming mental health services for children, youth and families (pp. 127-153). Baltimore: Paul H. Brookes Publishing.

Walker, J. S., & Schutte, K. (2004). Practice and process in wraparound teamwork. *Journal of Emotional & Behavioral Disorders, 12*, 182-192.

Walker, J. S., & Schutte, K. (2005). Quality and individualization in wraparound team planning. *Journal of Child & Family Studies, 14*, 251-267.

Part 2
Building and Supporting the Workforce

Chapter 4

Recruitment and Development of Staff

It is a fine thing to have ability, but the ability to discover the ability in others is the true test.

—Elbert Hubbard

INTRODUCTION

Programs are only as valuable as the presence of available resources to support them. In this case, staff are the most valuable commodity. While staff are clearly the most important resource in a program, there are significant challenges and considerations to make in developing a workforce. This process begins with determining the qualifications of the staff that will be needed. Many factors are involved in this decision including the quality and availability of training programs, accreditation concerns, and funding expectations. In addition to formal training and experience requirements, there are the special considerations that can make the difference between a marginal and an exceptional employee. Such considerations include consistent values, work ethic, capacity for relationship building, valuing supervision and ongoing training, and the ability to work within a team approach. Once staff are hired, there should be strong value placed on orientation, training, and reflective supervision to ensure the development and retention of a quality workforce. This ultimately supports the youth and families that programs are trying to serve, as continuity with practitioners is an important ingredient to success. While positions are carefully designed, plans are made for recruitment, and staffing options are evaluated, administrators must simultaneously determine ways to nurture those that are chosen to support the youth and families who are being empowered.

WORKFORCE CHALLENGES

As federal and state agencies place an emphasis on the importance of attending to the needs of youth with significant mental health challenges, there has also been recognition of the difficulty in building a workforce. The supply of well-trained mental health practitioners available to work with youth and families is significantly lacking, particularly in rural areas (Peterson, West, Tanielian, & Pincus, 1998). There is a shortage of practitioners at all levels. Paraprofessionals, staff with bachelor or masters degrees, and supervisory-level staff are all in demand. This concept was acknowledged by the President's New Freedom Commission on Mental Health (2003), as the report emphasized the need to recruit and train practitioners to assist in the transformation of the service delivery system for youth with serious emotional challenges.

Despite the fact that adherence to system of care principles is increasingly being accepted as the benchmark for quality service for youth with emotional challenges, the training programs have not consistently provided this in their curricula. In regards to the training that is needed when adhering to the wraparound process (see Chapter 3 in this volume), Burchard, Bruns, and Burchard (2002) describe higher education programs that "stress values, skills and attitudes that are inconsistent with those associated with the wraparound process" (p. 82). They further describe training programs as using curricula that are unidisciplinary, deficit focused, and failing to see family members as partners rather than clients (Burchard et al., 2002). Additionally, the programs do not give enough attention to the concept of recovery-oriented behavioral health care and the importance of building natural and community supports to maximize families and youth's capacities for recovery.

An additional challenge in the recruitment and retention of a workforce is related to the ever-changing nature of who the youth in need are. More and more youth in need represent ethnic minorities and specialty populations. African American, Latino, Asian American, and American Indian accounted for 39 percent of all children in 2000 (U.S. Bureau of the Census, 2000). This can present both linguistic as well as cultural competency issues that can discourage practitioners from taking positions. Working with specialty populations has become a challenge to the workforce in that many feel poorly prepared or supported in working with these youth. While, historically, services have been primarily focused on school-age youth, mental health needs are now more identified in both very young and transition-age youth. This has also presented new challenges to staff in learning specialized assessment and intervention techniques.

Finally, there are unique requirements for the positions of home-based practitioners and supervisors that may present programs with hiring challenges. Many potential staff decide that evening hours, on-call rotations, and the need for flexibility are requirements that are less than desirable. While these same characteristics may appeal to some, to many they are seen as too demanding. Potential staff must also be comfortable with the concept that families may have multiple challenges that require focused and intensive intervention with a strong need for dedication and persistence.

STAFF ROLES

As staff are being interviewed, clear descriptions of their potential roles are essential. Job descriptions should be given to potential hires to ensure a clear understanding of expectations. Potential staff may have misconceptions or a frame of reference regarding services that will represent a fundamental misalignment in job match and capacity. Some strategies to assist potential staff in this level of understanding also include sharing descriptions of what a typical day looks like and having existing staff describe their duties. Program materials (e.g., an orientation guide for families or program descriptions), if shared, will assist in a broader-level understanding as well. If staff are expected to work within a team-based approach, clarification of this process should also occur. In addition, assignments that may occur on a rotating basis, such as on-call crisis intervention, should be discussed. Exhibits 4.1 and 4.2 offer examples of home-based practitioners' and supervisors' job descriptions.

RECRUITMENT EFFORTS

The advertising and job postings that are developed when recruiting staff are most effective when the values and principles of the program are highlighted. From the moment that a potential staff person becomes aware that a home-based services position is available, the emphasis should be on the importance of family empowerment. There may be a human resources director who is the point of contact for potential staff, and awareness of the values of the program should be clearly understood by this person, as potential staff often first contact the human resources director. Potential staff members are often most concerned with finding programs that are in alignment with their personal values, goals, and beliefs. Likewise, programs are most successful when searching for a match between organizational values and individual values. This process of "person-organizational fit" seeks congruence between individual and organizational values (Spector, 2007). A mutual investment in empowering families and a shared understanding and value placed on the wraparound principles are the most important elements to consider when recruiting new staff. Lessons learned from staff selection for evidence-based practices include the fact that implementation was impeded when the interviewing process did not focus on hiring staff with congruent attitudes regarding the model and population served as well as openness to change. Intelligence, enthusiasm, and strong supervision offset a lack of credentials, experience, and skills (Wieder & Boyle, 2007).

Ongoing marketing and networking can also impact the recruitment process positively. A newsletter can be developed that is sent to community partners such as other service providers, schools, child welfare agencies, juvenile justice systems, and caregivers. The newsletter can serve to keep others in the field aware of the work that is happening within the program and field in general as well as providing information on current job openings and developments. Managers can also network within the community to make positions known. Staff can be encouraged to make referrals for potential new hires. Table 4.1 identifies additional strategies to consider in the recruitment process.

DESIRED STAFF CHARACTERISTICS

Experience and education definitely are important qualifications for staff, although there are additional considerations that may be equally significant. Many of the most beneficial characteristics are not related to either experience or education. This section discusses important characteristics for home-based services practitioners.

Table 4.1
Recruitment Process Strategies

Strategy	Person Responsible
Staff take opportunities to share the vision, principles, strengths, and successes of program with community members and partners.	All Staff
Staff are informed on how to respond to job inquiries at all levels and respond promptly.	All Staff
Job opportunities are posted internally, and internal candidates are treated fairly and with respect.	All Staff
Recruitment bonuses are considered for current employees, consumers, family members, board members, or other partners.	All Staff
Interview process is highly organized and timely, so as to not lose potential candidates.	Human Resources
Hiring bonuses are offered.	Administration
Advertising includes college and university career centers, newspapers, job services, notifications in community, and Web site notifications.	Human Resources
Participating in job fairs, career days, and speaking engagements in community as available is useful.	Human Resources Management
Internships and practicum experiences can be offered.	Management
Radio and television announcements are made.	Human Resources
Quality marketing materials are distributed.	Administration

Characteristics of Practitioners

Dunst, Trivette, Davis, and Cornwell (1994, p. 176) after reviewing the empowerment literature listed six attitudes and beliefs that characterized effective practitioners:

1. *Positive attributions toward help-seeker and helping relationships.* Helpers who see those asking for help in a positive manner are able to develop and maintain much more of a collaborative working relationship that produces good outcomes than those who do not.

2. *Emphasis on help-seeker responsibility for meeting needs and solving problems.* When helpers can focus not on the blaming of those in need for causing their problems but rather on the need to develop competencies to overcome challenges that are often results of societal barriers, change is more likely.

3. *High expectations regarding the capacity of help-seekers to become competent.* Helpers are most effective when at their core, they see families as competent and able to change with the guidance and support of professional and natural supports.

4. *Emphasis on building on help-seeker strengths.* Helpers who naturally assist others in building on their strengths to minimize the effects of needs facilitate lasting changes rather than a short term fixes.

5. *Proactive stance toward helping relationships.* Good helpers develop strategies that are able to build family functioning before the crisis occurs. The shift of empowering families in this fashion leaves behind the notion that helping families is defined by protecting and rescuing families when stressors or crisis occurs.

6. *Promotion efforts as the focus of help-giving.* Prevention efforts address issues before a problem occurs, and treatment efforts address issues once they have developed. In contrast to both, promotion efforts focus on identifying skills that enhance an individual's capacity to function.

Dunst et al. (1994, pp. 178-179) have also identified eight help-giving behaviors, which include the following:

1. *Practices reflective listening.* Reflecting listening occurs when someone is able to paraphrase and communicate accurately back to the speaker the points he/she is trying to make. The experience of being understood and empathized with is often communicated when this happens.

2. *Assists help-seekers in identifying, clarifying, and prioritizing aspirations as well as needs.* Helpers are able to balance their understanding of families and individuals when they focus on determining hopes and wishes as well as needs and concerns. This supports the development of competency enhancing interventions.

3. *Offers help before it is requested.* Families feel supported when workers identify supports before being asked, using the input from the assessment and ongoing relationship to anticipate needs before there is crisis. Careful attention to how needs are communicated, both verbally and nonverbally, is critical in this process as well.

4. *Offers help that is normative in terms of family culture.* The helping relationship is functioning best when helpers are able to work alongside families to identify interventions that appreciate and support their cultures.

5. *Offers help that is congruent with family's appraisal of problems and needs.* It is important to consider how the family prioritizes and interprets its needs and desired interventions. The plan should fully reflect what the family identifies and prioritizes. Both the youth and family are best served when there is support in focusing on the thoughts and priorities of both youth and their caregivers to determine a common focus.

6. *Promotes the development of family skills to decrease need for help.* Helpers that see their role as developing the family's capacities rather than being

"needed" by the family to support it ultimately serve the family much better and in a way that will produce long-lasting results.

7. *Promotes sense of cooperation and joint responsibility with family to meet needs.* Help-giving methods should always occur collaboratively and in a way that respects the family's ultimate authority in making decisions. Families should always feel that the goal of services is to ultimately leave the worker out of a job. This mentality is reflected in the mutual collaboration throughout all stages of service delivery.

8. *Promotes decision making occurring at the family level.* Families need to feel that they can refuse, redefine their needs and interventions, and ultimately guide the entire help-giving process to be most engaged and benefitted.

The following characteristics are also valuable in home-based practitioners.

Organization. A home-based practitioner is faced with several tasks and responsibilities that require good organizational skills. Responsibilities and commitments that are made to the families must be honored in a manner that is timely and reflects quality work. Families are often desperate for help, and strategies that truly empower families must be done "with" families not "to" families. This requires a strong level of organization to ensure that an adequate amount of face-to-face time with families is scheduled or facilitated. The ability to prioritize and make the most efficient use of time is needed to accommodate the ever-changing needs of families.

In addition to overall strong organizational strategies needed for the practitioner's own work flow, it is necessary to assist families and others with their personal organizational strategies. Staff, as they assist the family in determining action plans, must have the ability to follow up on tasks that the family and/or youth have agreed to do. As organization may be a weakness of some family members, it may be necessary to teach strategies. In coordinating services with schools, other service systems, and natural supports, it is critical that good planning and organization takes place so that progress is not sabotaged.

Flexibility. When providing services that are in alignment with wraparound principles, the valuing of youth and family input regarding service needs requires practitioners to be highly responsive and flexible. The shift from practitioners being in the expert role to families and youth being considered the experts on their own needs means that services will always be individualized (Walker, 2008). This requires openness to change, input, and nontraditional interventions. Home-based services practitioners must put the needs of the youth and families above the needs of the program. When families are in need, it is the job of the practitioner to be present and available, as this is when the greatest impact can occur. The relationship between families and practitioner is significantly positively impacted when this happens. In accomplishing this task, there is a strong need to be flexible and accommodating. The home-based practitioner must negotiate the demands of meetings, create documentation, and prioritize the needs of families.

Capacity for Supervision. When providing services to support youth and families with significant needs, there is a strong need for supervision and support. The experience of being a practitioner can be overwhelming. Practitioners will be affected by high levels of emotionality, crisis situations, and the demands of the position. Practitioners who are open to the support that supervisors can provide offer a characteristic that has been proven to benefit both practitioners and families. Some staff embrace the concept of supervision, while others see it as an obstacle and therefore passively or actively resist supervision. The experience of being in supervision requires the capacity to honestly reflect on both strengths and weaknesses in a way that can promote growth. Additionally, potential staff who are not threatened by supervisory oversight possess a needed characteristic. Supervisors can assist practitioners in managing the stress of the position, their reactions to situations that may occur during visits, and emotions related to working with those in need. Without support, or with an unreceptive attitude toward supervision, it is more likely that services to families will suffer. A reflective practice model can offer this type of support. Practitioners who experience a reflective practice model receive a number of benefits that can, in turn, enhance the therapeutic experiences of the families who they serve. A reflective practice model allows practitioners to reflect on frustrations and challenges within the parameters of a supportive relationship. When this occurs, it encourages practitioners to see their reactions and experiences as "normal" and as part of the therapeutic process. This ownership allows a processing of experiences that, without such, could become obstacles to the therapeutic process (Heffron, 2005). Additionally, the reflective practice model facilitates a strength-based orientation for both the practitioner and the family. This practice does not encourage ignoring needs, but rather it identifies the utilization of strengths already present to mitigate needs and concerns. Last, the reflective practice model supports learning in a manner that is most relevant to the adult learner—in the here and now and relevant to current experiences. This may create an opportunity to see how past practices may not be relevant or need modification based on current research. Table 4.2 shows the benefits of reflective practices.

Nonjudgmental Stance. The staff who meet with families in need are a precious resource that represents not only the program but perhaps an overall impression of home-based services. Staff who evoke a feeling of judgment are damaging to the self-esteem of both youth and caregivers, and at worst may prevent a family from getting the help it needs and deserves. Staff who are nonjudgmental are able to relate to a belief system for youth and their families that is nonblaming and free of stigma. Potential staff should demonstrate this attitude in discussions of youth and family needs as well as in their gestures and nonverbal communications.

Respect for Importance of Issues Related to Boundaries and Ethics. Home-based services can challenge any level of staff in the area of boundaries and ethics. Due to the intensity of needs, presence in the home environment, and the desire to help, it is likely that guidance in these areas may be needed. Home-based practitioners may often, especially in rural areas, be the only aid available to the family. This may stir up feelings of guilt, empathy, and a desire to overextend oneself. Staff may have trouble accepting that they cannot be all things to the families who they serve. It is crucial to be able to identify when a family's needs go beyond what a staff person can offer (Wasik & Bryant, 2001). Staff who demonstrate an appreciation for the complexity of these issues and the openness to consulting with others related to this are essential to serving families effectively. The characteristic of openness in discussing the topic is by far more important than knowledge or experience, as no one can ever be fully prepared for the challenges in this area.

Table 4.2
Benefits of Reflective Practice

- An opportunity to compare and examine beliefs and program mission with current research and thinking;
- An opportunity to explore how program practices reflect the mission and beliefs;
- An opportunity to explore how personal history, culture, and experiences affect relationships with families and other professionals;
- A way to think about patterns and systems not just one event;
- An opportunity for practitioners to experience observation, listening, and inquiry as an approach to understanding relationships;
- The development of a common language and shared vision for the work; and
- An opportunity to influence agency practices.

Positive View of How Needs Are Manifested in Youth and Families. Quite frequently, the most pressing concern that caregivers have is to manage a youth's behavior. The potential staff member must believe that behavior is reflective of a need in order to support the mission and value base of family-centered home-based services. This means that the behavior is present due to an unmet need that the youth is experiencing. For example, a youth who frequently yells at his mother in the morning, when she pushes him to get out of bed, is not merely "oppositional" but experiencing an unmet need, perhaps due to sleep challenges. This is challenging when caregivers exhibit difficult behaviors as well. This may be the most frustrating experience for home practitioners, although an orientation of need-based behavior improves understanding and tolerance. Ultimately, this belief system, as well as skill, supports true change, as it appreciates what is driving the behavior and promotes problem solving that is more effective.

Behavior Management Strategies That Reflect Respect and Strength-Based Orientation. With youth who experience emotional and behavioral challenges, an approach to behavioral management that is punitive, embarrassing, and disrespectful to youth may result in temporary change but does not support recovery and positive growth. More importantly, punitive and disrespectful strategies, such as forcing a child to squat against a wall, can be retraumatizing or traumatic in and of itself. Proactive behavioral interventions are the goal. Interventions should include direct and positive strategies, which can change behavior by focusing on adaptive or socially appropriate skills that can replace negative behaviors (Nelson, Roberts, & Smith, 1998). These interventions should reflect the strengths of the youth. Staff who can promote positive opportunities for youth to excel, and therefore divert their acting-out behavior, are a rare but needed find in home-based services.

Empathy. Empathy is considered one of the highest if not *the* highest level emotion that people experience. It is something that needs to be experienced in order to develop—hence, the reason for the benefit of this ability in home-based services. Youth may not have experienced empathy on a consistent basis for various reasons, and their caregivers are often overwhelmed and in need of empathy as well. The experience of being understood on an emotional level can be one of the most valuable characteristics a home practitioner can offer a family.

Awareness and Openness to Wraparound Principles and Empowerment Theory.
Potential staff may or may not be aware of the complete list of principles and characteristics of family-centered care, although their capacity to adhere to and exemplify
them must be present. Candidates should reflect an understanding that an awareness
of the wraparound principles (see Chapter 3 in this volume) and empowerment theory
(see Chapter 1 in this volume) is needed, although this further develops through a
commitment to continued learning and growth. It is therefore critical to ask specific
questions about to a potential staff member's viewpoints related to these areas or willingness to subscribe to them.

Characteristics of Supervisors

Spector (2007, pp. 170-173) identifies five core tasks of leaders who are hoping
to affect change within an organization. As supervisors hope to instill a philosophy of
empowerment that supports the wraparound process (see Chapter 3 in this volume),
the following five tasks are beneficial:

1. *Developing clear and consistent sense of purpose and direction.* Staff that are
   continually reinforced in a shared understanding of purpose and goals are more
   likely to demonstrate the values and principles within their work and organization.

2. *Demanding performance goals.* When staff are supported in identifying high
   performance goals as well as given the resources and autonomy to achieve
   these goals, they are often successful.

3. *Enabling upward communication.* Supervisors that support the communication
   upward allow for vital information that front-line workers have to be a part of
   higher-level decision making.

4. *Forging an emotional bond between employees and organizations.* When
   supervisors recognize the importance of developing and sustaining a positive
   relationships between staff and leaders, there are benefits in retention of staff
   and commitment to the program values.

5. *Developing future change leaders.* Investing in the development of future leaders ensures that both in the present and in the future a cadre of staff are available to ensure commitment to the mission of the program.

Provide Reflective Supervision. The skills that are needed by the effective supervisor
promoting a reflective practice model (see "Capacity for Supervision") are the same
skills that are needed in the practitioner and, ultimately, in the caregivers to create
positive relationships. These skills are described by Gilkerson and Ritzler (2005) as
"the capacity to (1) listen carefully, (2) demonstrate concern and empathy, (3) promote reflection, (4) observe and highlight the parent-child relationship, (5) respect
role boundaries, (6) respond thoughtfully in emotionally intense interactions, and (7)
understand, regulate and use one's own feelings" (p. 431). In order to provide reflective supervision, a supervisor needs to demonstrate specific characteristics amenable
to the process. The first and foremost capacity is the ability to value the relationship above all else. The relationship must be safe, supportive, and respectful. Staff
must feel as if they are free to process their weaknesses without fear of negative

consequences. Value is placed on being reflective and able to relate both positive and negative feelings regarding being in the helping role. The supervisory "role" is somewhat suspended in the sense that a hierarchy must be eliminated in order for the safety and protective environment of reflective supervision to take hold. Another capacity is the ability to relate to staff in a way that promotes growth. This may mean addressing difficult topics or guiding a staff member in addressing a complex and emotionally charged issue. Supervisors must develop strategies for keeping staff engaged while addressing issues or concerns.

Use Strength-Based Coaching. The importance of a supervisor using the principles and beliefs of a strength-based orientation is critical to the success of this philosophy being embedded into service delivery. This strength-based model views all people as having strengths as well as the capacity to recover and transform their lives. Supervisors reflect this orientation in their practice with individuals and families by truly knowing the families they serve, having frequent contact with them that reflects respect, promoting clients as capable and "heroes," and assuming an advocacy perspective (Rapp & Goscha, 2006). This same perspective should be reflected in the supervisor's relationships with staff. This may be a shift for some supervisors, as it is often not the supervisor's past experience with his/her own supervision. To provide this type of coaching and support, the supervisor must believe in the strength-based approach. It is not something, in either care provision or supervision, that can be provided without a comfort level with the general principles. Supervisors must be able to "see" staff members' strengths and build on them in a way that promotes growth. This does not mean ignoring issues or concerns, but strategies for addressing these concerns are focused upon in a different manner than a deficit-based approach. Providing supervision from this perspective supports the practitioners in what is considered a parallel process. What they experience in terms of support can then be transferred to the family, benefiting both in the process. This style of supervision serves to preserve staff members' capacities to manage a variety of tasks and prevent burnout, as it is more attentive to the issues that can become overwhelming in service provision.

Support Practitioners With Various Duties. Supervisors of staff in home-based programs need to remain attentive to the variety of duties that are a part of the job responsibilities for the front-line practitioner. The supervisory process needs to be mindful of this challenge and assist in developing strategies to ensure a comprehensive service delivery. Practitioners may need assistance in scheduling, time management, and concurrent documentation strategies. This means that supervisors must have the skills or abilities to support skill development in all areas of the job expectations. This often occurs best when supervisors are able to listen to staff and determine development needs. The supervisor's ability to recognize the strengths of staff is crucial in problem-solving strategies to ensure that comprehensive services occur. Additionally, most practitioners have areas in which they feel more competent and comfortable. Therefore, support for the development of skills in other areas is often needed.

Support Assessment and Documentation. Strong supervisors have the ability to monitor a number of families' services in a manner that is thorough and comprehensive. As practitioners complete assessments, supervisors will need to ensure that assessments remain comprehensive and result in an accurate picture of the strengths and needs of the family. This assessment will need to become the basis for service planning and must represent the uniqueness of each family. The notion that assessment is an ongoing process and not a single event must also be supported by supervisors as staff continues to serve families. Staff may be in need of support in documenting the good work that has occurred within the home. Third-party billing expectations must also be met, and oversight for this process is crucial to funding. Building a mentality that documentation is useful to both practitioners and families is also a role of the supervisor. Finding ways and opportunities to demonstrate this concept through encouragement of language that is understood by youth and families, documenting with families, and actual use of service plans, crisis plans, and transition plans should be a skill of all supervisors. Although much of the services and strategies that are used in home visits are the result of family input, it is often necessary to support the development of options for service delivery that reflect clinical understanding of the youth's needs as well as an ongoing strategy that supports recovery. Documentation, if valued and completed appropriately, should tell the story of the family in its movement from recognizing challenges to living and coping effectively with the needs of all members of the family. This can be invaluable in the present as well as if there is a need for services in the future.

Assist Staff in Service Planning. Service planning is a task that is often seen as overwhelming and daunting for staff. Unfortunately, it can feel that way for families as well. Supervisors are needed to assist staff in developing strategies to ensure that a comprehensive, easily managed and understood plan is developed for youth and families. This also includes ensuring that the plan is individualized and reflective of the assessment that is the foundation of the plan. Supervisors should first assist staff with ways to communicate the goals of service planning to families; this ensure that families are aware of what to expect in the process. Once this occurs, the development of a strategy that ensures that the assessment information translates into a plan should be discussed. For some, this may be a form that is shared with the family, or there may be another method to identify and discuss the needs and strengths identified in the assessment. Supervisors, who continually demonstrate using the service plan in supervision, assist staff in remembering to use the plan as a guide. Newly identified strategies or strategies that are no longer effective should always be modified in collaboration with the youth and family. Supervisors who continually remind staff of this assist in creating a process in which the service plan becomes a working document that accurately reflects what is happening in service delivery.

Support Staff in Appropriate Transition. Staff may become focused on the development and implementation of interventions that assist the family in moving toward change. Once change and growth occurs, and are present, it is often difficult to shift to transferring the skills to the family and natural supports. The value of planning for an appropriate time and manner in which to terminate services is significant and should not be overlooked. Walker (2008) describes successful transitions as ones that "anticipate and prepare for transition will in advance and maintain transition supports past the actual point when a setting or situation changes; and are coordinated, while also managing and sharing information in a way that is both efficient and respectful to the child and family" (p. 5). Due to the strong value of this stage of service delivery, this process must be well supported by supervisors. The complexity of issues related to transition should be understood and reflected in the supervisory process.

Manage Crisis. Just as front-line staff need to assist families in the managing of crisis, supervisors must have the skills to support staff in this process as well. Supervisors must be able to acknowledge the identification of a crisis situation, even when they may disagree with staff regarding the assessment. Staff must always feel supported, especially when they are away from the office and deem a situation to be critical. Supervisors must have the capacity to support staff immediately and completely. Characteristics of supervisors that manage crisis effectively include the following:

- *Accurate assessment of crisis.* This respects the fact that it is helpful not to overgeneralize but truly listen to the person in crisis to understand the uniqueness of the situation.

- *Thinking creatively and quickly.* Good supervisors are able to think quickly and in a manner that reflects "out of the box" and creative solutions.

- *Ability to remain calm and promote others in remaining calm.* This capacity is critical in that the practitioners are looking to the supervisors to provide guidance that will lead to an acceptable outcome. This can only be accomplished with a there is a calm understanding of the crisis.

- *Focus on the here and now in developing a plan.* The focus of crisis management is to develop a plan that will work in the present and understands the factors that are impacting the situation currently. Exploring past history may be unnecessary and even disruptive to the process. Helpful supervisors will not consider the crisis managed until a plan is in place that everyone is happy with and can be implemented. Follow-up to support the completion of all assigned tasks and commitments is also important (Shapiro & Koocher, 1996).

Once a crisis is over, it is critical for supervisors to have the skills to process and debrief the staff. It is equally important for supervisors to have the insight and ability to determine when they are in need of debriefing or when another person should assume the role of processing the crisis.

Develop Collaborative Supervision Plans. Just as service provision should be guided by a service plan, staff members' professional development should be recognized and guided by a plan. The plan should reflect a collaborative process in which concerns, needs, strengths, and agency expectations are appreciated. Staff that are interested in developing competencies that could contribute to the agency or team's mission should be encouraged and supported. The plan should be used to monitor the effectiveness of the training and supports that are implemented.

INTERVIEW PROCESS

Interview Techniques

In order to determine if potential staff subscribe to the values and principles of family empowerment (see Chapter 1 in this volume) and the wraparound process (see Chapter 3 in this volume), two techniques known as behavioral simulation and behaviorally anchored interviewing are helpful. Behaviorally anchored interviewing involves asking potential staff to give specific examples from their pasts to illustrate how they have responded to challenges and opportunities. Behavioral simulation involves giving applicants role play situations to demonstrate behaviors that reflect their values and beliefs (Spector, 2007). Exhibit 4.3 identifies questions that encourage potential staff members to demonstrate values and past behaviors in relationship to help-giving practices, beliefs, and attitudes.

Youth and Families in the Interview Process

In the interview process, it is helpful to use youth and families to give input regarding the qualifications of potential staff. This may be done by allowing families and youth to sit in on group interviews or, if time allows, in a one-on-one interview with candidates. Youth have perspective regarding the ability to relate to potential staff that may not be seen in the same way by anyone else. Additionally, family members have a unique perspective and investment that no one else may have in finding a staff member that is right for the job. Family members and youth may be assisted in developing questions but should be encouraged to determine what is important for them to know and assess from the interview process. This involvement in the process can be invaluable. It clearly communicates to families and youth their importance in program development while giving practitioners important insights into the best candidates to serve families.

PREPARING STAFF FOR HOME VISITING

Initial Training Program

Whether staff are seasoned or new to the field, preparation prior to the provision of services is valuable in a number of ways. The orientation process exposes all staff to the same concepts, values, principles, and procedures. Even experienced staff may have functioned differently in another work environment or program. In a team approach, it is essential that staff operate from the same set of principles and procedures to ensure quality care. Families without a team of practitioners who adhere to the same principles are often left confused and even more frustrated than before help was offered. Additionally, fidelity to a model may be one of the most important ways to ensure that the advantages of researched and proven strategies benefit all families. This means that careful explanation of what is expected and what fidelity entails should be provided in the orientation as well as throughout employment.

While it is necessary to orient all new staff to general principles and procedures, it is wise to consider that most new staff will not be able to absorb or put the information into perspective through orientation activities alone. What does occur is the opportunity to expose staff to concepts and lay a foundation that supports ongoing growth and development. The vital follow-up to orientation is ongoing supervision and processing of situations and experiences as they occur. Orientation activities may include didactic presentation of information, case examples (see Appendix A in this volume for a sample case study), and supervision planning, which highlights red flags for seeking support and a plan for ongoing development.

Concepts that are commonly misunderstood by all levels of staff can be reviewed in a discussion format. Even if the "myths" or common misunderstandings related to home-based services are reviewed, they may not be fully understood until the issue surfaces and is processed in upcoming service provision. The following section discusses issues related to service provision that can build awareness and heighten sensitivity.

Common Myths and Misconceptions Regarding Home-Based Services

Families Benefit More From Practitioners Than Natural Supports. When mental health practitioners forget to value a social support network, no matter how different or informal it may be, they miss opportunities for support and growth. Practitioners should never "trump" natural supports or inadvertently push them out of the families' lives. Families should be invited and encouraged to identify and continue using the natural supports that they have in place. Natural supports may include friends, family members, or community members that the family sees as supportive. In some cases, they are also paid practitioners who have the main qualifications of personal life experiences and an understanding of the communities they live and work in. The types of support that natural supports can offer may include skill building, emotional support, crisis intervention, community networking, obtaining resources, and concrete help (Apple et al., 1997). The supports, if given permission and invited by the family, should serve on the Child and Family Team (CFT; see Chapters 1, 3, and 7 in this volume). Social support research suggests that people go first to friends, relatives, and neighbors for information and help. Natural supports may help to overcome obstacles, such as limited access to mental health services, and stigma, especially with families of racial and ethnic minorities (Moss-Torres, & Lazear, 2004). There is a role for both practitioners and natural supports in assisting families. The value of natural supports should always be recognized, promoted, and developed to remain in place long after formal services end.

Home-Based Services Are Not as Important as Therapy for Youth With Serious Mental Health Conditions. It should never be assumed that youth with significant mental health conditions cannot benefit from services other than formal therapy. Several studies have shown that case management for youth with emotional challenges helps improve youth's positive adjustment, family functioning, and the stability of community living environments (Hoagwood, Burns, Kiser, Ringeisen, & Schoenwald, 2001).

A study was conducted by Mosier et al. (2001) to evaluate the effectiveness of in-home programs working with youth with behavioral and emotional problems. The program, in contrast to traditional office-based therapy offered a range of services within the home including in-home observation and assessment, crisis intervention, case management, school contacts, delivery of reinforcement for met goals, client and family education, and development of social supports for the family. The study demonstrated that the program was effective in reliably and significantly reducing behavioral and emotional problems in youth who would typically be served in inpatient settings.

Often, youth have been through years of formal outpatient therapy services or inpatient and residential programs. Some youth may not be capable or willing to discuss their feelings and issues with an interventionist through the use of language. This does not mean that they cannot progress or are missing an important component of treatment. At times, true growth, capacity building, or development occurs through an experience rather than a conversation. The resolution of some issues often begins with creating an environment supportive of growth and change. Youth exposed to trauma benefit more from stability and predictability in their environment than being forced or pressed to process verbally what occurred. Additionally, some mental health conditions (e.g., psychotic disorders) are best supported by building coping skill capacity and developing natural and community supports. Recovery is definitely possible for everyone, regardless of the disorder, and home- and community-based services may best support this process.

Families, Once Engaged, Have a Steady Climb Toward Change and Improvement. Practitioners need to remember that the experience of engaging in services is hard work. Even the most engaged family may temporarily "disengage" or regress in a manner that may be misconstrued as lack of motivation or focus. Treatment is, more often than not, an up and down curve rather than an upward climb. The periods in which a "lull" or regression takes place should be valued as a critical time; these periods should not be used to label the family or see it as failure, but, rather, it is a time to remain even more dedicated and committed to the family.

Youth Embrace and Appreciate Change in Their Caregivers. When youth have experienced dysfunctional behaviors in their caregivers, they may have adapted to their reality in a way that can be difficult to understand. By as early as 6 to 8 months of age, children have developed attachment patterns that reflect the type of caregiving they have experienced. One type of dysfunctional attachment is known as a role-reversed attachment disorder. When this occurs, the child begins to parent his/her caregivers and feels a sense of control as well as the need to preserve this role.

The controlling patterns are seen in two forms, controlling/nurturing and controlling/punitive. The controlling/nurturing pattern occurs when the child is overly solicitous, and the controlling/punitive pattern occurs when the child is overly bossy and punitive. Both patterns should be understood as a protective stance for the child that serves to minimize the effects of the caregivers' negative behaviors. Although, this is a dysfunctional adaptation and requires the child to bear most of the psychological burden related to the relationship, it would not have developed or remained in place if it did not serve a purpose for the child (Zeanah, Mammen, & Leiberman, 1993).

If the difficulties and patterns of behavior have been long standing, the youth may not see alternatives or even reasons why change should occur. The caregivers' behaviors that need support may be intergenerational patterns of behavior that have been accepted and normalized. At times, the challenges that caregivers have may be advantageous to youth (e.g., poor supervision or inconsistent discipline). Although it may seem that the changes that come about from home-based services are positive ones, they are also unfamiliar and confusing changes for youth. Often, youth are more comfortable with what they know and can predict than what they cannot. For these and other reasons that may be unique to the individual, change is scary and often rejected.

Safety Issues

Safety should always be of utmost importance in the provision of home- and community-based services (see Table 4.3). Newly hired staff should be told clearly that policies relating to safety should be strictly followed, and the use of their

Table 4.3
Safety Issues

- Car safety issues: Seatbelts, locking vehicle, passengers, insurance and registration, managing distractions, car seat requirements, familiarity with route, cell phone availability.
- Warning signs related to drug or illegal activity within the home.
- Advising administrators prior to visit and upon return.
- Leaving copy of schedule with secretary/supervisor.
- Procedures for getting support from supervisor while in the field.
- Procedures for reporting incidents.
- Guidelines on ways to communicate needed conditions for safety with families.

supervisor for support in this manner is recommended if there are any questions or concerns. Standard safety rules typically include notifying the administrator upon leaving and returning from a visit, traveling with a cell phone, and being familiar with the route to and from the home (Klass, 2008).

Prior to going to a home that has not been visited before or is new to the practitioner, there should be phone contact to advise the family of the purpose of the visit and outline important conditions that can optimize safety. Families should be asked if they are comfortable with the practitioner coming to the home and if all family members, as well as anyone staying with the family or likely to be present, are comfortable with a practitioner coming to the home. For instance, if a mother indicates that her husband is not comfortable with the practitioner, this should be a red flag to suggest that the mother come to the office for the first session and the issues be assessed further. Practitioners should emphasize the voluntary nature of this service and the recommendation that only family members or family supports that want to be involved be present during the first visit. Many programs have two staff go to the first visit to ensure a safer experience. The administrator or appointed staff member should be aware of when the practitioners leave and when they return. A phone call should be made from the office staff to the practitioners if they are not back within the allotted time frame.

Practitioners should be alerted to warning signs that the home environment may be unsafe related to possible drug or other illegal activity. Practitioners should also be empowered to leave a home immediately if they feel uncomfortable, and they should be advised that there will not be negative consequences for acting on their "gut" instincts.

Car safety issues, such as use of seatbelts, driving with enough gas, ensuring the car is in proper condition, having insurance and registration information, and eliminating distractions when driving, should be established and reviewed with practitioners.

Procedures should also be described for entering a home without a caregiver present. Typically practitioners are encouraged not to enter a home without a caregiver present. If practitioners are asked to transport youth or family members, the appropriate releases and sharing of procedures with caregivers should be reviewed. Practitioners should be advised of what should occur when a child is transported back to the home. If a caregiver cannot be present, practitioners should arrange, ahead of time, for an adult to leave the child with if necessary.

Practitioners should also feel empowered to request that animals be kept tied up or away from them during the visit if they feel uncomfortable. Also, if any family members have contagious illnesses, the practitioner should not feel obligated to visit the home.

Overview of Documentation Expectations

All staff should be given a complete orientation related to the expectations for documentation. It is best not to make assumptions related to a common understanding of documentation standards. Many employers have different expectations that may or may not be acceptable at another organization. Issues related to documentation should include a listing of required documents and time frames at the various stages of service delivery. It is helpful to provide sample packets that include mock documentation. Elements that should be included can be bulleted or included in orientation training. The expectation for language that is expected to be used in documentation should also be clarified. Using appropriate language that is also written in consumer friendly and familiar language is often challenging and needs supervisory support.

Time Management and Organizational Skills

It is wise for programs to invest time acknowledging and coaching newly hired staff in the skills of time management and organization (see Table 4.4). These can be overwhelming issues that can sabotage a practitioner's ability to meet the requirements of the position and adequately meet the needs of families. Strategies for planning a balance of time in the office completing paperwork, making calls, and attending meetings, as well as time in the field, should be shared. Practitioners can benefit from clear expectations of what is required for direct and indirect services, and how to make decisions related to priorities. Practitioners should be able to check in with a supervisor daily to review their scheduling and learn needed skills in this area.

Practice Standards and Parameters

Every program should have a program description and a list of expected activities related to the various stages of service delivery. While there are typically listed activities that are considered best practice, there should be some provision for recognizing family choice in service provision and the types of interventions that may or may not be requested. Practitioners should be familiar with what is considered best practice and model components, and the importance of discussing variations with their supervisor. Exhibit 4.4 offers sample practice parameters.

Peer and Supervisory Support

Practitioners should be oriented to the strong need for home- and community-based practitioners to not feel alone in the service delivery process and the strong need to review home-visiting activities with their supervisor on a regular basis. Reminding new staff of the need for administrative, clinical, and reflective supervision to be successful is recommended. Supervisors should also model this and remain true to their promises of being available for support. Peer supervision or the use of a peer mentor is also a helpful strategy when developing new staff. The peer mentor and supervisor should be clear about

Table 4.4
Types of Tools for Managing Time and Tasks

- Calendar of required meetings.
- Resource directory.
- Listing of needed phone numbers.
- Policy and procedure manuals.
- List of needed client information: family member's names, addresses, phone contacts, emergency contacts, etc.
- Sample formats for letters.
- Documentation checklists with time frames.
- Form for recording contacts.

their various roles and communicate with the new staff together related to how they will all work. Peer mentors are often used to assist the new staff in following procedures and completing documentation. They also can be helpful with organization and time management, offering useful strategies that are known to assist practitioners in managing tasks.

CONCLUSION

Staff who are best suited for working in a home- and community-based program are often difficult to find. The important characteristics, such as a congruous value base and relationship skills, must be looked for in the hiring process. When a new staff member is hired, it is important to appropriately train and support him/her in being the best staff person possible to meet the needs of the families served. This is an investment that should not be rushed or shortchanged. Supervisors must not forget the value of their support as well as the length of time that it may take to feel comfortable with the multiple tasks of home visiting.

References

Apple, K., Bernstein, S., Fogg, K., Fogg, L., Haapala, D., Johnson, E., et al. (1997). Walking our talk in the neighborhoods. Building professional/natural helper partnerships. *Social Policy, 27*(4), 54-63.

Burchard, J. D., Bruns, E. J., & Burchard, S. N. (2002). The wraparound approach. In B. Burns & K. Hoagwood (Eds.), *Community treatment for youth: Evidence-based interventions for severe emotional and behavioral disorder* (pp. 64-90). New York: Oxford University Press.

Dunst, C., Trivette, C. M., Davis, M., & Cornwell, J. C. (1994). Characteristics of effective help-giving practices. In C. J. Dunst, C. M. Trivette, & A. C. Deal (Eds.), *Supporting and strengthening families: Methods, strategies and practices.* Cambridge, MA: Brookline Books.

Gilkerson, L., & Ritzler, T. (2005). The role of reflective process in infusing relationship-based practice into an early intervention system. In K. Finello (Ed.), *The handbook of training and practice in infant, preschool mental health* (pp. 427-452). San Francisco: Josey-Bass.

Heffron, M. (2005). Reflective supervision in infant, toddler, and preschool work. In K. Finello (Ed.), *The handbook of training and practice in infant, preschool mental health* (pp. 114-136). San Francisco: Josey-Bass.

Hoagwood, K., Burns, B., Kiser, L., Ringeisen, H., & Schoenwald, S. K. (2001). Evidence-based practices in child and adolescent mental health services. *Psychiatric Services, 52,* 1179-1189.

Klass, C. S. (2008). *The home visitor's guidebook: Promoting optimal parent and child development* (3rd ed.). Baltimore: Paul H. Brookes Publishing.

Mosier, J., Burlingame, G. M., Wells, M. G., Ferre, R., Latkowski, M., Johansen, J., et al. (2001). In-home, family-centered psychiatric treatment for high-risk children and youth. *Children's Services: Social Policy, Research, and Practice, 4,* 51-68.

Moss-Torres, C., & Lazear, K. J. (2004). *Successmakers: The story of a natural helper team— An EQUIPO approach to supporting and strengthening families in our communities.* Tampa, FL: University of South Florida, Louis de la Parte Florida Mental Health Institute.

Nelson, J. R., Roberts, M., & Smith, D. J. (1998). *Conducting functional behavioral assessments.* Longmont, CO: Sopris West Educational Services.

Peterson, B., West, J., Tanielian T., & Pincus, H. (1998). Mental health practitioners and trainees. In R. W. Manderscheid & M. J. Henderson (Eds.), *Mental health: United States 1998* (pp. 214-246). Rockville, MD: Center for Mental Health Services.

President's New Freedom Commission on Mental Health. (2003). *Achieving the promise: Tranforming mental health care in America. Final report* (DHHS Publication No. SMA-03-3832). Rockville, MD: Author.

Rapp, C. A. & Goscha, R. J. (2006). *The strengths model: Case management with people with psychiatric disabilities* (2nd ed.). New York: Oxford University Press.

Shapiro, D., & Koocher, G. (1996). Goals and practical considerations in outpatient medical crisis. *Professional Psychology: Research and Practice, 122,* 109-120.

Spector, B. (2007). *Implementing organizational change: Theory & practice.* Upper Saddle River, NJ: Prentice Hall.

U.S. Bureau of the Census. (2000). *Census data reports and profiles.* Retrieved June 3, 2010, from http://www.census.gov/main/www/cen2000.html

Walker, J. S. (2008). Workforce: Staffing the transformation of children's mental healthcare systems. *Focal Point: A National Bulletin on Family Support and Children's Mental Health, 22*(1), 3-4.

Wasik, B. H., & Bryant, D. M. (2001). *Home visiting: Procedures for helping families* (2nd ed.). Newbury Park, CA: Sage.

Wieder, B. & Boyle, P. (2007). Staff selection as a core component of evidence based practices implementation: Findings from Ohio's study of integrated dual disorders treatment (IDDT) program development. In C. Newman, C. Liberton, K. Kutash, & R. M. Friedman (Eds.), *The 19th annual research conference proceedings: A system of care for children's mental health: Expanding the research base* (pp. 71-74). Tampa: University of South Florida, Louis de la Parte Florida Mental Health Institute, Research and Training Center for Children's Mental Health.

Zeanah, C. H., Mammen, O. K., & Lieberman, A. F. (1993). Disorders of attachment. In C. H. Zeanah (Ed.), *Handbook of infant mental health* (pp. 332-349). New York: Guilford.

Exhibit 4.1
Job Description: Family-Centered Intensive Home-Based Worker

Position: Family-Centered Intensive Home-Based Worker

Desired Qualifications:

- Experience working with youth with emotional and behavioral challenges and their families.
- Demonstrated understanding and acceptance of wraparound principles and family-centered services.
- Experience practicing in a family-driven, youth-guided, culturally and linguistically competent, and community-based manner.
- Experience in provision of home- and community-based services from a strength-based perspective.
- Openness and flexibility in tailoring the service/support delivery system to meet the therapeutic needs of the youth and family by being willing to listen and learn from the youth and family through an individualized assessment and service planning process.
- Excellent oral and written communication skills.

Roles and Responsibilities:

- Provide strengths and needs assessment for youth and families.
- Provide immediate stabilization, crisis planning, and intervention services.
- Provide case management and skill development for youth and families.
- Develop, with youth and families, a strength-based and individualized service plan based on the strengths and needs assessment.
- Ensure that services are individualized, family driven, youth guided, culturally competent, and community based.
- Ensure that youth and families are supported in transitioning from formal services to an empowered family system with natural and community supports.
- Provide needed documentation and communication with partners.
- Provide services from a team-based approach supporting other staff members as needed.
- Provide evening and weekend coverage as needed.
- Participate in individual and group supervision to enhance service delivery.
- Participate in ongoing trainings and staff development.

Exhibit 4.2
Job Description: Supervisor for Family-Centered Intensive
Home-Based Worker

Position: Supervisor for Family-Centered Intensive Home-Based Worker

Desired Qualifications:

- Extensive experience working with youth with emotional and behavioral challenges and their families and/or three to five years supervising home- and community-based workers.
- Demonstrated competence in directing and supporting services in adherence to wraparound principles and family-centered services.
- Ability to support workers from a strength-based perspective utilizing a reflective practice model.

Roles and Responsibilities:

- Recruit, orient, and train staff.
- Assist in the development and evaluation of home-based program policies, procedures, and curriculum.
- Provide administrative oversight and clinical supervision to staff.
- Support staff in documentation and service planning needs.
- Provide home-based services in coordination with team members.
- Ensure adequate staffing patterns and emergency coverage as needed.
- Evaluate staff on a regular basis to ensure quality services.
- Oversee referral process and assist staff in making level-of-care decisions.
- Collaborate with partner agencies to improve network of professionals available to families.
- Create a culture of respect, trust, safety, and professionalism.

Exhibit 4.3
Interview Questions for Potential Staff

Questions Regarding Core System of Care Principles

Family Driven

How would you describe the importance of services being family driven?
Can you give examples of how this can be reflected in service delivery?

Youth Guided

How would you describe to caregivers the importance of services being youth guided?
What are some ways to negotiate youth-guided services when youth and caregivers do not have the same perspective?

Culturally Competent

How would you define cultural competence?
Give some examples of what happens when services are not culturally competent?

Community Based

What benefits to youth and families do you see to keeping youth in their home communities?
Why is community such an important aspect of a youth's life?

Questions Regarding Help-Giving Attitudes and Beliefs

Positive attributions toward help-seeker and helping relationships.

What are your thoughts about what occurs for families prior to them asking for help? What types of experiences might families have experienced prior to getting help?

Emphasis on help-seeker responsibility for meeting needs and solving problems.

How would you describe the process of change for families in need?
How would you describe the role of the practitioner vs. the role of the family/youth?

High expectations regarding the capacity of help-seekers to become competent.

What does it take for youth and families to develop new capacities?

Emphasis on building on help-seeker strengths.

When deciding on a place to start working with a family, what would be your strategy?
What considerations do you make when designing interventions?

Proactive stance toward helping relationships.

How should a family supporting a youth with special challenges be supported in coping with crisis or potential crisis?
How might you assist a family that has difficulty identifying areas in which to intervene?

Promotion emphasis as the focus of help-giving.

How can a practitioner best support a family and youth with special needs?

(Continued)

Exhibit 4.3 *(Continued)*

Questions Regarding Help-Giving Behaviors

Reflective listening.

How would you describe ways in which you can offer families and youth the experience of being heard?

Assist help-seekers in identifying, clarifying, and prioritizing aspirations as well as needs.

When first meeting families and youth, what are you focused on developing an understanding about?

Offer help before it is requested.

When you as a practitioner within the home recognize needs, what would be your next steps?

Offer help that is normative in terms of family culture.

Can you describe ways in which you seek to show the family you recognize its culture and can work with them?

Offer help that is congruent with family's appraisal of problems and needs.

Describe ways in which you listen to and then respond to the family's descriptions of problems and views on intervention?

Promote the development of family skills to decrease need for help.

What are your views regarding the goal of service provision?

Promote sense of cooperation and joint responsibility with family to meet needs.

How would you describe how the family and practitioner interact throughout the service delivery process?
How would you describe the goal for the family/practitioner relationship?

Promote decision making occurring at the family level.

What is important to consider in how decisions are made regarding service delivery?

Exhibit 4.4
Sample Practice Standards

Orientation Activities

Phone contact or letter within forty-eight hours of receipt of referral
Phone contact reviewing home visit procedures
Mailing of orientation materials
Assessment and discussion of family preferences for assessment process (who present at first visit, location of visit, etc.)

Assessment Activities

Assess caregiver-child interaction
Assess family interaction
Assess child individually
Provide crisis intervention as needed
Observe child in school setting
Observe child in day care setting
Interview teachers, other providers, natural supports
Orient family and youth to program
CFT development
Organize CFT and first meeting
Orient CFT members to mission/function
Crisis plan development
List strengths and needs and seek family input
Hold CFT meeting and develop plan

Intervention Components

Provide MD and other providers with copy of plan
Summarize CFT meeting in minutes and provide members with copy
Send monthly updates to family, MD, department of child welfare, probation, other providers, and CFT members
Provide family members and youth with information regarding diagnosis and pertinent interventions
Provide family members with linkage to resources
Assist family members in developing a resource binder with plans, individualized education plans (IEPs), resources, and information
Orient family to psychiatric services and prepare for visit
Accompany family to visit
Meet with teachers to assess school issues and functioning
Monitor functioning with teachers, day care, and other providers
Review crisis plans monthly or after each crisis
Contact families after MD appointments to ensure understanding of MD recommendations
Make contact with all family experiencing crisis the following day to ensure stability
Help family maintain entitlements
Group leaders contact family weekly and write weekly reports of group curriculum and child progress

(Continued)

Exhibit 4.4 *(Continued)*

Assist family with ongoing recovery planning
Provide family with information regarding planning for transitions such as summer vacation, school breaks, or moves
Provide ongoing coordination with CFT members
Develope linkages to the community and build natural supports
Provide ongoing development of strengths and resiliency
Provide ongoing reassessment every ninety days or with significant changes
Provide family with plan for respite needs
Assess caregiver functioning if needs are present in greater detail
Assist caregivers in understanding temperament of child and how it relates to mental health needs
Meet with siblings to assist them in supporting client needs
Prepare family for IEP meetings and attend as invited
Attend meetings of other providers as pertinent

Chapter 5

Supervising and Supporting Staff

When someone does something good, applaud! It makes two people happy.
—Samuel Goldwyn

The greatest good you can do for another is not just to share your riches, but to reveal to him his own.
—Benjamin Disraeli

INTRODUCTION

This chapter discusses supervising home- and community-based practitioners in a manner that will parallel the philosophical underpinnings of the service delivery process itself. The same skills, values, and assumptions that are made when supporting families should be a part of the supervisory process. Supervisors must be aware of their vital importance to the success of programs. The supervisory process is a complex task that has many facets. The areas of importance related to administrative, reflective, and clinical supervision are described with differentiations made between the individual and group process.

SHARING A PHILOSOPHY OF SUPERVISION

Protective Environment

The term "supervision" has a negative connotation for many. Employees fear that making a mistake will cause them to be judged harshly or, worse yet, lose their jobs. It evokes a feeling for many that they are unsafe and vulnerable. When a person has authority or power over another person, it is challenging to build a relationship that can support growth in a way that does not feel threatening. Most do not fully trust the process of exposing weaknesses to a supervisor. This capacity does not usually come naturally or without effort on the parts of both supervisors and supervisees. Changing this mentality may be considered a daunting task, although it is one that can be accomplished.

Before becoming a supervisor, a person should consider past experiences being supervised as well as his/her own basic philosophy regarding supervision. Both of these areas have relevance for how a person, on a conscious and subconscious level, will be able to carry out the supervisory duties. Past experiences, both good and bad, should be considered as strong influences of how the supervisor will interpret a supervisee's actions, relate to a supervisee, and focus his/her strategies and attention. The supervisor's job is complex as well as integral to the service delivery process. A supervisor must be clear on his/her own vision, markers for success, and values that are important to communicate to supervisees. A lack of clarity will only make the supervisor's guidance feel fragmented and inconsistent to the supervisees.

Supervision should always be communicated as a process that is meant to support learning, growth, and reflection on the process of being in the helping role. Some young practitioners may believe that this process is expected to last only until they have reached the ability to be independently licensed or "experienced" enough to no longer need supervision. The value in life-long learning and the need to process clinical experiences throughout the supervisee's career should always be emphasized. This, in many cases, helps to relieve pressure and the expectation that the person being supervised needs to "know it all." Additionally, it supports the safety of the supervisory environment by normalizing the fact that all practitioners need guidance and do experience emotions and thoughts in the process of helping that merely reflects their status as humans. Just as it is much more powerful to support youth and families from a strength-based orientation, the same is true for practitioners. Taking opportunities to identify strengths is mutually beneficial for staff and managers, as it allows staff to feel success and utilize their skills. As needed skills are identified and developed, it is most helpful to utilize those strengths to mitigate needs.

Although framing supervision in a positive light is important, the supervisor's attitudes, actions, and reactions to a supervisee are what pave the way to a safe and beneficial supervisory relationship. Staff should be given an understanding of how issues are identified and worked on through the supervisory relationship. There should be no surprises regarding expectations, job duties, policies, and procedures. Respect should be at the forefront of all interactions, and supervisors should make time to process their reactions or feelings prior to discussing the issues with staff. This supports the commitment to handling issues in a professional manner in which learning and growth can occur.

Reflective Practice

Reflective practice is based on the premise that the ability to be an effective practitioner is largely dependent on the ability of the practitioner to process the experiences of being in the helping role. When practitioners visit families and become intimately involved with the routines and family environment, there are often feelings and reactions that can be difficult to understand and process. Practitioners may reexperience their own past traumas if, in the process of helping families, they witness difficulties similar to their own. This does not mean that past experiences will interfere with the ability to be objective. Past experiences merely make up who the practitioner is, and they becomes woven into the fabric of helping. They only become barriers when the opportunity to recall, recognize, and put the experiences into perspective does not occur. A reflective practice model recognizes the need to process these events, and the model places reflection at a level of high importance. Additionally, reflective process facilitates the ability to give pause in order to consider multiple perspectives to a problem or situation within a family. The supervisory relationship supports this process. When relationships are central to all that occurs within a home- and community-based program, there must be trust, support, and growth that exists between staff, caregivers, and youth. When agencies function in this manner, there are seven characteristics that may result. These characteristics are as follows:

- Mutuality of shared goals;

- Commitment to evolving growth;

- Commitment to reflecting on the practitioner's own work;

- Respect for individuals;

- Sensitivity to a context that recognizes the influence of environment on an individual;

- Open communication; and

- Expectations for all staff to operate from a relationship-based mentality (Bertacchi, 1996).

As part of the supervisory process, the supervisor fosters this environment and the development of these characteristics by a commitment to a reflective process. The reflective practice model, although profound in its benefits, is somewhat simplistic in the way in which it occurs. Staff are encouraged to discuss what is occurring with the families while exploring their own worries, fears, and frustrations as well as feelings of success. During the supervisory process, staff are allowed to set the agenda, move at a pace they are comfortable with, and do the majority of the talking. Supervisors do not dominate the sessions or use them as an opportunity to promote their own agendas. The benefits to staff, and therefore ultimately to families, when reflective practice is used are many. These include the following:

- An opportunity to consider the link between program mission and current research, reinforcing the importance of adherence to program values and principles;

- An opportunity to explore how the practitioner's personal history, culture, and experiences affect relationships with families as well as other professionals;

- A way to think about patterns and systems—not just one event;

- An opportunity for practitioners to experience observation, listening, and inquiry as an approach to understanding relationships;

- The development of a common language and shared vision for the work; and

- An opportunity to better understand and influence agency practices (Copa, Lucinski, Olsen, & Wollenburg, 1999).

Reflective supervision can only take place when a supervisor and supervisee have developed a relationship that will allow for the needed support, guidance, and direction to take place. A safe relationship recognizes each person's strengths and weaknesses but is not threatened by the notion that one person has power over another. Because this is so important, as much as possible, a supervisor must attempt to suspend the hierarchy of supervisor-supervisee and replace it with a coach or guide mentality. The experience of reflective supervision includes the promotion of three key elements. The first element, reflection, means considering what an experience really means. A supervisor guides the process of questioning what occurred and determining next steps. This occurs in a nondirective and supportive manner. A supervisor also reflects this element by empowering staff to assess their own work performance, limits, and strengths.

The second element, collaboration, reflects sharing the responsibility and control of power. Power, although it has many implications, refers, in this context, to knowledge. Both supervisor and supervisee work together as a team to ensure quality care occurs. In the supervisory relationship, collaboration is reflected by clear expectations for both parties and a mutual understanding of the logistics related to the supervision.

The third element, regularity, reflects the need for a strong commitment by both parties for supervision to occur on a regular basis. The time should be held sacred with no interruptions (Parlakian, 2001). When the basic elements of reflective practice occur in combination with the needed supervisory skills of self-awareness, observation, and flexible responses, supervisors demonstrate a

Figure 5.1
Elements of Reflective Supervision

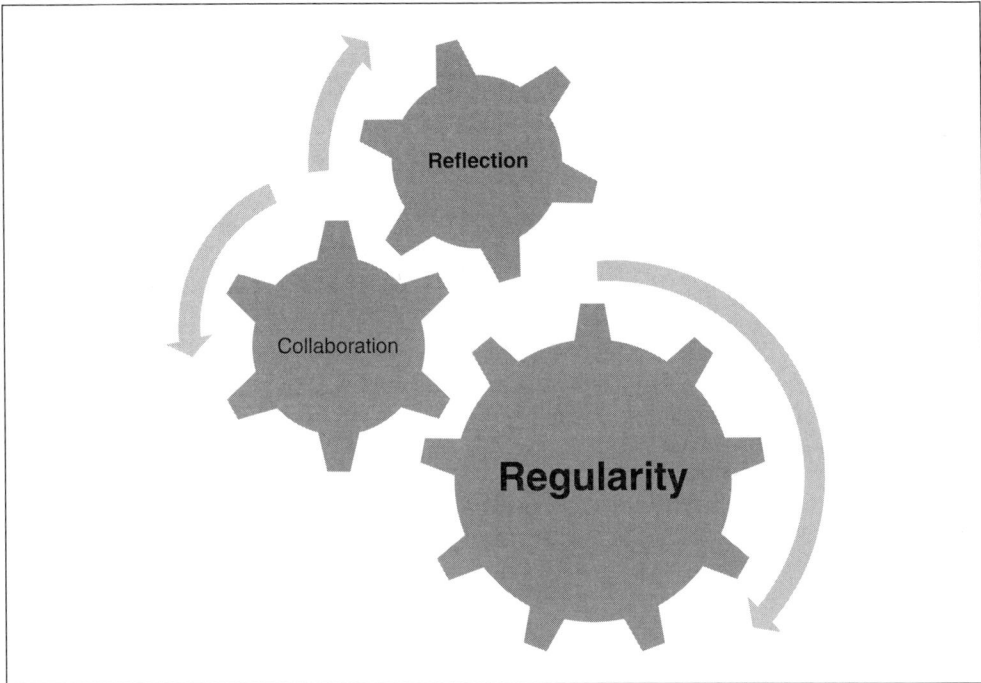

commitment to reflective practice and reflective leadership (Parlakian & Seibel, 2001; see Figure 5.1).

Parallel Process

The parallel process (see Figure 5.2) occurs when a supervisor acknowledges and contains the feelings of a supervisee in the same manner that the supervisee does for the caregivers. This ultimately allows the caregivers to, in turn, support their youth in the same accepting and nurturing manner that both they and the supervisee have experienced (Sharlin & Shamai, 2000). The feelings of the supervisees can be related to their own responses as well as the result of experiencing the feelings of the family. Often, families are feeling a sense of despair. This feeling can easily be transferred to the practitioner who, in turn, feels somewhat immobilized by an overwhelming sense of despair. Growth occurs within the context of a relationship. While practitioners seek to empower caregivers to relate to their youth in a positive and supportive manner, they too have the same need. The same positive results that can occur through a safe and secure relationship between a practitioner and family occur within a supervisor-supervisee relationship. When a supervisor encourages a supervisee to express feelings and concerns, a feeling of being understood and supported results. This empowers the supervisee to support this same experience with the family. The caregivers can, in turn, give the youth the same experience.

Figure 5.2
Parallel Process

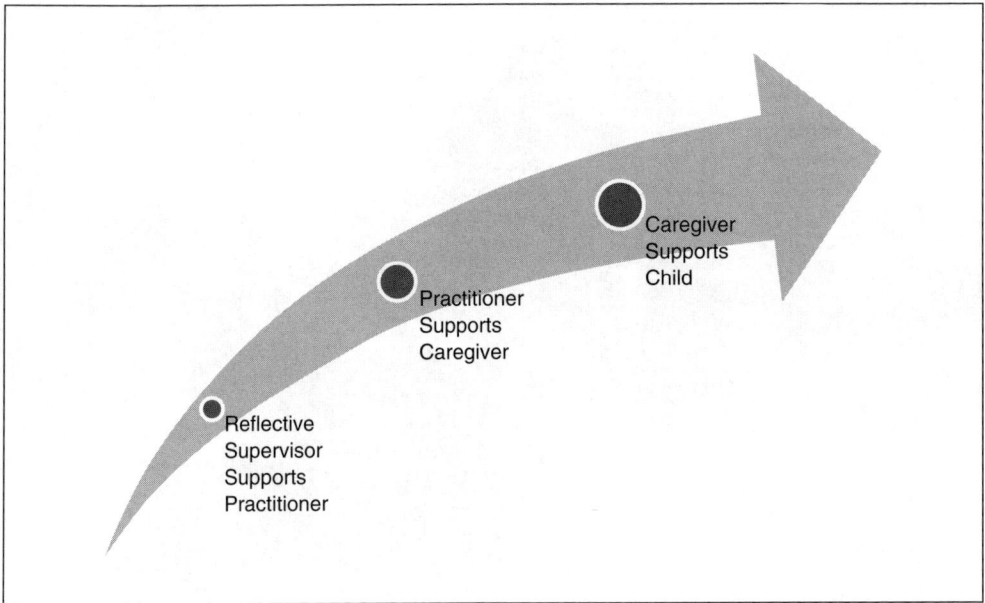

Caregiver
Supports
Child

Practitioner
Supports
Caregiver

Reflective
Supervisor
Supports
Practitioner

STRATEGIES FOR INDIVIDUAL SUPERVISION

Administrative Supervision

An important component of supervision includes administrative oversight. The administrative supervisor must attend to a plethora of issues within a home- and community-based program. Issues include hiring, staffing, retention, and oversight of areas such as time management, organization, and compliance with policies and procedures. Staff should always be recognized as resources to be valued. Administrative supervision is best received when it is implemented in a supportive and strength-based manner. This does not mean ignoring needs or concerns. Meeting expectations related to timeliness, documentation, and organization of duties is a skill that may be challenging to develop. Supervisors must develop strategies to help assess their strengths and needs related to these areas. Once acknowledgement and mutual agreement related to the assessment of needs and strengths occurs, a strength-based plan for developing these areas can occur. As with families, the use of strengths in this process makes change more possible. Addressing issues from this perspective typically feels more empowering and will show results more quickly than a deficit-based or punitive approach. When staff are able to feel success in these areas, it serves two important functions. First, it supports job satisfaction and staff retention. Second, a contented, well-functioning employee can only be more therapeutic and positive with families.

Clinical Supervision

Clinical supervision refers to the clinical guidance and support that allows a practitioner to provide professional, appropriate, and quality services to youth and families. From an ecosystemic structural model of supervision, the supervision as well as the therapy evolves from a network of relationships that include the youth, families, treatment team, supervisor, agency, and trainers. Just as practitioners guide families in developing and utilizing the network of relationships and supports available to them, the supervisors do the same for the practitioners. The supervisory relationship serves as a point of reference for developing the practitioner's capacity to be as effective as possible with the family (Lindblad-Goldberg, Dore, & Stern, 1998). A supervisor working from this orientation promotes the same principles and values in the supervisory relationship that represent what is to occur within the therapeutic experience (Haber, 1996). Clinical supervision in many programs happens both individually as well as in a group format. Clinical supervision encompasses many areas including the development of the practitioner, assurance that documentation and services are appropriate, and guidance in the process of service delivery. When a new staff person begins employment, it is helpful to engage in a needs and strengths assessment of the staff person's professional abilities. Specific dedication to the identification of strengths is helpful and reflects the same orientation that practitioners are working from. Areas to explore might include work behaviors, knowledge, skills, and strengths. The basic principles related to empowerment (see Chapter 1 in this volume) and the wraparound process (see Chapter 3 in this volume) should be prioritized for consideration. Additionally, capacities related to the provision of services throughout the various phases and the activities related to the phases should be incorporated. Exhibits 5.1 and 5.2 suggest areas for consideration and sample questions that can be used to explore strengths.

Once a comprehensive and collaborative assessment has occurred, an individual development plan can be built around the priorities of the staff person. This places value and focus on the areas that are a priority to the staff person, increasing the likelihood that investment will occur. The plan can then guide the various components of clinical supervision and the focus it will take. See Exhibit 5.3 for a sample format.

Developing and Maintaining a Relationship

The development and ability to maintain a relationship takes investment and time. Despite the fact that a supervisor is in a position of power, this does not mean the relationship cannot be safe, predictable, and supportive. A staff person will internalize the meaning of relationship with a particular supervisor based on the experience of three core conditions. These conditions include the ability to demonstrate respect, consistency, and a value for the supervisory process. Each one of these areas has important activities and tasks associated with it. Table 5.1 outlines method for developing and maintaining the relationship.

STRATEGIES FOR GROUP SUPERVISION

Developing a Shared Goal

Group supervision is the practice of providing clinical supervision in a group setting. In general, the most commonly identified goals of both supervisors and

Table 5.1
Methods for Promoting a Positive and Supportive Supervisory Relationship

- Dispel the myth that experience supersedes the need for reflective supervision.
- Promote the notion that discussing needs, frustrations, or feeling overwhelmed is a needed and positive characteristic that does not reflect negatively on the practitioner.
- Preserve supervision time without intrusions, phone calls, or cancellations.
- Model openness and flexibility in thoughts and ideas.
- Do not overreact to mistakes or concerns.
- Identify strengths in practitioners' actions and promote the development of such.
- Acknowledge the benefits of and support efforts to explore areas of weakness.
- Allow the practitioner to set the pace and agenda.
- Weave successes and newly obtained skills into future sessions in a way that consolidates learning.
- Attend to and invest in the developing relationship.

supervisees include the development of knowledge related to services; the imparting of skills; and mutual support, which is sometimes referred to as a "restorative function" (Carter, Goodyear, Enyedy, & Arcinue, 2009). While a supervisor typically organizes and develops the group, the goals of the group should be mutually determined. A supervisor may choose to discuss options for what the group can accomplish, although, it is more beneficial when the group as a whole decides the focus. All members of the supervisory group should be encouraged to give input. The group may decide to present cases with a specific focus or learning point being explored throughout the presentation of cases. Topics may be specific clinical strategies such as engagement or utilizing strengths or values and principles of empowerment theory (see Chapter 1 in this volume) or the wraparound process (see Chapter 3 in this volume). Most groups use case presentations as a format for supervision and may have some time for didactic presentation strictly related to a concept or subject area. Case presentations have been identified in some cases as being the most beneficial strategy for learning (Ravets, 1993; see Appendix A for a sample case presentation). The group will need to determine which formats they will utilize. If the group decides to take turns presenting cases, some discussion should take place around the subjects of taking turns, what types of cases should be chosen, and how long the presentations should be. Some additional areas to consider when case presentations are utilized include the following:

- Allowing for a balance of time between case presentation and group discussion;

- Encouraging staff to present cases related to their areas of expertise;

- Encouraging both challenging and less complicated cases; and

- Determining a plan for topic selection.

Ensuring Safety in the Group Process

Once the group is comfortable with a common goal or set of goals as well as a focus if so chosen (see "Developing a Shared Goal"), the discussion can begin regarding the rules of the group. Determining rules will help members feel safe because possible concerns about how the group will operate can be addressed. It is important that this process be facilitated but not dominated by the supervisor. All members can be asked to consider what they fear or worry may happen in the group as well as what they look forward to. Rules typically encompass the areas of communication patterns or styles, time, frequency, confidentiality, or follow-up to difficult topics. Members may want to have assurances that the group will start and stop within a specific time frame, that feedback will be constructive, and that a certain level of confidentiality will be maintained. In research conducted by Doxsee and Kivlighan (1994), group members felt particularly challenged in situations where participants felt misunderstood, attacked, and disconnected from the group. It was also discussed that dealing with member absences or changes in structure were challenging.

The supervisor needs to set a positive tone for the meaning and function of the group. This can be accomplished by reiterating benefits, encouraging a strength-based orientation, and assuring staff that exposing weaknesses will not be seen negatively. The supervisor may want to give examples related to these areas and always model and reinforce these concepts. As part of ensuring safety, the supervisor should acknowledge the possibility of conflict and engage the group in discussion of how this should be addressed. Members should be encouraged to keep discussions related to the group within the group setting, as having individual conversations with members and supervisors outside of the group sets up negative dynamics and mistrust.

As the group begins meeting, it is important for the supervisor to vigilantly attend to dynamics and issues that may need to be addressed or facilitated. Supervisors should ensure that one member is not dominating the group, that established rules are being followed, and that members who are not engaged are encouraged or supported in doing so. Skills related to attending to group cohesion, assessing communication patterns and dynamics, and understanding the roles members take in the group are critical ones for supervisors to develop. More complex issues that need observation include the development of coalitions within the group, problem-solving patterns, and conflict management (Prieto, 1996). With careful attention to the possible dynamics, both good and detrimental to the group, the members will benefit from an environment that remains therapeutic and able to handle conflict and change.

Meeting the Needs of the Group

When considering the general needs of members in the group to gain knowledge, skills, and process challenges, there are a number of benefits to group supervision. Staff are able to gain exposure to a wider variety of cases and skills of others; there is a greater quantity of information that can be shared; they develop skills in the delivery and reception of feedback; and they have opportunities for vicarious learning. Staff also benefit from experiences in which strategies for intervention are addressed, and problem-solving skills are fostered (Bernard & Goodyear, 2004; Hoese, 1987). If an appropriate environment is fostered, the psychological benefits of having a safe place to share personal reactions and feeling validated can be significant.

As the group will assuredly have multiple levels of expertise and experience, it is challenging for the supervisor to keep the group engaged in learning on multiple levels. The needs of members may be varied, although, through the facilitation skills of the supervisor, a balance related to depth of conversations can be achieved. Group supervision rarely is the only form of supervision, and if individual learning needs are obvious, the supervisor can address them in individual supervision. What needs attention is the assurance for both the one in need and the group that the issue will be addressed.

A common goal and area of focus is typically determined prior to the group beginning the supervisory process. As the supervisor observes the growth and development of the group, it is necessary to remind staff to evaluate their progress. The group will move through developmental phases, which means recognizing accomplishment of goals and reformulating new ones. Specific issues that appear to be recurring themes or concerns may need to be identified as possible areas to explore once goals have been accomplished to keep the group progressing. Some agencies have chosen to identify performance indicators as measures of success in grasping new skills or concepts.

Determining Scope of Group Supervision

The supervisory process should always include a variety of approaches and functions. Group supervision is not intended to meet all supervisory needs. The supervisor of a home- and community-based team must recognize administrative, clinical, and reflective supervision needs that can and should occur in both group and individual sessions (see "Strategies for Individual Supervision"). Administrative issues, depending on their nature, may be discussed in staff meetings; individual issues related to work performance should not be addressed in a group setting. Reflective practice sessions are effective in both individual and group settings (see "Reflective Practice"). Clinical supervision can also occur within both settings. When issues arise for a staff member in group supervision that point to growth needs, the staff member can address these issues more comprehensively one on one. The scope of group supervision is limited and meant to augment and enhance the individual supervisory process with a unique set of benefits.

ADDRESSING CONCERNS

Preparing Staff for Process

The process of supervision should always include, prior to the inception of any problems, a discussion on how the disciplinary process occurs. This should be discussed verbally, and a copy of the agency's policy should be referenced and located for the staff to refer to as needed. Of primary importance is the need to relate to staff that the process of supervision is meant to be supportive, and identifying concerns and addressing them through this process is an illustration that progress is being made. There is great value in discussing weaknesses, frustrations, and areas of concern. The supervisor must differentiate between when a situation is representative of a learning situation and when an issue warrants discipline. Examples of situations that may require a warning for a staff person include gross ethical or boundary violations, policy violations, or repeated failures to engage in suggested activities to make improvements in a behavior. Staff should be prepared for the identification of an issue that needs to be corrected and that this will result in a work improvement plan. When a staff person develops this plan mutually with the supervisor, it is then the obligation of the supervisor to monitor that person to make sure that the tasks that need improvement are completed.

Setting Clear Expectations and Obtaining Feedback

At the beginning of employment, a review of the staff person's job description should take place. When job descriptions are somewhat vague, time should be spent discussing the details of what is expected. It is helpful to give examples of how more experienced staff arrange required meetings, duties, and home visits into their workday. A listing of required meetings, trainings, and other duties should be given. The supervisor should expect that staff may need suggestions on a time management system and organizational strategy that will ensure a smooth transition into the position. The supervisor must normalize the adjustment period and welcome suggestions, questions, and feedback. Supervisors should encourage staff to give feedback regarding how they best receive information, comments, or feedback, and ask for assurances that they understand what is being asked of them.

Developing a Work Improvement Plan

While a supervision plan is a working document that guides the areas and ways in which employee development should occur, a work improvement plan is designed to specifically focus on an area in which a particular employee must improve. Work improvement plans are reflective of the disciplinary process, which supports the strategies that are identified to ameliorate the problem area. A work improvement plan should be done in collaboration with the staff person in a manner that appreciates the strengths of the staff person as well as the person's needs. The objectives of the plan should be measurable and easily tracked, so that both the staff person and supervisor can continually monitor improvement. Objectives should also be reachable and realistic. The interventions should clearly identify the responsible person, frequency of the problem, and what is to occur. The plan should be reviewed on a regular basis, and time limits should be identified for completion of interventions to meet the objectives. At the time of review, the staff person should be encouraged to suggest alternative interventions, if progress is not occurring.

Maintaining a Relationship

The challenge of maintaining a relationship despite the need to address concerns is familiar to most supervisors who have experienced disciplinary actions. The strength of the relationship prior to the corrective action often is a factor in mediating the challenges of this situation, although it can still be difficult even when a strong relationship is in place. Acknowledging the difficulty in the situation and exploring the reactions of the staff person may be helpful. Despite the importance of acknowledging feelings, careful attention should be paid to continuing the process of administrative and clinical supervision. The presence of a disciplinary issue should not overshadow the process and preoccupy both the supervisor and supervisee to the point that progress cannot take place. If a supervisor begins to overcompensate by not addressing future concerns or giving needed feedback, it will ultimately hurt the genuineness and effectiveness of the supervisor-supervisee relationship. Conversely, if a supervisor is too harsh and does not appreciate small gains, it will injure the morale of the staff person—often to the point that progress is sabotaged as well. Ideally, a supervisor should continue to interact in the same manner that has been present from the beginning, with the ability to integrate into the supervisory experience the ability to provide a safe environment for staff despite challenges and setbacks.

PEER MENTORSHIP AND SUPPORT

Valuing Peer Support

Peer mentors can extend the impact of the supervisory relationship into a realm that develops the skills of a new staff member in a uniquely valued manner. Peer mentors do not supplant or replace a supervisory relationship but contribute a new and varied experience that may not happen with a supervisor. This may be the case for a variety of reasons, the most commonly identified barrier being time constraints. Perhaps another reason peer mentors offer a unique set of contributions to staff development is the knowledge that occurs from simply being in a parallel role day in and day out as that of the mentee. This provides immediate relevance to what the mentee is seeking guidance for and sometimes only occurs through frequent exposure to the tasks at hand. Supervisors may have lost sight of techniques related to time management and work behaviors that can significantly impact a mentee's ability to manage the tasks at hand. When a new staff person or one who is in need of additional support is matched with a mentor, there is an immediate opportunity for growth and positive outcomes for the entire team. Mentees who are approached in a supportive manner by another member of the team will typically feel more comfortable and accepted by the team. This translates into greater comfort asking questions, exposing areas that need growth, and relating more confidently and positively to families. The mentor usually facilitates relationship development with the team, which results in overall benefits to the program. When a staff person feels connected and able to work effectively with the team, the mutual benefit to everyone becomes apparent more quickly, as the mentee can begin to contribute to the team tasks. It behooves the team to invest in the mentee, as the stronger the individual, the stronger is the team as a whole.

Because lack of turnover is closely linked to family satisfaction, the process of peer mentorship has positive effects in this area as well. Staff who feel welcomed and supported are more apt to persist through the learning curves and challenges of new jobs. A peer mentor can normalize the learning curve and put into perspective feelings of failure and inadequacy. Fears regarding performance that a mentee may not feel comfortable addressing with a supervisor can be brought to light with a mentor. When this occurs, it often encourages staff to continue to use the available supports and feel comfortable with the learning process. If problems are present, a mentor can suggest a timely intervention with the supervisor, which can address the issues before they become unmanageable. All of these interventions reduce the likelihood of burnout and problems associated with it. Ultimately, new staff who develop competence and feel supported by tools to do their job will be less taxing on the team as a whole and begin contributing to the team mission much earlier.

Using Peer Mentors

Mentorship, in general, has been given many definitions and is associated with many disciplines. Collins (1994) defines mentorship as follows:

An interdisciplinary helping relationship between two individuals who are at different stages in their professional development. The mentor-the more professionally advanced of the two-facilitates the development and advancement of the protégé-the junior professional-by serving as a source of social support beyond what is required solely on basis of their formal relationship (p. 414).

In this definition, there may be a situation in which there is a power differential such that the mentor is not necessarily at the same level as the mentee in terms of position. This type of mentorship is common although different than peer mentorship because of the power differential. Peer mentorship is when employees at the same level are in an intentional relationship designed to provide support and teaching between the more experienced employee and the less experienced employee (Ensher, Thomas, & Murphy, 2001). Two broad categories have been used to describe the function of mentors. The first category is coaching, in which development related to service provision takes place. This may take the form of role plays, observing sessions, processing sessions, or case discussion. The second category is psychosocial role modeling, in which the mentor attempts to develop professional skills and behaviors in the mentee through observation and imitation. Examples of activities related to this category may include modeling practitioner and family interactions; fostering a sense of acceptance with the team and families; and discussing practitioner roles, interactions, and behaviors (Kram, 1983). Additional skills that may be fostered include time management, knowledge to do the job, accessing resources, work aids, listening to concerns, answering questions, and orienting to the culture of the organization and community (Kram, 1985; Young & Perrewe, 2004).

There are a number of skills that should be developed in mentors, which should be introduced through training and reinforced in supervision. Peer mentorship is an investment that supervisors as well as the entire team make to promote staff development and overall competence. Mentors should be clear about what their roles are and be able to communicate these roles clearly to the mentees as well as the team. This fosters a common understanding that can support the rest of the team in endorsing the process. A mentor should also be able to communicate clearly with the mentee and determine when misunderstanding or further need for clarification is present. When working with the mentee, there should be a focus on important points and areas for development that are relevant to the mentee's learning needs and the program's mission. The learning style of the mentee may be significantly different than that of the mentor, creating a need for the mentor to understand adult learning principles. The learning needs must be assessed, and a clearly specified plan for growth should be mutually determined between the mentor and mentee. As progress is made, it will be necessary for the mentor to assess and clearly articulate to the mentee, as well as the supervisor, performance and goal attainment information (Eby, 1997; Isabella, 1985; Trautman, 1999).

Developing Mutual Investment in Success

The multiple benefits to the mentee in a mentorship relationship are obvious. But, there is much to be gained by both the mentor and the mentee. A successful mentorship relationship should have a bidirectional benefit, which is the responsibility of both parties to ensure (Cohen et al., 2007). This responsibility must be an investment that needs patience and commitment to flourish. Both the mentor and the mentee should be able to see past their own markers for success and focus on the mutual success of the experience. Developing the workforce has obvious implications for the program as well as the families who are served. The success of the relationship benefits everyone.

Just as a therapeutic relationship is a process, so too is the mentorship relationship. Mentors should invite mentees to make their needs known and to feel safe in the process. This takes an investment of time and fostering of the appropriate learning environment. Feedback and support should be presented from a strength-based framework, just as the supervisory process should. Mentors should also attend to boundary and confidentiality issues as well. Mentees should make use of their time with mentors by preparing discussions and asking questions that would foster their growth. If concerns arise or difficult feelings, mentees who take the opportunity to discuss the concerns create opportunities for continued growth and development that may be otherwise stalemated.

CONCLUSION

Supervisors must remain vigilant to the needs of the practitioners who they support. The work of home- and community-based services can be challenging and taxing, especially without adequate support. This occurs in a number of ways, which ultimately reflect the quality of the professional relationship that is developed. The supervisory relationship is a complex one, and its importance should not be underestimated. The support of the team as well as the individual staff members must also take place in a complimentary fashion.

References

Bernard, J. M., & Goodyear, R. K. (2004). *Fundamentals of clinical supervision* (3rd ed.) Boston: Allyn & Bacon.

Bertacchi, J. (1996). Relationship-based organizations. *Zero to Three, 17*(2), 1, 3-7.

Carter, J. W., Enyedy, K. C., Goodyear, R. K., Arcinue, F., & Puri, N. N. (2009). Concept mapping of the events supervisees find helpful in group supervision. *Training and Education in Professional Psychology, 3*(1), 1-9.

Cohen, M. S., Jacobs, J. P., Quintessenza, J. A., Chai, P.J., Lindberg, H. L., Dickey, J., et al. (2007). Mentorship, learning curves and balance. *Cardiology in the Young, 17*(Suppl.2), 164-174.

Collins, P. M. (1994). Does mentorship among social workers made a difference? An empirical investigation of career outcomes. *Social Work, 39*, 413-419.

Copa, A., Lucinski, L., Olsen, E., & Wollenburg, K. (1999). Promoting professional and organizational development: A reflective practice model. *Zero to Three, 20*, 3-9.

Doxsee, D. J., & Kivlighan, D. M. (1994). Hindering events in interpersonal relations groups for counselor trainees. *Journal of Counseling & Development, 72*, 621-626.

Eby, L. T. (1997). Alternative forms of mentoring in changing organizational environments: A conceptual extension of the mentoring literature. *Journal of Vocational Behavior, 51*, 125-144.

Ensher, E. A., Thomas, C., & Murphy, S. E. (2001). Comparison of traditional, step-ahead, and peer mentoring on protégés' support, satisfaction, and perceptions of career success: A social exchange perspective. *Journal of Business and Psychology, 15,* 419-438.

Haber, R. (1996). *Dimensions of psychotherapy supervision: Maps and means.* New York: Norton.

Hoese, J. (1987). An exploratory investigation of group supervision: Trainees, supervisors and structure. *Dissertation Abstracts International, 48,* 2285.

Kram, K. E. (1983). Phases of the mentoring relationship. *Academy of Management Journal, 28,* 608-625.

Kram, K. E. (1985). *Mentoring at work: Developmental relationships in organizational life.* Glenview, IL: Scott, Foresman.

Kram, K. E., & Isabella, L. A. (1985). Mentoring alternatives: The role of peer relationships in career development. *Academy of Management Journal, 28,* 110-132.

Lindblad-Goldberg, M., Dore, M. M., & Stern, L. (1998). *Creating competence from chaos: A comprehensive guide to home-based services.* New York: W. W. Norton.

Parlakian, R. (2001). *Look, listen, and learn: Reflective supervision and relationship-based work.* Washington, DC: Zero to Three.

Parlakian, R., & Seibel, N. L. (2001). *Being in charge: Reflective leadership in infant/family programs.* Washington, DC: Zero to Three.

Prieto, L. R. (1996). Group supervision: Still widely practiced but poorly understood. *Counselor Education and Supervision, 35,* 295-307.

Ravets, P. (1993). Group supervision: A multiple case study. *Dissertation Abstracts International, 54,* 2768.

Sharlin, S. A., & Shamai, M. (2000). *Therapeutic intervention with poor, unorganized familes: From distress to hope.* New York: Haworth Clinical Practice Press.

Trautman, S. (1999). *Technical peer mentoring handbook: The art of sharing what you know with the person working next to you.* Seattle, WA: Solution Strategies.

Young, A. M., & Perrewe, P. L. (2004). The role of expectations in the mentoring exchange: An analysis of mentor and protégé expectations in relation to perceived support. *Journal of Managerial Issues, 16,* 103-126.

Exhibit 5.1
Strengths and Needs Assessment for Staff: Sample Assessment Domains

Knowledge

> Empowerment Concepts
> Wraparound Principles
> Recovery and Resiliency Concepts
> Mental Health Conditions in Adults and Children
> Child Development
> Principles of Crisis Intervention
> Behavior Management
> Adult Learning Theory

Skills

> Listening and Reflecting
> Demonstrating Empathy
> Provision of Feedback
> Structuring Therapeutic Relationship
> Assessment
> Service Planning
> Transition Planning
> Designing Meaningful Interventions
> Assessing Progress and Needed Changes in Services

Work Behaviors and Skills

> Time Management
> Organization
> Documentation Skills
> Use of Supervision
> Capacity to Manage Team Dynamics
> Stress Management
> Balance of Work and Leisure

Exhibit 5.2
Sample Questions for Strengths Discovery With Staff

What are the areas related to service provision that are most meaningful to you?

Can you describe a situation in which an initial session seemed to really go well? What about not so well?

Have there been crisis situations in which you felt that your actions were especially supportive and facilitated a positive outcome?

When stressed, what activities as part of your job refuel you?

What about service provision seems to come naturally to you?

What has been the greatest compliment that a family has given you? What about a coworker or supervisor?

Exhibit 5.3
Supervision Plan

Staff Member Name _____

Supervisor Name _____

Date of Plan _____

Review Date _____

Identified Needs   Identified Strengths

1.   1.

2.   2.

3.   3.

4.   4.

5.   5.

Goals/Objectives/Interventions

Goal

_____

_____

Objectives (What will show us progress is occurring?)

_____

_____

_____

Interventions (Describe the strategy and person responsible)

_____

_____

_____

Training Opportunities and Expectations

_____

_____

_____

Signature of Staff Member _____

Date _____

Signature of Supervisor _____

Date _____

Chapter 6

Determining a Model for Service Provision

First, have a definite, clear practical ideal; a goal, an objective. Second, have the necessary means to achieve your ends; wisdom, money, materials, and methods. Third, adjust all your means to that end.

—Aristotle

When people base their lives on principle, 99 percent of their decisions are already made.

—Anonymous

INTRODUCTION

The design and type of service provision model should take into account multiple variables, as it has broad implications for the success of a program. If a program has not yet been developed, it is helpful to hear the voices of youth and families, community members, and all levels of staff within the organization. Other factors to consider include staffing resources, clinical focus, cultural influences, and the community's preferences for service provision. This chapter reviews the benefits and challenges of a multidisciplinary team approach as well as an individual or small team approach. The adherence to values and principles is discussed, regardless of the approach that is chosen. The roles of the members within the team ultimately working together to enhance family's experiences are outlined.

GENERAL PRINCIPLES

Adherence to Wraparound Principles

A program that is strongly guided by principles that are proven to be effective will empower staff to provide quality services and families to experience positive outcomes. As a program is being developed, it is important that all levels of staff are familiar with the wraparound principles (see Chapter 3 in this volume) and the research that supports them. Upper management should have as strong an understanding as the core staff, as there are numerous decisions related to staffing, fiscal issues, and management that, when made, will have implications for the program. In addition to all levels of staff agreeing to the service provision model, it is important to include family and community members in an orientation of the guiding principles. This is especially important if the concepts are new ones in an area, or there is a change from a different orientation. This can be provided in community forums that offer education on topics relevant to families as well as in publications regarding the program. This common knowledge, although cursory, will give community and family members a common ground from which to operate, if they are later involved in service provision.

Mutual Investment of Staff and Community

Manifesting the wraparound principles in everyday interactions is a process and not an event. A staff person must be open to continual support and guidance from team members and supervisors in this area. Additionally, staff would do well to appreciate how family and youth have a lot to teach and contribute in this area as well. There is often a paradigm shift in operation that must continually be challenged and addressed, or the values will not become a natural part of a staff person's thinking. Investment occurs at several levels. It is most commonly developed and reinforced when change is seen as a result of services that reflect a family-driven, youth-guided, culturally competent, and community-based commitment. Actually witnessing the changes in outcomes, attitudes, and the lives of families has great impact. Investment also is developed through vicarious learning experiences that are plentiful in a team environment.

When community and staff members interact on behalf of families, it is critical that a common level of understanding and agreement regarding guiding principles takes place. When services are coordinated through a planning process, such as a Child and Family Team (CFT) meeting, there is an obvious opportunity to unify approaches and techniques. Families will become overwhelmed, confused, and frustrated if this does not occur. Some CFTs choose to discuss the values and principles prior to working together and agree to conform to a common method of service provision. The staff person who takes on the role of coordinating the service planning process can use a variety of formats to ensure that this occurs. Discussions may not be enough, and therefore a written agreement regarding following the values and principles, and how the team will function, may be developed. It is often difficult to operationalize the

Table 6.1
**Areas in Which Common Understanding Is Needed for Child
and Family Team Members**

- Meaning and manifestations of values and principles that guide the planning process (family driven, youth guided, culturally competent, community based, recovery and resiliency minded).
- Roles of individual members.
- Way in which conflict will be addressed.
- Rules for CFT membership and functioning.

Table 6.2
Characteristics of Well-Functioning Teams

- Effective communication (direct, open, formal and informal means).
- Coordination of efforts.
- Mutual support.
- Cohesion.
- Mutual investment.
- Member satisfaction.
- Collective task meaningfulness.

Source: Hoegl & Gemuenden (2001); Li, Li, & Wang (2009).

principles consistently, and staff, as well as community members, will need to agree to support one another in this process (see Table 6.1).

MULTIDISCIPLINARY TEAM APPROACH

A multidisciplinary team consists of staff members who represent the various helping professions (e.g., social work, psychology, psychiatry, counseling, and nursing). Other related disciplines (e.g., occupational therapy) may be a part of the team, depending on the population or focus and resources available. The team members work together to meet the needs of the family utilizing their unique skills and training, increasing a family's options for interventions (see Table 6.2). The team, although consisting of multiple types of professionals, works synergistically to meet the needs of the family with a common philosophy and value base. The team typically functions in a collaborative manner, with the team leader/supervisor taking responsibility for overseeing service provision. Supervisors' values are their proven experience with families, commitment to the values of the program, and ability to support team functioning, not their degrees. It is helpful to eliminate the notion of hierarchy related to degree or experience and value all members for fulfilling their various roles. While it is necessary to value the different roles and unique expertise of individuals, much of what supports success and positive outcomes with families is not related to degree. Paraprofessionals should not be devalued because of their lack of an advanced degree. Research studies from decades back have demonstrated that paraprofessionals achieve clinical outcomes equal or better than those of professionals in many circumstances. Education, training, and experience, although valuable, do not appear to solely predict positive outcomes. Overall change in a client's level of functioning was also greater when paraprofessionals provided the service in a study conducted by Hattie, Sharpley, and Rogers (1984) in follow up to the 1979 study by Durlak (1979; Wasik & Roberts, 1994). Relationship skills, communication skills, and familiarity with the communities being served appear to have a significant impact on outcomes (Hiatt, Sampson, & Baird, 1997, Wasik & Roberts, 1994). Paraprofessionals are more often associated with programs that value intensity and frequency of services within the home environment, and adhere strictly to a model that has proven outcomes. Both of these variables are also present in home- and community-based programs that serve youth from an empowerment perspective.

Benefits and Challenges

There are numerous benefits for team members, supervisors, and family members when a multidisciplinary team approach is utilized (see Table 6.3). Team members have the opportunity to be exposed to multiple perspectives that may reflect the various training and disciplines. The benefit of being exposed to another's perspective is far reaching. It provides opportunities to extend learning, develop new strategies, and remain flexible in thinking and interventions. Reviewing cases in a group format or discussing concepts or strategies give staff opportunities to improve problem solving as well as decision making (Carrilio, Cohen, & Goldman, 1980, Carrilio, 2007; Bruder, 1996; Wasik & Bryant, 2001). Especially when discussions involve difficult situations, such as ethical issues, there can be a great deal of learning that takes place. The experience of observing the thought processes of others and working as a group to determine a plan can be self-validating and improve staff confidence as well as overall competence. This process helps staff understand and process their own reactions to difficult situations as well. All of the above benefits serve staff well for a number of other reasons. Morale, staff burnout, stress, and feelings of being overburdened can all be mitigated by a supportive team approach.

Supervising in a team approach also has numerous benefits. When one person is telling a supervisor what is occurring within service provision, it is possible that the experiences are being filtered through that person's own lens. When multiple practitioners serve a family, the entire team's perspectives are brought to bear, and the dynamics in the interactions between team members is observed as well. Often, the family dynamics become replicated in the way that the team begins to interact, and this can be very telling of what needs to be addressed or supported in the process for both the family and the team. This process of supervision also allows for all team members to hear the same feedback at once, lessening the possibility for miscommunication or misrepresentation of supervisory suggestions. When supervisors join with the team in discussing service provision and family issues, it also serves to keep supervisors more connected to what is occurring in the field. This insight is also best understood by having a regular opportunity to assess and impact team functioning and dynamics. These issues are being reflected either positively or negatively in the service provision whether members are consciously aware of it or not.

When families experience a multidisciplinary team approach, they are exposed to an experience that can be different from an approach that is not multidisciplinary. Families have options for services that may not be available if staff resources and roles were more limited. Families also benefit from the multiple perspectives in that they optimize opportunities to best understand family needs and strengths. Families are also able to get their needs met in a coordinated and integrated manner. The benefit

Table 6.3
Benefits of Multidisciplinary Team Approach for Families,
Team Members, and Supervisors

Families	Team Members	Supervisors
• Experience broader range of skills and perspectives. • Experience more comprehensive level of support. • Foster skills in communicating with various members or within a group. • Experience likelihood of experiencing staff burnout or frustration.	• Better manage stress and burden of service provision. • Benefit from insights and skills of others. • Provide more specialized and focused services. • Better utilize strengths and talents.	• Better ensure that family needs are met. • Strengthen staff morale and competency. • Offer opportunity for cross-training and development of broader perspectives in workers. • Offer an opportunity to better understand individual strengths and needs for supervision.

to a unified approach and value base minimizes the family's feelings of confusion regarding conflicting approaches and interventions. Table 6.3 illustrates the many benefits of a multidisciplinary approach to families, team members, and supervisors.

Roles Within Team

The beauty of a multidisciplinary team is that not only are multiple disciplines typically represented but a broad range of skills and knowledge is present as well. Especially in rural areas where service options are minimal, it is ideal when a team can fully support a family's needs. The team may have members who have special skills and knowledge in areas that allow them to function as consultants or specialists in certain areas (see Table 6.4). These areas may relate to specific systems that touch the lives of youth (e.g., school, community programs, child welfare, or juvenile justice). They may also include specialty knowledge and skills in such areas as trauma, attachment disturbance, behavior disorders, or mood disturbances. Some members of the team may be exceptional at locating resources or better understand the needs of particular age groups.

A team usually consists of a team leader and approximately six to eight additional members who represent different disciplines and levels of staff. Psychology, psychiatry, social work, counseling, and nursing are some of the disciplines that may be represented. When supporting youth with serious emotional challenges, a blending of paraprofessionals and practitioners may be the best approach to offer a continuum of care (Landy & Menna, 2006). When younger children are being served, there may be developmental specialists, physical therapists, or occupational therapists because of the strong interplay between mental health and developmental issues. In older youth, there may be team members focused on vocational, employment, or housing issues.

The team must be clear about the roles of each of its members and consider the benefit in remaining flexible to meet the unique needs of individual families. Service provision should be driven by the needs of the family not the program, and therefore each family should not necessarily have the same interventions or utilize team members in the same manner as another family. The team leader, team

Table 6.4
Potential Specialty Roles of Team Members

- Managing pace and timing of accepting new families.
- Monitoring crisis intervention plans and need for development.
- Resource specialist.
- Behavior management specialist.
- School advocate.
- Community liaison.
- Parenting support specialist.
- Infant mental health specialist.
- Transition youth specialist.

as a whole, and team members all serve specific roles. The team leader provides oversight for team functioning, oversight of clinical and service provision, and administrative issues related to the program. This person should be someone who understands the needs of the community and the families who are served, and the team leader should have the ability and experience to support others in their service provision. The type of degree may not always be the marker for the best candidate. Billing requirements may require the leader or supervisor to be a masters level practitioner, although, if this is not a barrier, consideration should be given to other levels of staff who best meet the above criteria. One member of the team should be identified as the facilitator or manager of each family's services. This role can be served by all levels of staff. It requires the ability to coordinate service planning and team communication. Many teams use the term "lead case manager" to identify this role, and each team member serves this role for several families on his/her caseload. Often, teams maintain a caseload of no more than ten families per practitioner, and the practitioner only serves as a lead case manager on three to five of the ten. The team, as a whole, serves to support all families who may be served by the program when crisis situations occur, or the entire team serves as a "bank" of resources that can be consulted at any time.

A team leader should assign new referrals by matching the needs of the family to the strengths of the practitioner when possible. As the first stage of service delivery is assessment, this may be completed by one or more members of the team as needed. If one member of the team has knowledge in a particular area that may be utilized in the assessment process, it is helpful to integrate this person into the assessment process. Once the assessment is completed and a service plan is developed, this process will clarify how or if other members of the team are needed to assist in service provision. Although a multidisciplinary team has the capacity to utilize several members in service provision, this decision should be made based on the preferences and needs of the family. Clinical oversight and recommendations should be made to the family, so an informed decision can be made if certain conditions appear relevant to this decision. Young children, for instance, may be overwhelmed by too many practitioners.

Commitment to Healthy Team Functioning

A team that functions well results from commitment at all levels of the program. An organization should reflect support to the team functions in its consideration of policies, procedures, and staffing patterns. A team leader must prioritize the healthy functioning of the team as a process that should be facilitated and overseen on a continual basis. Effective team management has been described by Seifter and Economy (2001) as consisting of strategies in the following eight areas:

1. Empowering the team members doing the work;

2. Fostering individual responsibility;

3. Clarifying roles;

4. Creating shared leadership;

5. Fostering horizontal teamwork;

6. Facilitating effective listening and communication;

7. Striving for consensus; and

8. Strongly committing to the mission.

Individual team members should make a commitment to address both positive and negative interactions or concerns with members of the team in a way that will promote strong team functioning. Acknowledging others' strengths and successes lays a foundation for relationships that can also tolerate discussing difficulties.

Stages of team development and changes, in such areas as team composition or focus, can impact a team's functioning. A team may go through stages of development known as forming, storming, norming, and performing (McDonald, 2005). In the stage of forming, the group members are just beginning to know each other, and several points of clarification need to occur before they can function cohesively and effectively. Tasks during this stage include clarifying focus, identifying group strengths and weaknesses, and creating a system of communication and a process for dealing with conflict.

The storming stage will occur with all teams in varying degrees. This period of time is characterized by adjustment to the newness of the situation and how the group will function as a whole. Conflict is often a part of this stage. It is crucial that the group remains goal focused, clarifies the team's communication needs, and uses the established procedures for conflict resolution.

The norming stage is often welcomed by members as the team begins to see its value and invests in continued growth. There is a sense of progress and mutual benefit. Although change for the better has begun, it is important to continue to foster communication and conflict resolution. Successes and progress should be recognized and applauded. Challenges are best reframed as opportunities for growth.

In the performing stage, the team is functioning as a system, and there is a high degree of mutual support and respect. Continued acknowledgement of successes should occur while the group is vigilant for regression. While stability is comfortable, this is a time for new growth and the taking on of new goals.

These stages may not always be sequential, and changes in team composition or unresolved issues may result in a need to move through some or all of the stages again as a group. Table 6.5 identifies some strategies for fostering healthy team development and functioning.

Table 6.5
Strategies to Promote Healthy Team Development

- Supervisor modeling strength-based supervision.
- Supervisor promoting a safe and supportive learning environment.
- Provision of reflective supervision in group and individual formats.
- Attention to stress level and management of team.
- Retreats and planning sessions.
- Opportunities for training and development.
- Crisis debriefing when providing or involved in crisis services.
- Consistent and available supervision as needed.
- Decisions made with input from team.
- Feedback loop when team members offer suggestions for change.
- Team-building activities.

Communication Within Team

A strategy for effective communication within the team should be discussed and developed. Especially when several members of the team are involved, an effective system must be established to ensure that everyone is up to date and coordinated in their interventions. Some programs accomplish this task by meeting every morning to discuss family issues and needs. When crisis intervention has occurred or continued needs are present, the team can be informed or decide on next steps.

The team can also develop mechanisms to support communication that are reflected in natural processes and the structure of the program. Locating staff in common areas so that interaction is frequent and easier to facilitate is one strategy. Documentation that can be reviewed by the team as needed and a process for doing so can also be a way to share daily updates. Staff can also meet at the end of the day to process what has occurred and prioritize needs of the families and team.

Family Needs

Families who support youth with serious emotional challenges may experience multiple areas of need. A team approach can often best facilitate the acquisition of these needs and ensure comprehensive, intensive, and ongoing services. Staff members who have the support of a team can feel less burdened and possibly better able to balance work/life needs. Staffing patterns are more easily managed if the team is familiar and able to attend to family needs when staffing conflicts occur.

INDIVIDUAL OR SMALL TEAM APPROACH

Benefits and Challenges

When a program assigns individual or small teams to serve families, there are benefits and challenges (see Table 6.6). Some families, especially those where difficult situations have occurred in the past, are suspicious and distrustful. This results

Table 6.6
Benefits and Challenges of Small Team Approach

Benefits	Challenges
• Less opportunity for communication issues. • Less stress for family in forming relationships and establishing trust. • Opportunity for more focused care and reduced caseloads.	• Strain of meeting family needs. • Increased need to be a generalist. • Management of time off and burnout.

in families feeling less comfortable with several practitioners. The ability to limit the number of practitioners who the family must interact with can be beneficial. Young children and older youth may benefit from not having to deal with multiple relationships due to developmental and life-stage issues that make this challenging. Some cultures or communities are more open to this type of approach and would feel less inclined to embrace services if a multidisciplinary team approach were the only methodology. There are also fewer concerns regarding communication with the family in terms of giving conflicting messages. Communication issues are also less of an issue between team members. Challenges include limitations regarding staff coverage and response capacities. The family may not be able to be seen as quickly in emergency situations or when a need for greater frequency of visits occurs. The staff as well have less resources or the ability to allow others to fill in for them when feeling overwhelmed or challenged. Supervisors also have less ability to hear many perspectives on how families are progressing, and the need for field supervision may be more demanding.

Comprehensive Services

Individual or small teams may have limitations to their service provision capabilities. The commitment to ongoing assessment and resource linkage is necessary to ensure that family needs are not ignored. Practitioners should be aware of new insights on the part of family, youth, natural supports, teachers, or other practitioners who may reflect on a previous understanding of issues and needs. Options for referrals to needed services that may develop should be available, and the process for how to do so should be familiar to staff. Staff should also be prepared to consider when another practitioner may be needed or when a decrease or discontinuation of their services may be warranted.

Communication Needs

An individual or small team will need to consider strategies for communicating to the family, supervisor, and other team members. When teams of two are involved intensely with a family, the possibility of triangulation or splitting may occur. To prevent this from happening, there should be clear and consistent communication between all involved. The practitioners should spend time discussing with the family how communication will occur, as some families may not be fully aware of how important service coordination is and how confidentiality impacts this. Youth and families should be advised of a team's documentation procedures and how access to chart information occurs. If a family member requests a practitioner not to share information with another practitioner, there are several factors to consider. If the issue will sabotage or interfere with treatment, the family should be alerted to the practitioner's concerns. Certainly, if the information is about someone's well-being or reflects mandatory reporting requirements, the information must be dealt with appropriately. If this request reflects dysfunctional family dynamics, supervisory support should assist the practitioner in confronting the request from a clinical standpoint. Supervisors will need to consider meeting with team members together to gain insight on how service collaboration is occurring. Team members should agree to be open with regard to potential conflicts or issues on service provision, as this may be more likely to occur when fewer members are spending significant amounts of time with individual families.

DIRECT SERVICE SUPPORT WITHIN SYSTEM OF CARE

Working in Concert With Wraparound Facilitator

When a wraparound program (see Chapter 3 in this volume) is being utilized, the direct services that are being provided by the home- and community-based program will be coordinated through a wraparound facilitator. This process may occur differently according to the particular program, but the overall role of the facilitator is to manage, coordinate, and oversee the process of service delivery that has been outlined in a individualized plan. Some CFTs commission practitioners after needs and strengths are assessed and request specific types of services. Other teams may request practitioners to consult with the family and team regarding their assessment of needs and options for service delivery. Regardless of how services begin, the facilitator will always work to ensure that services remain focused, related to the plan, in line with the wraparound principles, and coordinated. The facilitator will typically ask that the practitioners and family prepare a report for monthly team meetings regarding successes or challenges and commit to not changing plans without informing the facilitator and discussing any changes with the team at the scheduled team meetings.

Clarifying Roles and Communication

Many practitioners maintain communication with other practitioners and members of the CFT in order to inform their service provision. If practitioners are addressing homework issues within the home environment, it is appropriate to communicate with teachers regarding progress at school. This function serves a different role than that of the facilitator. The facilitator is concerned that duplication not occur and that the family and youth are getting their needs met. Facilitators often meet with families on a weekly basis to discuss the wraparound process and their satisfaction with services; weekly meetings also help facilitators monitor crisis planning needs. Facilitators may have meetings with members of the CFT to ensure that interventions are effective and happening as they have been agreed upon. CFT members will need to agree to maintain communication with the facilitator and be aware that these conversations may be referenced with families. If CFT members have issues with families, the wraparound facilitator should work to develop ways to address these issues openly with the family in order to move the services forward. The facilitator will need to make decisions regarding how issues will be addressed at meetings, although the wishes of the family and youth are always of primary consideration. Along with this is the need to consider what is best practice, in line with the wraparound principles, and most appropriate. All of these considerations and options should be discussed with the family. Typically, team members are asked to inform the facilitator of issues prior to the CFT meeting, so that they are placed on the agenda pending discussion with the family. Issues that do not seem appropriate for the meeting should not be ignored but addressed in a more appropriate manner that can be determined with support of a supervisor.

Preparing Family for Child and Family Team Meetings

Practitioners who use the service plan as a guide typically are having conversations on a regular basis regarding the effectiveness of interventions and status regarding progress. Prior to a CFT meeting, this conversation should take place in a focused manner to allow both the family and the practitioner to relate strengths, needs, and progress. The goal is for there to be agreement on the report that will be made to the CFT. The report could indicate that the intervention needs adjustment, that new needs are present, or that success has occurred. The practitioner may be more conscious of the impact of this report to the team, especially when youth are sensitive to criticism or other systems, such as child welfare, are involved. This should not change the report, but the feelings of the youth or family should be acknowledged and assisted as needed. At times, the practitioner may assist a youth or caregivers in this experience within the CFT meeting.

CONCLUSION

The model from which service provision takes place is a decision that is impacted by the agency, community, culture, and staff resources. There are benefits to a multidisciplinary team approach that, if appropriate, can be beneficial for families. This type of approach also has advantages for supervisors and staff in terms of minimizing feelings of burden and stress regarding the needs of families. Small team or individual service provision has distinct benefits and challenges as well. Flexibility to adjust the type of model that is used, depending on the preferences of the families, may be the ideal situation for families as well as staff.

References

Bruder, M. B. (1996). Interdisciplinary collaboration in service delivery. In R. A. McWilliam (Ed.), *Rethinking pull-out services in early intervention* (pp. 27-48). Baltimore: Paul H. Brookes Publishing.

Carrilio, T. E. (2007). *Home-visiting strategies: A case-management guide for caregivers.* Columbia: University of South Carolina Press.

Carrilio, T. E., Cohen, R. G., & Goldman, A. R. (1980). The team method of delivering services to the elderly: An interim report. *Journal of Jewish Communal Service 52*, 56-62.

Durlak, J. (1979). Comparative effectiveness of paraprofessional and professional helpers. *Psychological Bulletin, 86*, 80-92.

Hattie, J. A., Sharpley, C. F., & Rogers, H. J. (1984). Comparative effectiveness of professional and paraprofessional helpers. *Psychological Bulletin, 95*, 534-541.

Hiatt, S., Sampson, D., & Baird, D. (1997). Paraprofessional home visitation: Conceptual and pragmatic considerations. *Journal of Community Psychology, 25*, 77-93.

Hoegl, M., & Gemuenden, H. (2001). Teamwork quality and the success of innovative projects: A theoretical concept and empirical evidence. *Organization Science, 12*, 435-449.

Landy, S., & Menna, R. (2006). *Early interventions with mult-irisk families: An integrative approach.* Baltimore: Paul H. Brookes Publishing.

Li, F., Li, Y., & Wang, E. (2009). Task characteristics and team performance: The mediating effect of team member satisfaction. *Social Behavior and Personality, 37*, 1373-1382.

McDonald, T. (2005). Building an effective team. *Health Care Registration: The Newsletter for Health Care Registration Professionals, 15*(2), 3-4.

Seifter, H. & Economy, P. (2001). *Leadership ensemble: Lessons in collaborative leadership from the world's only conductorless orchestra.* New York: Times Books, Henry Holt.

Wasik, B. H., & Roberts, R. N. (1994). Home visitor characteristics, training, and supervision: Results of a national survey. *Family Relations, 43*, 336-341.

Wasik, B. H., & Bryant, D. M. (2001). *Home visiting: Procedures for helping families* (2nd ed.). Newbury Park, CA: Sage.

Part 3

Assessment of Youth With Serious Emotional Challenges and the Families Who Support Them

Chapter 7

Assessment Principles and Components

The beginning of knowledge is the discovery of something we do not understand.
—Frank Herbert

No pessimist ever discovered the secret of the stars or sailed an uncharted land, or opened a new doorway for the human spirit.
—Helen Keller

INTRODUCTION

The assessment process is an essential element in the provision of home- and community-based services. The process of discovery, if administered from an empowerment perspective has tremendous opportunities beyond the assessment process. The primary goal of determining strengths and needs of the family to inform a strength-based, family-driven, youth-guided, and individualized plan is but one result of this process. The experience for families engaging in an assessment process of this type exemplifies the principles of empowerment, wraparound, recovery, and resiliency. This supports the development of a mutually satisfying, collaborative, and professional relationship with trust at its center. The comprehensive nature of the assessment is outlined in this chapter to support the ecological perspective of the many influences within the home, school, and community that impact a family. This chapter also discusses the necessary components of the assessment process and offers information related to fulfilling these components.

GOALS OF ASSESSMENT

Developing a Unique Perspective of Youth and Family

The goals of the assessment process are realized when careful attention is given to both the process and context of the assessment. The investment in laying a foundation for meaningful, relevant, and useful data to be identified is essential. Families and youth often need assistance in empowering them to be full assessment partners. Practitioners must emphasize to youth and families the value and importance of their input in the assessment process. Information should be considered from the context of the home, school, and community within the unique cultural perspective that the family holds. Information is not able to be properly put into context unless the norms, traditions, rules, and meaning of interactions within the home, school, and community are understood. Families and youth may not consider, without encouragement, that natural supports, community members, extended family, and other practitioners may have vital information to round out a picture of what the family does well and what it needs help with. Families are encouraged to describe their unique social support networks and available resources within their communities (Yoe, Santarcangelo, Atkins, & Burchard, 1996). The ways in which information is compiled are varied. Informal conversations, which may include family and youth telling stories or sharing discussions with other caregivers, often provide good insight into a family's functioning in a way that is comfortable for the family. Other strategies for gaining information include screens, checklists, questionnaires, and scales. These tools are used to obtain information regarding signs and symptoms of mental health challenges. They may be completed by either the caregivers or the practitioner. Additionally, observing youth and caregivers directly offers insight that can significantly improve understanding of the issues (Rosin Jesien, Whitehead, & Begun, 1996; Carrilio, 2007; Yoe et al., 1996). If the focus of the assessment remains true to the beliefs of home- and community-based services, the end result will be an identification of the youth's and family's strengths, resources, concerns, needs, and priorities. This information is best understood by an ongoing commitment to recognizing the ecological influences, the history relevant to the family as well as the present situation (Early & Poertner, 1995; Olson & Hains, 1992).

Planning for Crisis Stabilization

Families who have been attempting to cope for extended periods of time are likely to feel overwhelmed and are often in a state of distress. Many families who have youth with emotional challenges have experienced multiple stressors that have resulted in such issues as family strain, marital discord, school issues, supervision concerns, respite needs, financial concerns, and community pressure. Families at the point of assessment may be characterized as feeling a sense of hopelessness and helplessness (Sharlin & Shamai, 1995). Often, the interventions that a family may have received, or is currently receiving, have been deficit based and focused on the individual child only. In this case, it is more imperative than ever to respond to the family's distress and communicate the benefits of interventions being family focused. If a family is in need of stabilization, this must be acknowledged and addressed before a clear picture of family strengths and needs can be obtained. The practitioner must work in partnership with the family to assess what resources or interventions are needed to stabilize the family. A discussion regarding safety, basic need, and immediate crisis concerns should be facilitated and supported by the practitioner in order to arrive at a plan. Reviewing the current situation and past crisis situations provides important information (Rotto, McIntyre, & Serkin, 2008). An initial crisis/stabilization plan should be developed with clear delineation of roles, interventions, and a plan for follow-up. The initial plan should be considered a starting place that will likely evolve and need to be changed, possibly several times, before the initial Child and Family Team (CFT) meeting. The practitioner must be dedicated to careful and thorough follow-up. At the time of the CFT meeting, a more comprehensive plan, which can enlist the help of all members of the team, can be created. One characteristic that a successful crisis plan typically has is heavy reliance on natural and community supports resulting in a lack of reliance on formal supports.

Preparation for Service Planning: Identifying Youth and Family Team Process

When home- and community-based services are a part of a formal wraparound process that follows the model to fidelity, there will be a monthly CFT meeting that practitioners will be expected to attend. The services are identified, coordinated, and reviewed at each team meeting as part of the development of an individualized service plan. When home- and community-based services that are not a part of a formal wraparound process develop a plan, they too may use a CFT meeting to accomplish service planning. The composition of the team can vary from just the practitioner and family to a complex host of players depending on the wishes of the family. Regardless, the family, as part of the assessment process, will need to be assisted in understanding how the CFT process is beneficial to the planning process. The family and youth may not have encountered the CFT concept previously and may need examples of what they can expect. The definition of a CFT is a helpful place to start. A useful definition has been offered in *The Wraparound Process User's Guide: A Handbook for Families,* (Miles, Bruns, Osher, Walker and National Wraparound Initiative Advisory Group, 2006): "A group of people-chosen with the family and connected to them through natural, community and formal support relationships-who develop and implement the family's plan, address unmet needs, and work toward the family vision" (p. 9). The youth and family may need to be supported in voicing questions or concerns about the CFT process, as it may evoke some degree of anxiety, especially if it is an unfamiliar process. Table 7.1 offers sample questions and answers related to the CFT process.

Families and youth may wonder about the confidentiality of what is discussed and have concerns about practitioners providing more information than is necessary to develop a plan. These and other issues should be addressed, and assurances can be

Table 7.1
Common Questions and Answers Regarding Youth and
Family Team Formation and Functions

What is the purpose of a CFT?

The CFT serves to gather together a group of unique individuals who support the youth and family. The members of the team may be paid or unpaid supports as well as representatives of services or systems that the family and youth are involved in. The team will mutually invest in ensuring that the youth and family have a voice in determining what needs to be accomplished, in what manner, and how success will be determined. A facilitator will guide and support the development of a plan that will coordinate interventions in a way that appreciates the culture, strengths, and vision of the family.

Why is it important for CFT members to meet monthly?

To form a well-functioning team, which is fully aware of what the family's vision is, everyone's presence and active involvement is needed. The family and youth's needs and strengths often change and develop over time, and present differently as time goes by. The experience of seeing how everyone can come together, work for the benefit of the family, and effect change is very powerful for the family. Recognizing progress is a vital way to keep the process from feeling overwhelming. A monthly meeting can ensure that this takes place and that the interventions are truly still relevant to what the family needs.

What if an important person does not want to be a part of the CFT?

At times, members are not willing or able to come to CFT meetings. The meeting times and locations can be altered to accommodate logistical issues if needed. If a potential member still cannot or does not want to participate, the facilitator will work with the family and youth to find an alternative way, if possible, to get input from this person.

What if the youth or caregivers are uncomfortable with the process?

If the process is uncomfortable to either the youth or caregivers, the process must be modified. No exceptions! For this process to be successful, every effort must be made to support the people that the plan is all about.

---

given that all members of the team are only chosen and allowed to participate if the family is comfortable with their involvement. Table 7.2 assists in the identification of questions that can assist in the development of a CFT.

Family members determine whose involvement would be helpful, and standard operating procedures, such as confidentiality, are attended to and monitored by the facilitator. At any time, the family can ask the facilitator to address concerns or even remove someone from the team if warranted. The range of tasks that the CFT will be asked to accomplish should be clarified to the family. The family and youth should be reminded that their voices will always have the greatest influence, and the team will work to support their wishes and preferences. These tasks include *collaborating with* and *assisting* the family in the following:

- Participating in a needs and strengths assessment and cultural discovery;
- Providing input into the prioritization of needs;
- Supporting the family vision;

Table 7.2
Practitioner Questions to Assist Family in Identifying
Child and Family Team Members

- Who are the people involved in your family/child's lives in a meaningful way?
- Who are the people you turn to for support?
- Who are the people that have been "hired" to support your family?
- Who are the important representatives of services or supports that your child may be involved in?
- Who are the peers or adults that your child uses or could use for support?
- Are there any family members who should be included?

- Providing input on the utilization of strengths;

- Developing an individualized and strength-based plan;

- Identifying and reporting on outcome measures;

- Ensuring coordination and access to services;

- Assisting in the development/monitoring of a safety/ crisis plan;

- Assisting in identifying and planning for fransitions;

- Assisting in the development of natural and community supports; and

- Assisting in developing an individualized recovery plan and postdischarge crisis plan.

The above, as well as additional roles of the CFT, are described in a clear and comprehensive manner in *Phases and Activities of the Wraparound Process* (Walker et al.) for programs that choose to follow the wraparound process to fidelity. Programs should consider the benefits of following the wraparound process to fidelity and using measures such as the Wraparound Fidelity Index 4.0 (WFI-4) and Team Observation Measure (TOM) available through the National Wraparound Initiative, Research and Training Center on Family Support and Children's Mental Health, Portland State University. Exhibit 7.1 provides a sample document that can be given to the families to clarify the role of CFT members.

Committing to a Comprehensive and Individualized Plan

The end result of the assessment process should be a comprehensive and individualized plan that is a reflection of what is discovered in the needs and strengths assessment and cultural discovery. Although family members prioritize and focus on what is most relevant and important to them, the plan should guide a process of fully meeting the needs of not only the individual youth but the family as a whole. This process may occur in stages but supports the youth's and family's needs in all domains and areas that impact functioning. This ecological perspective does not limit interventions to solely address mental health needs but appreciates how most, if not all, areas of a youth's and family's lives potentially impact emotional needs. The assessment process should uncover specific examples of how needs and strengths are manifesting in the family's lives, so that the plan truly reflects an understanding of how the family functions. Assumptions should never be made related to how needs or strengths are demonstrated as well as how the family perceives them.

GUIDING PRINCIPLES OF ASSESSMENT

Achieving a Family-Driven Assessment

The concept of a family-driven assessment represents an evolution from the mentality that practitioners know what is best for youth to a belief that families have the critical knowledge of who their youth are and what may work best. In the past, the value of family input has taken many twists and turns despite the fact that one of the most influential founders of the social work movement, Mary Richmond, articulated "family voice and choice" as early as 1922. Mary Richmond (1922) stated, "individuals have wills and purposes of their own, and are not fitted to play a passive part in the world" (p. 258). In the early to mid 1900s, there was little, if any, family involvement in the treatment of youth. Caregivers were not allowed to participate and knew little about what was occurring typically behind closed doors in a hospital or office setting. In the 1950s and 1960s, family therapy, as a movement, emerged, led by such pioneers as Virginia Satir and Murray Bowen. Later in the 1960s and 1970s, the early intervention field began to develop models in which a family focus and empowerment were the primary characteristics of programs that served youth with developmental disabilities. In the mental health field, the 1980s brought about a challenge to the traditional caregiver-blaming mentality with regard to youth with emotional concerns. The work of advocates in the 1980s, in which a family focus and increased involvement in the care and decision making regarding their youth, led to a systems of care framework emerging in the 1990s (Duchnowski & Kutash, 2007). As family involvement and collaboration is one of the main corollaries of this framework, the original conceptualization of family-centered soon moved to "family-driven." This process also saw many developments. Initially, the practitioner-centered practice could be characterized as caregiver blaming, uninviting of caregivers into the process, and adversarial at best. Gradually a family-focused process emerged in which caregivers were allowed into the process but clearly in a one down position. Family allied services evolved next, in which the family was recognized as the consumer of services, and families and practitioners worked together to develop goals. Family-centered services took this further by stating that families know what is best, and practitioners are one down to families. Finally, the concept of family-driven emerged (Caplan, Blankenship, & McManus, 1998). Osher, Osher, and Blau (2006, as cited in Duchnowski & Kutash, 2007, p. 3) proposed a definition of family-driven care that evolved out of a partnership between practitioners and families represented by the national office of the Federation of Families for Children's Mental Health and the federal Substance Abuse and Mental Health Services Administration. This definition stated as follows:

> Family-driven means families have a primary decision making role in the care of their own children as well as the policies and procedures governing care of all children in their community, state, tribe, territory and nation. This includes: chosing supports, services, and providers; setting goals; designing

and implementing programs; monitoring outcomes; participating in funding decisions; and determining the effectiveness of all efforts to promote the mental health and well being of children and youth.

Practitioners who strive to achieve this value, also must subscribe to the guiding principles of family-driven care, which should direct their practice. The need to provide families with understandable, accurate, and complete information necessary to make choices and the concept of shared decision making and responsibility are clearly pertinent to the assessment process (Osher et al., 2006). When these principles are considered, the end result should produce an environment in which practitioners and families value one another, strengths are identified and utilized, a common vision is embraced, resources are pooled, and respect and understanding truly exist (Duchnowski & Kutash, 2007).

The application of these principles within the assessment process not only ensures that the family's preferences are facilitated, but, most importantly, it optimizes the likelihood that the assessment has meaning. Meisels and Provence (1989) identified several practices that reflect family-driven principles, which are especially relevant to younger children. These practices include the ideas that

- Evaluation and assessment are parts of the intervention process;

- Informed consent and collaboration with families is essential;

- The process must reflect cultural awareness;

- Results should not be based on one source of information; several contexts should be reflected based on family concerns and child characteristics; and

- Reassessment should occur frequently to reflect the rapid changes in young children's development.

Guiding assessment in a family-driven manner builds a level of comfort and trust that can become the foundation for a meaningful collaboration. When consideration is shown for a family's preferences and input, it gives a clear message that the family's ideas and insights are truly valued. Family members who are comfortable with the process are also more likely to feel free to state their concerns, fears, and ideas without worry that they will be judged.

There are times when a family's and youth's input related to the conditions of the assessment has significant meaning, which represents more than a preference. Some youth, as well as their families, may have experienced negative and even traumatic experiences related solely to an assessment process. Youth may believe that assessment means hospitalization or admission in a facility away from their families. Caregivers may have been embarrassed, shamed, or overwhelmed with feelings of guilt when considering their youth's difficulties. Especially when youth are very young, engaging in an assessment for the first time evokes many fears. Failure to recognize and accommodate the youth's and family's emotional needs related to the assessment will unnecessarily stress or traumatize the family, resulting in a poor understanding of the youth's needs and strengths.

A family-driven assessment has many components and reflects the family's input in a number of areas. Families know best how the time, location, and duration of the assessment interview will impact its effectiveness. Some caregivers may offer the suggestion that the assessment not persist longer than a certain amount of time due to the youth's temperament or ability to tolerate the process. Conversations related to the best way in which to obtain the information needed from all members are essential as well. If properly supported, caregivers have an unlimited amount of knowledge about how their families operate and are best able to demonstrate their capabilities and needs. Giving family members options related to their level of involvement is ideal. Some siblings may be reluctant or worried about giving input. They may need time to form a level of comfort and a relationship with the practitioner before this can occur. The family and youth must also be fully informed on the components of the assessment, the needed information, the way in which the information will be used and communicated, and the results of the assessment. Mendenhall (1990) described a family-centered assessment where, prior to the assessment, the family was fully informed who would be a part of the assessment team, what would be evaluated, and how the assessment would be conducted. After the assessment, information should be given related to how information was interpreted during the assessment, what the information means, and how the data will be used.

A practitioner who supports a family-driven assessment displays a number of behaviors throughout the process. The first priority in the assessment must remain the family and not the obligations or pressures of the program. If the assessment appears overwhelming to the family, it must be stopped or adjusted as appropriate. If a practitioner identifies a look of concern, this must be acknowledged and questions or issues addressed. Practitioners should invite family members to offer input related to the process at any time. Questions should always be encouraged and answered fully. Practitioners should speak in a way that is easily understood and respectful, free of jargon, and in first-person language. When the assessment is completed, the family should be given the opportunity to process the experience, especially with regard to its validity. Feedback and results should be discussed and concerns prioritized. The family should then be encouraged to give input related to the next step—the planning process. The family should be offered written reports that are respectful and in the language of the consumer (Rosin et al., 1996).

Supporting a Youth-Guided Assessment

There are multiple benefits to the meaningful engagement of youth in the assessment process. Regardless of age, a meaningful assessment can only occur if the youth have been supported in offering their insights, concerns, and uncovering unique assets. Involving youth fully in the treatment and ongoing planning provides benefits for youth, caregivers, and practitioners (Walker & Child, 2008).

It is more likely that the assessment data will be relevant and useful if the conditions have been optimized to ensure a youth's ability to reflect and report needs, strengths, and concerns. The perspective of the youth may be different from the caregivers' report. Assumptions should never be made related to behavior, as a well-thought-out and comfortable interview process is more likely to result in a truer understanding of the youth's needs.

There are a number of considerations in determining the way in which the assessment will take place, which can ensure the youth's meaningful participation and comfort level. First, the youth should be given information related to the purpose of the assessment and the components that make up the assessment. This discussion can lead to determining options related to how the assessment can occur. The same questions that were asked of the caregivers, such as time, location, duration, and level of involvement of all members, should be asked of the youth. When the family is meeting as a unit, practitioners should attempt to remain present and available to all members, not allowing caregivers to dominate the discussion or minimize youth input. Caregivers can be engaged by encouraging youth to share in the assessment process and emphasizing the importance this has for positive outcomes. Youth who feel misunderstood or falsely represented will likely resist services and supports. Youth should be asked to contribute to the discussion during the process and as the assessment results are being discussed in a way that will clarify any misconceptions or differences of opinions.

Fully Appreciating the Impact of Culture

In the assessment process, there should always be a strong attempt to understand how the family's culture impacts the assessment. This should be not be accomplished by assuming that all individuals from the same cultural orientation share the same types of traits. Although many cultures share similar traits, it is even more relevant to understand what is driving observable behaviors and beliefs. Most are not aligned with only one cultural influence but a variety of cultural influences. This may be illustrated by considering the various impacts of ethnicity, family culture, and a rural versus city orientation to life. Not only is it critical to understand the impact that culture has on a family but the impact it has on the practitioner as well. There must be an awareness of biases and beliefs, which may be transmitted to the family in either a conscious or unconscious manner. Many factors influence how a person's behavior manifests including past experiences, beliefs, values and traditions, and the influence of relationships (Cornett, 2009). Each individual and family should be seen as individuals despite their ethnicity or cultural orientation. Not all people that identify themselves as being a specific ethnicity or orientation are alike.

Culture as a concept is often minimized in terms of the amount of influence that it has on a person. The far-reaching effects of culture may be overlooked. The definition of culture, shared by Maschinot (2008), emphasizes this concept: "Culture is a shared system of meaning, which includes values, beliefs, and assumptions expressed in daily interactions of individuals within a group through a definite pattern of language, behavior, customs, attitudes, and practices" (p. 1).

A number of considerations should be made when structuring and conducting the assessment. Families may have clear opinions related to how questions are asked, who answers questions, and the appropriateness of youth giving their input. Culture impacts a family's understanding of mental health issues as well as its level of comfort in discussing the issues. The way in which interactions with practitioners unfold is influenced by culture as well. If a practitioner's style of interaction is not adjusted to be in line with what is considered respectful and appropriate, the assessment results may be skewed or misunderstood. Family culture, including the hierarchy of the family, roles of members, ways in which decisions are made, beliefs, and traditions, is relevant information. Ethnicity may have strong influences on the way in which families care for, discipline, and communicate with their children. Communication is broad in the sense that it has many components. There are differences in what is considered appropriate topics, the value of communication in general, and how the caregivers believe the teaching of language should occur.

As part of the assessment process, a cultural discovery should take place. This is often completed in a conversational format that is guided by a list of areas to explore. Many programs have developed tools that can be adapted to include additional questions or topics for discussion that may be specific to different parts of the country. In conducting the cultural discovery, it is helpful to recognize that most individuals have difficulty answering many questions related to culture, as it is so engrained in their personalities that it is difficult to recognize and explain. Giving examples and observing patterns of behavior to discuss often gives families better opportunities to teach practitioners how their families work (see Table 7.3).

Appreciating the Comprehensive Nature of the Assessment

In appreciation of an ecological perspective, the assessment must include all areas of a youth's life. How the individual functions within his/her home, school, and community should be considered. The developmental and other relevant history information should be included as well. The strengths and needs assessment should be comprehensive in the sense that it captures a picture of what is occurring in all domains of a youth's and family's lives.

The Child and Adolescent Needs and Strengths (CANS) assessment is one example of a format for assessing both the individual and family functioning. The CANS consists of dimensions that relate to both needs and strengths for the youth and family. Anchors that are standard across the dimensions are used to rate the level of strength or need. The item structure has four levels of rating that is associated with levels of action needed. For the needs, the action levels are as follows:

1. No evidence: No action needed.

2. Watchful waiting, prevention: Efforts are needed to monitor this need or engage in activities to ensure that it does not become worse.

3. Action: The need is interfering in a notable way with the child's or family's life and something should be done.

4. Immediate or intensive action: This is a priority for intervention. The need is dangerous or disabling. (Lyons, 2004, pp. 221-222)

For the strengths, the action levels are as follows:

1. A strength that can serve as the centerpiece of a strength-based plan.

2. A strength that exists and can be used in strength-based planning but not as the focus.

3. A strength has been identified, but must be built.

4. No strength has been identified. (Lyons, 2004, p. 222)

The CANS assesses strengths and needs in several domains related to the youth and family. The state of Indiana uses the CANS Indiana Comprehensive Multisystem Assessment on a statewide basis within the behavioral health system overseen by the Department of Mental Health and Addictions. The domains include Life Domain Functioning, Child Strengths, Acculturation, Caregiver Strengths and Needs, Child

Table 7.3
Cultural Discovery

Questions for Caregivers

- Who are the people that you consider your family?
- How would you describe your ethnicity?
- What are you most proud of regarding your ethnicity?
- How do you share with your children ideas about their ethnicity?
- Do you feel others understand your views, values, and traditions?
- Do you have trouble understanding other's views, values, and traditions?
- What is your preferred language?
- Is communication ever a barrier for you?
- How would you describe the most important roles of a caregiver?
- How would you describe how children should behave in the home, school, or community?
- What is your preference for how I offer you information? Verbal or written? language?
- What are your favorite activities?
- What family activities are most enjoyable?
- How does your family celebrate holidays and birthdays?
- What do you want most for your children?
- How do you interact with extended family?
- Does your family have friends that are a big part of your life?
- Are others at your house often?
- What are special rules that your family has?
- Does your family belong to a faith community?
- What does your family do in times of stress?
- Who do you call in times of need?
- How would you describe family routines?
- How would you describe your beliefs about relationships with practitioners?
- How would you feel most comfortable sharing concerns or needs?

Questions for Youth

- Who would you describe as your family?
- Do you have friends that spend a lot of time with your family?
- When is it easiest or most difficult to share your ideas with adults?
- Is it comfortable for you to talk about what you do well?
- How does your family spend time together?
- Does your family have certain ways of doing things at mealtimes?
- Do you feel your family has ways of doing things that are different than other families?
- What language do you like to speak in?
- Do you ever have a hard time understanding how others do things?
- Does your family have an identity or ethnicity that is talked about?
- How would you describe your family?
- How does your family expect kids to act?
- What are the jobs of the caregivers?

Behavioral/Emotional Needs, Child Risk Factors, and Child Risk Behaviors. Additional modules require a more in-depth assessment of needs in such areas as school, development, family/caretaker, regulatory functioning, and trauma (Lyons, Cornett, & Walton, 2009). The assessment information is meant to inform a service plan, so that plans are developed based on input from the youth and family and reflect what is needed. The

CANS is also used as a decision support model to make recommendations regarding the needed level of care. Various versions of the CANS exist, which represent nuances in the items that are chosen in order to best reflect the geographical areas, culture, or systems in which youth are served. The Starting Early Together (SET) program is part of the Systems of Care Initiative located within the Allegheny County, Pennsylvania, Department of Human Services, Office of Behavioral Health. This program has developed a section related to service needs that is entitled Care Intensity and Organization (Lyons, Ryan (Cornett), & Duran, 2007). See Exhibits 7.2, 7.3, and 7.4 for examples of CANS assessments.

In addition to a needs and strengths assessment, developmental and life history, and cultural assessment, it is important to consider the transition needs of the youth and family. Youth and families are especially vulnerable when transitions, although a natural part of the life cycle, occur. Such transitions include movement through the developmental stages, entry into school/preschool, changes in day care, changes in residence, movement to different schools, or transitioning to independence or adult services. In addition to recognizing the above types of transitions, the assessment process should also recognize that the family will ultimately need to transition from services. An assessment of what needs to occur to make this a successful transition will need to take place. This type of planning begins as soon as the assessment process is completed in the same way that an individualized service plan will begin. These processes should be integrated and support one another.

Building a Strength-Based Assessment

Youth have historically been represented as either victims or "problem children." This has been especially true for youth who represent minority cultures and come from low-income backgrounds. As well, the period of adolescence throughout the decades has been described as pathologic and devoid of significance and value (Cheon, 2008). The mental health field as a whole continues to operate from a deficit-based perspective. This is evident in the focus on diagnosis that forces practitioners to first think of problems and develop plans related to the problem areas. In the diagnostic process, the identification of strengths is not recognized as an integral component. The building of strengths, although increasingly recognized as valuable, is not the indicator of success. The outcome for treatment remains the mitigation of problems. Weick, Rapp, Sullivan, and Kisthardt (1989) identify three negative dynamics that arise when a problem-focused approach is used. These include the problem being seen as a deficit or inability in the individual solely; the problem being defined by the practitioner; and the problem driving the treatment process, so that overcoming the deficiency becomes the sole focus. Despite this stark reality, there has been progress in the conceptualization of strength-based services over the past twenty years. See Table 7.4 for a comparison of strength-based versus deficit-based assessments.

In offering assistance to youth and their families, perhaps the greatest gift is the installation of hope. Youth may have lost all sense of hope and see themselves and the world through a lens of negativity. When youth are offered hope and encouraged through the recognition of their strengths, capabilities, and resources, a relationship that supports motivation for change and growth evolves (Laursen, 2004). The strength-based perspective attempts to redirect the focus from what is wrong or "abnormal" to what is possible in the future. Youth and families must be seen in

Table 7.4
Strength-Based vs. Deficit-Based Assessment

Strength-Based

- Respects view of consumer and family.
- Format is conversational.
- Values natural supports.
- Identifies hopes and aspirations.
- Assessment is ongoing and relationship based.

Deficit-Based

- Professional sets agenda.
- Focused on problems and deficits.
- Client insight is devalued.
- Emphasizes need for formal services.
- Professional identifies priorities.

Source: Rapp and Goscha (2006).

light of their abilities, talents, and capacities as well as their needs. This allows for a process in which youth and families can clarify their values and develop a family vision for the future (Saleebey, 1996).

The strength-based perspective is also congruous with both the ecological and recovery-oriented perspectives. The significance of this is great, as it allows for the theoretical perspectives to be appreciated and reflected in practice. When a problem-based assessment is utilized, it typically results in an individualistic rather than social-environmental explanation of the "problem." The strength-based assessment forces the practitioner and family to look globally at all areas of a youth's and family's lives that contribute to successes (Weick et al., 1989). Resilience, as a concept, appreciates the strengths that youth may possess, which both protect them from adversity and are often born out of exposure to trauma. Resilience describes the insight, skills, abilities, and knowledge that both youth and families develop as challenges and adversity are encountered. It is an ongoing growth process that continually matures and develops to empower individuals to cope effectively with challenges (Garmezy, 1994). The landmark Kauai Longitudinal Study was designed to identify what factors are significant in protecting youth from the adverse effects of challenging life circumstances. The study analyzed the impact of a variety of risk factors that were identified as biological and psychosocial conditions as well as stressful life events in 698 Asian and Polynesian children born in 1955. Data was collected at birth, in the postpartum period, and at ages 1, 2, 10, 8, 32, and 40 (Werner, 2000; Werner & Smith, 1989, 1992; Werner, Randolph, & Masten, 1996). The results of this study demonstrate the importance of the focus on, and development of, strengths in individuals, their social support systems, and their communities. In the 1992 follow-up study, Werner and Smith emphasized that individuals have self-righting tendencies that allow for self-correction of the life course. Relationships are crucial in this process, and it is never too late to change a life trajectory towards aspiration, accomplishment, and recovery (Saleebey, 1996).

Strength-based assessment paves the way for strength-based practice by initiating treatment through a process that rejects a deficit model and focuses on capacities. This process is less stigmatizing and engages youth in a manner that is more likely to produce outcomes (Cox, 2006). This approach is part of a comprehensive and holistic approach to supports and services for youth with serious emotional challenges. While identifying needs as a point of intervention, identifying strengths and talents gives practitioners a context and a focus for development (Epstein, Harniss, Pearson & Ryser, 1999). Strength-based assessment is described by Epstein and Sharma (1998) as "the measurement of those emotional and behavioral skills, competencies, and characteristics that create a sense of personal accomplishment, contribute to satisfying relationships with family members, peers, and adults; enhances one's ability to deal with adversity and stress; and promotes one's personal, social, and academic development" (p. 3).

The beliefs that compliment this definition are as follows:

1. All children and families have unique strengths.

2. Focusing on these strengths results in increased motivation and outcomes.

3. The failure to demonstrate a skill should be seen as an opportunity to learn.

4. Service plans that focus on strengths are more likely to have family agreement (Epstein et al., 2003; Epstein, 1999).

Home- and community-based practitioners may use a conversational style to identify the presence of strengths that consider the major domains and influences in a youth's and family's lives. This often produces a plethora of information, as the questions are open-ended and encourage a thoughtful process. Formal assessments, such as the Behavioral and Emotional Rating Scale (BERS) (Epstein & Sharma, 1998), are available as well. The BERS includes five subscales: interpersonal strengths, family involvement, intrapersonal strengths, school functioning, and affective strengths.

The focus on strengths does not disregard the presence of needs. When strengths are identified and strategies are put in place to develop strengths, there remains an appreciation of what areas are not so strong. Service plans should reflect an awareness of both needs and strengths, although the focus of intervention and methods in which change occurs is through the building and development of strengths. It is also important to remember that emotional and behavioral strengths are not mutually exclusive of emotional and behavioral deficits. A child with high levels of strengths versus a child with low levels of strengths may need different types of interventions (Epstein et al., 1999).

Using Assessment as a Tool for Change

The assessment process itself can serve as a change agent. By engaging with the family in a respectful and supportive manner, the experience of being "heard" and understood often leads to a new level of understanding regarding what can occur and what is already occurring that is useful and able to be built upon. Families as well as youth may not have experienced the recognition that change is even possible. The identification of possibilities and feelings of hope are often seen as the most important elements in the therapeutic process. In addition to this recognition is the opportunity to see the family's needs and strengths in a comprehensive manner. Caregivers may be focused on behavior or an emotional need and have not considered the contribution that other factors may be making in the situation. Building up the family's resources and knowledge in relevant areas is a service that will augment the child's functioning in the most needed areas.

A needs and strengths assessment that is most useful provides information about what is needed in a youth's and family's lives. It is a common practice for practitioners to make recommendations that reflect a service rather than a need. If a child does not want to attend school for instance, the need, if properly assessed, may be related to any number of factors. If a treatment practitioner did not remain open to these possibilities and merely stated "the child needs therapy to process why he isn't going to school," the intervention is much less likely to be successful. An assessment of what the behavior actually represents may lead to another type of intervention that could more efficiently address what is occurring. The child may feel bullied on the bus, for example, and need the adults in his/her life to take charge. This type of openness to listening to the child and family can lead to meaningful interventions that produce better outcomes for families.

The data that is developed from the assessment process may seem overwhelming. The process of prioritizing and focusing on one goal at a time ensures that youth and families can see some success. The comprehensive nature of the assessment should be recognized therefore as providing valuable information that will not get lost in the process. A plan for how to integrate new goals as progress occurs or the family feels ready for an additional focus should be discussed. The information should be seen as a valuable, written down and recorded process that is a baseline for understanding what needs to be done. The likelihood that this information will change as reassessment occurs is great but does not diminish its value.

PREPARING YOUTH AND FAMILY FOR ASSESSMENT

Orienting Youth and Family to the Assessment Process

The orientation process is meant to ensure that the family and youth are fully informed of what the assessment process is and how it can be conducted in a family-driven and youth-guided manner. The information that is given as well as received in this process should result in the identification of how the assessment process can best work for the youth and family who are being assessed. Although there may be components of the process that need to occur, the way in which this happens should be flexible in order to respond to the family as needed.

There is a wide variance in the understanding of what an assessment is for both youth and caregivers. It is likely that caregivers have a traditional understanding of what assessments are, which may have been influenced by past experiences or exposure to what they have seen or read in the media. Both youth and their care-givers may be worried about the process and the ramifications for being open and honest. There should be information regarding the comprehensive nature of the assessment as well. It may appear intrusive to families if a rationale for this is not offered. In addition, if the questions do not appear related to the family's concerns, they may not feel understood or attended to. Confusion, as well as suspicion, may also arise if the areas that are assessed appear to be beyond the scope of the assessment or the practitioner. The purpose of the assessment in recognizing all needs and linking to resources should be explained (Beckman & Bristol, 1991). It should also not be assumed that the principles of empowerment (see Chapter 1 in this volume) and the wraparound process (see Chapter 3 in this volume) will be familiar or even comfortable to the family and youth, as it does represent a paradigm shift in the way in which services are received. The principles that appear to be the most misunderstood or worrisome are related to family-driven/youth-guided processes and the strength-based premise. Many family members as well as practitioners see the family-driven/youth-guided principles as meaning that practitioners will rely on families to know what their options for care are. The practitioner's role should be explained as informing and giving recommendations that represent best practice and allowing families to make choices. In regards to strength-based services, families often worry that this philosophy will ignore needs. It is helpful to offer an orientation to assessment from both a written and oral perspective. Materials that can be left with the family, which are written in the language of the consumer, are valuable.

There is much information to provide that can fully inform a family and youth of what will occur in an assessment process. It is helpful to frame the components that make up a good and thorough assessment process. The family should be advised that it will be given choices regarding the way in which the components can occur. The role of the family, youth, and practitioner should also be clarified. The principles on which the assessment process is based should be explained and described. The options for tools and methods of obtaining the information should be discussed, and how the information will be used should be clarified. The fees, confidentiality, and reporting formats should be detailed and understood. Lastly, the family and youth should be asked if there are any conditions, barriers, or worries about the assessment process that can be addressed to ensure that it does not unduly stress the family. The orientation process should not be rushed, and assessment should not begin until the family feels comfortable and requests that the process begin. Figures 7.1 and 7.2 provide sample pages from an orientation book for young children (Houchens, 2008, pp. 5, 9).

Engaging Youth and Family

Engaging the youth and family is a process and not an event. Giving consideration to the ways in which relationships are formed can assist a practitioner in being mindful of the important elements. Engagement is essentially a relationship that facilitates the work that needs to be accomplished. Initial reactions are often impactful and difficult to overturn once an opinion is formed. Eye contact that is culturally sensitive and appropriate will invite a level of comfort. Body language is also important to attend to. Family members want to feel that they are being listened to and that their thoughts are valued and considered. Interrupting, looking away, fidgeting with objects, and not acknowledging what was said are blocks to engagement. As the practitioner listens to a family member, a level of self-awareness, good listening skills, and appropriate responses are essential (Bailey, 1991). As the family makes its assessment of how the practitioner will be of value to the family, all of these areas are being taken into consideration.

Figure 7.1
Sample Orientation Information Regarding Assessment

A caseworker named Cindy came to our house to talk to us.

She asked us lots of questions. She wanted to know what things we were already good at and what things we wanted to do better.

I said that I wanted to do better in school and Mommy said she wanted me to behave better.

Reprinted with permission from Crystal Houchens.

Figure 7.2
Sample Orientation Information Regarding Child and Family Teams

Cindy said that one of our first steps was to do an assessment of our strengths and needs. While we were in the process of finding our strengths and needs we made a crisis intervention plan and formed a team of all the people who would be helping us out.

The crisis intervention plan had steps in it that explained what we should do it I or Mommy had a really bad day and didn't know what to do.

Our Family Team had Mommy, Grandma, my teacher Miss Marie, My caseworker Cindy, and ---of course--- ME in it.

Reprinted with permission from Crystal Houchens.

COMPONENTS OF ASSESSMENT PROCESS

Assessing Caregiver Strengths and Needs

There is nothing more impactful and important to youth than the relationship they have with their caregivers. There is great importance in understanding the functioning of the caregivers in order to strengthen needed areas by utilizing their innate capabilities. It is important to communicate the tremendous significance of the caregivers to the youth and validate the need to find ways to meet caregivers' needs to, in turn, assist the youth. Interviewing the caregivers through a strength-based format can yield a great deal of information, although observation and information from referral and support networks also offer relevant data.

Assessing Individual Strengths and Needs

It is important to understand as clearly and comprehensively as possible how youth function and who they are as individuals. Youth should never be forgotten as part of a family system, although their functioning in other environments (e.g., school and community) is a relevant and a significant part of their lives. Input from relevant others, such as teachers, will also be necessary to provide important perspectives of those who interact with youth on a regular basis. Time should be given to developing a relationship with youth and facilitating their sharing of their perspectives and concerns. Through time spent with youth in multiple environments, which are part of their routines, their strengths and needs will become apparent.

Determining Family Strengths and Needs

The family is the system in which an individual develops and builds skills for interacting with others and the broader community. The dynamics that affect youth include the ways in which the caregivers function, the relationships they have with their individual caregivers, the relationships they have with their siblings, and the overall tone and quality of their relationships with their families as a whole. Family characteristics that represent resiliency, such as adaptability, communication, and mutual investment in one another, are strong influences in youth development. The understanding of how a family operates and the ways in which interventions can most be helpful should be a part of every assessment process.

CONCLUSION

The assessment process is the foundation on which service planning is built. Without this strong foundation, interventions would be weak at best. At worst, these interventions would be irrelevant and ineffective in impacting change. The initial assessment, although it has time frames, will be an ongoing learning process. New information and understandings may evolve, as the relationship between practitioners and families strengthens. This ever-changing understanding should always be used to modify and rebuild a functional service plan.

References

Bailey, D. B. (1991). Issues and perspectives on family assessment. *Infants and Young Children, 4*(1), 26-34.

Beckman, P. J., & Bristol, M. M. (1991). Issues in developing the IFSP: A framework for establishing family outcomes. *Topics in Early Childhood Special Education, 11*(3), 19-31.

Caplan, E., Blankenship., K., & McManus, M. (1998). Family participation in policymaking. *Focal Point: A National Bulletin on Family Support & Children's Mental Health, 12*(1), 1-32.

Carrilio, T. E. (2007). *Home-visiting strategies: A case-management guide for caregivers.* Columbia: University of South Carolina Press.

Cheon, J. W. (2008). Convergence of a strengths perspective and youth development: Toward youth promotion practice. *Advances in Social Work 9*, 176-190.

Cornett, S. (2009). *The impact of culture: Early childhood mental health continuing studies guidelines.* Retrieved January, 9, 2010, from http://www.iaitmh.org/cmhc/csg/5-ImpactCulture.pdf

Cox, K. F. (2006). Investigating the impact of strength-based assessment on youth with behavioral or emotional disorders. *Journal of Child and Family Studies, 15*, 287-301.

Duchnowski, A. J., & Kutash, K. (2007). *Family-driven care.* Tampa: University of South Florida, The Louis de la Parte Florida Mental Health Institute, Department of Child and Family Studies.

Early, T. J., & Poertner, J. (1995). Examining current approaches to case management for families with children who have serious emotional disorders. In. B. J. Friesen & J. Poertner (Eds.), *From case management to service coordination for children with emotional, behavioral, or mental disorders: Building on family strengths* (pp. 37-59). Baltimore: Paul H. Brookes Publishing.

Epstein, M. (1999). The development and validation of a scale to assess the emotional and behavioral strengths of children and adolescents. *Remedial & Special Education, 20*, 258-262.

Epstein, M. H., Harniss, M. K., Pearson, N., & Ryser, G. (1999). The Behavioral and Emotional Rating Scale: Test-retest and inter-rater reliability. *Journal of Child & Family Studies, 8*, 319-327.

Epstein, M. H., Harniss, M. K., Robbins, V., Wheeler, L., Cyrulik, S., Kriz, M., et al. (2003). Strength-based approaches to assessment in school. In M. D.Weist, S. W. Evans, & N. A. Lever (Eds.), *Handbook of school mental health: Advancing practice and research* (pp. 285-300). New York: Kluwer Academic/Plenum Publishers.

Epstein, M. H., & Sharma, J. (1998). *Behavioral and Emotional Rating Scale: A strength-based approach to assessment.* Austin, TX: PRO-ED.

Garmezy, N. (1994). Reflections and commentary on risk, resilience, and development. In R. J. Haggerty, L. R. Sherrod, N. Garmezy, & M. Rutter (Eds.), *Stress, risk, and resilience, in children and adolescents: Processes, mechanisms, and interventions* (pp. 1-18). Cambridge, England: Cambridge University Press.

Houchens, C. (2008). *A children's guidebook to intensive youth services.* Unpublished manuscript.

Laursen, E. K. (2004). Creating a change-oriented, strength-based milieu. *Reclaiming Children and Youth, 13*, 16-21.

Lyons, J. S. (2004). *Redressing the emperor: Improving our children's public mental health service system.* Westport, CT: Praeger.

Lyons, J. S., & Bell, S. (2003). Young adults' needs and strengths assessment: An information tool for young adults with mental health challenges. Winnetka, IL: Praed Foundation.

Lyons, J. S., Cornett, S., & Walton, B. (2009). *Child and adolescent needs and strengths: Comprehensive multisystem assessment (birth to 5)*. Winnetka, IL: Praed Foundation.

Lyons, J. S., Ryan (Cornett), S., & Duran, F. (2007). *Child and adolescent needs and strengths, (early childhood): An information integration tool for young children ages birth to eight*. Winnetka, IL: Buddin Praed Foundation.

Mashinot, B. (2008). *The changing face of the United States: The influence of culture on child development*. Washington, DC: Zero to Three.

Meisels, S. J., & Provence, S. (1989). *Screening and assessment: Guidelines for identifying young disabled and developmentally vulnerable children and their families*. (A Report of the National Early Childhood Technical Assistance System). Washington, DC: Zero to Three/ National Center for Clinical Infant Programs.

Mendenhall, J. (1990). *Family-centered assessment: Six central elements*. Eagan, MN: Project Dakota Outreach.

Miles, P., Bruns, E. J., Osher, T. W., Walker, J. S., & National Wraparound Initiative Advisory Group (2006). *The wraparound process user's guide: A handbook for families*. Portland, OR: National Wraparound Initiative Resource and Training Center on Family Support and Children's Mental Health, Portland State University.

Olson, P. P., & Hains, A. H. (1992). Birth to three time line. In S. Robbins (Ed.), *Toward parent and professional partnership: Guidelines for Wisconsin's individualized family service plan* (p. 7). Madison, WI: Division of Community Services.

Osher, T. W., Osher, D., & Blau, G. (2006). *Shifting gears to family-driven care: Ambassadors tool kit*. Rockville, MD: Federation of Families for Children's Mental Health.

Rapp, C. A., & Goscha, R. J. (2006). *The strengths model: Case management with people with Psychiatric disabilities* (2nd ed.). New York: Oxford University Press.

Richmond, M. (1922). *What is social casework? An introductory description*. New York: Russell Sage Foundation.

Rosin, P., Jesien, G. S., Whitehead, A. D., & Begun, A. L. (1996). *Partnerships in family-centered care: A guide to collaborative early intervention*. Baltimore: Paul H. Brookes Publishing.

Rotto, K., McIntyre, J. S., & Serkin, C. (2008). Strengths-based, individualized services in systems of care. In B. Stroul & G. Blau (Eds.), *The system of care handbook: Transforming mental health services for children, youth and families* (pp. 401-435). Baltimore: Paul H. Brookes Publishing.

Saleebey, D. (1996). The strengths perspective in social work practice: Extensions and cautions. *Social Work 41*, 296-305.

Sharlin, S. A., & Shamai, M. (1995). Intervention with families in extreme distress (FED). *Marriage and Family Review, 21*, 92-122.

Walker, J. S., Bruns, E. J., Vandenberg, J. D., Rast, J., Osher, T. W., Miles, P., et al. (2004). *Phases and activities of the wraparound process*. Portland, OR: National Wraparound Initiative, Research and Training Center on Family Support and Children's Mental Health, Portland State University.

Walker, J. S., & Child, B. (2008). *Involving youth in planning for their education, treatment, and services: Research tells us we should be doing better*. Portland, OR: Research and Training Center on Family Support and Children's Mental Health, Portland State University.

Weick, A., Rapp, C., Sullivan, W. P., & Kisthardt, W. (1989). A strengths perspective for social work practice. *Social Work, 34*, 350-354.

Werner, E. E. (2000). Protective factors and individual resilience. In J. P. Shonkoff & S. J. Meisels (Eds.), *Handbook of early intervention* (2nd ed.) (pp. 115-132). New York: Cambridge University Press.

Werner, E. E., Randolph, S. M., & Masten, A. S. (1996). *Fostering resiliency in kids: Overcoming adversity.* Proceedings of the Consortium of Social Sciences Associations, Washington, DC.

Werner, E. E., & Smith, R. S. (1989). *Vulnerable but invincible: A longitudinal study of resilient children and youth.* New York: Adams, Bannister, Cox.

Werner, E. E., & Smith, R. S. (1992). *Overcoming the odds: High risk children from birth to adulthood.* Ithaca, NY: Cornell University Press.

Yoe, J. T., Santarcangelo, S., Atkins, M., & Burchard, J. D. (1996). Wraparound care in Vermont: Program development, implementation, and evaluation of a statewide system of individualized services. *Journal of Child and Family Studies, 5*, 23-39.

Exhibit 7.1
Clarifying Roles of Child and Family Team Members

Concepts

The following concepts, which are called "wraparound principles," are the fundamental beliefs of how services should be offered to youth and families:

- *Voice and Choice*: The youth and family must be full and active partners throughout the assessment, treatment planning, and service delivery process. Families and youth make choices that are informed by staff giving them options about how services are delivered, what types of services are offered, where services are delivered, and by whom.
- *Youth and CFT:* The wraparound approach must include the family and youth making a decision regarding who will be on a CFT that is designed to make decisions about care. A team may consist of the caregivers and youth, providers, and many others such as teachers, family members, ministers, coaches, or other service providers who are in a youth's life.
- *Community-Based Services:* Wraparound services are most effective when practitioners understand the community that a youth and family lives in and offers supports in the places where they interact such as home, school, and the community.
- *Cultural Competence:* The process must be built on a solid understanding of the unique values, preferences, and strengths of children and families, and their communities.
- *Individualized and Strength-Based Services:* Services and supports must be individualized and built on the strengths of the family and youth, and services must meet the needs of youth and families across life domains to promote success, safety, and permanence in home, school. and community. Everyone's plan is unique and special in order to meet his/her needs.
- *Natural Supports:* This value reflects the strong benefit of utilizing the people in a family's life who they would normally turn to first. If families are not able to identify natural helpers, practitioners can assist in developing them. This way, when services end, there are ongoing supports that every youth and family can benefit from.
- *Continuation of Care:* There must be unconditional commitment to serve the youth and family.
- *Collaboration:* It is of utmost importance that all services and supports are coordinated and that good communication between CFT members occurs.
- *Outcome-Based Services:* The CFT will develop a plan for how to determine success at meeting goals. One way is to measure progress by using an assessment process that will be reviewed at treatment planning time and at least every six months if services remain in place that long.

Youth's and Families' Roles

- Help the CFT understand the family's and youth's wishes, preferences, and areas that need to be focused on.
- Work with the resource facilitator and CFT to determine how services are going.

Wraparound Facilitator's Roles

- Collaborate with family and youth to identify needs and strengths.
- Coordinate the development of a crisis plan and monitor its effectiveness.
- Organize and facilitate CFT meetings.
- Ensure that everyone involved is following the above principles and that plans are moving things forward.
- Assist the family and youth in determining when they are ready to prepare to discontinue wraparound services and what needs to be in place afterwards.
- Ensure that the family and youth feel prepared to determine and coordinate meeting their needs in a way that is best for the family and youth in the future.

(Continued)

Exhibit 7.1 *(Continued)*

Child and Family Team Members' Roles

- Provide services or supports as agreed upon and inform resource facilitator of any challenges or needed changes.
- Attend monthly meetings to assist in identifying strengths and needs, supporting crisis plan development and updates, and designing plans to help in a coordinated fashion.
- Give feedback between meetings to resource facilitator if a decision needs to be made.
- Discuss any new issues or concerns that should be brought up at meetings with the resource facilitator prior to the meetings so adequate time and family involvement/feedback can be obtained.

Signature of CFT Member: _____

Date: _____

Exhibit 7.2
Young Adult Needs and Strengths Assessment

Functioning
  Physical/Medical
  Family
  Peer/Social Experience
  Intellectual/Developmental
  Knowledge of Illness
  Independent Living Skills
  Residential Stability
  Transportation
  Caregiving Roles
  Intimate Relations
  Monitoring
  Treatment
  Self-Care
  Medication Compliance

Mental Health
  Adjustment to Trauma
  Anti-Social Behavior
  Impulse Control
  Depression/Anxiety
  Psychosis
  Consistency across situations
  Consistency over time
  Motivation for Care
  Personality Disorder

Culture
  Language
  Cultural Identity
  Ritual
  Cultural Stress

Education/Vocational
  Educational Functioning
  Educational Attainment
  Job Functioning

Risk Behaviors
  Danger to Self
  Danger to Others
  Social Behavior
  Sexually Inappropriate Behavior
  Crime
  Environmental Cues
  Victimization

Substance Abuse
  Alcohol/Drug Use
  Duration of Alcohol/Drug Use
  State of Recovery

Strengths
  Family Involvement
  Spiritual/Religious
  Vocational/Career
  Educational
  Interpersonal
  Relationship Permanence
  Talent/Interests
  Inclusion
  Service Permanence
  Coping and Enjoying
  Resiliency
  Resourcefulness

Caregiver Needs and Strengths
  Physical/Behavioral
  Involvement with care
  Knowledge
  Resources
  Organization
  Safety

(Continued)

Exhibit 7.2 *(Continued)*

The basic design for rating NEEDS is:

A rating of **'0'** reflects *no evidence*,

A rating of **'1'** reflects a *mild degree of the dimension*,

A rating of **'2'** reflects a *moderate degree of the dimension*, and

A rating of **'3'** reflects a *severe or profound degree of the dimension*

The basic design for rating STRENGTHS is:

A rating of **'0'** reflects *a significant strength that is present*,

A rating of **'1'** reflects *that a moderate level of the strength is present*,

A rating of **'2'** reflects that *a mild level of the strength is present*, and

A rating of **'3'** reflects that *the strength is not present.*

Source: Lyons & Bell (2003, pp. 2-3).

Exhibit 7.3
Domains for Child and Adolescent Needs and Strengths:
Early Childhood (CANS: EC)

Domain One: Child Strengths

1. Family Relationships
2. Extended Family Relationships
3. Interpersonal
4. Relationship Permanence
5. Curiosity
6. Playfulness
7. Creativity/Imagination
8. Special Skills/Talents
9. Adaptability
10. Persistence
11. Self-esteem/Self-confidence

Domain Two: Functioning

12. Motor
13. Sensory
14. Developmental/Intellectual
15. Communication
16. Medical/Physical
17. Family
18. Social/Emotional
19. Self Care/Daily Living Skills
20. Parent/Child Interaction
21. Early Care/Education Settings
22. Social Behavior

Domain Three: Challenges

23. Attachment
24. Failure to Thrive
25. Anxiety
26. Adjustment to Trauma
27. Oppositional Behavior
28. Aggression
29. Depression
30. Atypical Behaviors
31. Sleep
32. Impulsivity/Hyperactivity
33. Attention
34. Current Environmental Stressors

Domain Four: Care Intensity and Organization

35. Service Intensity
36. Funding/Eligibility
37. Transportation

(Continued)

Exhibit 7.3 *(Continued)*

38. Service Permanence
39. Service Coordination
40. Service Access/Availability
41. Cultural Appropriateness of Services

Domain Five: Caregiver Strengths and Needs

42. Supervision
43. Involvement with Care
44. Knowledge
45. Organization
46. Cultural Diversity
47. Language
48. Spirituality
49. Physical Health
50. Behavioral Health
51. Substance Use
52. Education
53. Employment
54. Housing
55. Financial Resources
56. Social Resources

Source: Lyons, Ryan (Cornett), & Duran (2007).

Exhibit 7.4
Indiana Comprehensive Child and Adolescent Needs
and Strengths (CANS) Birth-5

ASSESSED DOMAINS

Child Functioning

1. Family
2. Living Situation
3. Preschool/Daycare
4. Social Functioning
5. Recreation/Play
6. Developmental
7. Motor
8. Communication
9. Medical
10. Physical
11. Sleep
12. Relationship Permanence

Child Strengths

13. Family
14. Extended Family Relationships
15. Interpersonal
16. Adaptability
17. Persistence
18. Curiosity

Acculturation

19. Language
20. Identity
21. Ritual
22. Cultural Stress
23. Cultural Differences

Caregiver Needs and Strengths

24. Supervision
25. Involvement
26. Knowledge
27. Empathy for Child
28. Organization
29. Social Resources
30. Residential Stability
31. Physical
32. Mental Health
33. Substance Use
34. Developmental

(Continued)

Exhibit 7.4 *(Continued)*

35. Accessibility to Care
36. Family Stress
37. Safety

Child Behavioral/Emotional Needs

38. Attachment
39. Regulatory
40. Failure to Thrive
41. Depression
42. Anxiety
43. Atypical Behaviors
44. Impulsivity/Hyper
45. Oppositional
46. Adjustment to Trauma

Child Risk Behaviors

47. Birth Weight
48. Pica
49. Prenatal Care
50. Labor and Delivery
51. Substance Exposure
52. Parent or Sibling Problems
53. Maternal Availability
54. Self Harm
55. Abuse/Neglect
56. Social Behavior

School Module (1)

57. Preschool/Daycare Quality
58. Preschool/Day Care Behavior
59. Preschool/Day Care Achievement
60. Preschool/Day Care Attendance

Developmental Module (2)

61. Cognitive
62. Self Care/Daily Living

Family/Caregiver Module (3)

63. Self Care/Daily Living
64. Culture Stress
65. Employment/Education
66. Education Attainment
67. Legal
68. Motivation for Care
69. Financial Resources
70. Transportation

(Continued)

Exhibit 7.4 *(Continued)*

Trauma Module (4)

71. Sexual Abuse*
72. Physical Abuse
73. Emotional Abuse
74. Medical Trauma
75. Natural Disaster
76. Witness to Family Violence
77. Witness to Community Violence
78. Witness/Victim-Criminal Acts

*Sexual Abuse Module

79. Emotional Closeness to Perpetrator
80. Frequency
81. Duration
82. Force
83. Reaction to Disclosure

Adjustment

84. Affect Regulation
85. Re-experiencing Trauma
86. Avoidance
87. Increased Arousal
88. Numbing of Responsiveness
89. Time Before Treatment

Regulatory Module

90. Eating
91. Elimination
92. Sensory Reactivity
93. Emotional Control

Source: Lyons, Cornett, & Walton (2009).

Chapter 8

Assessing Caregivers' Strengths and Needs

*What children take from us, they give . . . We become people who feel more
deeply, hurt more deeply, and love more deeply.*

—Sonia Taitz

*The central struggle of parenthood is to let our hopes for our children out-
weigh our fears.*

—Ellen Goodman

INTRODUCTION

The critical impact that caregivers have on youth has long been recognized. In 2000, *Neurons to Neighborhoods: The Science of Early Childhood Development* (Shonkoff, Phillips, & Board on Children, Youth, and Families (États-Unis), Committee on Integrating the Science of Early Childhood Development, 2000) compiled the most current and up-to-date research on early childhood development. One of its main conclusions was as follows: "Children grow and thrive in the context of close and dependable relationships that provide love and nurturance, security, responsive interaction, and encouragement for exploration. Without at least one such relationship, development is disrupted and the consequences can be severe and long-standing" (p. 7). Despite this long-standing recognition, what seems to have sometimes lagged behind in supporting youth with serious emotional challenges is the clinical focus on empowering caregivers to meet the unique needs of their youth. Often practitioners, when asked to intervene with a youth struggling with mental health conditions, focus heavily on individual interventions and miss opportunities to build and support caregivers' capacities. This chapter assists the practitioner in identifying the structure and essential elements of the caregiver assessment. This process will result in an initial understanding of the caregivers' strengths and needs related to core capacities, which will later be used to construct a service plan.

STRUCTURING CAREGIVER ASSESSMENT

Prior to an assessment process taking place, it is of utmost importance that caregivers and youth are fully engaged in the process. This process can be described as a mutual discovery of needs and strengths that will later be used to develop a plan for intervention (see Chapter 7). Caregivers may feel threatened by the notion of assessing their functioning, and previous experiences in which they felt blamed for their youth's behaviors may underlie this. A discussion with caregivers regarding the rationale of the needed assessment components can alleviate concerns. The first point that should be clarified is the notion that all caregivers have challenges as well as strengths related to caregiving. Attending to and valuing strategies and skills that are particularly useful may be a new experience for caregivers. Each caregiving element discussed below is to be thought of on a continuum. A caregiver, for instance, may have some strategies that periodically allow the skill to be manifested, but this easily falls apart under stress. Understanding where these strengths and challenges lie leads to successful intervention plans and ultimately wellness and recovery for the family. This can and should be communicated in a supportive manner that is in line with the concept that no one is more important to youth than their caregivers. Each component of the caregiver assessment has purpose and value related to the goal of understanding needs and strengths. The interview gives caregivers an opportunity to reflect on their abilities without the youth present. Caregivers can feel free to explore their own needs, feelings, and reactions to their youth in this setting. Observing interactions within the family is critical in that it allows for an understanding of dynamics that caregivers may be unable to explain. Caregivers should also be asked to permit review of pertinent records that will help the practitioner gain an understanding of past or current experiences with services. Reviewing the records with the caregivers or minimally asking caregivers to relate their experiences with other service providers also ensures an environment of mutuality. Later in the assessment process, when the practitioner meets with the youth and hears their perspective on family functioning, this too will be integrated into the overall assessment. The order in which the assessment of caregiving capacity takes place can be individualized to meet the needs of the family, and the components typically overlap one another.

ESSENTIAL ELEMENTS OF CAREGIVER ASSESSMENT

This section lists areas that should be considered in the assessment of caregiving needs and strengths. Youth with serious emotional disturbances require a great deal of caregiving support, and a comprehensive understanding of caregivers' abilities in this area is therefore a necessary component. The order in which these areas are assessed is not important, and additional areas may be relevant based on the uniqueness of each family. The impact of each element on youth is discussed to substantiate the relevance of each element. In addition, specific areas to understand, questions to ask, important observations, and possible causative factors for challenges are offered to guide the assessment of each element. Last, strategies on synthesizing the information are discussed to assist in arriving at a conclusion regarding the level of need or strength within each area.

Ability to Provide for Basic Needs of Youth

Critical Nature of Element. As Maslow has so clearly described in his 1943 paper, *A Theory of Human Motivation,* all of us are first in need of having our physiological needs met. Maslow defines physiological needs as the availability of food and water, and the presence of the bodily functions of breathing, sex, sleep, homeostasis, and excretion (Maslow, 1943). If the basic elements of physiological needs are not met, the higher order needs of safety, love and belonging, esteem, and self-actualization will not occur. Interestingly, this too is how the attachment relationship unfolds. Infants, as their basic needs are met, will begin to develop a sense of security that later evolves into a loving relationship and bond with their primary caregivers.

Erickson and Egeland (2002), report that the most commonly studied form of neglect is physical neglect. The definition that they offer for basic needs includes the availability of adequate food, water, shelter, and clothing. For purposes of this assessment element, this definition will be utilized. Youth who do not have their basic needs met will likely develop a host of challenges in several areas. The Pennsylvania Child Welfare Training Program, University of Pittsburgh (2009), has developed materials that illustrate the effects of abuse and neglect on youth (see Table 8.1).

Facilitating a Conversation. The discussion of basic needs may be one that is somewhat sensitive. Bringing recognition to the fact that there is a broad range of beliefs and practices in this area, which vary between families and cultures, will again communicate the desire to appreciate each family's uniqueness. The following will guide the exploration of this element:

- *What are the caregiver's beliefs about basic needs?* It is important not to assume that the caregiver automatically identifies basic needs in the way that has been previously outlined. Additionally, if two caregivers are involved, there may be a lack of agreement about this. Although it would be rare for caregivers not to agree that all youth need food, water, clothing, and shelter, how they interpret what these needs are is the critical element. Additionally, the practitioner wants to use this as an opportunity to learn if there are any cultural influences unique to the family that need to be considered.

Questions That May Evoke Understanding

What are your thoughts about diet and nutrition? Does your child have any specific needs in this area?

What are your thoughts about clothing needs for your child? Does your child have specific demands or issues regarding clothing?

How do you feel homelessness would affect your child?

Have there been any conflicts regarding these areas with your partner or spouse?

Table 8.1
Possible Effects of Neglect

Infants/Toddlers	Preschoolers	School-Age Youth	Adolescents
Physical Slow Growth Poor Muscle Tone Poor Motor Control Delayed Fine and/ or Gross Motor Development Impaired Brain Development	*Physical* Delayed Physical Growth Frequent Illness Poor Coordination and Muscle Strength	*Physical* General Physical Delays Poor Coordination Poor Visual Spatial Skills Frequent Illness	*Physical* Frequent Somatic Complaints and Illnesses Sensory, Motor, and Coordination Challenges Delayed Puberty
Cognitive Generalized Cognitive Delay Communication Delays Failure to Explore Environment Poor Problem-Solving Skills	*Cognitive* Poor Concentration Poor Attention Span Poor Thinking and Reasoning Skills Speech and Language Delays	*Cognitive* Egocentric Thinking Poor Organization of Thoughts Speech Challenges Poor Academic Skills and Performance	*Cognitive* Poor Sequence of Thought Poor Perspective Taking Ability Poor Academic Ability
Social Poor Attachment Relationship With Primary Caregiver(s) Unresponsive to Adults or Overly Affectionate Poor Play or Peer Interaction	*Social* Difficulty With Separation From Caregiver Withdrawal From Adults and Peers Immature Play Skills	*Social* Inability to Use Adults for Support Poor Friendship Making Skills Inappropriate Reactions to Praise or Constant Seeking of Approval Poor Ability to Understand Social Cues and Expectations	*Social* Immature Social Interactions Strained Adult Relations Poor Understanding of Others' Feelings Poor Adherence and Understanding of Social Rules
Emotional Depression Anxiety Clingy Behavior Poor Regulation of Emotion Self-Stimulation: Thumb Sucking, Rocking, Head Banging Tantrums or Aggression	*Emotional* Excessively Fearful Poor Self-Esteem Depression Lack of Initiative Poor Regulation of Emotion Self-Stimulation	*Emotional* Lack of Self-Confidence Frequent Emotional Outbursts Poor Ability to Delay Gratification Poor Coping Strategies Depression Anxiety	*Emotional* Mood Disorders Aggressive or Impulsive Behavior Intense or Volatile Emotions Unrealistic Goals for Future Identity Confusion

Source: Pennsylvania Child Welfare Training Program, University of Pittsburgh: School of Social Work Online Curricula (2009).

Do you believe that others within your community or extended family see these issues differently than you?

Do you have some practices or beliefs regarding these issues that are unique to your family?

- *What are the strategies the caregivers have used to meet needs?* Learning about specific routines related to basic needs and the prioritization of these routines gives useful information.

Questions That May Evoke Understanding

Can you talk about the routines you have for buying food and preparing meals?

How do you go about getting clothing for your child?

- *If there has been difficulty in this area, to what extent and duration?* Understanding the extent and duration of the problem helps practitioners appreciate the possible effects and patterns of coping that the youth and family have developed, which is again useful in service planning.

Questions That May Evoke Understanding

Do you feel that this has been a challenging area for you?

Are there others who feel this has been a challenge?

How long has this been a problem?

How would you describe what occurred?

- *If there have been stressors in this area how would the caregiver describe these stressors and their impact?* Learning about what the caregivers perceive to be the challenges assists in later developing interventions that will assist in this area. Resources and strategies that have compensated for these stressors are also important to identify for later use as interventions to support continued growth in this area.

Questions That May Evoke Understanding

What do you think are some of the reasons this has been challenging?

Were there ways that you worked through these challenges?

Were there others who were able to help in this area?

Opportunities for Observation. When meeting with caregivers within the home, there are obviously opportunities to observe the home environment, which will contribute to a better understanding of the assessment of basic needs. The home that appears well stocked with food suggests the availability of food. In addition, attending to the routines that are present around these issues and the youth's reactions to these routines contributes to an understanding in this area. If home visits occur near typical mealtimes, and there is no evidence of recent or upcoming food preparation, this can lead to a discussion that may impact understanding in this area. Attending to other factors that may impede the caregivers' capacities in this area is helpful as well. Frequent visitors, lack of structure, or discipline issues may get in the way of routines that ensure youth's needs being met. This, however, does not always translate into the caregivers' capacities to provide for the youth, especially those that are very young. Being aware of the condition of the home will also pesent possible ways to help at the intervention stage. As the assessment process continues and services begin to be provided, it is important to be continually aware of patterns that will help substantiate either the lack of, or presence of, a problem in this area.

Possible Causative Factors for Challenges in This Area. Ayoub and Jacewitz (1982) have identified that intellectual challenges, substance abuse, and physical illness, in some circumstances, are associated with child neglect. Caregivers who experience mental health challenges (e.g., anxiety, depression, or psychosis) are often unable to prioritize the needs of their youth. Paxson and Waldfogel (2002) list poverty, caregivers' work status, and absence of fathers within the family structure as contributing to child neglect. Although research gives us some understanding of possible factors, practitioners should not make assumptions. Discussing if and how these factors actually interfere with the ability to provide basic needs will lead to specific and useful interventions.

Formulating the Assessment: Putting It All Together. The ability to provide for basic needs is an area in which the indication or presence of challenges warrants action on some level due to the concern for the well-being of the youth. When this area is of concern, there is often a history of services being provided, either to the caregivers or youth, that can be reviewed to gain a broader perspective. In addition, when there is concern, the referral itself may have come from a youth-serving agency, physician, or other mental health professional. Regardless of the source of information, this offers insight that will contribute to an overall assessment. When reviewing information and discussing this with caregivers, a past history of problems is much less of a concern when caregivers are able to acknowledge and discuss the issue. When history suggests problems, it is ideal if the caregivers can demonstrate change. Recognizing change and growth is important in the provision of home-based services. Strategies would be needed to prevent a reoccurrence from happening in the future or when the caregivers are under stress. When determining the level of strength or need in this area, it is important to compile what was learned from all components of the assessment and decide if the youth's needs are met in terms of food, water, shelter, and clothing. In making this determination, the culture of the family must be respected, and practitioners should not impose their own values or beliefs on the family unfairly. If basic needs are provided for the youth, but there is a need to improve the amount or quality of what is provided, a practitioner can determine if the caregivers are in need of outside supports or resources to improve the situation. When some level of need is apparent, the various components of the assessment should address possible reasons for this (e.g., level of understanding regarding needs, financial strain, or perhaps emotional or psychological issues). It is critical to determine sources of the problems because interventions will be different if the sources are financial versus emotional or psychological in nature. Caregivers who have emotional issues that interfere with the provision of basic needs (e.g., depression or unresolved feelings of anger or rejection from their own past) often do not want or intend for their youth to be neglected. Interventions may be successful in this area. At the phase of assessment, an understanding of caregivers' needs in this area can be expected, but determining capacity can only be more fully understood once interventions take place.

Ability to Ensure a Safe Environment for Youth

Critical Nature of Element. Everyone is in need of safety and security. When safety needs are not being met, the focus will rapidly shift to preoccupation with making this occur. Youth will be stalemated in their development if their safety needs, whether physical or emotional, are not met. Physical safety refers to the absence of hazards that can harm youth. Emotional safety refers to the presence of an environment that supports acceptance, belonging, and security. Toddlers are faced with the developmental task of exploring and beginning to form relationships with other adults who can continue to support their growth. When safety and security needs are not met, there are usually delays in toddlers manifesting these capacities. This has an impact on all areas of development. Taking opportunities to explore fosters cognitive development in numerous ways. Problem-solving skills, exposure to new concepts, and learning through experience are just a few of the skills developed through exploration. Emotional and social areas of development are hindered as well in failed opportunities to develop a secure attachment to caregivers and learn skills related to forming new relationships. A toddler may appear distrustful, experience confusion, or develop low self-esteem (Michigan Association of Infant Mental Health, 2005). Even speech and motor development will not be mastered if toddlers are insecure in their own abilities and willingness to take risks. Older youth who are not afforded a safe environment are often shaky in their mastery of various developmental tasks and may exhibit regression periodically. Older youth may not have coping strategies or ego strength sufficient to protect them from ordinary and everyday stressors. In more extreme cases, when youth are exposed to chronic situations in which they are fearful, a chronic state of hyperarousal and overall sense of helplessness may occur. Additionally, youth may experience dissociative episodes when memories or emotions are activated related to their safety needs (Perry, 2001). Behaviors may be difficult to understand and leave youth, as well as caregivers, feeling powerless and misunderstood. Table 8.2 summarizes the safety needs of youth.

Facilitating a Conversation. In the assessment of safety, caregivers may have difficulty discussing this sensitive topic, as it may make them feel embarrassed, defensive, and judged. When the source of the referral revolves around safety, caregivers may feel a need to explain or discuss the issue more openly. The following will help in discussing this element and developing an assessment of this capacity:

- *How do caregivers perceive the safety needs of their youth?* Do the caregivers see emotional as well as physical safety as areas to consider? Are the perceptions consistent with the youth's developmental and emotional needs?

Questions That May Evoke Understanding

Can you describe what your child needs in order to feel safe in your home?

How has this changed over time?

Are there any special considerations that you can identify in regards to your child's safety needs?

- *What types of planning or interventions occur to prevent safety from being an issue?* How well can the caregivers anticipate situations that may be problematic? Are there strategies in place to keep the youth safe? How effective have the strategies been?

Questions That May Evoke Understanding

Do you have routines or things you have done to prevent problems from occurring?

Table 8.2
Safety Needs of Youth

Physical Needs
- Environment free of hazards.
- Level of supervision meets developmental needs.
- Caregivers respond appropriately to injury or fears.

Emotional Needs

- Supportive comments given by caregivers.
- Acceptance of youth demonstrated.
- Caregivers protect youth from verbal or physical abuse of siblings or others in home.
- Sense of belonging and connectedness to family.

When someone else in the home is caring for your child, such as a babysitter, what are the things you tell them to do to keep your child safe?

Have your strategies worked?

- *What are the caregivers' reactions when issues occur in the area of safety?* Can the caregivers solve problems when issues occur? Do emotional reactions get in the way? Are there experiences of anger, blame, or shifting of responsibility to other family members?

Questions That May Evoke Understanding

What is your initial reaction when problems occur?

How do you feel about your typical reaction?

What are your emotional reactions to problems?

- *How do youth react to the caregivers when the caregivers try to support them in this area?* Do youth appear to perceive the caregivers as supportive? Do the youth's reactions suggest difficulty accepting help?

Questions That May Evoke Understanding

Can you describe how your children react when you attempt to keep them safe?

What do you think about their reactions?

- *If problems are present in the area of safety, what are the issues that contribute to this?* Do the caregivers have insights into issues that impact their abilities to meet the youth's needs?

Questions That May Evoke Understanding

Are there issues that may have contributed to this problem?

How do you feel these issues can be addressed?

- *If there are problems present in the area of safety, what is the extent and duration of these problems?* Are the problems in this area consistent, subtle, or obvious? If there is no consistent pattern, what were the factors that contributed to the problem emerging? Do the caregivers have insights into the pervasiveness and severity of the issue?

Questions That May Evoke Understanding

Have the challenges in this area changed over time?

How long has this problem been present?

How much of a problem has this been?

Opportunities for Observation. When meeting with the family within the home environment, there now becomes a heightened ability to understand how the environment impacts the youth and family. When considering safety needs, practitioners are able to identify if the home has obvious hazards that will put the youth in danger or if it appears that appropriate provisions have been made. Practitioners can also attend to how the caregivers respond in the event that their youth are in an unsafe situation. Reactions that reflect concern and address the danger are ones that would appropriately support the youth. If the caregivers react with heightened emotionality, it is important to consider how the youth react and if, consequently, the youth are kept safe. If the youth are overwhelmed emotionally by the caregivers reactions, it is helpful to attend to how the youth relate this feeling and how the caregivers respond. Caregivers who are able to keep their youth safe physically and emotionally will anticipate problems and determine strategies that will help avoid them. Caregivers fostering acceptance and security will compliment appropriately, provide encouragement, and offer assistance to youth who are struggling. In addition, if others are emotionally abusive or threatening to youth, this will be addressed.

Possible Causative Factors for Challenges in This Area. When considering the assessment of safety issues, several factors may be worthy of consideration. Understanding possible causative factors is most relevant when determining interventions, as it can support a truer picture of caregivers needs. Caregivers who struggle with safety issues may be experiencing their own mental health or substance use challenges, which interfere with their abilities to focus adequately on their youth. When this occurs, it may become apparent that caregivers want what is best for their youth, but they are handicapped in their abilities to ensure that this occurs. Some caregivers may have past unresolved issues that result in impaired psychological functioning, which may be displayed by anger or resentment toward the youth. These feelings may be rooted in their own past experiences and may appear to the practitioner as misperceptions about the youth's intentions and behaviors. Caregivers may have experiences in their early childhoods in which their own safety needs were met with anger or abuse. In this case, caregivers who have been traumatized in this manner may not be able to acknowledge their youth's needs and may even dissociate (Crittenden, Lang, Claussen, & Partridge, 2000).

Formulating the Assessment: Putting It All Together. Safety, along with the ability to provide for basic needs, is one element in which a need is present if the youth is at risk some or all of the time or if the strategies for ensuring safety need improvement. There may be excellent supervision and provisions for safety within certain time frames or situations but not in others. The quality of the supervision may be marginal and leave room for improvement. The safety needs may be met primarily by the siblings in the home. In assessing this area of caregiver functioning, the important elements to be aware of include level of awareness in the caregivers, openness to support, and the factors that make ensuring safety challenging for the caregivers. When caregivers struggle in this area and are open to support, this is always a better scenario than when a desire for support is not present. When caregivers do not recognize this issue or disagree about the presence of the issue, the practitioner will need to ensure that the youth can be kept safe. Caregivers show strength in this area when it is consistently attended to and skills are in place to anticipate and predict needs. Caregivers who demonstrate paying attention to their youth's reactions and needs show an additional strength of attunement and connectedness that is extremely beneficial to youth.

Presence of Structure Within the Home

Critical Nature of Element. Structure refers to the ability to establish and maintain healthy routines and schedules for a balance of leisure time, chores, responsibilities, and quiet time. A household that provides a sense of structure also supports a sense of predictability and consistency regarding the when, what, who, where, and how of each day. Routines may revolve around mealtimes, before- and after-school times, and bedtime. Klass (2008) defines rituals as the "everyday routines that make up the shared lives of parents and their children" (p. 227). She further explains that "the safe and predictable space that a child finds in these everyday patterns is much like the traditional rituals, such as religious services, holidays, or birthday celebrations" (p. 227) The value of routines and rituals is the formation of an identity as a member of a family, a shared understanding of values and beliefs, and a support for continued growth and development. As these are the times that may result in the most behavioral concerns, it is helpful to have consistency and predictability about what will occur. Caregivers, who assist their youth in understanding precisely what is expected of them and what will occur if it does not happen, are more likely to contain behavioral issues and reduce unnecessary anxiety or frustration in their youth. Youth who are not provided with assistance in structuring their time often report feeling bored or unchallenged, and problems may occur. Youth who are challenged with emotional or behavioral issues have a strong need for structure. Booth and Jernberg (1999) state that "although all children benefit from the predictability of structure, this dimension is most important for children who are overactive, unfocused, over-stimulated or who have an anxious need to be in control" (p. 18).

Facilitating a Conversation. When introducing the topic of structure to the caregivers, there is a need to have a common understanding of what is meant by structure within the home. Many caregivers will need assistance separating the overall structure of the home from what actually occurs for the youth. Understanding both of these components is helpful, especially when the family's needs and experiences with structure are different than the youth's. The following questions will assist with this element:

- *What are the caregivers' beliefs about the need for structure within the home?* This question will offer an understanding of the value the caregivers place on structuring the home environment. It may also lead to discussion regarding the caregivers' own experiences with this as children. This will help to more fully understand the caregivers' perspectives as well.

Questions That May Evoke Understanding

How would you describe the activities and goings on within your household from day to day?

How important do you feel it is for children to have help with planning their daily activities?

How do you think it affects children when there are frequent changes in the household in terms of who is present in the home and what occurs within the home?

How would you describe your child's need for structure compared to yours or the siblings within the household?

- *How is the youth's time structured within the home?* Gathering specific information regarding how the youth's time is spent and how predictable or planned his/her day is helps to substantiate whether structure is a problem area.

Questions That May Evoke Understanding

Can you describe your child's activities on a typical school day?

How does your child usually spend his/her time on the weekends?

Does your child have chores or responsibilities?

What types of things does your child like to do in his/her free time?

Does your child rely on you to help him/her plan his day?

Is this the same from day to day?

- *How predictable and consistent are the family's patterns and routines?* When caregivers are asked to relate examples regarding routines, it gives them the opportunity to think more specifically about the topic. Questions that are too general may not help to grasp an understanding.

Questions That May Evoke Understanding

How would you describe your family's routine for meals?

Do you eat meals around the same time every day?

How would you describe your activities around bedtime and in the mornings?

Are there different rules for weekdays and weekends?

Would you describe your household as a busy one with lots of visitors?

Do most days seem the same or different?

If days are not often the same, what are some reasons for that?

- *How do the caregivers determine what the youth's needs in terms of structure are?* The practitioner wants to learn if the youth's unique needs are clear to the caregivers in this area and how well the caregivers can attend to the youth's way of communicating these needs.

Questions That May Evoke Understanding

What would you say your child does to show you if he/she needs more or less structure?

Can you think of some examples where this occurred?

What have you learned over time about your child's needs in this area?

How does your child respond to changes in the routine?

Is it challenging to figure out ways to help your child in this area?

Is what your child needs from you in this area difficult to make happen?

- *Do the caregivers perceive that there are any challenges in providing structure?* This question helps to determine if issues interfere with the provision of structure within the home. In addition, do the caregivers feel challenged in how this need may be different from time to time with the child?

Questions That May Evoke Understanding

Is what your child needs from you in this area difficult to make happen?

Do you feel your child has the right amount of structure?

Is it hard to figure out when and how the need changes from time to time?

What do you feel gets in the way of this?

What might you or others have done that has made this easier?

Opportunities for Observation. As the practitioner interacts with the family and takes opportunities to learn how the family functions, there are many areas to attend to in terms of structure. Table 8.3 illustrates some of these areas.

Possible Causative Factors for Challenges in This Area. When there are challenges for the caregivers in the area of structure, it may well be that the caregivers do not recognize the level of chaos or unpredictability. Some caregivers may have been in an environment of unpredictability or change as long as they can remember. Their determination of this being problematic may be different than the practitioner. It is important for the practitioner to recognize this and not make assumptions that it is problematic for the youth. Cultural and family differences are important to understand in this circumstance. When youth clearly are in need of more structure, as evidenced by their remarks or behavioral disturbances that clearly are linked to lack of structure, caregivers may be preoccupied or overwhelmed with their own issues. Often, caregivers are able to express this and relate challenges in managing various household duties, challenges in caring for the various needs of their youth, depression, anxiety, or other mental health challenges as being related to problems in this area.

Formulating the Assessment: Putting It All Together. Clearly, youth benefit from some degree of structure within the home. Caregivers who do not have regular routines of any sort, or strategies to determine how the youth are affected, may be at the highest level of need in this area. Caregivers who assess that they do not have

Table 8.3
Observing Structure Within the Home

- Do the youth or caregivers make comments about what should (or usually) occur during time frames when you are present?
- Do the caregivers and youth refer to routines and activities when they discuss issues or successes?
- When entering or leaving the home, are there activities that are occurring on a regular basis?
- Are there frequent visitors or mention of visitors?
- Do the caregivers assist the youth in setting expectations for what they are to do? Do the youth make these determinations alone?

regular routines or predictability, and believe change would be beneficial to the youth, have a level of need that is mediated somewhat by their desire for change. Typically, it is wise to pay close attention to youth who relate needs in this area. If youth are pointing this out, it is most likely disruptive or reflective of unique needs of the youth who are not being understood or met. As in most of the elements, it may be the case that what is described and what is seen within the home does not match. In this case, pointing this out to caregivers in a supportive manner can either confirm or negate the assessment, although strong emphasis should be placed on what is observed. Caregivers who have creative, consistent, and effective strategies for this clearly show strengths in this area. Caregivers may display the ability to be flexible with their youth, yet still maintain structure and consistency. Additionally, caregivers who provide for the unique needs of all of their youth in ways that are different, yet effective, are displaying significant skills in this area.

Capacity for Disciplining and Limit Setting

Critical Nature of Element. Providing discipline and limit setting to youth in a manner that is empathetic and supportive has numerous positive effects. These youth will be less likely to experience behavior problems and antisocial behavior (Brenner & Fox, 1998; Chamberlain & Patterson, 1995, as cited in Houck & LeCuyer-Maus, 2002). When youth experience limit setting that provides clear limits, gives reasons, and is done in an empathetic manner, they are better able to develop self-regulation (Houck & LeCuyer-Maus, 2002). In addition, it has been found that the more youth are given opportunities to learn from their own reactions and behaviors, the more they are able to do this on their own (Kopp, 1982). Youth who have particular challenges with anger control or behavioral control are particularly in need of extra support in this area. Youth need to know that caregivers will be available and present to ensure that support, teaching, and limit setting will occur as needed. This, although often resisted by youth, also affords them a sense of security in knowing that when they become "out of control," the caregivers will assist them in regaining control. When caregivers are functioning well in this area, the youth in the home are typically more relaxed and secure that their needs will be me. Authoritative caregiving has been defined as providing clear expectations and high demands in an emotionally supporting and responsive manner. This form of caregiving is thought to provide the most support for the development of behavioral control and social competence (Baumrind, 1991). Youth with emotional challenges may be impulsive and unable to read the social cues of others. This puts them at a disadvantage for successfully relating to others and maintaining behavioral control. In this case, the caregivers are in need of coaching these skills and using limit setting and discipline as a way to do this. These strategies, which may be preventative as well as a reaction to poor choices, serve to promote skill development in the youth. Youth can then internalize the need for and ability to execute needed skills to support their social and emotional growth.

Facilitating a Conversation. Most caregivers who have youth with emotional challenges experience difficulties in behavioral management. Helping caregivers to share how well they can determine the needs of their youth for limit setting and strategies to provide this will be the goal. The following questions will assist in the interview process:

- *How do the caregivers feel about the need for limit setting and determining when it is needed?* The focus of this question is to ensure that the practitioner understands the basic values and beliefs about limit setting that the caregivers have. The understanding of this should, as with every element, be filtered through a cultural lens. Maybe even more so than other areas, this element has different manifestations for what is seen as normal within the various cultures.

Questions That May Evoke Understanding

How would you describe what you believe children need in terms of discipline?

What do you think your child needs from you in this area?

How do you decide that you need to discipline your child?

Do you do this in the same way for all your children? Do they have different needs in this area?

- *What are the strategies caregivers utilize with regard to limit setting?* It is helpful to understand the range of strategies that are currently used as well as in the past. Allowing and supporting the caregivers in relating their reasoning for the various strategies is beneficial.

Questions That May Evoke Understanding

What are some of the ways you are comfortable teaching and enforcing limits with your child?

What typically happens when your child misbehaves?

Are your strategies different in the home versus the community?

- *How do the caregivers decide that their strategies are appropriate or need to change?* This question helps the practitioner determine how the developmental level of the youth is considered in disciplining. In addition, it helps provide an appreciation for the level of planning and problem-solving capacity within this process. How the caregivers see the changing needs of the youth and how they have responded to this will be learned as well.

Questions That May Evoke Understanding

How do you decide if your strategies are the right ones?

Do you do this alone or with the help of others?

What have been some of your strategies in the past?

How are these strategies different now?

How do you decide if you want to change your strategies?

- *What do caregivers see as barriers or supports to successful limit setting and disciplining?* This clarifies what may be underlying challenges as well as successes in this area.

Questions That May Evoke Understanding

What makes limit setting difficult?

What makes it easier to do?

Are there people that help or hinder the process?

Are there certain situations in which things go better or worse?

Opportunities for Observation. In a home-based assessment process, there can and should be opportunities to learn the everyday routines and nuances of the home. Caregivers seen in home visits may or may not need to support their behavior or direct their interactions. If the opportunity arises, the timing of when the caregivers choose to intervene should be observed. How the caregivers communicate—the clarity, tone of voice, and content of what they say—needs to be assessed. In addition, the ability to enforce and follow up with the interaction should be considered. Family members may also give clues to how consistent these interactions with everyday experiences are. If this occurs, caregivers can be asked to discuss how closely the current interactions match what typically occurs. If opportunities for observing this do not appear naturally, practitioners can ask caregivers to allow them to observe a time when rules are enforced (e.g., chore time).

Possible Causative Factors for Challenges in This Area. Caregivers who have difficulty providing consistent, nurturing, and supportive limit setting do so for a number of reasons. Caregivers who may not have experienced this in their own childhoods may not have the benefit of this being part of their set of learned or valued skills. In addition, some early childhood experiences, especially when they include abuse and neglect, put caregivers at risk of misperceiving both their youth's and their own reactions. When a high level of emotion may be involved, it may be too much for some caregivers to tolerate. Being aware of how caregivers and their youth interact is also of value in understanding possible causes for concern in this area. Some caregivers may have perceptions about relationships and behaviors that support a youth being more of a caregiver than a youth. This puts the youth in the position of meeting the needs of the caregivers, and in this role reversal pattern of attachment, a youth's discipline needs are distorted and inconsistently met. When caregivers are struggling with mental health or stressors (e.g., financial, transportation, employment, or relationship issues), they may be less likely to attend to and enforce limits. Although these are common causes of concern, it is best to appreciate the uniqueness of each family and be open to other causes and stressors.

Formulating the Assessment: Putting It All Together. Some caregivers are open and accepting of the challenges they have in the area of discipline and limit setting.

They may also have insight into the causes and ways they compensate for these challenges. Alternatively, some caregivers may be focused on the youth being to blame and have difficulty accepting their role in the issues. If the caregivers are knowledgeable about developmental needs, put this knowledge to use in forming strategies, and can assess appropriately the usefulness of their strategies, there is much strength in this area. It is even more helpful when caregivers are able to be flexible and assess when their youth is in need of differences in their approaches. Youth who are labile in their mood may especially need alternate strategies for support. When caregivers consider their role to be one of support and coaching, the opportunities for growth are more likely. Caregivers ultimately model for youth coping strategies and the development of emotional regulation when they are also able to discipline in a calm and focused manner. When needs are present in this area, they may be discovered through input from the youth. It is important to find ways to appreciate the perspective of the youth and try to utilize this information during the service planning process to facilitate change.

Provision of a Nurturing Home Environment

Critical Nature of Element. Nurturance is described as the element that is present when a youth flourishes and develops. Nurturance is the communication of positive feelings, love, and affection. It encourages and supports growth and makes challenges more easily tolerated. The manner in which this is experienced varies greatly among cultures and families. Some families are physical in their interactions, and others are more verbal. Regardless of the way that youth experience affection and support, it is essential for all youth to experience. Youth who are able to experience warmth and affection will demonstrate a greater capacity for growth in all areas of development. Development is supported and occurs within the context of the caregiver-youth relationship. Whether the developmental task is a caregiver encouraging a youth to take a step, negotiating rules with peers, or taking steps towards independent living, it is the feeling of being nurtured and supported that has the most impact. Additionally, youth who experience nurturance are able to develop the capacity to nurture themselves. When considering qualities related to nurturing, sensitivity to a youth's cues, emotional availability, and responsiveness all contribute to positive influences on all areas of development (Landy & Menna, 2006). Although youth with serious mental health challenges may sometimes appear not to need their caregivers, nurturing interactions are essential to supporting their ability to cope and interact with others. When caregiving interactions are lacking in nurturance, it appears to contribute to overall levels of depression and insecurity in youth (Lempers & Clark-Lempers, 1997).

Facilitating a Conversation. Nurturance is an area that a caregiver often has difficulty "explaining" how and why things occur in the way that they do during the interview process. It is a characteristic that is complex and difficult to even have insight about. Caregivers who have had an absence of nurturance in their past are especially challenged in their ability to perceive their own and their youth's experiences in this area. The following questions guide the exploration of nurturance:

- *What are the caregivers' perceptions and beliefs in regards to youth needing nurturance?* The caregivers, in response to discussion in this area, are given the opportunity to verbalize how important this is to them and what role nurturance plays in the family. Some caregivers firmly believe that displaying affection interferes with their abilities to discipline their youth. Understanding their beliefs may be facilitated by asking about their own experiences.

Questions That May Evoke Understanding

What are your thoughts about children's need for love and support?

What are your thoughts about how this should happen for children?

How would you describe your own children's needs for this?

How would you describe your own experiences of this?

Is it something that is seen as important for you?

- *How do the caregivers express positive feelings and support toward their youth?* This question can help to gain an understanding of the natural ways that this occurs within the home and if there are times when it is absent or challenging for the caregivers.

Questions That May Evoke Understanding

What are ways you feel comfortable in showing positive feelings toward your child?

Can you describe any special routines and times in which you are able to do this (e.g., bedtime)?

How would you describe what you do when you leave or greet your child?

- *Is there ever a time when nurturing is more or less difficult?* This will allow for insight into how the caregivers are able to continually meet the youth's needs for love and belonging even when they are challenged. It will also help to determine situations that promote or hinder this capacity?

Questions That May Evoke Understanding

Are there times when it is easier than others to show your children you care for them?

What are things or situations that occur to help or hinder this?

Are there people that support or hinder you in doing this?

Opportunities for Observation. Table 8.4 describes characteristics that can be observed within the home setting to substantiate needs or strengths in the area of nurturance.

Possible Causative Factors for Challenges in This Area. There are many issues that can interfere with caregivers' abilities to effectively nurture their youth. Making assumptions regarding what those are can only lead to alienation from the caregivers, and a better strategy is to work alongside the caregivers to best understand their experiences. Undoubtedly, caregivers sometimes are compromised in this area because of past abusive or neglectful experiences that they may or may not even be aware of. Some may have cultural practices that are open in their displays of affection. Related to this is the fact that ways in which girls and boys receive and accept affection may be different in some families. Caregivers may, at the time

Table 8.4
Characteristics of Nurturance

Caregiver-Youth Relationships Demonstrating Nurturance	Caregiver-Youth Relationships Needing Nurturance
• Mutual enjoyments. • Initiation of physical contact on part of both both youth and caregivers. • Good eye contact, positive affect demonstrated. • Appropriate roles and boundaries. • Positive verbalizations; age-appropriate communication. • Appropriate amount of time spent together. • Ability to tolerate frustrations; balanced perspective regarding youth's strengths and limitations. • Demonstrated belief by youth that needs will be met.	• Interactions appear strained and difficult. • Low level of physical contact; little initiation of physical contact. • Minimal eye contact; flat or negative affect. • Skewed family boundaries. • Little time spent in interactions. • Extreme reactions to infractions or disappointments; difficulty reestablishing positive interaction following such. • Few bids for attention or expectation to have needs met.

of assessment, be overwhelmed and angry with their youth. Youth who experience behavioral and emotional challenges may exhaust their caregivers. It is also useful to consider that challenges in this area have also been improved by training caregivers in skills such as accepting youth's feelings, accepting their uniqueness, and recognizing their need for autonomy (Guerney & Gavigan, 1981).

Formulating the Assessment: Putting It All Together. Caregivers who exhibit strength in this area, talk openly and clearly about their attempts to nurture their youth. Recognizing challenging times and situations that make it more difficult is a skill as well. This allows for caregivers to seek support or develop strategies to ensure that positive interactions occur. When the home environment is consistently nurturing and supportive of the youth, and both caregivers and youth feel this to be true, there is obvious strength in this area. Most caregivers of youth with significant emotional challenges have difficulty managing behavioral issues in a manner that is empathetic and supportive as well. A need is present if caregivers are observed needing assistance or if input from either the youth or caregivers suggests that improvement is needed.

Ability to Reflect on Youth's Experiences and Communicate Empathy

Critical Nature of Element. Some things need to be experienced. What has been termed "reflective functioning" is one such thing. Reflective function has been described by Peter Fonagy and his colleagues as the "uniquely human capacity" (Fonagy, Gergely, Jurist, & Target, 2001) that allows for the understanding of the affective experiences of oneself and others. It is what is necessary for caregivers to have in order to accurately predict and understand what their youth need and are feeling (Slade, 2002). Humans have the need to experience reflective functioning in order to develop and foster this capacity in others. This experience allows youth to begin to understand, at a very young age, that they have feelings, intentions, and needs. Once this is understood, youth are then able to make sense of their internal experiences and communicate them. Later, as youth experience interpersonal relationships outside of the caregiving relationship, they are able to use this ability to understand others and how to interact with them. This capacity, which is essential to healthy social functioning, occurs when caregivers consider their youth's feelings and communicate this understanding. The ability to empathize cannot be fully mastered unless multiple experiences of having been empathized with have occurred.

Facilitating a Conversation. Reflective functioning is an area that can best be explained to caregivers prior to the interview as *the way in which you understand what your children need and let them know you know how they are feeling.* Caregivers can relate to the importance of this occurring, as they often describe the importance of this occurring for them in the provision of services. The discussion of this can be guided by the following questions:

- *How do the caregivers see their abilities for reflecting on the youth's experiences and communicating understanding of this to them?*

Questions That May Evoke Understanding

Can you give examples of being able to interpret what your child is experiencing?

How would you describe your ability to understand what your child needs or is feeling?

How would you describe what your child experiences when you attempt to make him/her feel understood?

Can you describe times when this is overwhelming or challenging for you?

- *Are there situations or times when reflective functioning is easier or more challenging than others?* This question helps to assess how consistently reflective functioning occurs for the caregivers and if there are certain times when support may be needed to do this.

Questions That May Evoke Understanding

Have there been times in the past when understanding your child's thoughts and needs was more or less challenging than others?

Do certain situations result in you feeling less able to understand and support your child?

Opportunities for Observation. Table 8.5 illustrates how a practitioner may observe caregivers demonstrating capacity for reflective functioning and communicating empathy.

Possible Causative Factors for Challenges in This Area. Some caregivers may be extremely limited in their ability to experience their own and others' emotional experiences. In addition, some may have challenges in demonstrating and feeling empathy. Both of these are developed through actual occurrences of the experiences. These experiences typically occur within the youth-caregiver relationship, although other relationships can take the place of this. Therapeutic relationships can also be the

Table 8.5
Observing Reflective Functioning and Communicating Empathy

- Do the caregivers attempt to explain the youth's intentions or feelings on his/her behalf (e.g., "He's looking at you like that because he is feeling nervous that you are here")?
- Do the caregivers refer back to past emotional experiences the youth experienced and relate them to the present (e.g., "Last time she went to my mom's house, she was afraid I wasn't coming back, and I think she is remembering and starting to worry about that now")?
- Are the caregivers able to verbalize an understanding of how they understand the youth and link it back to their own thoughts and feelings (e.g., "When he is yelling and I think he is feeling angry about what happened at school, it also makes me think about how I felt when I was his age, and I wonder if I understand it correctly")?
- When a youth is distressed, do the caregivers acknowledge his/her experience and discuss how he/she must be feeling (e.g., "I am guessing you are feeling angry that your friend said those things, and that must be hard for you")?
- Do the caregivers' tones of voice and actions match with the statements they are making (e.g., while making the comment to the youth that he/she must be overwhelmed and angry with a situation, are the caregivers laughing or smiling about what has occurred)?

gateway to building capacity in this area. Other times, caregivers have the capacity for reflective functioning, but certain issues trigger emotional reactions in them that may cause them to ignore or distort their youth's experiences.

Formulating the Assessment: Putting It All Together. Listening carefully to what caregivers relate during the interview process gives clues to capacity in the area of reflective functioning, but observations are the most valuable component of the process. Especially when there are challenges in this area, the perception of how it occurs is not always within caregivers' conscious awareness. In assessing if this is a need, the feedback of the youth may support or give clarity to areas that need improvement. Caregivers who are attempting to understand their youth's experiences are much better off than those who are not, even when their perceptions are incorrect. The youth may repeatedly say things such as "that's not right or that's not why I did that," and guidance and support can take place within the interaction to communicate needs and feelings. The motivation or desire to understand what another may be thinking is what is critical (Fonagy et al., 2001).

Ability to Understand and Support Youth's Unique Characteristics

Critical Nature of Element. Every person wants other people to know who he/she is as a person and what he/she needs. Youth who are fortunate have caregivers who provide support for their unique characteristics. T. Berry Brazelton and Stanley Greenspan (2000) state in their book, *The Irreducible Needs of Children: What Every Child Must Have to Grow, Learn, and Flourish,* "Babies learn to love while being respected as unique" (p. 81). Every person can be described as having varying degrees of the nine temperament characteristics: sensitivity, activity level, intensity, adaptability, regularity, approach/withdrawal, persistence, mood, and distractibility (Kristal, 2005). Youth with serious emotional challenges are particularly in need of having caregivers who are highly attuned to their needs, as it may be a challenge for the youth to understand their own emotions. Responding in ways that are acceptable to the youth is a part of this as well. Some strategies may be seen by the youth as intrusive or hindering them in some manner. Caregivers who are functioning optimally in this area not only understand what their youth need but support them in a way that is experienced positively by the youth. As youth grow and mature, the strategies for assisting a youth with difficult temperament characteristics change as well. Having an understanding of how this occurs can also significantly impact a youth. When considering other needs of youth with mental health challenges, it is of great benefit when caregivers understand mental health issues in general and specific to their youth. Understanding a youth's mental health condition is critical on a number of levels. Initially, it can support the youth to get the appropriate care. Caregivers who are familiar with warning signs of mental health challenges are therefore armed with the information they need to reach out for further evaluation and support. Even after a youth is diagnosed and receiving treatment, familiarity with risk factors for mental health issues assists in identifying additional concerns, exacerbations, or regressions that can be addressed. Once a mental health issue has been identified, it is also of significant benefit when caregivers understand causes, manifestations, and appropriate interventions related to their youth's challenges. Youth with mental health challenges may be subjected to misunderstanding, blame, and harsh judgments, which only serve to further alienate them and harm their sense of self. Gowan and Walker (2009) indicate that stigmatization goes beyond name calling. When internalized, it can lead to feelings of shame and self-disgust. This only further complicates the youth's ability to cope. When caregivers contribute to this experience, it can have even more deleterious effects. Youth need their caregivers to help combat the effects that stigma generated from extended family, peers, or community members may have on them. Additionally, and perhaps more importantly, it is essential for caregivers to support youth in seeing themselves in a positive manner and understanding the principles of recovery. As caregivers have the most impact on the development of their youth, it is important that they see the uniqueness in their youth's experiences and help align interventions that are best suited for the youth and family.

Facilitating a Conversation. Caregivers can feel supported in questions on temperament characteristics when reminded that sometimes a youth is difficult to understand and that experiences in which this occurs are challenging for both youth and caregivers. This perhaps normalizes the concept that some caregivers may feel challenged in this area and that strategies can be determined to help if problems exist. The discussion can be guided by the following questions:

- *Do the caregivers have a unique profile of the youth that reflects awareness of who he/she is?*

  Questions That May Evoke Understanding

  Do you have a way of describing who your child is—likes and dislikes, attitudes and preferences, and reactions to others and his/her environment?

  How would you describe what has remained the same and what has changed in your child's development?

- *Do the caregivers struggle with how to support youth in his/her reactions to others and his/her environment?*

Questions That May Evoke Understanding

How would you describe how you are able to assist your child in coping with his/her reactions?

Can you describe situations in which you can predict problems may occur?

How has it been for you as your child grows and develops?

- *How do the caregivers see mental health challenges in terms of origin, causes, and contributing factors?*

Questions That May Evoke Understanding

How would you describe your beliefs and understanding of mental health issues in youth?

Have you experienced others not seeing this in the same way as you?

Is it a challenge to understand what your child has control over and what he/she does not? How would you describe your thoughts about this?

Opportunities for Observation. Depending on the age of the youth, temperament charactersitics may be substantiated as a concern by the youth expressing feeling misunderstood. Youth may give examples, both alone and with the caregivers present, in which this occurs. Caregivers may also make comments to support the assessment of this being a challenge, which then can be used to facilitate more discussion. When practitioners are astute to temperament characteristics, they can look for patterns in which these characteristics are displayed and how the caregivers respond. When reactions occur over and over, and caregivers either do not take opportunities to support or attempt support that are not in line with the youth's needs, there is a need for intervention.

Possible Causative Factors for Challenges in This Area. Well-intentioned caregivers may have challenges in understanding who their youth is. Caregivers who have not been with their youth since birth may be more handicapped than others in this experience. It is useful to consider that it is not merely a caregiver capacity but a youth capacity to cue and express needs. When youth are particularly challenged in this area, the dyad may be impaired. In terms of understanding mental health challenges, exposure, education, past experiences, and cultural understanding may all have an impact.

Formulating the Assessment: Putting It All Together. The caregivers' interviews and observations contribute information that should be seen on a continuum. No caregivers can possibly understand every situation and reaction that a youth has, but they should be able do so much of the time. The comments and strategies that are used can be determined as more or less effective with the caveat being that this may evolve and change as services progress.

Ability to Advocate for the Needs of Youth and Family

Critical Nature of Element. Of all the wraparound principles (see Chapter 3), the concept of family driven is perhaps the most emphasized. The emphasis is on caregivers being in the position of making decisions regarding services and supports, and sharing responsibility for the implementation of plans (Osher, Penn, & Spencer, 2008).

Before this can occur, the caregivers must have not only the ability to understand what is best for their youth but the confidence to express this understanding. Caregivers may have felt discounted and blamed, and their capacity for effective advocacy may be compromised. The way in which they seek support may in fact alienate them from their youth's support systems. Caregivers who can effectively advocate for the needs of their youth optimize their youth's opportunities for the most effective support available. In addition, the capacity to form productive and collaborative relationships with youth's teachers, service providers, and significant others is then felt in a positive way by the youth.

Facilitating a Conversation. Caregivers are often comfortable talking about their experiences in advocating for the needs of their youth. They may be less comfortable discussing the effectiveness of their techniques, but support a practitioner can offer in developing skills in this area may offset their reluctance. The following questions will assist in the interview process:

- *What experiences have the caregivers had in the area of advocating for the youth's needs?*

Questions That May Evoke Understanding

If you have been in experiences in which you have had to explain what your child needs to others, how has that gone for you?

Do you feel successful in your attempts at doing this?

Are there times when this is easier or more difficult?

- *What are barriers in the area of advocating the youth's needs? What makes it easier?*

Questions That May Evoke Understanding

Are there issues or feelings that you may have about advocating for your child's needs that make it difficult?

What could make this less challenging?

Have you experienced support from others in this area?

What are some characteristics that you have that support this happening?

Opportunities for Observation. Within the assessment process, there are characteristics that can be observed within the interview, which may support an understanding of capacity in the area of advocating for the needs of the youth and family. A caregiver who clarifies misperceptions, or challenges or corrects practitioners' inappropriate summary of what has been said, demonstrates an assertiveness and confidence that can predict skills in the advocacy area. Also, caregivers who continually make comments about their youth's needs demonstrate an awareness that is at the foundation of this ability.

Possible Causative Factors for Challenges in This Area. Several factors may contribute to challenges in the area of advocating for youth's needs. Caregivers who are blocked by their own experiences now overshadowing their youth's experiences may misinterpret their youth's needs. Some caregivers may not have experienced or have a cultural orientation that supports expressing needs clearly. Others may have experienced such challenging situations that they have chosen to withdraw from the situation.

Formulating the Assessment: Putting It All Together. Few caregivers would say that advocacy is never a challenge for them. The severity of needs in this area is related to the perceptions of the caregivers, the risk to the youth, and the complexity of advocacy needs that the youth may have. Determining a baseline for where the caregivers are, related to this capacity, is the most useful, and then strategies can be built to maximize potential.

BRIDGING TO THE NEXT PHASE OF ASSESSMENT

Assessment should always be presented as an ongoing process. Gaining the most comprehensive understanding of the youth and family does not occur simply in the initial phase of assessment but evolves throughout the service delivery process. The caregivers' assessment is not complete without input from the youth, appropriate records review, and observation of interactions. Caregivers can be supported in naturally beginning to focus more on their youth's functioning and family functioning with appreciation for their need to move freely in their discussion of needs.

CONCLUSION

It is critical for practitioners to assess the needs and strengths of caregivers when attempting to assist youth with mental health challenges. There is no one more influential to a youth than his/her caregivers. This process must be comprehensive and strengths based. When this occurs, it assists in forming a trusting relationship between practitioners and families that ultimately facilitates the growth and development of the youth in need.

References

Ayoub, C., & Jacewitz, M. M. (1982). Families at risk of poor parenting: A model of service delivery, assessment, and intervention. *Child Abuse and Neglect, 6,* 351-358.

Baumrind, D. (1991). The influence of parenting style on adolescent competence and substance use. *Journal of Early Adolescence, 11,* 56-95.

Booth, P. B., & Jernberg, A. M. (1999). *Theraplay: Helping parents and children build better relationships through attachment based play* (2nd ed.). San Francisco, CA: Jossey-Bass.

Brazelton, T. B., & Greenspan, S. I. (2000). *The irreducible needs of children: What every child must have to grow, learn, and flourish.* Cambridge, MA: Perseus Publishing.

Brenner, V., & Fox, R. A. (1998). Parental discipline and behavior problems in young children. *Journal of Genetic Psychology, 159,* 251-256.

Chamberlain, P., & Patterson, G. R. (1995). Discipline and child compliance in parenting. In M. H. Bornstien (Ed.), *Handbook of parenting: Vol. 4. Applied and practical parenting* (pp. 205-225). Hillsdale, NJ: Lawrence Erlbaum Associates.

Crittenden, P. M., Lang, C., Claussen, A. H., & Partridge, M. F. (2000). Relations among mothers' dispositional representations of parenting. In P. M. Crittenden & A. H. Claussen

(Eds.), *The organization of attachment relationships: Maturation, culture and context* (pp. 214-233). New York: Cambridge University Press.

Erickson, M., & Egeland, B. (2002). Child Neglect. In J. Myers, L. Berliner, J. Briere, C. Hendrix, C. Jenny, & T. Reid (Eds.), *The APSAC handbook on child maltreatment* (2nd ed., pp.3-20). Thousand Oaks, CA: Sage Publications.

Fonagy, P., Gergely, G., Jurist, E., & Target, M. (2002). *Affect regulation, mentalization, and the development of the self.* New York: Other Press.

Guerney, L. F., & Gavigan, M. A. (1981). Parental acceptance and foster parents. *Journal of Clinical Child Psychology, 10,* 27-32.

Gowan, L. K., & Walker, J. S. (2009). Stigmatization. *Focal Point: Research, Policy, & Practice in Children's Mental Health, 23*(1), 3-6.

Houck, G. M., & LeCuyer-Maus, E. A. (2002). Maternal limit-setting patterns and toddler development of self-concept and social competence. *Issues in Comprehensive Pediatric Nursing, 25,* 21-41.

Klass, C. S. (2008). *The home visitor's guidebook: Promoting optimal parent and child development.* (3rd ed.). Baltimore: Paul H. Brookes Publishing.

Kopp, C. B. (1982). Antecedents of self-regulation: A developmental perspective. *Developmental Psychology, 18,* 199-214.

Kristal, J. (2005). *The temperament perspective: Working with children's behavioral styles.* Baltimore: Paul H. Brookes Publishing.

Landy, S., & Menna, R. (2006). *Early Intervention with multi-risk families: An integrative approach,* Baltimore: Paul H. Brookes Publishing.

Lempers, J. D., & Clark-Lempers, D. S. (1997). Economic hardship, family relationships and adolescent distress: An evaluation of a stress-distress mediation model in mother-daughter and mother-son dyads. *Adolescence, 32*(126), 339-357.

Maslow, A. H. (1943). A theory of human motivation, *Psychological Review, 50,* 370-396.

Michigan Association of Infant Mental Health. (2005). *Guidelines for comprehensive assessment of infants and their parents in the child welfare system* (2nd ed.). Ann Arbor, MI: Author.

Osher, T., Penn, M. & Spencer, S. A. (2008.) Partnerships with families for family-driven systems of care. In: B. A. Stroul & G. Blau (Eds.), *The system of care handbook: Transforming mental health services for children, youth and families* (pp. 249-273). Baltimore: Paul H. Brookes Publishing.

Paxson, C., & Waldfogel, J. (2002). Work, welfare, and child maltreatment. *Journal of Labor Economics 3,* 435-440.

Pennsylvania Child Welfare Training Program, University of Pittsburgh: School of Social Work Online Curricula. (2009). *Effects of abuse and neglect on child development: Handout #4.* Retrieved June 7, 2010, from http://www.pacwcbt.pitt.edu/Curriculum/Core%20103/Handouts/HO%204%20Effects%20of%20Abuse%20and%20Neglect%20on%20Development.pdf

Perry, B. D. (2001). Violence and childhood: How persisting fear can alter the child's developing brain. In D. Schetky & E. Benedek (Eds.), *Textbook of child and adolescent forensic psychiatry* (pp. 221-238). Washington, DC: American Psychiatric Press.

Shonkoff, J. P., Phillips, D., & Board on Children, Youth, and Families (États-Unis). Committee on Integrating the Science of Early Childhood Development (Eds.). (2000). *From neurons to neighborhoods: The science of early childhood development.* Washington, DC: National Academy Press.

Slade, A. (2002). Keeping the baby in mind: A critical factor in perinatal mental health. *Zero to Three, 22,* 10-16.

Chapter 9

Assessing Infants, Toddlers, and Preschoolers Within the Context of Family and Community

If there is anything that we wish to change in the child, we should first examine it and see whether it is not something that could better be changed in ourselves.

—Carl Jung

Teach us delight in simple things.

—Rudyard Kipling

INTRODUCTION

Infants, toddlers, and preschoolers, although often considered "too young to remember" or resistant to stress, may very well be the most vulnerable population of youth served. The intimate connection between development and mental health functioning is of critical importance. When mental health challenges occur, children may have serious and significant consequences within their overall development. An understanding of developmental milestones is first necessary to interpret how and to what extent mental health challenges have affected development. The following sections support the process of assessing all areas of a child's functioning and form a basis for service plan development.

STRUCTURING THE CHILD'S ASSESSMENT

The assessment of an infant, toddler, or preschooler should never occur in the absence of the primary caregiver. This concept has been well established in early intervention literature as well as early childhood mental health research (Greenspan & Meisels, 1996). In considering the structure of the assessment, the needed components include caregiver interviews, observation of children and caregivers, assessment of child with caregivers present, and review of pertinent records.

DEVELOPMENTAL FUNCTIONING

Importance of Understanding Developmental History

To best understand how an infant, toddler, or preschooler is currently functioning, it is necessary to know how development has unfolded from birth to the present time. Development may be uneven, and patterns may be present that support a more thorough understanding of the child. Paying attention to the presence of stressors as well as supports during the various developmental stages offers additional insights that may be useful in the service planning process.

Motor Development

Motor development is crucial to assess because it supports a child's ability to move about and explore the world, which is a critical need for children. A child who is challenged in this area may be experiencing a medical or neurological problem that needs to be addressed. Motor development refers to the development of both fine and gross motor skills. Table 9.1 identifies both gross and fine motor tasks in children from 0 to 6 years of age.

In addition to the assessment of the child's ability to meet developmental milestones, the child's coordination, muscle tone, strength, and motor planning should be considered. The child's ability to demonstrate fluid and coordinated movements develops with time and practice. As infants, the first area in which control is developed is the head. An infant's movements are often awkward, although there should be improvement in this with practice. It is helpful to ask caregivers how long a skill has been in place and if the level of coordination related to this skill is improving. As children develop, coordination typically continues to improve in both fine and gross motor skills. It is possible to have coordination challenges in only one area as well as both. Muscle tone can be low or high. Children with low tone appear slumped or challenged in supporting themselves in various positions. A child may try to compensate by locking joints or leaning on objects or caregivers. Children with high tone appear stiff and rigid. They may keep their hands closed tightly or walk on their toes. When being held, high-tone children may not appear comfortable or mold into the caregivers. Children who struggle with strength do not display the ability to sustain interactions that would be developmentally appropriate. They tire easily and do not persist in play. When this is a significant problem, the child may appear distressed by breathing heavily, have skin changes, or have blue lips and fingernails. Motor planning is the child's ability to initiate action and sequence movements. In infants, the ability to imitate actions would be slow or impaired if there are motor planning challenges. As a child becomes older and attempts more complex tasks, the ability to move through space in a coordinated manner may appear compromised. The ability to climb, jump, and judge space and intensity of movement may appear impaired. In summary, the ability to meet developmental milestones, as well as the presence of coordination, strength, tone, and motor planning, should be considered.

Caregiver Interview: In discussing motor development with caregivers, the following explanation and sample questions are helpful:

Motor development refers to your child's ability to use and coordinate his/her large and small muscles. It also relates to strength and endurance related to physical tasks.

Infants: Does it seem as if your infant changes in this area from month to month? How would you describe your infant's ability to move around and explore his/her surroundings? Does your infant seem to become tired easily when attempting a physical task? Does your infant seem to have enough strength? How would you describe your infant's ability to grasp and handle small objects? Do you have any concerns that your infant is lagging behind in physical development? Has anyone else voiced concerns?

Toddlers: Describe your toddler's skills in moving around and handling objects. Is your toddler developing more coordination with physical tasks? Does your toddler appear to enjoy physical activity or become frustrated with certain tasks? Does your toddler seem to give up on tasks quickly or tire easily? Does your toddler seem to have the strength needed for physical tasks?

Table 9.1
Motor Development

By 3 Months (Gross Motor)

- Opens and closes fists
- Holds head upright
- Raise upper body with arms when lying on stomach
- Attempts to stand when held in standing position on hard surface
- Rolls from side to back

By 3 Months (Fine Motor)

- Reaches for objects
- Puts hand in mouth
- Focuses briefly on a close-by object
- Grasps objects placed in palm

By 6 Months (Gross Motor)

- Rolls from back to stomach and stomach to back
- Sits with support, may sit unsupported
- Lifts head while in supine position
- May pull self to standing
- Pushes up easily with arms

By 6 Months (Fine Motor)

- Grasps feet
- Moves objects from hand to hand
- Uses raking grasp to pick up objects
- Imitates actions such as clapping

By 12 Months (Gross Motor)

- Walks around furniture
- Walks with adult support, may walk alone
- Throws objects such as a ball
- Shifts sitting position easily

By 12 Months (Fine Motor)

- Uses pincer grasp
- Can bang small objects together
- Tries to imitate scribbling of others
- Can put objects in and out of containers
- Holds cup and brings to mouth easily

By 2 Years (Gross Motor)

- Runs easily
- Climbs on objects
- Walks up and down stairs easily with support
- Jumps forward and up and down
- Easily picks objects up while walking

(Continued)

Table 9.1 *(Continued)*

By 2 years (Fine Motor)

- Can put puzzle pieces together
- Enjoys scribbling
- Builds tower of at least four blocks
- Turns and twists objects such as door handles
- Turns pages in a book

By 4-5 Years (Gross Motor)

- Walks on tiptoes
- Stands on one foot
- Easily throws and catches
- Climbs on playground equipment
- Walks up and down stairs unassisted and by taking alternate steps
- May be able to skip
- Hops

By 4-5 Years (Fine Motor)

- Copies shapes
- Draws person with body
- Manipulates buttons and zippers
- Uses silverware easily
- Beginning to print letters

By 6 Years and Early School Age (Gross Motor)

- Alternates feet when skipping
- May be learning to swim
- May be beginning to ride a bike
- Easily kicks a ball
- Plays and climbs easily on playground equipment
- Runs smoothly and confidently

By 6 Years and Early School Age (Fine Motor)

- Prints name
- Holds pencil correctly
- Uses scissors
- Can trace around objects
- Displays consistent preference for left or right hand

Source: Landy (2002).

Do you feel as if your toddler is developing the way he/she should be? Has anyone voiced any concerns?

Preschoolers/School Age: How would you describe your child's skills in activities such as climbing, running, and walking? Is your child improving his/her ability to move faster and in a more coordinated way? Do you have any concerns regarding strength or endurance? Can your child imitate simple drawings and movements? Have you or anyone else had concerns about your child's motor skills?

Sensory Processing

Sensory processing refers to a child's ability to fully utilize the senses of sight, taste, touch, sound, and smell, as well as his/her ability to monitor reactivity to these experiences. In the assessment of the infant's ability to react to sound, it is helpful to be aware of how this develops. Infants from 0-1 months will begin to evidence an awareness of sounds, which is seen in their pausing their breathing, displaying startle reactions, changing their expressions, tensing their bodies, or widening their eyes. These are more primitive reactions and further develop as an infant matures. Into the second and third months of life, infants display the capacity to respond to a voice and then search with their eyes for sounds. By the end of the first year, they should be able to localize sounds that are hidden, come from below them, and later from above them. It is helpful to use these benchmarks when asking caregivers to describe how they determine if their child is able to hear normally. In addition, asking caregivers if the children have had their hearing tested is important and will offer helpful information.

In the assessment of an infant's ability to react to visual experiences, practitioners should be familiar with the developmental sequence of this activity. An infant's abilities in this area are not fully developed for quite some time after birth. Initially, within the first month, it is considered on track for infants to respond to brightly colored objects approximately eight to ten inches away from them. The response may only be brief, lasting two to three seconds. As their vision further develops, infants are later able to follow a person moving toward them and then an object moving in the midline or from side to side. By the end of three months, infants should be able to follow an object downward and then upward. It is helpful to also ask caregivers if any vision screenings have occurred. Table 9.2 provides some guidance regarding sensory reactivity as described in the *Diagnostic Classification of Mental Health and Developmental Disorders of Infancy and Early Childhood*, revised edition (*DC 0-3 R*; Zero to Three, 2005).

> ***Caregiver Interview:*** In discussing sensory processing with caregivers, the following explanation and sample questions are helpful:
>
> Sensory refers to your child's ability to use the senses of sound, sight, touch, taste, and smell, as well as how he/she reacts to these experiences.
>
> *Infants:* Do you have any concerns that your infant's abilities are not what they should be in this area? Does your infant cry, avoid, or become irritable with certain types of sensory experiences?
>
> *Toddlers:* Do you have any concerns about your toddler's abilities in this area? Did you have any concerns when your toddler was younger? Does your toddler demonstrate preferences to certain types of sensory experiences? Does your toddler avoid certain experiences?
>
> *Preschoolers/School Age:* Do you or anyone else have any concerns about your child's abilities in this area? Have there been concerns in the past? Have you needed to put accommodations in place to help your child with his/her senses? Does your child have strong reactions to certain types of experiences?

Table 9.2
Sensory Reactivity

Indications of Overreactivity to Sensory Stimulation

- Fearfulness
- Crying
- "Freezing"
- Trying to get away from stimulus
- Increased distractibility
- Aggression
- Excessive sartle reaction
- Motoric agitation
- Restricted tolerance for variety in food textures, tastes and smells

Indications of Underreactivity to Sensory Stimulation

- Lack of response
- Ignores social interactions or encouragement
- Withdrawal from stimuli
- Inattentiveness
- Fatigability
- Apathetic appearance

Cognitive Development

Cognitive development is important to assess because it impacts all other areas of development. This is an area in which early intervention is critical. Table 9.3 indicates tasks related to cognitive development in 0- to 6-year-olds.

Caregiver Interview: In discussing cognitive development with caregivers, the following explanation and sample questions are helpful:

Cognitive development refers to your child's cognitive abilities such as learning, understanding, planning, and anticipating actions.

Infants: Does your infant remember or anticipate your actions? Is your infant aware of what is occurring around him/her? Does your infant imitate your actions and try to get you to do things for him/him? Does your infant give up on difficult tasks or keep trying?

Toddlers: Does your toddler remember things? Do your toddler's actions show you that he/she understand routines and familiar situations? Does your toddler show you through words or actions that he/she has questions and can put ideas together?

Preschoolers/School Age: How does your child do with self-help activities? Can your child do tasks like sorting and recognizing colors? Has anyone in a preschool/school setting questioned your child's abilities? Does your child seem to be progressing in his/her abilities in this area?

Table 9.3
Cognitive Development

By 3 Months

- Observes hands
- Develops ability to regulate internal states (body rhythms and arousal)
- Attends briefly to activity
- Attentive to environment
- Recognizes familiar people
- Begins recognizing routines

By 6 Months

- Imitates other's gestures
- Intentionally throws objects down to watch them fall
- Demonstrates stranger anxiety
- Focuses on activity or person for up to 2 minutes
- Demonstrates object permanence

By 12 Months

- Points to objects in pictures
- Attempts to determine how things work
- Plays alone briefly
- Imitates other's actions in play
- Follows one-step directions
- Listens to simple books being read
- Beginning to understand simple cause and effect

By 2 Years

- Begins to pretend in play
- Plays independently for short periods
- Points to at least five body parts
- Sorts items by color
- Sorts items by size
- Attentive for longer periods

By 4-5 Years

- Engages in complex pretend play
- Understands function of most common household objects
- Identifies around six shapes
- Counts to ten
- Understands daily routines and events
- Distinguishes between girl and boy, he and she
- Names some letters and numbers

By 6 Years and Early School Age

- Consistently knows shapes, colors, and sizes
- Understands games and simple rules
- Understands concepts of big/small, short/tall
- Grasp concepts of numbers
- Understands concept of left and right

Source: Landy (2002).

Speech and Language Development

Table 9.4 indicates tasks related to speech and language development.

Caregiver Interview: In discussing speech and language development with caregivers, the following explanation and sample questions are helpful:

Speech and language development refers to your child's ability to understand what is said to him/her and to express thoughts and ideas with others.

Infants: How does your infant communicate with you about getting needs met? Does your infant show you that he/she understands what you are saying? If your infant is making sounds, when did this begin and how has this developed?

Toddlers: How do you feel your toddler has developed in this area? Was there a time that his/her development was really noticeable in this area? Do others have problems understanding what your toddler is communicating? Does your toddler show you through actions that he/she understands what is said? Does your toddler become frustrated when trying to communicate?

Preschoolers/School Age: Do you or anyone else have concerns in this area? Does your child use language as part of pretend play? Can your child find words to express himself? Do others understand your child most of the time? Does your child show you that they understand what is being said to them? Is communication a frustration to your child?

Social and Emotional Development

Table 9.5 describes social and emotional development in 0- to 6-year-olds.

Caregiver Interview: In discussing social and emotional development with caregivers, the following explanation and sample questions are helpful:

Social and emotional development refers to how your child experiences and expresses his/her emotions and abilities to interact with others.

Infants: Can you describe the type of emotions your infant displays? How does your infant react to your emotions or facial expressions? How would you describe how your infant relates to you and others? How does your infant relate to other children?

Toddlers: What types of emotions do you see your toddler expressing? Has this changed and developed as he/she has grown? Does your toddler have any difficulties with emotional expression? Is your toddler aware of other's emotional expressions? Are there differences in how your toddler relates to peers and adults? How would you describe your toddler's socialization with others of the same age?

Table 9.4
Speech and Language Development

By 3 Months

- Experiments with sounds, makes cooing noises
- Responds to those speaking
- Laughs and squeals with delight
- Cries when in need
- Babbles and repeats simple sounds

By 6 Months

- Reacts to tone of voice
- Imitates sounds
- Expresses joy and frustration
- Repeats syllables
- Responds to some words
- Reacts to hearing name

By 12 Months

- Identifies "mamma" and "dada" for specific people
- Uses words to demonstrate surprise such as "oh"
- Begins to use a few words
- Points and gestures for needs
- Responds to being told "no"
- Understands many words and responds to simple requests

By 2 Years

- Listens to a story
- Responds to questions
- Understands more than can say
- Can say two-word sentences
- Recognizes names of family members
- Points to body parts

By 4-5 Years

- Can speak five-word sentences
- Uses all parts of speech
- Uses future tense
- Identifies colors
- Knows family members names and own last name
- Remembers simple songs
- Uses possessives
- Uses words to distinguish gender

By 6 Years and Early School Age

- Easily communicates ideas
- Asks questions
- Is easily understood
- Knows name and address
- Begins to recognize pragmatics of language
- Uses plurals correctly

Source: Landy (2002).

Table 9.5
Social and Emotional Development

By 3 Months

- Develops a social smile
- Enjoys interaction with others
- Communicates with face and body
- Imitates some gestures
- Responds to soothing
- Expresses basic emotions
- Comfortable with holding and interaction

By 6 Months

- Enjoys play/interactions with others
- Responds to others emotional expressions
- May cry when in response to hearing another's cry
- May cry when separated from caregivers
- Shows fear in distressing situations
- Demonstrates preference for caregivers

By 12 Months

- Shows hesitancy with strangers
- Reacts to caregivers' responses to situations
- Begins to imitate others
- Prefers regular caregivers
- With adult support, can take turns and play simple games
- Engages primarily in parallel play
- Has an item, such as a blanket or stuffed animal, for comfort
- Likes to be around others
- May react to another's distress by becoming distressed or trying to help

By 2 Years

- Increasingly interacts with other children in play
- May have increased separation distress
- Identifies self in mirror
- May have difficulty in sharing
- Enjoys games with others such as hide and go seek
- Points out emotions of others
- Begins to be defiant at times
- Communicates distress or joy/pleasure with caregivers

By 4-5 Years

- Asks to be around other children
- Can play with others independently for longer periods
- Can tolerate separation from caregivers
- Understands and follows simple social rules and routines
- Enjoys praise and approval of peers
- Develops preferences in peer group and friendships
- Displays less volatile emotions

(Continued)

Table 9.5 *(Continued)*

By 6 Years or Early School Age

- Enjoys group games
- Understands and expresses distinctions between basic emotions
- Understands differences in adult and child interactions
- Begins to understand complex emotions such as pride, jealousy, and shame
- Has a "best" friend
- Demonstrates complex social pretend play
- Is anxious to please and follow rules
- Usually plays with gender-specific toys and same-sex peers

Source: Landy (2002).

Preschoolers/School Age: Does your child seem to have a wide range of emotional expressions? Do you have any concerns in this area? Does your child express his/her emotions well? Does your child do well understanding other's emotional reactions? How does your child play with others? How would you describe how your child relates to you and other adults?

Self-Help Skills Development

Self-care/daily living skills refer to a number of tasks that reflect a child's growing ability to take care of his/her own physical needs and to become responsible for dressing, doing household chores, eating, toileting, and preparing for sleeping. Self-care/daily living skills are often reflective of cognitive ability. This is important to assess and monitor because of the limitations that this places on children when it is suboptimal. Children are at times excluded from some environments, if skills in this area are not present. This area, if underdeveloped, causes challenges in caregiving that are often overwhelming. Table 9.6 identifies self-help skills in children from 0 to 6 years of age.

Taking responsibility for household tasks is also related to self-help skills development, and typical milestones may include the following:

- *By 1 Year:* A 1-year-old may show interest in imitating household tasks (e.g., sweeping, dusting, or vacuuming) but is far from able to complete these tasks alone.

- *By 2 Years:* Children of this age will often assist in simple clean-up tasks as long as the task is modeled for them and they can physically accomplish the task. Their attention span is limited at this age, and there will be a need for consistent support and direction.

- *By 3 Years:* A child will be able to complete simple chores (e.g., setting a table, feeding a pet, or cleaning spills) independently if supervised by an adult.

- *By 4 Years:* Children will be able to complete many simple chores that start to involve more than one step (e.g., sorting and folding clothes). They can understand and adhere to routine and daily tasks with support and reminding.

- *By 5 Years and Early School Age:* A child will begin to follow through with simple routines without ongoing monitoring by an adult.

Table 9.6
Self-Help Skills

By 3 Months

- Seems familiar with dressing and caregiving routines
- Sucks from bottle or nipple well
- Enjoys bath time
- Opens mouth when presented with bottle or nipple

By 6 Months

- Holds bottle
- Picks up objects
- Shows anticipation of routines
- Opens mouth when spoon fed
- Feeds self finger food such as crackers

By 12 Months

- Sips from a cup with assistance
- Begins to use a spoon
- Participates in dressing
- Cooperates and assists in bathing
- Responds to requests to get familiar objects

By 2 Years

- Easily drinks from cups
- Takes off clothes and assists in dressing
- Feeds self
- Begins to engage in toilet training
- Unbuttons large buttons
- Responds to and remembers routines related to eating, sleeping, and dressing

By 4-5 Years

- Typically dresses self
- Usually toilet trained
- Feeds self with little spilling
- Serve self food from packages
- Washes self with help
- Uses utensils easily

By 6 Years and Early School Age

- Brushes/combs hair independently
- Washes hands regularly
- Takes care of toileting tasks without help
- Cuts food
- Can keep toys and clothes in proper location with direction
- Ties shoes
- Picks appropriate clothing

Source: Landy (2002).

Caregiver Interview: In discussing self-help skills development with caregivers, the following explanation and sample questions are helpful:

Self-help skills development refers to the skills your child is developing in caring for him-/herself in such areas as feeding, dressing, and grooming.

Infants: Is your infant demonstrating an interest in feeding him-/herself and becoming more independent in this area? Does your infant assist in dressing and grooming activities?

Toddlers: Has your toddler developed an ability to initiate and assist in dressing him-/herself? Describe your toddler's use of utensils and a cup during meals? How does your toddler respond to bathing, brushing teeth, or wiping his/her nose? Does your toddler assist in these activities? If you have begun toilet training, how is that going?

Preschoolers/School Age. Does your child participate in self-care activities? Are there problems in this area at home or school? Has your child continued to develop abilities in this area?

Sleep Issues

Sleep is one of the primary reasons families seek intervention because of the impact this has on caregivers and siblings. The bedtime routine and actual amount of time spent asleep may be of concern to caregivers. Infants typically sleep fourteen to eighteen hours a day. Sleep does not have a regular circadian rhythm till approximately 6 months of age. In early childhood, children sleep approximately eight to twelve hours per day, and naps may continue throughout the day until the ages of 3 to 5. Night waking is at times a concern. In infants, night waking is a common occurrence. Typically infants should be able to return to sleep easily or with caregivers support. Intermittent nightmares are also common during toddler and preschool development. They may be present when a child is attempting to master developmental tasks. In assessing sleep concerns, the following questions can help with evaluating sleep issues:

- How much does the infant or child sleep during the day and night?
- Describe the activities that take place to assist the child in going to sleep or returning to sleep.
- Is the sleep routine variable or predictable?
- How does the sleep routine of the child affect the family?
- What are the sleeping arrangements?
- Does the child have nightmares or night terrors?
- Have the sleep problems changed over time?

Caregiver Interview: In discussing sleep issues with caregivers the following explanation and sample questions are helpful:

Understanding your child's sleep patterns and if there are any concerns in this area is important.

Infants: Describe your infant's patterns related to sleep? Has the amount of time your infant sleeps become longer since birth? Do your infant's sleep patterns cause disruption for your family?

Toddlers: How would you describe your toddler's routine related to sleep? Are there any ways that sleep could be improved? How does your toddler's sleep routine impact your family?

Preschoolers/School Age: How would you describe your child's nighttime routine? Does your child take a nap? Are there challenges related to getting to sleep or staying asleep? Has this affected your family in any way?

MENTAL HEALTH FUNCTIONING

Depression

Infants, toddler, and preschoolers, who are attempting to cope with feelings of sadness or depression are compromised in their ability to attend to the tasks of development (see "Developmental Functioning"). Many practitioners and caregivers do not believe that an infant can experience depression, despite the fact that researchers and practitioners began documenting this condition in the early 1940s when Anna Freud and Dorothy Burlingham (1944) recorded the reactions of young children removed from their caregivers during World War I. The two researchers documented a distinct grief reaction that started with protest, continued to despair, and, finally, the children appeared disconnected, withdrawn, developmentally delayed, and almost resolved to their fate. A child who is traumatized in any way may first develop a traumatic response that can develop into depression and meet criteria for a depressive disorder. There are children in whom it is difficult to identify a specific trauma, although they appear depressed. A child may exhibit signs of depression despite the fact that caregivers cannot identify a specific trauma. At times it is a challenge for caregivers to identify or even believe a specific environmental condition may contribute to depression in young children. These factors may include a chaotic home environment, poor or limited interaction from caregivers, or preoccupation of caregivers with their own stressors. The assessment of depression in young children should meet the criteria outlined in the *DC 0-3 R*. Both the *DC 0-3 R* and the *Diagnostic and Statistical Manual of Mental Health Disorders,* fourth edition, text revision (*DSM IV-TR*; American Psychiatric Association, 2000) consider the symptoms of depression to include depressed/irritable mood, diminished interest or pleasure, weight loss/gain, insomnia/hypersomnia, psychomotor agitation/retardation, fatigue or energy loss, feelings of worthlessness, diminished ability to think/concentrate, or recurrent thoughts of death or suicidal ideation. Clinical observations and manifestations of these symptoms are listed in Table 9.7. In addition, the *DC 0-3 R* states that all of the following general characteristics must be present to diagnose a child with major depression:

1. The disturbed affect and pattern of behavior should represent a change from the child's baseline mood and behavior.

Table 9.7
Manifestations of Depressive Symptoms in Young Children

- Depressed or irritable mood may be displayed by little variation in emotional expression, few smiles, infrequent laughter, and easy and frequent crying. The infant or toddler may display poor coping skills and difficulty recovering from frustration.
- Diminished pleasure or interest in activities may be displayed by little interest in play and poor response to caregivers' encouragement to play. The child may appear unhappy or withdrawn during play.
- When assessing the presence of appetite or sleep disturbance, there should be a change from a previously established pattern that is now the consistent experience for the child. Due to the dynamic nature of the child's development, this may be difficult to assess, so weight changes or fatigue may help guide this.
- Diminished ability to think or concentrate may be illustrated in giving up easily on completing tasks while playing; poor ability to sustain attention, despite strong motive to do so; and poor persistence in general.

2. The depressed mood or anhedonia must be persistent and, at least some of the time, uncoupled from sad or upsetting experiences. Persistent is defined as present most of the day, more days than not, over a period of at least 2 weeks.

3. Symptoms should be pervasive, occurring in more than one activity or setting and in more than one relationship.

4. Symptoms should be causing the child clear distress, impairing functioning or impeding development.

5. Disturbances are not due to a general medical condition or the direct effect of a medication or substance. (Zero to Three, 2005, pp. 25-26)

Caregiver Interview: In discussing depression with caregivers the following explanation and sample questions are helpful:

If your child has experienced ongoing sadness or withdrawn behavior, he/she may be depressed.

Infants: How would you describe your infant's mood throughout the day? Have there been changes in this? Does your infant at times appear unhappy? Is it difficult to get your infant to respond to you or others? Have there been situations that have been stressful for your infant? Does your infant's development seem to be on track to you? Has it changed?

Toddlers: How is your toddler's mood throughout the day? Does your toddler recover from upsetting situations or seem hard to console? Is your toddler easy to interact with? Does it take a lot to get your toddler to respond to you or others? Does your toddler seem to enjoy play? Has there been a change in your toddler's skills or abilities?

Preschoolers/School Age: Do you or others have any concerns in this area? How would you describe your child's mood most of the time? Is it difficult to engage your child in play? Have there been changes in how your child relates to you and others? If this has been a problem, what have you done to help the situation? Has anything helped?

Anxiety

Infants, toddlers, and preschoolers, who are preoccupied with worries or fears, may experience significant challenges in their ability to relate to others, accept support and nurturing from others, and focus on growth and development. Beyond this, caregivers who are attempting to assist a child who is anxious are also challenged in their task of being responsive and supportive to the child. This experience may interfere with the attachment relationship (see "Attachment") making the caregivers feel inadequate in meeting the child's needs. In the worst-case scenario, caregivers may reject or withdraw from the child to protect themselves from the negative feelings of perceived rejection. Anxiety in adults may be described as debilitating and one of the worst possible feelings. It is no different in infants and young children, and can stalemate development and result in regression. The challenge in assessing anxiety in young children first becomes the determination of the presence of clinically significant anxiety versus temperament characteristics or otherwise normative anxiety. Important considerations in this determination are the persistence of the problem and to what degree the problem interferes with functioning. The *DC 0-3 R* (Zero to Three, 2005, p. 21) states that all of the following criteria must be present to consider an anxiety disorder substantiated:

- The anxiety or fear causes the child distress or leads the child to avoid activities or settings associated with the anxiety or fear.

- The anxiety or fear occurs during two or more everyday activities or within two or more relationships (pervasive).

- The anxiety or fear is uncontrollable at least some of the time.

- The anxiety or fear impairs the child's functioning related to expected development.

- The anxiety or fear is persistent.

Table 9.8 shows the clinical manifestations of anxiety.

Caregiver Interview: In discussing anxiety with caregivers, the following explanation and sample questions are helpful:

If your child experiences worry or fears, he/she may be suffering from anxiety.

Infants: Does your infant demonstrate fears or worry in situations that you would not expect? How easily can you comfort your infant when he/she appears distressed? Are there situations you avoid because you are worried about your infant's reaction? What are your infant's reactions that tell you he/she may be worried or unsettled?

Table 9.8
Clinical Manifestations of Anxiety

- There may be excessive distress when separated from caregivers, manifested by excessive crying, inability to be consoled, inability to be distracted, self-injurious behavior, and statements of worry or fear.
- There may be persistent and excessive worry regarding separation from caregivers, manifested by scanning the environment, clingy behavior, statements regarding possibility of something bad happening, and lack of exploratory behavior.
- Thre may be frequent startle reactions, hypervigilance.
- There may be nightmares and poor ability to go to sleep and stay asleep.
- There may be somatic complaints.

Toddlers: Does your toddler ever appear nervous or worried? Does this keep your toddler from social interaction or normal routines? Have you needed to put strategies in place to help your toddler cope with fears or worries?

Preschoolers/School Age: Does your child show you through his/her words or actions that he/she is unsettled or worried at times? Are there certain times that your child displays worries? What have you done to help your child with worries? Has this interfered with your child's activities?

Trauma Reactions

Trauma is an experience that can have serious implications for children of all ages. Children may experience developmental arrest, developmental regression, depression (see "Depression"), anxiety (see "Anxiety"), cognitive disturbances, and perhaps, most significantly, impairment in their abilities to use the attachment relationship (see "Attachment"). More specifically, research has indicated that children may develop abnormal patterns in their abilities to express their feelings, unusual or deviant patterns of behavior, distractibility, inattention, disturbances in eating and elimination patterns, poor sleep, and delays in motor and language acquisition (Scheeringa & Gaensbauer, 2000). Children may develop distorted views about their safety, the safety of others, and view others as threatening and harmful to their own well-being. It is also true that children respond to trauma in an individualized fashion, and the duration of these reactions may range from short term to long lasting. Table 9.9 shows factors that may affect the way a child responds to trauma.

The child's response to trauma is impacted by a number of variables and impacts his/her ability to cope with ongoing stressors. One variable that has significant impact is the child's temperament. In considering temperamental variables, it is important to be aware of what the child's temperament consists of and how these variables are received and supported within the home. A child who is adaptable and comfortable with change will use this to his/her benefit in the face of trauma. If a child is challenged in this capacity, caregivers who are aware and able to assist the child in this area can make a significant difference for the child. The child's developmental status is significant as well. If a child is focused on attempting to master major developmental tasks, his/her emotional reservoir may be more easily drained. A child's age is also an

Table 9.9
Factors Affecting Response to Trauma

- Temperamental variations
- Age and developmental stage
- Caregivers responses and ability to support the child
- Presence of environmental supports
- Intellectual ability
- Degree of structure and predictability within the home
- Presence of age-appropriate explanations regarding trauma
- Ability of the child to integrate the taumatic experience
- Caregivers abilities to predict child's need for support in the presence of traumatic reminders and ability to demonstrate support to child
- Degree of perceived threat or harm to child and/or significant others

important factor. Children who are preverbal may incorporate memories in a manner that is harder to access and process. The ability to use cognitive appraisal and restructuring to reassess and reframe troublesome issues is a helpful skill that older children develop. The use of this skill to mediate anxiety is a particular advantage and may not be available to a younger child. Of all the age groups, children under the age of 5 are the least resilient when it comes to trauma. Early childhood trauma can have the greatest impact due to its ability to alter fundamental neurochemical processes, which in turn affect the growth, structure, and functioning in the brain. If the child has caregivers who can provide a basic feeling of being safe and a predictable routine, a child will stabilize much faster than if this is not present. A child may need the opportunity to process what occurred with an adult and gain an understanding that will also help with feelings of anxiety. A child's magical thinking or errors in cognition may contribute to less-managed anxiety. The type of trauma needs to be understood as well. There are various types of trauma (e.g., medical; disasters, such as flooding or tornados; abuse; neglect; separation from caregivers; exposure to domestic violence or violence in the community). The *DC 0-3 R* (Zero to Three, 2005, pp. 15-16) indicates that the criteria for traumatic stress disorder include a response to a traumatic event, which includes the following:

1. Symptoms of reexperiencing the trauma in the form of posttraumatic play, repeated statements or questions about the trauma, nightmares, distress at exposure, or dissociation;

2. A numbing of responsiveness that may include restricted range of affect, social withdrawal, regression, or constricted play;

3. Increased arousal that may include night terrors, night waking, attentional difficulties, or startle response; and

4. Signs of fear or aggression that began after the trauma (e.g., separation anxiety, fear of dark, aggression towards peers or animals, sudden new fears, or reenactment).

Caregiver Interview: In discussing trauma reactions with caregivers, the following explanation and sample questions are helpful:

Understanding your child's reactions to any situation that may have been traumatic or scary to him/her is important.

Infants: Do you have any concerns that your infant has experienced or witnessed a difficult situation? Has your infant been separated from you? Have you noticed any regression in your infant's development? Does your infant appear to be on guard or worried at times? Have there been any changes in the way your infant responds to you or others? Is your infant easily agitated or subdued since a stressful situation?

Toddlers and Preschoolers/School Age. Do you have any concerns that your child has experienced or witnessed a difficult situation? Has your child experienced separations from caregivers? Has your child demonstrated nightmares, night fears, or changes in behavior after a difficult situation? Do certain situations make your child uncomfortable or react in a way that is unusual for him/her? Have there been disruptions in your child's routines due to his/her reactions or worries?

Attachment

Attachment refers to the special relationship between a child and his/her caregivers, which is established within the first year of life. As infants experiences getting needs met throughout the first months of life, they begin to associate gratification and security within the caregiving relationship. This ultimately leads to feelings of affection, and by 8 months of age, an infant will typically exhibit a preference for the primary caregiver. Infants who do not experience their needs being met or responded to in a consistent and predictable pattern will typically develop insecure patterns of attachment. The benefits of a secure attachment have been researched significantly and are far reaching. Levy (1998) summarizes these benefits as promoting positive development in self-esteem, independence, and autonomy; impulse control; conscience development; long-term friendships; prosocial coping skills; relationships with caregivers and adults; trust, intimacy, and affection; empathy; compassion; behavioral and academic performance; and the ability to form secure attachments with their own children when they become adults. Table 9.10 provides signs of attachment disturbance in young children.

Caregiver Interview: In discussing attachment with caregivers, the following explanation and sample questions are helpful:

Attachment refers to your child's relationship to his/her caregivers.

Infants: Do you feel able to comfort your infant? Is it difficult to understand what your infant wants from you? Do you feel your infant prefers you to others? How does your infant react to strangers and separation from you?

Toddlers: How do you feel about you and your toddler's interaction? Do you feel your toddler is too clingy? How does your toddler react to you after

Table 9.10
Signs of Attachment Disturbance in Young Children

- Lack of preference for primary caregiver
- Indiscriminate affection with unfamiliar adults
- Lack of expectation for getting needs met
- Lack of comfort seeking when hurt or upset
- Comfort seeking in an odd manner
- Excessive clinginess
- Poor ability to tolerate separation
- Strange or mixed reactions to reunion with caregivers
- Low level of compliance with caregivers
- Controlling behavior
- Lack of exploratory behavior
- Low level of affection or physical contact within dyad

a separation? Does your toddler seek help from you when hurt or needy? Does your toddler display preferences for you when with other adults?

Preschoolers/School Age: How would you describe your child's relationship to you? How does your child handle separations from you? Do you feel special to your child? What does your child do to seek out your attention? How does your child react to you when he/she is sick or upset?

Aggression

Important considerations in the assessment of aggression include the following: the severity of the aggression, pervasiveness of behavior, ability to use caregivers' support to discontinue behavior, and frequency of the behavior. Aggression may be present for a variety of reasons including caregiver concerns, modeling of inappropriate behavior, poor impulse control, regulatory and sensory concerns, or depression.

Caregiver Interview: In discussing aggression with caregivers, the following explanation and sample questions are helpful:

Understanding if your child has either threatened to or hurt other children or adults is important. Aggression is not rated in infants. Verbal as well as physical aggression is considered.

Toddlers: Have there been situations in which others have been hurt by your toddler? Can you describe the situation? What were the results of this situation? Were there things that you or others have done to make the situation better? Have other caregivers refused to care for your toddler due to this?

Preschoolers/School Age: Do you or others have any concerns in this area? If so, can you describe situations in which this is a concern? Has anything helped the situation? What does your child say about this problem? Has this caused any disruptions or limitations in your child's activities? Has your child been asked not return to school settings because of this?

Oppositional Behavior

Oppositional behavior is a significant concern for caregivers and teachers. It is one of the most common reasons for referral for a mental health assessment. The American Academy of Child and Adolescent Psychiatry (2009) describes oppositional defiant behavior as follows:

> All children are oppositional from time to time, particularly when tired, hungry, stressed or upset. They may argue, talk back, disobey, and defy parents, teachers, and other adults. Oppositional behavior is often a normal part of development for two to three year olds and early adolescents. However, openly uncooperative and hostile behavior becomes a serious concern when it is so frequent and consistent that it stands out when compared with other children of the same age and developmental level and when it affects the child's social, family and academic life.

Behavioral difficulties may range from significant to mild and may interfere with a child's functioning in varying ways. In determining how to rate this oppositional behavior, it is important to remember that etiology is not a factor in the rating. Although a child may be experiencing ineffective caregiving, which explains the oppositional behavior, it is still present. Oppositional behavior refers to reactions toward adults, not peers. Table 9.11 provides the characteristics of oppositional behavior in children over the age of 3.

> *Caregiver Interview:* In discussing oppositional behavior with caregivers, the following explanation and sample questions are helpful:

> How your child reacts to authority figures is important. Do you have any concerns in this area? Do any adults who interact with your child have concerns in this area? How does your child respond to being told what to do? Does your child become angry easily or often with authority figures? What has been done to help your child in this area?

Impulsivity/Hyperactivity

Impulsivity/hyperactivity refers to both a child's ability to control impulses as well as his/her activity level. Both of these areas need to be considered as problematic only when they impairs functioning, are observed in more than one setting, and are outside the realm of what is considered normal for the child's age and development. Both of these behaviors may result in disruptions in relationships and interfer with the development of new skills. Attention deficit hyperactivity disorder (ADHD) is considered appropriate as a diagnosis according to the *DSM-IV-TR* if

> 6 or more of the following symptoms of hyperactivity or impulsivity have persisted for at least 6 months: often fidgets with hands or feet or squirms in seat, often leaves seat in classroom or other situations, often runs about or

Table 9.11
Characteristics of Difficult Oppositional Behavior in Children Over 3

- "Hostile defiance" rather than attempts to negotiate or avoid punishment
- Consistent pattern of refusal to comply to adult requests
- Temper tantrums
- Loss of temper
- Arguing with adults
- Anger and vindictiveness
- Blaming others for mistakes
- Annoying or provoking others

climbs excessively in situations in which it is inappropriate, often has difficulty playing or engaging in leisure activities quietly, is often on the go, often talks excessively, often blurts out answers, often has difficulty awaiting turns, and often intrudes on others. (American Psychiatric Association, 2000, p. 92)

Caregiver Interview: In discussing impulsivity/hyperactivity with caregivers, the following explanation and sample questions are helpful:

Impulsivity/hyperactivity refers to difficulties your child may have controlling activity levels and actions in a way that should fit with his/her developmental abilities.

Infants: Does your infant's activity level concern you? Have you needed to find ways to prevent your infant from getting hurt due to his/her activity level? What happens as the result of your infant being active?

Toddlers: Have you or anyone else had concerns in this area? What do you think would be a normal level of activity? Does your toddler run and climb excessively? Do you or others have trouble controlling your toddler? Does your toddler require more supervision than others his/her age?

Preschoolers/School Age: Do you or others have any concerns in this area? Does your child need a high level of supervision? Does your child seem to make poor decisions over and over again, despite being taught otherwise? Does your child have difficulty sitting down to eating or engaging in activities like circle time in school? Describe your child's activity level?

Attention

Attention is something that develops with age and should be considered problematic only within the framework of the child's developmental capacities. Attention is considered problematic when an infant or child cannot focus long enough to complete a task or activity. Ways in which this may be presented include distractibility, shifting from activity to activity, not finishing tasks, or rapidly shifting attention. An infant may not be able to focus for more than five to six seconds on a person, toy, or interaction. Young children may appear to not play for periods of time that would seem normal for their age, often show confusion about what is occurring, miss parts of conversations or pieces of information, and may not attend to self-care tasks.

Caregiver Interview: In discussing attention with caregivers, the following explanation and sample questions are helpful:

Understanding if your child has difficulties attending to tasks as well as interactions with others is important. Infants are not rated here.

Toddlers: Have you or anyone else had concerns in this area? Does your toddler seem different in this area than others his/her age? Does it take a tremendous amount of energy to keep your toddler's attention for more than ten seconds? Does your toddler switch from activity to activity excessively?

Preschoolers/School Age: Do you or others have any concerns in this area? Does your child seem to have enough attention to function in play or other activities? How does this interfere in his/her routines? Does your child give up quickly on tasks? How have teachers described your child in this area?

FUNCTIONING WITHIN EARLY CARE/EDUCATION SETTINGS AND THE COMMUNITY

Early Care/Education Settings

Infants, toddlers, and preschoolers may spend the majority of their days with alternate caregivers. It is critical that these environments meet the needs of these children. It is clear that the same parenting practices and caregiving techniques that are taught in the home need to be promoted within early care/education settings. These experiences are often critical in supporting growth and development, and allowing the children to feel positive about relationships with others outside of the home. Early care and education settings have the potential to impact a child's development, school success, and overall life success. The quality of the day care environment is important to consider as well as the day care facility's ability to meet the needs of the child within a larger caregiving context. It is important for infants and children to be supported in ways that appreciates their individual needs and strengths. When assessing early care/education settings, practitioners should look for ways that the parents or children can indicate that the unique qualities of the children are being accepted and embraced. The following are indicators of an appropriate early care/education setting:

- The infants or children seem comfortable with caregivers and the environment;
- The environment allows for movement and space for materials;
- The environment offers a variety of experiences and opportunities;
- Caregivers appreciate individual differences of children;
- Caregivers seem to understand children's feelings and thoughts;
- Caregivers provide appropriate structure to the children's days; and
- The schedule reflects balance of activities and allows for quiet times/breaks.

Caregiver Interview: In discussing early care/education settings with caregivers, the following explanation and sample questions are helpful:

Early care/education settings refer to your child's ability to get his/her needs met in these settings.

Infants: How would you describe the input you receive from staff at early care settings regarding your infant? How do you feel regarding the care that your infant receives? How do you feel your infant has adjusted to this setting?

Toddlers: Can you describe the input you receive from staff at early care settings regarding your toddler's behavior and responses to staff and other children? Does your toddler seem to enjoy this setting? What observations have you made of your toddler in this setting?

Preschoolers/School Age: Can you describe your child's past and current early care/educational experiences? What are your child's attitudes regarding preschool/school? Does your child's teacher seem to understand his/her needs? How does your child get along with other children in school?

Community Settings

Social behavior refers to the child's behavior within a social setting that may or may not need sanctioning by an adult. A child who is unable to function appropriately in a social setting may be kept from participating in these types of activities. This may interfere with the child's opportunity to further develop in this area. Caregivers may have concerns about allowing children to be in problematic social situations. These include the children harming others or themselves, caregivers' lack of willingness or energy to adequately supervise and support the children's challenges, and caregivers' embarrassment regarding the inappropriate behaviors. In assessing whether there are challenges in this area, the following considerations should be made:

- What are the caregivers' understandings of age-appropriate behaviors?
- What types of behaviors are present, and how long lasting are they?
- Can the child discontinue behaviors considered inappropriate with adult intervention?
- Do the behaviors threaten either the child or others?
- Does the child's behaviors result in caregivers avoiding certain situations?
- Does the child enjoy social situations?

Table 9.12 provides examples of typically developing patterns of social behavior.

Caregiver Interview: In discussing community settings with caregivers, the following explanation and sample questions are helpful:

Community settings refer to your child's behavior in social settings.

Table 9.12
Typically Developing Patterns of Social Behavior

- Infants will demonstrate voluntary efforts to initiate action with others and sustain interaction with them. Infants will change interaction patterns based on facial expressions.
- Toddlers will use the reactions of their primary caregivers to guide their own reactions (social referencing). Toddlers can comply with simple directions and restrictions.
- Preschoolers will generally cooperate with caregivers and need less ongoing support and guidance to maintain control in social setting. They are able to remember rules and have internalized basic standards of behavior.
- Early school-age children are able to regulate their actions through discussion. They have internalized standards of behavior and rely less on others to enforce basic standards. They are capable of judging their own behavior and the behavior of others.

Infants: How would you describe your infant's responses to social settings? Does your infant now or in the past have reactions that make outings difficult? What are other adult's reactions to your infant?

Toddlers: How would you describe your toddler's behavior in public settings? How do other adults respond to your toddler in public settings? Do you need to plan for or have strategies to make outings go well?

Preschoolers/School Age: How would you describe your child's behavior in public settings? Have there been times this did not go well? Are there activities that are avoided for your child because of his/her behavior? How would you describe other adult's reactions to your child?

STRENGTHS DISCOVERY

This section focuses on the attributes, traits, talents, and skills of youth, which can be useful in developing strength-based treatment plans. Within a system of care approach, identifying strengths is considered an essential part of the process (Miles, Burns, Osher, Walker, & National Wraparound Initiative Advisory Group, 2006). A focus on strengths that both the youth and the family have to offer allows for a climate of hope and optimism, and has been proven to engage families at a higher level. Strength-based assessment has been defined as "the measurement of those emotional and behavioral skills, competencies, and characteristics that create a sense of personal accomplishment; contribute to satisfying relationships with family members, peers, and adults; enhance one's ability to deal with adversity and stress; and promote one's personal, social, and academic development" (Epstein & Sharma, 1998, p.3). The benefits of a strength-based assessment include involving caregivers and youth in a service planning experience that builds on what a youth and family are doing well, facilitates positive expectations for the youth, and empowers family members to take responsibility for the decisions that will affect their youth (Johnson & Friedman, 1991; Saleebey, 1992).

Interpersonal Skills

The infant or child's capacity to relate to others in a positive manner is a capacity that can be of great benefit in numerous ways. Youth who are perceived by others as pleasant to associate with usually are blessed with a greater number of social interactions as well as longer periods of time in interaction with others. The importance of a youth experiencing positive interactions with others has been researched extensively and is now proven in numerous brain development studies. *From Neurons to Neighborhoods: The Science of Early Childhood Development* (Shonkoff, Phillips, & Board on Children, Youth, and Families (États-Unis), Committee on Integrating the Science of Early Childhood Development, 2000) included as one of its core concepts the notion that "human relationships, and the effects of relationships on relationships, are the building blocks of health development" (p. 4). It furthers this concept later when referring to the importance of relationships on brain development in stating that "developmental neurobiologists have begun to understand how experience becomes integrated into the developing architecture of the human brain. . . . brain development therefore depends on an intimate integration of nature and nurture throughout the life course" (p. 54). Not only do youth who are inept at relating to others have greater and more sustained interactions with others but they are more likely to get their needs met. Infants and young children who evoke positive reactions in others are responded to in a more positive manner than those that are less sociable. Even if a young child's methods for getting his/her needs met when upset or stressed are less than desirable, if that same child has built up positive relationships with caregivers and other adults, he/she will benefit. Caregivers and authority figures also tend to be less reactive and more nurturing to youth who are interpersonally strong when the need for correction or discipline occurs. Table 9.13 provides manifestations of interpersonal skills in infant, toddlers, and preschoolers/school age children.

> ***Caregiver Interview:*** In discussing interpersonal skills with caregivers, the following explanation and sample questions are helpful:
>
> Interpersonal skills refer to how well your child relates to others and how he/ she is perceived by others. How easy is it for you and others to engage your child? Do adults or other children enjoy being around your child? How does your child do in social settings?

Positive Temperament Characteristics

All individuals have characteristics that are easily recognized by others and are stable throughout their lifetimes. These characteristics remain the predominant or "default" reactions to others and the environment but may be modified as a youth matures and receives support as needed. The originally defined components of temperament as defined by Thomas and Chess (1977) include sensitivity, intensity, activity level, adaptability, approach/withdrawal, persistence, rhythmicity, quality of mood, and distractibility. Sensitivity refers to the level of stimulation needed to cause a reaction. Some individuals experience a high threshold for sensory stimulation, which allows them to tolerate or ignore experiences that others with a low threshold are bothered or annoyed by. Intensity refers to the level of response that a youth has.

Table 9.13
Interpersonal Skills

Infants	Toddlers	Preschoolers/School Age
Smiles	Reactions to others are synchronous	Prefers peers
Establishes eye contact	Acknowledges new people with gestures and/or words	Initiates conversation with adults
Imitates others	Establishes appropriate eye contact	Accepts praise
Initiates physical contact	Develops awareness of social boundaries	Shares successes
Laughs	Responds to humor	Develops appropriate interpretations of social cues

Activity level refers to the quantity and type of activity level that the youth experiences. Approach/withdrawal refers to the skills a youth has in handling new situations. Persistence involves the ability of the youth to continue to attempt a task or experience that is difficult. Rhythmicity refers to a youth's natural ability or need for regularity in bodily functions, sleep, arousal, and activity. Quality of mood is considered the youth's general mood, which may be cheerful or fussy and irritable. Distractibility refers to a youth's ability to remain focused on an activity or interaction. When a youth is considered to have an "easy," temperament he/she has the characteristics of regular rhythm, positive approach, adaptability, moderate intensity, persistence, pleasant mood, and normal activity level. These characteristics not only make a youth less challenging to interact with but contribute to the youth's own experiences as being less challenging.

> *Caregiver Interview:* In discussing this area with caregivers, the following sample questions are helpful:

> Would you describe your child as easy or difficult to interact with in general? Is your child typically predictable in his/her sleeping and eating patterns? When your child reacts to a situation, is it with more or less intensity than others? Does your child give up on things easily? How would you describe your child's normal activity level? What is your child's mood most of the time? Does your child focus well on activities or tasks?

Creativity/Imagination

Toddlers and preschoolers may exhibit the characteristic of creativity/imagination in varying ways and to different degrees. Creativity reflects the ability to think "out of the box." Children who demonstrate this ability are able to accept explanations,

Table 9.14
Manifestations of Creativity in Toddlers and
Preschoolers/School Age Children

Toddlers

- Explores art and music
- Pretends with objects
- Develops pretend play without objects
- Develops pretend play with pther inanimate objects (e.g., dolls)
- Tells stories
- Has imaginary friends
- Develops ability to use objects in alternative ways (e.g., block can be a phone)

Preschoolers/School Age

- Finds enjoyment in drawing and creating
- Offers interpretations of artwork reflecting feelings and experiences
- Can play independently for extended periods of time
- Enjoys music and sings songs about life experiences
- Enjoys dress-up activities
- Tells detailed stories
- Displays greater capacity for the abstract

solutions, and alternatives to problems. This allows them to accept changes more easily and therefore cope with challenging situations more successfully. This will also result in expanding play sequences as well as developing opportunities to play when other children would be limited in this capacity. When children are rigid in their thinking, this makes them more challenging to discipline, socialize, and interact with. Rigid thinking is as frustrating for the child as it is for caregivers, due to the inability to control changes and life events. Creativity/imagination is often manifested in artistic, musical, and literary abilities as well as skills in the dramatic arts. This is demonstrated by a child's interest in thinking broadly and expressing his/her ideas, feelings, and experiences. The emotional benefit may be anxiety reducing and compliments verbal methods of processing feelings. Some children who are challenged in their ability to process their feelings verbally can compensate by using creative means. Manifestations of creativity in toddlers and preschoolers/school-age children are provided in Table 9.14.

Caregiver Interview: In discussing creativity/imagination with caregivers, the following explanation and sample questions are helpful:

Creativity/imagination should be assessed for preschoolers/school-age children only. Creativity/imagination refers to a child's ability to come up with new ideas and to be good at problem solving. Does your child enjoy telling stories or having imaginary friends? Does your child demonstrate the ability to come up with ways to cope with a problem? During play, does your child use toys only for their intended use or in various ways? Would your child be good at "brainstorming" ideas or avoid doing this if asked?

Table 9.15
Categories of Intelligence

Linguistic Intelligence "Word Smart"	Skills in speaking, writing, understanding meaning of words, debating, and explaining concepts or their point of view. May be interested in drama, journaling, or writing stories.
Musical Intelligence	Skills in playing instruments, recognizing songs and patterns/rhythms, or singing.
Interpersonal Intelligence	Skills in listening, responding with empathy, awareness of other's feelings, awareness of social cues, forming relationships with peers and adults.
Intrapersonal Intelligence	Skills in being aware of own feelings, strengths, and weaknesses. Develops within a caring, nurturing relationship with caregivers.
Visual Spatial Intelligence	Skills in puzzle building, legos, construction toys, copying designs, sense of direction.
Logical/Mathematical Intelligence	Skills in sorting and classifying, sequencing, understanding number concepts, understanding shapes.
Bodily/Kinesthetic Intelligence	Skills in physical coordination, sports, hands-on tasks, crafts, and expressing feelings through the body.

Special Skills/Talents

The presence of special skills or talents has been a characteristic of resilient youth noted in several longitudinal studies (Werner, 1990). Youth who demonstrate capacity in this area can focus their time, attention, and skills in a manner that is both enjoyable and supportive of their growth and development. A youth who spends time demonstrating a special skill is often encouraged by both peers and adults in a way that develops self-concept and self-esteem. A talent that is truly of benefit to a youth is enjoyable and not imposed on him/her by adults. Youth should demonstrate their own initiative to participate in this activity. This is manifested by the youth initiating the activity, conversing about the activity, and planning for continuation of the activity (see Table 9.15). This certainly can be supported by the adults in the youth's life, but, to fully be of use to the youth, it should be his/her own investment. As Howard Gardner (1983) has described, the concept of multiple intelligences can be used to identify areas in which a youth may have special skills or talent.

Caregiver Interview: In discussing special skills/talents with caregivers, the following explanation and sample questions are helpful:

It is helpful to identify if your child has demonstrated special skills or talents that would be beneficial to continue to foster. Does your child show a special

Table 9.16
Manifestations of Strong Self-Esteem

- Child accepts compliments
- Child points out successes
- Child tries difficult tasks
- Child socializes well with peers
- Child accepts correction
- Child gves others compliments

interest in certain activities? Does your child seem to be able to develop skills in a certain area? Does your child use special skills or talents in his activities, play, or school environments? How would you describe that this developed and what have you found supports this?

Self-Esteem

Self-esteem refers to the youth's belief that he/she is worthwhile, competent, and able to succeed. It is hard to imagine how this would not be considered an essential characteristic for a youth to have. A youth is constantly exposed to new tasks, changes, and challenges that are tolerated by this core belief. A youth who does not reflect a strong sense of self is handicapped in numerous ways. Youth will not typically attempt or sustain new activities or tasks, nor will they achieve the same capacity without self-esteem. Self-esteem is further developed as a youth experiences making friends, achieves developmental milestones, and learns new skills, experiences love and support, experiences encouragement for efforts, and feels valued. Positive self-esteem is associated with positive mental health, academic achievement, good behavior, and frustration tolerance. Poor self-esteem is more often associated with negative behavior, frustration intolerance, poor academic achievement, social withdrawal, and poor peer relations. Table 9.16 provides manifestations of strong self-esteem.

Caregiver Interview: In discussing self-esteem with caregivers, the following explanation and sample questions are helpful:

How your child feels about him-/herself and his/her abilities is called self-esteem. Infants are not rated here.

Toddlers: How would you describe your toddler's confidence in and his/her abilities? Do you have any concerns in this area? Are there certain situations in which you see issues? Does your toddler show excitement about his/her accomplishments?

Preschoolers/School Age: How would you describe your child's feelings about him-/herself and his/her abilities? How does your child show this to you? Does your child point out to you and others things that he/she does well? How does your child respond to praise?

Positive Relationships With Extended Family or Other Adults

The relationships that young children experience with extended family and other adults can be of great significance. Often, the significant others in a child's life serve to support him/her with additional experiences of unconditional love and acceptance. In addition, the other adults in a child's life assist in supporting the caregivers so the child's experiences with his/her caregivers are improved.

> *Caregiver Interview:* In discussing positive relationships with extended family or other adults with caregivers, the following explanation and sample questions are helpful:
>
> It is important to understand if extended family members are a part of your child's life and if these relationships are helpful to your child. Does your child's extended family play a part in your child's life? What types of activities do your child and extended family members do together? How would you describe the importance of these relationships to you and your child?

CONCLUSION

Infants, toddlers, and preschoolers can be complex to assess. The interplay between development and mental health challenges should never be overlooked. The way in which issues present is related to temperament, family circumstances, and overall level of development. The assessment process should never be rushed in young children, and multiple interactions should be utilized to gain as accurate an understanding of the child as possible. Additionally, caregivers are in need of support to understand the areas that are being assessed. Mental health intervention with young children is often their first interaction with practitioners, and it is critical to instill a positive understanding of how services should occur.

References

American Academy of Child and Adolescent Psychiatry. (2009). Facts for families: Children with oppositional defiant disorder. No. 72. Retrieved June 16, 2010, from http://www.aacap.org/es/root/facts_for_families/children_with_oppositional_defiant_disorder

American Psychiatric Association. (2000). *Diagnostic and statistical manual of mental disorders* (4th ed., text rev.). Washington, DC: Author.

Epstein, M. H., & Sharma, J. (1998). *Behavioral and Emotional Rating Scale: A strength-based approach to assessment.* Austin, TX: PRO-ED.

Freud, A., & Burlingham, D. (1944). *Infants without families.* New York: International Universities Press.

Gardner, H. (1983). *Frames of mind: The theory of multiple intelligences.* New York: Basic Books.

Greenspan, S. I., & Meisels, S. J. (1996). Toward a new vision for the devlopmental asessment of infants and young children. In S. J. Meisels & E. Fenichel (Eds.), *New visions for the developmental assessment of infants and young children* (pp. 11-26). Washington DC: Zero to Three Press.

Johnson, M. K., & Freidman, R. M. (1991). Strength-based assessment. *Program Update, 7,* 10-11.

Landy, S. (2002). *Pathways to competence: Encouraging healthy social and emotional development in young children.* Baltimore: Paul H. Brookes Publishing.

Levy, T., & Orlans, M. (1998). *Attachment, trauma, and healing: Understanding and treating attachment disorder in children and families.* Washington, DC: Child Welfare League of America Press.

Miles, P., Bruns, E. J., Osher, T. W., Walker, J. S., & National Wraparound Initiative Advisory Group. (2006). *The wraparound process user's guide: A handbook for families.* Portland, OR: National Wraparound Initiative, Research and Training Center on Family Support and Children's Mental Health, Portland State University.

Saleebey, D. (1992). *The strengths perspective in social work practice* (2nd ed.). New York: Longman.

Scheeringa, M., & Gaensbauer, T. (2000). Posttraumatic stress disorder. In C. H. Zeanah (Ed.), *Handbook of infant mental health* (2nd ed.) (pp. 364-381). New York: Guilford Press.

Shonkoff, J. P., Phillips, D., & Board on Children, Youth, and Families (États-Unis), Committee on Integrating the Science of Early Childhood Development (Eds.). (2000). *From neurons to neighborhoods: The science of early childhood development.* Washington, DC: National Academy Press.

Thomas, A., & Chess, S. (1977). *Temperament and development.* New York: Brunner/Mazel.

Werner, E. E. (1990). Protective factors and individual resilience. In S. J. Meisels & J. P. Shonkoff (Eds.), *Handbook of early childhood intervention* (pp. 97-116). New York: Cambridge University Press.

Zero to Three. (2005). *Diagnostic classification of mental health and developmental disorders of infancy and early childhood* (Rev. ed.). Washington, DC: Author.

Chapter 10

Assessing School-Age Children Within the Context of Family and Community

We cannot always build the future for our youth, but we can build our youth for the future.

—Franklin D. Roosevelt

Keep true to the dreams of thy youth.

—Friedrich von Schiller

INTRODUCTION

Assessment is an essential function of service delivery. An adequate amount of time should always be given to this task. The ecological approach clearly demonstrates the complexity of multiple influences in a person's life. The school-age child is sometimes considered to be at a stage of development where the strong relationship between mental health functioning and development is less apparent. Although the stage of development of school-age children is more consolidated and stable than a toddler, it is nonetheless a significant area to consider. This, along with all other areas in a child's life, must not only be considered from the individual perspective but the family perspective as well. This chapter outlines the many areas to include in a comprehensive assessment of a school-age child.

STRUCTURING THE SCHOOL-AGE CHILD'S ASSESSMENT

The way in which the assessment unfolds should be individualized to meet the needs of the family. The assessment components serve as a guide for the practitioner to discuss the options of how to include or modify the needed components with the family. It is important not to be rigid about the way in which the assessment is completed, as the results will not be accurate if the assessment does not fit the culture of the family.

FUNCTIONING BY LIFE DOMAIN

There are many facets that make up the whole picture of a school-age child's level of functioning. No one area remains untouched by the other areas. A youth's life is complex, and the understanding of how all the pieces fit together and impact one another is essential and reflects an ecological approach. A comprehensive assessment includes functioning in the areas of youth and family strengths, development, mental health functioning, behavior, community life, school, home, health and wellness, substance abuse as well as the presence of risk factors. Each domain has several items to assessed related to that domain, which will result in an in-depth understanding of how strengths and needs present in each area.

DEVELOPMENTAL FUNCTIONING

Importance of Understanding Developmental History

Obtaining a thorough developmental history gives the practitioner a context for understanding and appreciating the abilities as well as challenges that are presently occurring. A comprehensive developmental history should be prioritized as a task of assessment, as it informs the practitioner of possible discontinuities or changes in development as well as how the caregivers feel about the child's progression in this area. Caregivers who have concerns, frustrations, or worries related to their school-age child's development should be supported by the practitioners.

Motor Development

Middle childhood is a time in which youth refine their fundamental motor skills. The fundamental motor skills are typically acquired and refined in such tasks as running, galloping, jumping, hopping, skipping, throwing, catching, striking, and kicking. As youth continue to develop these skills, they eventually demonstrate the ability to master more complex motor skills. These types of skills are needed typically for team sports. Along with greater finesse and ability, balance and reaction time improves (Patrick, Spear, Holt, & Sofka, 2001). Fine motor skills are also improved during this period. This is demonstrated in handwriting and drawing skills as well as the ability to grasp and handle small objects (Davies, 2004). Gross motor developmental milestones typically have a wide range of what is considered normal variation. Fine motor milestones have a more narrow range. Difficulties in meeting developmental milestones may be described by caregivers as clumsiness, lack of coordination, poor handwriting, or poor athletic ability. When a youth's development is significantly delayed and impairment in academic and daily living occurs, a diagnosis of developmental coordination disorder may be appropriate. The prevalence of this disorder is up to 6 percent for 5- to 11-year-olds (Wolraich, Felice, & Drotar, 1996).

Speech and Language Development

By the time a youth reaches middle childhood, there should be a fundamental ability to use language in a functional manner. It should feel comfortable and meet a youth's needs for relating to others. Youth in this phase of development present with a wide range of abilities, and there are many developments from the beginning to the end of this age range. Youth by age 6 will typically have a working vocabulary and sense of grammatical structure that meets their needs for communicating. A first-grader will typically know the meaning of approximately 8,000 words. This number will grow to approximately 80,000 words by high school (Zembar & Blume, 2009). As the youth moves through this phase of development, there is continued development in the ability to use abstract words, understand the pragmatics of speech, and clearly organize and sequence conversations (Santrock, 1993; Davies, 2004). Others who are listening to a youth should be able to identify a beginning, middle, and end to narratives that are shared. Youth in this stage of development are not confined by literal interpretations and can demonstrate this by making interpretations of what a person intended to say by considering context and the multiple meanings of words. This leads to the ability to comprehend simple jokes and simple sarcasm. Youth during middle childhood are honing their skills in understanding active and passive voice, correct use of subject-verb and noun-pronoun agreement (Zembar & Blume, 2009; Davies, 2004).

The skill of taking the perspective of another is a significant development in this stage. Preschoolers (see Chapter 9 in this volume) remain egocentric in their orientation and fragile in their ability to consider others' ideas and structure their conversations to appreciate others' ideas. As they mature, the words that are used, the tone, inflection. and manner in which they speak can be altered depending on who they are speaking to.

School-age children can anticipate how an adult versus a child will think differently about the way in which they communicate the same concepts. Youth will also demonstrate the ability to show others that they understand their perspective in spoken and unspoken ways. A youth may alter the course of the conversation based on this understanding or use gestures to demonstrate understanding of what another is thinking. This skill allows for conversations to be extended and maintained, and for others to want to converse with the youth.

Problems in speech and language can be identified by both school-age children and caregivers in a number of ways. Caregivers may address an inability to understand a youth's words. This has almost always been identified in early stages of development. When caregivers identify an inability to understand the meaning of what their child is attempting to communicate, this may or may not have been as apparent in younger years. Basic skills may have been mastered, but as language expectations and attempts are made at more complex skills in communicating, the deficits may be more notable. A youth with challenges in this stage of development is unable to clearly construct sentences and sequence ideas in a way that results in understanding for others. This demonstrates an expressive language difficulty. Conversely, a youth may not be able to understand what is said to him/her, representing a receptive language challenge. Stuttering is another manifestation of difficulties that may be seen (Wolraich, Felice, & Drotar, 1996).

Cognitive Development

Determining the need for cognitive testing or the presence of cognitive issues can occur in a number of ways. One of the best measures of cognitive ability is a child's academic history. A youth who has cognitive challenges, depending on the degree, will most likely have been evaluated for special education. Obviously, all youth who have poor grades do not have cognitive deficits, but this is a first avenue to consider. In addition, youth should demonstrate the ability to independently care for themselves and attend to the activities of daily living. This may require reminders to attend to such tasks, although a youth's ability to remember how to complete the task should be present. Tasks such as telling time and counting money should be mastered.

Youth in this stage of development are sharpening their skills in the areas of logic and reasoning. These areas show growth and refinement, as the youth moves through middle childhood, but are not fully developed even by the end of this period. Youth may be better able to demonstrate logic and reasoning with concepts that are concrete and familiar, but applying this to abstract concepts is still challenging (Collins, 1984). Thinking, in general, is more logical and sequential, and the perspective of another can now be more fully recognized and appreciated. This is demonstrated by anticipating others' actions, acknowledging such in conversations, and altering behavior to appreciate others' perspectives.

Social and Emotional Development

During middle childhood, youth become increasingly focused on forming relationships outside of the family. Their friends become of primary importance to them (Jellinick, Patel, & Froehle, 2002). They are also aware of the need to develop relationships with teachers and adults in the community who are in a role of authority over them. Youth who are developing typically should identify a group of friends that they prefer to associate with. There may be one person who is considered a youth's "best friend." The skills of functioning within small and larger groups should also be in development. Taking into account individual temperament and environmental situations, a youth developing typically should not feel undue stress or display behavior that results in sanctions from adults when interacting with others. The youth who feels challenged periodically, who can use the help of another adult or peer, is developing typically.

Emotionally there is a wide range of skills that are developing in school-age children. Youth should be able to identify a wide range of emotions when they are witnessed or experienced.

Sensory Processing

In the simple act of walking out of a school building and onto a playground, the brain is most likely barraged with an enormous amount of sensory stimulation. The sights, sounds, feel of the breeze, and the need to negotiate and respond to the movements of multiple students are all registered by the brain and responded to in a variety of ways. This processing of information is identified as sensory integration by Horowitz and Rost (2007), which is defined further as "the processing of information that our eyes, ears, skin, muscles, joints, mouth, nose and sense of balance delivers to the brain" (p. 3). A school-age child should demonstrate an ability to cope with sensory input in a manner that does not result in distress or behavioral issues. All individuals will experience a range of preferences, dislikes, and automatic responses that manifests how they experience sensory processing. The experience of being stressed, tired, or emotionally distraught may mitigate the effectiveness of coping strategies that are typically successful in meeting challenges related to sensory experiences. These should be isolated situations that are difficult, yet, with adult support or altering the situation, the challenges are overcome.

There are several types of sensory input that individuals must respond to, which are generally characterized as auditory, visual, taste/smell, touch, body position, and movement. A youth may be overreactive or underreactive to the various types of experiences. When the brain demonstrates a high sensory threshold, it takes a great deal of input for the brain to respond. This is demonstrated by underreactivity. (For example, if the child has a high sensory threshold, his/her brain can be exposed to much more stimuli before a reaction is noticed than the child who has a low threshold and reacts quickly.) A low sensory threshold is present when it takes very little input for the brain to recognize and respond to it. This is seen in the actions of a hyperreactive individual. Hypersensitivity or hyposensitivity may coexist, as the brain does not necessarily process all types of sensation in the same manner (Ayres, 2005).

Difficult reactions to sensory experiences are challenging for youth, and behaviors are representative of their need to protect themselves from an overwhelming, often aversive, neurological experience. Youth may demonstrate these challenges in their activity level, behavior, social interaction, and emotional responses. Youth may appear over- or underactive in particular situations. It may be difficult for them to attend and focus their attention in certain situations. They may have great difficulty beginning or stopping an activity or appear disorganized in their actions. Many youth with challenges appear clumsy and uncoordinated. Behavior may be characterized as difficult and resistant to intervention. Youth may appear easily frustrated and have difficulty coping with conditions or transitions. They may cry easily or exhibit an overall lack of response. Socially, youth may seem to avoid social situations or demonstrate poor boundaries. Their interactions with adults may seem overly dependent or, on the contrary, disconnected and overly independent (Kranowitz, 1998). The school-age child who demonstrates both strong reactions or hyporeactivity in any sensory modality with an accompanying behavioral or emotional response should be considered in need of intervention. Table 10.1 identifies sample questions related to development.

Table 10.1
Interview Questions Related to Developmental Functioning

Questions for Caregivers

- In the various areas of development what do you see your child doing well?
- Are there certain situations that assist your child in functioning his/her best?
- Do you see your child running, jumping, and climbing with the same degree of ease as others his/her age?
- Do you have concerns that your child is uncoordinated or clumsy?
- Can your child manipulate small items such as utensils in the way that is typical for his/her age?
- Do you have any concerns that your child does not understand what is said to him/her?
- Do you have concerns that your child has difficulty expressing him-/herself?
- Do others understand your child?
- Do you have concerns that your child has any learning challenges?
- Does your child have difficulty with daily living tasks?
- Does your child have difficulty retaining information that he/she has learned?
- Does your child have difficulty making and keeping friends?
- What have you observed related to how your child interacts with others?
- Does your child have difficulty expressing or coping with his/her emotions?
- Does your child have strong preferences for sounds, sights, touch, textures, smells?

Questions for Youth

- What subjects in school do you feel best at? What subjects do you feel are the most difficult?
- Are there things at home or school that you need help understanding how to do?
- Do others understand you when you talk to them?
- Is it hard to find the right words when you are talking to others?
- Do you enjoy playing sports or activities in gym class? When you play on the playground or in gym, what do you do well? What do you do not so well?
- How is it for you making friends? Do you have a best friend?
- Do you feel other kids are nice to you?
- How do you get along with teachers and other adults?
- When you get frustrated, what do you usually do?
- Can you usually figure out how you are feeling?
- What do you feel like most of the time?
- Do sounds ever bother you? At school or at home?
- Do blinking lights bother you? Do any other kinds of lights bother you?

MENTAL HEALTH FUNCTIONING

Mood and Affective Functioning

School-age children typically have many interests, activities, and a desire to interact with their peers. They are generally positive about their lives and the future. They often become irritated with limits that are set by caregivers, mandates given by authority figures, and dynamics that occur within their peer groups. These irritations and frustrations should be short lived and not result in behaviors that result in ongoing problems. Youth in this age range are typically fun-loving, laugh with friends, and positive about themselves.

Youth who are struggling in this area may present with a number of signs and symptoms that do more than reflect individual differences and temperament; rather, they reflect interference with functioning. Youth often experience depressive disorders that are biologically based, and in this case it is common that caregivers are experiencing depression as well. There also may be stressors at school, within their peer groups, within the family environment, or losses that contribute to depression. There are common symptoms and behaviors that are present in youth's feelings, behaviors, and thoughts. A youth who describes, relates, or is observed to be sad, irritable, bored, or unable to find pleasure in activities is often depressed. Accompanying behaviors may include withdrawal, low energy level, defiance, irritability, or regression in functioning. The way in which a youth thinks is usually negatively affected when depression is present. When negative events occur, a youth experiencing depression may distort the meaning of this event. The youth may see the cause of this event as being related to him-/herelf and believe that it will negatively affect other areas of his/her life and impact the future. The youth also may have experienced ongoing negative distortions about him-/herself, the world, and the future, which significantly influence how the new stressor is interpreted (Asarnow, Jaycox, & Tompson, 2001). Youth who are suffering with depressive disorders may represent a continuum of experiences that may range from a serious, life-threatening condition to a lower-level, negative view of themselves and the world, which is a chronic pattern of thinking and behaving. Although, serious, life-threatening depression requires immediate intervention, all levels of depression should be acknowledged and treated.

Thought Disorder/Psychosis

Thought disorder and psychosis are neuropsychiatric symptoms that may represent a range of medical or psychiatric conditions. A thought disorder is manifested by unusual associations that impede communication. A person's thoughts are disorganized, incoherent, nonsequential, or illogical. A delusion is a false belief that does not represent developmental age or cultural orientation. Hallucinations are sensory perceptions in the absence of an actual sensory stimulus (Morrison & Anders, 1999).

In determining the presence of psychotic behavior or thought disorder, it is important to recognize that school-age children are often limited in their ability to relate internal experiences, sensations, and perceptions. The disordered thinking and psychotic processes are often contributing or associated factors in behavioral disturbances, developmental lags, social skill deficits, problem-solving challenges, poor judgment, and poor self-care skills. Socially, youth may become agitated, confused, or anxious. Although these symptoms tend to first present in adolescence, they do occur in younger children as well. The onset may be insidious, as evidenced by a steady increase in the number, frequency, and intensity of symptoms (Taylor, 1998; Torrey, Bowler, Taylor, & Gottesman, 1994).

Trauma Reactions

Trauma reactions may occur when a school-age child experiences an event that is considered overwhelming and leaves him/her feeling unable to cope. Broad thinking is necessary when identifying the types of events that may be considered traumatic, as the criteria for determining an "overwhelming" event may be individual or related to culture. Some examples of events that may be considered traumatic include abuse, neglect, witnessing violence, health procedures or conditions, natural disasters, or accidents. Several factors have been identified in predicting the severity of a trauma reaction as well as the differences in how individuals react to trauma. These factors are identified by Morrison and Anders (1999, p. 358) as

- Duration and severity of the stressful event;
- Overall emotional stability of the affected individual;
- Reactions shown by parents and extended family members;
- The community's social network; and
- Cultural and political factors.

If a traumatic event can be identified, screening should take place to identify potential signs and symptoms indicating that intervention may be necessary. Traumatized youth may experience overall regression in their developmental capacities. The younger youth are, the more likely that this regression is apparent in their presentation. In older youth, changes in the way they relate to others, care for themselves, or complete tasks may be more apparent. Younger school-age children may repetitively act out their memories of the trauma in an effort to master their anxieties through play. New fears, nightmares, or intrusive thoughts may become apparent. A sense of being "on guard" or hypervigilant is often noted. When confronted with a reminder of the incident, a child may reexperience the incident and become distressed, avoidant of the reminder, or disorganized. There may be physiological reactions such as a rapid heartbeat, dizziness, or difficulty breathing. It is also common to identify disturbances in mood in which a youth appears preoccupied, unhappy, worried, or frightened. Conversely, youth may exhibit a numbing of responsiveness in which it appears that they are disconnected or lack reactivity to interactions and their environment (Morrison & Anders, 1999; Davies, 2004). As a more severe reaction, a youth may dissociate, whereby the youth appears to be in an altered state of consciousness. This is a defensive reaction that youth utilize to protect themselves from overwhelming anxiety. When any or several of these symptoms are present and/or there is an interference with functioning, further assessment should occur.

Atypical Behaviors/Autism Spectrum Disorders

Atypical behaviors are often thought of in relation to autism spectrum disorders, which are a group of developmental disabilities that are characterized by atypical development in social, communication, and behavior. The symptoms are typically present before age 3, and there are often associated difficulties. These include learning, attention deficits, and sensory processing difficulties. The conditions that are identified as autism spectrum disorders include autistic disorder, Asperger's disorder, and pervasive developmental disorder not otherwise specified (Rice, 2009). The prevalence of autism spectrum disorders has been estimated at six per 1,000 youth (Newschaffer et al., 2007).

A number of repetitive behaviors are common in typically developing school-age children but may also represent atypical development, especially when seen in combination with self-injurious behavior (Wolraich, Felice, & Drotar, 1996). Difficulties may be present in such areas as motor, perceptual, socioemotional, language, and mental representation. Behaviors related to motor functioning may include toe-walking, rocking, head banging, spinning, sniffing, or repetitive movements. Perceptually, a youth may engage in self-stimulation or stare into space suddenly. From a socioemotional perspective, a youth may insist on rituals, fail to see another's point of view, or remain disconnected from others. In the area of speech and language, there may be limited ability to communicate with written or gestural communication, or echolalia (pathological repetition of what is said by others). In terms of mental representation, there may be an absence of representational play or an inability to solve false-belief problems (Kalmanson, & Pekarsky, 1987).

Substance Use/Abuse

Substance use is a serious issue with youth, which is most commonly underreported and misunderstood. Johnston, O'Mallery, and Bachman (2001) indicated that 30 percent of high school students surveyed reported that they had engaged in binge drinking, which is defined as having at least five drinks in a row. In addition, nearly 50 percent of U.S. students reported having used marijuana, and 29 percent have used another illicit drug by the end of high school. In lieu of these statistics, it should be considered that many older school-aged children have been exposed to substances.

Substance abuse and dependence are described by the American Psychiatric Association (2000) as

- Recurrent substance use despite negative consequences

- Loss of control over use, resulting in any of the following:

  - Failure to meet obligations at school, work or home

  - Recurrent use in physically hazardous situation

  - Legal problems

  - Persistent social and interpersonal problems. (p. 199)

Substance dependence includes the following additional criteria:

- Preoccupation with substance use, which takes up significant amounts of time and interferes with other activities

- Development of tolerance or withdrawal symptoms

- Increase in risk-taking and dangerous drug-related behaviors. (p. 192)

Table 10.2 identifies sample questions related to mental health functioning.

Table 10.2
Interview Questions Related to Mental Health Functioning

Questions for Caregivers

- Are there times your child appears or expresses sadness or lack of interest in activities or interactions with others?
- Does your child appear irritable?
- Are there times when this is better or worse?
- Does your child display worries, fears, or preoccupations?
- Does your child have sleep or appetite disturbance?
- Does your child ever share ideas or experiences that make you suspect he/she is not in touch with reality? Describe hallucinations and disordered thinking.
- Does your child become scared, worried, or on guard under certain circumstances?
- Does your child have nightmares related to a past negative event?
- Does your child have any behaviors such as toe-walking, rocking, head banging, spinning, sniffing, or repetitive movements?
- Do you have any concerns that your child is using substances?

Questions for Youth

- Do you have any activities that you really find enjoyable?
- Do you enjoy being around others?
- Is sleeping a problem for you?
- How would you describe your appetite? Do you eat enough or maybe too much? Has it changed?
- How would you describe your mood most of the time?
- Are there things that worry you? What do you do when you are worried? How often is it that you feel worried?
- Are there times when you use alcohol or drugs?

BEHAVIORAL CONCERNS

Oppositional Behavior

Oppositional behavior, at a level that becomes problematic, is identified by the American Academy of Child and Adolescent Psychiatry (2009) as

an ongoing pattern of uncooperative, defiant, and hostile behavior toward authority figures that seriously interferes with the youngster's day to day functioning. Symptoms of ODD [oppositional defiant disorder] may include:

- Frequent temper tantrums

- Excessive arguing with adults

- Often questioning rules

- Active defiance and refusal to comply with adult requests and rules

- Deliberate attempts to annoy or upset people

- Blaming others for his or her mistakes or misbehavior

- Often being touchy or easily annoyed by others

- Frequent anger and resentment

- Mean and hateful talking when upset

- Spiteful attitude and revenge seeking. (p. 1)

Oppositional behavior is a reflection of an unmet need that an individual is experiencing. Youth with behaviorial issues may be extremely frustrated, suffering emotionally, or unable to cope with stressors that may be beyond their control. In the assessment of behavioral issues, it is reasonable to expect that a full understanding related to etiology may not happen until the relationship with the youth and family is firmly established. Dynamics that may not be able to be verbalized may take time to be displayed so that the practitioner can gain a fuller understanding. Although the factors that contribute to the presence of behavioral problems are important to recognize, the assessment and identification of interventions can certainly begin without full recognition of all factors. This underscores the notion that assessment is an ongoing process. Oppositional behavior may or may not be identified by the youth. The culture of the family must be an integral part of the assessment as well.

Behavioral problems are quite frequently the most recognized and common reason why caregivers refer youth for services. All youth experience some degree of misbehavior and defiance throughout their development. When there is a distinct pattern of behavior that can be described as disobedient, negativistic, or provocative opposition to authority, a need for intervention is present. In middle childhood, most of the time, youth are capable of regulating their behavior and emotions when frustrated or restricted. If problems arise, they are quickly corrected and do not develop into a pattern. Youth who appear angry, attempt to provoke authority figures, or have frequent reactions that are intense and long in duration are developing in a manner that is atypical. Youth with concerning behavior are often described as unresponsive to social reinforcement, punishment, or their relationships with adults (Gard & Berry, 1986).

Conduct Problems

The American Psychiatric Association (2000) identifies conduct disorder as "a repetitive and persistent pattern of behavior in which the basic rights of others or major age-appropriate societal norms or rules are violated" (pp. 93-94). Behaviors that may be present include bullying, threatening or intimidating others, truancy from school, and frequent lying. Other types of behaviors that could result in sanctions include cruelty to animals, using weapons, stealing, vandalism, fire setting, running away, or major violations of caregivers' rules. To meet the criteria for conduct disorder, these behaviors must have caused social and occupational dysfunction (American Psychiatric Association, 2000).

Conduct and behavioral problems are typically the main reason why caregivers or referral sources request services for youth. Youth with conduct problems

Table 10.3
Interview Questions Related to Behavioral Functioning

Questions for Caregivers

- Does your child's behavior cause difficulties for him-/herself or others?
- Has it been challenging to find ways to assist your child in coping?
- In what circumstances do you feel your child does well in maintaining his/her behavior?
- Are there certain people your child responds especially well to?
- Have there been any incidents in which your child did something within the community that resulted in any legal issues?
- How does your child do managing anger?
- Do you know what circumstances in which this is more or less difficult for your child?
- Has your child had difficulties with aggression?

Questions for Youth

- Does the way that you act at home or school ever cause problems?
- When is it easiest for you to follow rules and behave well?
- When is it most challenging for you to follow rules?
- Do others complain about how you behave?

---

may receive high rates of service use and system involvement. Many receive acute hospitalization, residential treatment, special education services, and juvenile justice involvement (Foster & Jones, 2005). These issues may involve the safety of others and therefore cannot be easily overlooked. In the assessment process, it is critical to obtain the viewpoint of the youth, caregivers, referral sources, teachers, and community supports to fully understand how needs are manifesting.

Aggression/Anger Control Issues

Aggression is an area that evokes a great deal of concern in caregivers and practitioners alike. Many associate aggression with the symptoms of conduct disorder (see "Conduct Problems"), although this is quite frequently not a symptom. Loney, Frick, Clements, Ellis, and Kerlin, (2003) examined the emotional reactivity of adolescents with antisocial behavior problems. As identified in research with adults, psychopathic traits are associated with abnormalities in processing of emotional stimuli. This concept was measured by comparing recognition time for emotional words, both positive and negative. Just as with adults, psychopathic traits were associated with slower reaction time to emotional words in adolescents. Those that demonstrated problems of impulse control had faster recognition of emotional words. This suggests that different patterns of emotional reactivity may characterize distinct subgroups of youth with antisocial problems. Table 10.3 identifies sample questions related to behavioral concerns.

COMMUNITY FUNCTIONING

Social Behavior

By the time that a youth reaches school age, there should be a basic understanding of what is expected in social situations and expectations for behavior. Social behavior refers to how a person communicates with and reacts to others through speech, gestures, and body language. Youth are likely to experience challenges in this area occasionally, but positive experiences in this area should be the norm. There are facets to social behavior that should be considered in an assessment of youth's capacities in this area. Success in social behavior is significantly dependent on the presence of skills in processing both social interactions and internal reactions. The processing of social interaction and the behavior of others requires the capacity to accurately interpret the meaning of both verbal and nonverbal communication. Most of what is communicated does not happen in a verbal manner. "Paralanguage" is a term that includes the numerous gestures and nonverbal components of communications. This includes such things as eye contact, vocal inflection, fluidity of speech, volume of speech, pace of speech, body positioning, physical contact, and body and hand movements (McKay, 2009). Proxemics refers to the use of personal space. Vocalics refers to the use and meaning of pitch. Kinesis refers to the overall ability to read and interpret facial expressions and body language (Giler, 2000). Additionally, it is critical to be aware of internal reactions. Recognizing and understanding emotional reactions can significantly support the choices and ways in which people behave. This can lead to decisions to modify the situation, get support from another, or discontinue the interaction if needed.

There are numerous observations that can be made while assessing a youth's needs and strengths in the area of social behavior. These behaviors are represented in verbalizations, nonverbal interactions, and actions that occur in social interactions with both peers and adults. The observation should include the reactions of the youth as well as the reactions of the people the youth is interacting with. Specific skills to observe include the following:

- The manner in which conversation is initiated;
- The way in which the youth assessed the group's or individual's willingness to interact;
- Appropriateness of verbal responses—content, relevance to topic, and ability to show understanding of another's perspective;
- Appropriateness of nonverbal communication—congruence between actions, gestures and words, pitch, volume and pace of speech, use of touch and proximity to others, facial expressions, and eye contact;
- Ability to share conversation with others;
- Quality of social interactions—passive, assertive, or aggressive; and
- Ways in which interactions are terminated.

Recreational and Leisure Time

Werner and Smith (1992) state that the resilient youth is one "who loves well, works well, plays well and expects well" (p. 192). Recreational and leisure activities serve a number of positive functions for youth. Friendships are often developed in

Table 10.4
Interview Questions Related to Community Functioning

Questions for Caregivers

- Do you have concerns related to the way your child relates to others in public?
- Does your child behave as you would like in community settings?
- Does your child take part in community activities?
- Are there any community activities that you would like your child to be a part of that are not available to him/her?
- Are there adults in the community that have supportive relationships with your child?

Questions for Youth

- Do you spend time with kids and adults in your neighborhood?
- Do you have people outside of your family that are helpful to you?
- What do you like about your neighborhood or community?
- Are there activities that you take part in outside of your home?
- Do you have things you enjoy doing in your neighborhood?

relationship to the leisure activities that a youth engages in. Exposure to other youth and adults also offers opportunities to develop cooperation and negotiation skills, sharing abilities, and social behavior. When the home environment is stressful, leisure activities may serve to distract youth from these difficulties and provide experiences of success and mastery (Grizenko & Pawliuk, 1994). Activities also help to alleviate boredom, which may be a contributing factor in behavioral disturbances.

When assessing needs and strengths in this area, it is important to gain the perspective of both the youth and caregivers on several factors. It is more meaningful and positive for youth if there is a desire and investment on the part of the youth to engage in the activity. At times, activities are driven by the wishes or expectations of the caregivers and are not seen by youth as helpful or enjoyable. The frequency of the activities should be assessed as well. A healthy balance between expectations, school, and recreation should be present. A balance of activities that are solitary, family-oriented, and outside the family should also be present. When engaging in the activities, youth should be able to describe a sense of enjoyment and feel that the activity is not overly stressful or taxing of coping resources. Some youth describe activities that evoke a high level of frustration or stress that is not mediated by adults or worthwhile to the youth. Input from both caregivers and youth in the above areas can highlight areas in which interventions can be helpful and strengths that can be built on.

Participation Within Community

Interaction within the community broadens a school-age child's perspective and offers feelings of connection and well-being. Supportive adults who are present and available within the community can reinforce a feeling of being protected and able to take risks to extend youth's capacities. Youth who feel a sense of support from their communities are more likely to develop and accomplish goals. Community involvement fosters a sense of belonging. Informal relationships stemming from involvement in work, church, or neighborhood activities help develop a sense of self and individuality to negotiate the demands of everyday life. It also fosters a sense of shared experience, trust in an authority structure, membership in a group, and influence (McMillan, 1996). Table 10.4 identifies sample questions related to community functioning.

RISK BEHAVIORS

Putting Self at Risk

Suicidal ideation and suicide attempts exist among young people. The National Center for Injury Prevention and Control, Division of Violence Prevention (2008) reports that suicide is the third leading cause of death among 10- to 24-year-olds, most commonly by use of a firearm, suffocation, or poisoning. Additionally, in a nationwide survey, 15 percent of youth reported thinking of suicide, 11 percent had created a plan, and 7 percent had a made previous attempt. The assessment of suicidal ideation should never be ignored based on a youth's age or belief that it would not occur.

Many factors and sources of information should be considered in the process of assessing youth for suicidal ideation. For example, a youth's mood, behavior, thinking, and family history should all be considered when making the assessment. Youth and caregivers should be included as part of the assessment, and it is ideal if significant adults in the youth's life are able to offer input as well.

When assessing mood, a description of the quality of the youth's mood is relevant. Has the youth been sad, irritable, hopeless, or preoccupied, and for how long? Changes in mood and triggers for mood changes should also be explored. It is also helpful to get an overview of mood changes and how they have been managed over the past couple of weeks. The intensity of mood changes should be understood as well as the frequency and duration of mood changes.

The youth should be asked if there have been thoughts of harming him-/herself. If so, is there a method that has been considered, and is there accessibility to that method? Caregivers and other adults should be asked if the youth has made statements about wanting to die or planning to harm him-/herself.

The mental status of the youth should be assessed focusing especially on the presence of hallucinations or delusions and how these symptoms may or may not be part of the issue. There should be a determination of how the youth's behavior has been. If the youth has been volatile or markedly different from his/her norm, how have the caregivers responded?

The youth as well as caregivers should also be asked about a history of suicidal ideation, attempts, or intervention. What has occurred if a youth previously made a suicide attempt or disclosed ideation? Finally, what is the family's history of suicidal ideation, attempts, or mental illness? The weaving together of all pieces of information is necessary and relevant in determining if safety is present for the youth.

Putting Others at Risk

Youth may be at risk of harming another person intentionally or unintentionally. The intent to kill another person may not be present, but the likelihood of harm due to a variety of other factors may be present. Youth and caregivers must be interviewed to obtain information in this area so that an informed assessment can be accomplished. Youth should be asked directly if they are intending to harm another or believe that they may harm another under certain conditions. Youth

Table10.5
Questions Related to Risk Behaviors

Questions for Caregivers

- Does your child act aggressively with others?
- Does your child engage in behaviors that put him/her at risk?
- Do you have concerns that your child would harm him-/herself?

Questions for Youth

- Are there times when you are aggressive with others?
- Do you have thoughts of wanting to hurt anyone?
- Do you have thoughts of wanting to harm yourself?

---

who experience a great deal of anger may be able to report that if conditions (e.g., lack of supervision or the provoking of another) were present, harm to another may happen. Intent, plan, and accessibility of weapons should be discussed as it would be when screening for suicidal ideation. Knowing the youth's history related to harming others and conditions that may have been contributing factors are important. If a youth is aggressive toward others in an impulsive manner, it is often less concerning than when it appears calculated and planned. If youth respond to adult supports and interventions when aggression has either been threatened or occurred, a different level of concern is present than if supports are rejected.

It may be helpful to be knowledgeable about the risk and protective factors in an area that is being assessed. A number of risk factors related to the youth, his/her family, and community interactions have been linked to aggression. A youth who demonstrates hyperactivity, poor attention span, risk-taking behaviors, poor social skills, and a belief that retribution is necessary may be linked to aggressive acts. Within the family, harsh and ineffective caregiving, lack of caregiver involvement, caregiver criminality, child abuse, and rejection are risk factors for aggression. Characteristics of schools that may indicate risk are low school investment in youth, poor follow-through with discipline, and few allowances for differences (McEvoy & Welker, 2000). It is important to consider the accumulative effect of these risk factors and not assume that any or all may always lead to aggression. Protective factors in the youth include a positive view of his/her circumstances and ability to affect others, and stress-reducing strategies. The school factors that can contribute to positive outcomes are a positive and safe learning environment, high yet achievable standards, supports for academic and social success, and the presence of clubs and activities. Positive community supports and integration are protective as well (Catalano, Loeber, & McKinney, 1999). Protective factors can be developed at any time and can mediate a number of risks. Table 10.5 identifies sample questions related to risk behaviors. If there are any indications of suicidal or homicidal ideation, a risk assessment is necessary.

SCHOOL FUNCTIONING

Relationships With Teachers

When school-age children experience positive interactions with teachers who are perceived as supportive, there are definite academic, behavioral, emotional, and social benefits. In addition, when youth struggle with aggressive tendencies, this too is mediated by a positive relationship with a teacher (Meehan, Hughes, & Cavell, 2003). If youth experience difficulties in school, there may be perceptions on the part of youth that teachers are being unfair in their interactions with them. A youth may display a lack of respect, verbal or physical aggression, or noncompliance. The practitioner should explore youth's reactions to correction, positive interactions, and support in order to understand the quality of the youth-teacher relationship. The teacher's perspective should be sought, as this may be different from the youth's perspective. An understanding of the attitudes and behaviors that are present on the part of the teacher is needed. Teachers may be skilled in determining the needs of the youth and adapt their interactions to support the youth. On the contrary, the teacher may be rigid and display a lack of understanding of the youth's strengths, needs, and behaviors.

Relationships With Peers

Relationships with peers during the school years are of primary concern. Youth are much influenced by their peers and want to feel accepted and understood by their peers. There are situations that may evoke tension, but these situations should be resolved successfully most of the time. It is valuable to observe the youth interacting with peers, obtain reports from caregivers and other adults, and interview the youth to best understand the youth's relationships with peers.

There are numerous skills related to the ability of developing and maintaining peer relationships. A youth may have specific needs in some areas and strengths in others. Some of the skills to consider are as follows:

- Ability to initiate interactions;
- Ability to differentiate between friends, classmates, and peers in a way that guides appropriate interaction;
- Ability to maintain interactions and friendships;
- Ability to identify and negotiate conflict with peers;
- Ability to enjoy interactions with friends;
- Ability to play or interact with both large and small groups; and
- Ability to share friendships with others.

Understanding how relationships with peers have evolved in the past assists in developing an understanding of current struggles. If youth have a history of problems with peers and have resolved the problems, knowing the strategies that were used is helpful. These adaptive strategies can be used with similar difficulties when needed.

Academic Functioning

Academic functioning should be considered from a variety of perspectives. The youth's academic history should be examined. There may have been challenges present since the onset of school, or perhaps challenges slowly emerged as expectations became more difficult, which is a different situation than a youth who all of a sudden begins to have difficulties despite a history of success. If the assessment reveals that the onset of academic issues has been sudden, then considering situational stressors, trauma, or other factors is important. When poor grades are present, it is also helpful to understand what this represents and how grades are given. Is it related to poor homework completion, poor test grades, poor overall comprehension, or a combination of many issues? It is also helpful to know if any area identified above is an area of strength. If problems have occurred in the past, has there been a successful strategy in turning things around? If challenges are present, it is also helpful to know if testing has been administered to formally determine a child's capacities.

Although it is crucial to be aware of a child's grades, a comprehensive assessment related to academic functioning should consider other factors. Youth's perspectives related to their levels of effort or lack of effort in maintaining the grades they are making is useful information. A youth who is not meeting his/her potential, yet is making adequate grades, is just as much in need of intervention as a youth who is not making adequate grades. If a youth is demonstrating a great deal of motivation and effort with little support or perceived support, a conversation related to how to better manage expectations or preserve the youth's motivation may be appropriate. When considering academic functioning, it is helpful to consider the conditions that resiliency research has demonstrated are protective in the area of school functioning. When a student's environment provides stability, load balance, and participation, the conditions are optimal for promoting success (Antonovsky, 1991). Stability is offered to a youth when close and supportive relationships promote a stable and secure foundation from which to grow and develop. Caregivers, teachers, and significant others in a youth's life are all examples of adults who can serve this role. Load balance refers to how well the demands of an environment fit with the capabilities of the youth. When load balance is an issue, risk factors can be mitigated, and available support systems can be ameliorated. Participation is protective because it offers opportunities for meaningful involvement and contribution in the school and community. This promotes a sense of autonomy, independence, social competence, and success (Richman, Bowen, & Woolley, 2004; Benard & Educational Resources Information Center (U.S.), 1991). In appreciating an ecological perspective, all of these areas have relevance and should be understood when assessing academic functioning.

Attendance

Attendance is an area related to school functioning that is a mandated requirement and therefore closely monitored by the school. There can be a number of reasons why difficulties in attendance are present, many of which have little to do with the youth. There is great benefit in first getting the perspective of the youth and family in this area, as it acknowledges their ideas and will offer a context from which to begin understanding the issue. Caregivers and youth often have a different perspective on the significance as well as cause of this issue. If there are no issues reported with attendance, it is helpful to understand how the youth as well as caregivers prioritize this issue and what barriers they may have overcome in ensuring attendance. Their excellence and attempts in this area may highlight important competencies and strengths that can be used in other areas.

There are a number of factors that must be understood when considering the interventions that must be developed to assist an individual with attendance issues. The first issue may be the time frame in which attendance has been a problem. Making associations with the time frame are helpful, as there may be links that are pertinent and help explain the issue. Identifying new stressors, changes in routine, and issues within the home, community, or school may shed a great deal of understanding. In addition to the identification of stressors or issues, it is helpful to learn ways in which the youth has responded to stressors in the past. When a history of attendance issues has occurred in the past, the circumstances related to this should be explored. Finally, analyzing what may happen as a result of lack of attendance at both home and school should be considered. There may be secondary gains that can occur in a different manner that supports the youth in going to school.

Behavioral Concerns

In the overview of behavioral functioning within the school environment, there is a wide range of types of behaviors that may be displayed. The context, expectations, and responses to the behavior must all be identified as well. A youth may also display a pattern of behavior only in certain situations, as other variables either alter the behavior or keep problems from occurring altogether. Behavior at school may be in reaction to a directive or expectation. This type of response, reactive behavior, is usually driven by a need to avoid something. The youth may refuse to do something, cry, yell, ignore the teacher, or attempt to leave the setting. It may be unclear in some cases what the youth is trying to avoid, but, nonetheless, this is the motivation. When behavior is proactive, there is a need on behalf of the youth to cause something to occur. This too is a reflection of a need and may occur for such reasons as the youth having difficulty managing emotions, craving excitement or attention, wanting peer recognition, or needing to feel competent (Center for Mental Health in Schools at UCLA, 2008). Looking for themes, triggers, or clues to the need that is being reflected in a youth's behavior is key to designing the appropriate intervention.

In line with the ecological approach to understanding youth's needs, the environment, the individual, and the fit between the two must be assessed. Having a profile of how the youth reacts to transitions, manages activity level and patterns in such, reacts to internal and external triggers in terms of intensity, tolerates change, persists when challenged, and organizes tasks is important (Kristal, 2005). The environment has a number of factors to consider as well. These include the following:

- How stimulating is the school environment?
- How well can the school staff predict student needs?
- How have the staff responded to needs in the past and used this information to plan for the future?
- How do the staff recognize and respond to individual differences?
- How do the staff communicate concern and remain connected to their students?
- Do the staff demonstrate nontraditional and flexible responses?

If a youth has been identified as having challenges in particular areas, a school staff that can identify, predict, and support the challenges promotes a good fit between the youth and his/her environment. The situation in which youth are able to work at their potential and feel comfortable and supported throughout the school day is more likely if these factors are present. When assessing behavioral needs, all areas must be fully understood. Table 10.6 identifies sample questions related to school functioning.

Table 10.6
Questions Related to School Functioning

Questions for Caregivers

- What areas is your child most competent in related to school?
- Are there special adults at the school who your child relates well to?
- What does your child enjoy most about school?
- Are there behavioral concerns at school?
- Are there any issues related to attendance?
- How do teachers describe your child at parent-teacher conferences?
- Does the school do a good job meeting your child's needs?

Questions for Youth

- Do you enjoy school? What do you like and not like about school?
- What do you need to get better at in school?
- Do you attend school regularly?
- Are you happy with your grades? Are your parents happy with them?
- How do you get along with your teacher?
- Are there times you get in trouble at school?

FUNCTIONING WITHIN THE HOME

Behavioral Functioning

To understand how school-age children are operating behaviorally within the home, it must be clear what is expected and how these expectations have been communicated to the youth. The youth may or may not be able to demonstrate a clear and consistent understanding of rules and expectations. This may be related to unclear communication as well as an issue with the youth. The two scenarios have a different need being represented. If caregivers alter expectations frequently or in a manner that is not interpreted or understood by the youth, there may be a desire to comply but an inability to understand how. If a youth is not processing information well or has attention/impulse control issues, the reason for noncompliance may not be related to inconsistent messages.

It is helpful to identify patterns in behavior that can be demonstrated and/or explained. This allows for the assessor to gain further information or link possible triggers or environmental characteristics to the behavioral response. Getting input from all involved is important, as it clarifies the situation and corrects for making assumptions. Behavior within the home can be classified, as in the school environment, as reactive or proactive. Both have specific needs related to them, and looking for the responses before, during, and after the behavior is critical. If a youth's needs are continually ignored, reactions will continue to escalate because the youth feels that he/she is unheard. The behaviors and reactions of all family members related to the youth's needs must be understood, as all influences and interactions are a part of the problem as well as the solution.

Strategies for Getting Needs Met

Observing and interviewing youth and the family related to how needs are met should not be overlooked. Some youth may have a passive and poor ability to share their desires for help, emotional support, or concrete needs. This is a pattern that must be acknowledged and compensated for as part of a well-developed intervention plan. This pattern of behavior is often rooted in relationship issues between the caregivers and youth, which specific and well-informed strategies can address. The appreciation for how and why this has developed must be a part of the intervention plan. Other times, youth may have dysfunctional strategies for getting needs met. This too is reflective of youth and families who have unmet needs and need intervention as well. Caregivers may become overwhelmed and inadvertently support the inappropriate strategies. Gaining perspective from all family members and understanding the barriers and needs of the entire family is the only way to develop intervention strategies that can be successful.

HEALTH AND WELLNESS NEEDS

The ways in which school-age children feel physically on an everyday basis can significantly impact their social and emotional well-being. Many youth experience overall satisfactory health but complain of frequent headaches, stomach aches, or body aches. In an Australian study of 900 children ages 10 to 18, 33.7 percent experienced a headache once a month, 24.8 percent experienced one every few days and 4.6 percent described having one most of the time (King & Sharpley, 1990). It should also not be assumed that caregivers are aware of how a child feels on a regular basis, as many do not relate this information unless asked. Physical well-being is often related to such areas as activity level, energy, nutrition, oral health, and mental health. A history of hospitalizations, emergency room visits, doctor visits, related health care visits, and missed school or activities due to health issues and pain management are all relevant to best understand needs in this area.

SERVICE DELIVERY NEEDS

Coordination of Care

Many families experience a number of services and supports that are made available to them. Some services may be voluntary, and others are not. Family members may have multiple appointments and obligations for other children in the home, which further complicates their need for coordination of care. The practical nature of this activity is often a priority, as no single caregiver can be in two places at one time. Although this is overwhelming, an equally challenging issue is the coordination of strategies and viewpoints that the family is exposed to. It can be distressing to have multiple service providers suggesting strategies that conflict with one another. This area should be addressed and supported in a way that reflects what is best for the family.

Intensity and Duration

Although family members have definite opinions about the way in which services should occur, they may have difficulty deciding on the intensity and duration. Many families may be surprised at the suggestion that services be frequent in the beginning. Families often believe that services should begin on a less frequent basis and intensify as needed. It may improve the family's ability to engage and feel good about progress if services begin at the most appropriate level and lessen as progress warrants it. Table 10.7 identifies sample questions related to service delivery.

Table 10.7
Questions Related to Service Delivery

Questions for Caregivers

- What are some important factors for you related to the way in which you receive services? Time, place, strategies, service types, preferences regarding worker?
- Are services that your family receives difficult to manage and coordinate?
- Do you have any concerns about services in the home?
- At what level of frequency do you feel services should begin?

Questions for Youth

- Do you want someone to offer your family help in your home?
- How do you feel about help in your school?
- Do you have a preference about receiving help from a man or woman?
- How often do you think services should occur?

STRENGTHS DISCOVERY

Unique Skills/Talents

In the quest to understand what motivates youth as well as their families, there are often special interests and talents that are identified in school-age children. Youth may have a love for sports or other type of recreational activities. When youth find activities that they are interested in, enjoy, and find fulfillment in, there are multiple reasons why promoting exposure to these activities is in youth's best interests (e.g., it serves to build a youth's self-esteem, sense of mastery, social interaction skills, and improve mood). Fulfilling activities also promote a strategy for coping with stressors or conditions that youth have no control over. Similarly, if talents are identified, there may be significant benefits in promoting ongoing exposure to these activities. Youth must have a sense of investment and desire to fully benefit from engaging in these activities. If the motivation is solely on the part of caregivers or other significant adults, it can be seen as a burden on the part of the youth. Some youth demonstrate strong skills in such areas as, for example, interpersonal relationships or intelligence. When usable and strong skills exist, finding opportunities to maximize their use or preserve them are helpful for youth and can be the focus of interventions.

Resiliency Characteristics

Throughout the assessment process, there should always be a focus on identifying protective factors that are present or can be fostered. There is a plethora of research stemming from the Kauai Longitudinal Study (Werner & Smith, 1992). This study sought to identify the characteristics of high-risk youth, which protected them from developing mental challenges. Awareness of resiliency concepts is not enough. One must be diligent about both assessment and ongoing observation for protective factors and resiliency characteristics. Constantine, Benard, and Diaz (1999) presented an instrument that can be used to identify protective and resiliency traits in youth. The instrument looks at the presence of caring relationships with and high expectations from adults in the home, school, and community; meaningful participation in these areas and internal characteristics of social competence; autonomy; sense of self; and sense of purpose. This focused assessment along with ongoing observation and careful attention to clues related to resiliency can ensure these concepts are considered and utilized in promoting change.

Temperament Characteristics

Temperament is described by Jan Kristal in her book, *The Temperament Perspective,* as "a child's innate way of approaching and experiencing the world" (p. 5). Two psychiatrists, Stella Chess, M.D., and Alexander Thomas, M.D., are seen as pioneers in the study of temperament, initiating a longitudinal study in 1956 that resulted in data to later identify nine temperament characteristics. These characteristics were identified as sensory threshold, activity level, intensity, rhythmicity, adaptability, mood, approach/withdrawal, persistence, and distractibility. The majority of youth were identified as displaying characteristics of a positive mood; regularity in bodily functioning; high adaptability to change and transitions; positive responses to new people, places, and situations; and a mild level of intensity in their responses. This description was classified as an "easy" temperament (Thomas, Chess, & Birch, 1968). Youth who fit this description are typically responded to by adults in a more positive fashion and experience less distress when coping with challenges or daily routines.

In identifying areas of strength as well as need, it is helpful to assess these innate characteristics that make up who a youth is. These characteristics, if present, can be helpful to a youth in getting needs met, coping with stressors, and interacting with others. Adults are more inclined to form a relationship with a youth, continue to help a youth when needed, and provide meaningful assistance when they identify the youth as "easy" to interact with. Youth with temperament challenges are often misunderstood, seen as behavior disordered, and difficult to remain engaged with. When a youth demonstrates characteristics that are seen as helpful, these traits should be encouraged, further developed, and preserved at all costs. Specific strategies to promote competence should be identified, and strategies that inadvertently undermine or discourage a trait should be avoided. If a youth, for instance, has been identified as continually trying to master difficult tasks despite frustration, caregivers may want to find ways to break down the task into more manageable parts, if it becomes too challenging, in order to continue to reward and foster the youth's sense of persistence. Contrarily, if difficult traits are assessed (e.g., poor response to change or transitions), there are specific strategies that can be put in place to assist in the development of this area. All individuals have areas that are challenging to them, but typically, by adulthood, they have either found ways to avoid them or cope with them when necessary. This can be taught and promoted with youth so as to avoid unnecessary distress and promote success wherever possible.

The assessment of temperament is one that can take many forms. There are numerous temperament assessments that typically require caregivers to complete a questionnaire. Many of these assessments are targeted to specific age ranges and appreciate the developmental variations and tasks of a particular age range in the assessment process. For middle childhood, two such questionnaires are the Middle Childhood Temperament Questionnaire (MCTQ; Hegvik, McDevitt, & Carey, 1982) and the School-Age Temperament Inventory (SATI; McClowry, 1995). Surveying caregivers assists in the identification of patterns and traits that are also observed by

Table 10.8
Strengths Discovery

Questions for Caregivers Related to Youth

- What stands out in your mind about your child's strongest points?
- What are some behaviors you have seen in your child that help in coping or dealing with a challenging event?
- Are there adults and peers who your child has good relationships with outside the family?
- Are there special activities that come easy for your child or that he/she especially enjoys?
- Does your child deal well with change?
- What is your child's mood most of the time?
- Would you describe your child's reactions as intense or calm most of the time?
- Does your child participate in any activities in the community?
- Does your child seem to have a strong ability to cope with stressors?
- Tell me a story about your child that makes you smile.
- When you find your child easiest to care for, how would you describe his/her behavior and interaction with you?
- In what situations or circumstances do you find your child behaves or functions at his/her best?
- Is there a year in school that your child did better than others? What are your thoughts about what made that happen?

Questions for Caregivers Related to Their Strengths

- In what situations with your child do you feel most competent?
- Describe what you are most proud of in your role as a parent.
- When do you have the most fun with your child?
- Do you have activities that help you relax?
- Do you have friends and family that you can turn to for support?
- What strategies do you have to calm down when you are overwhelmed as a parent?
- What do you think are the most important things you do for your child as a parent?
- In what ways do you feel alike or different from your own parents?
- Do you have certain strategies that work when your child is very upset or in crisis?
- Do you feel comfortable asking others for help?
- What strategies do you have for talking to others about your child's needs?
- Are you able to predict situations that your child will have difficulty with?
- Can you describe a time when you felt really close to your child?

Questions for Youth

- What are you most proud of?
- What area in school do you feel best at?
- What would you like to be when you grow up?
- Are there things that you especially like to do?
- If you could plan your future, what would happen?
- What would your friends say about you?
- What are some skills that you feel especially proud of?
- What are some things that others believe you do well?
- What are some activities that you find enjoyment in?
- What would your friends say are the things you are good at?
- What types of tasks come easy for you?
- Are there some adults in your life that are helpful to you?
- Who do you like to spend time with?
- What do you do when you need to calm down?

Questions for Youth Related to Their Caregivers

- Can you describe a time when you really had fun with your parents?
- What is the best thing about your mom or dad?
- When is it easiest to listen to your mom or dad?
- What do you count on most from your mom or dad?
- What does your mom or dad do to make you feel better when you are upset?
- What would your mom or dad tell us he/she likes most about you?
- Do you have special activities that you only do with your mom and dad?

the practitioner. Observation of the youth is therefore another and often informative strategy for learning about innate tendencies and traits. Youth who are observed in their natural environments (e.g., home and school) are likely to demonstrate their styles of interaction and coping with stressors. Practitioners can also ask caregivers to set up scenarios that may likely lead to an illustration of temperament characteristics in order to better understand a youth's temperament. These situations could be responding to directives, asking to complete a task, or initiating transitions. If practitioners are present during natural times when these things occur (e.g., mealtimes, homework times, or chore time), it is likely that there will be much to observe. The practitioner must be careful to look for patterns across multiple observations and settings, and integrate caregiver feedback before making conclusions. Table 10.8 identifies sample questions related to strengths discovery.

CONCLUSION

The assessment of school-age children, as with other age groups, has a number of areas to consider. Youth's functioning within the home, school, and community should be assessed in a manner that appreciates their intrapersonal as well as interpersonal functioning. The school-age child is at the stage of development in which he/she is focused on developing relationships outside the family. Family relationships are important to youth, but often peer relationships are their main focus. When difficulties arise in this area, it can be overwhelming for the school-age child to focus on other areas as needed.

References

American Academy of Child and Adolescent Psychiatry. (2009). Facts for families: Children with oppositional defiant disorder. No. 72. Retrieved June 16, 2010, from http://www.aacap. org/es/root/facts_for_families/children_with_oppositional_defiant_disorder

American Psychiatric Association. (2000). *Diagnostic and satistical manual of mental disorders* (4th ed., text rev.). Washington, DC: Author.

Antonovsky, A. (1991). The structural sources of salutogenic strengths. In C. L. Cooper & R. Payne (Eds.), *Personality and stress: Individual differences in the stress process* (pp. 67-104). New York: Wiley.

Asarnow, J. R., Jaycox, L. H., & Tompson, M. C. (2001). Depression in Youth: Psychosocial interventions. *Journal of Clinical Child Psychology, 30,* 33-47.

Ayres, J. (2005). *Sensory integration and the child: 25th Anniversary edition.* Los Angeles: Western Psychological Services.

Benard, B., & Educational Resources Information Center (U.S.). (1991). *Fostering resiliency in kids: Protective factors in the family, school, and community.* Portland, OR: Western Center for Drug-Free Schools and Communities, Far West Laboratory.

Catalano, R. F., Loeber, R., & McKinney, K. C. (1999). School and community interventions to prevent serious and violent offending. *Juvenile Justice Bulletin.* Washington, DC: Office of Juvenile Justice & Delinquency Prevention.

Center for Mental Health in Schools at UCLA. (2008). *Conduct and behavior problems related to school age youth.* Los Angeles: Author.

Collins, W. A. (Ed.). (1984). *Development during middle childhood: The years from six to twelve.* Washington, DC: National Academy Press.

Constantine, N. A., Benard, B., & Diaz, M. D. (1999, June). *A new survey instrument for measuring protective factors in youth: The healthy kids resilience assessment.* Paper presented at the Society for Prevention Research National Conference, New Orleans.

Davies, D. (2004). *Child development: A practitioner's guide* (2nd ed.). New York: Guilford Press.

Foster, E. M., & Jones, D. E. (2005). The high costs of aggression: Public expenditures resulting from conduct disorder. *American Journal of Public Health, 95*, 1767-1772.

Gard, G. C., & Berry, K. K. (1986). Oppositional children: Taming tyrants. *Journal of Clinical Child Psychology, 15*, 148-158.

Giler, J. Z. (2000). *Socially ADDept: A manual for parents of children with ADHD or learning disabilities.* Santa Barbara, CA: CES Publications.

Grizenko, N., & Pawliuk, N. (1994). Risk and protective factors for disruptive behavior disorders in children. *American Journal of Orthopsychiatry, 64*, 534-544.

Hegvik, R. L., McDevitt, S. C., & Carey, W. B. (1982). Middle childhood temperament questionnaire. *Developmental and Behavioral Pediatrics, 3*, 197-200.

Horowitz, L. J., & Rost, C. (2007). Helping hyperactive kids: A sensory integration approach. Alameda, CA: Hunter House Publishers.

Jellinek, M., Patel, B. P. &, Froehle, M. C. (2002). *Bright futures in practice: Practice guide, mental health* (Vol. 1). Arlington, VA: National Center for Education in Maternal and Child Health.

Johnston, L. D., O'Mallery, P. M., & Bachman, J. G. (2001). *The monitoring the future national results on adolescent drug use: Overview of key findings, 2000.* Bethesda, MD: National Institute on Drug Abuse.

Kalmanson, B., Pekarsky, J. H. (1987). Infant-parent psychotherapy with an autistic toddler. *Zero to Three, 7*(3), 1-6.

King, N. J., & Sharpley, C. F. (1990). Headache activity in children and adolescents. *Journal of Paediatrics and Child Health 26*: 50-54.

Kranowitz, C. S. (1998). *The out-of-sync child : Recognizing and coping with sensory integration dysfunction.* New York: Perigee.

Kristal, J. (2005). *The temperament perspective: Working with children's behavioral styles.* Baltimore: Paul H. Brookes Publishing.

Loney, B., Frick, P., Clements, C., Ellis, M., & Kerlin, K. (2003). Callous-unemotional traits, impulsivity, and emotional processing in adolescents with antisocial behavior problems. *Journal of Clinical Child & Adolescent Psychology, 32*, 66.

McClowry, S. G. (1995). The influence of temperament on development during middle childhood. *Journal of Pediatric Nursing, 10,* 160-165.

McEvoy, A., & Welker, R. (2000). Antisocial behavior, academic failure, and school climate: A critical review. *Journal of Emotional and Behavioral Disorders, 8,* 130-140.

McKay, M. (2009). *Messages: The communication skills book.* Oakland, CA: New Harbinger Publications.

McMillan, D. (1996). Sense of community. *Journal of Community Psychology, 24*, 315-325.

Meehan, B., Hughes, J., & Cavell, T. (2003). Teacher-student relationships as compensatory resources for aggressive children. *Child Development, 74*, 1145-1157.

Morrison, J., & Anders, T. F. (1999). *Interviewing children and adolescents: Skills and strategies for effective DSM-IV diagnosis.* New York: Guilford Press.

National Center for Injury Prevention and Control, Division of Violence Prevention (2008). *Suicide prevention: Youth suicide.* Retrieved January 23, 2010, from http://www.cdc.gov/ncipc/dvp/suicide/youthsuicide.htm

Newschaffer, C. J., Croen, L. A., Daniels, J., Giarelli, E., Grether, J. K., Levy, S. E., et al. (2007). The epidemiology of autistic spectrum disorders. *Annual Review of Public Health, 28*, 235-258.

Patrick, K., Spear, B., Holt, K., & Sofka, D. (Eds.). (2001). *Bright futures in practice: Physical activity.* Arlington, VA: National Center for Education in Maternal and Child Health.

Rice, C. (2009). Prevalence of autism spectrum disorders—Autism and Developmental Disabilities Monitoring Network, United States, 2006. *MMWR Surveillance Summaries, 58*(SS-10), 1-24.

Richman, J. M., Bowen, G. L., & Woolley, M. E. (2004). School failure: An eco-international developmental perspective. In Mark W. Fraser (Ed.), *Risk and resilience in childhood: An ecological perspective* (2nd ed.) (pp. 133-160). Washington, DC: NASW Press.

Santrock, J. W. (1993). *Children* (3rd ed.). Dubuque, IA: Wm. C. Brown Communications.

Taylor, E. (1998). Advances in the diagnosis and treatment of children with serious mental illness. *Child Welfare, 77*, 311-332.

Thomas, A., Chess, S., & Birch, H. (1968). *Temperament and behavior disorders in children.* New York: New York University Press.

Torrey, E., Bowler, A. E., Taylor, E. H., & Gottesman, I. I. (1994). *Schizophrenia and manic depressive disorder: The biological roots of mental illness as revealed by the landmark study of identical twins.* New York: Basic Books.

Werner, E. E., & Smith, R. S. (1992). *Overcoming the odds: High risk children from birth to adulthood.* Ithaca, NY: Cornell University Press.

Wolraich, M., Felice, M. E., & Drotar, D. (1996). *The classification of child and adolescent mental diagnoses in primary care: Diagnostic and statistical manual for primary care (DSM-PC) child and adolescent version.* Elk Grove Village, IL: American Academy of Pediatrics.

Zembar, M. J., & Blume, L. B. (2009). *Middle childhood development: A contextual approach.* Upper Saddle River, NJ: Prentice Hall.

Chapter 11

Assessing the Transition-Age Youth Within the Context of Family and Community

Into the darkness they go, the wise and the lovely.
—Edna St. Vincent Millay

We stand today on the edge of a new frontier.
—John F. Kennedy

INTRODUCTION

Youth who have experienced mental health challenges often struggle with what this means for them and what the possibilities for recovery are. For so long, many youth have experienced their caregivers directing the treatment process in a way in which their voices have not been heard. During adolescence and young adulthood, feeling independent, capable, and positive about the future are primary needs. A deficit-focused approach to treatment and planning without youth input will simply not work. Identifying the possibilities for youth rather than the problems are more likely to keep the youth at the table and invested in continuing to work toward recovery. Too many youth see their eighteenth birthday as a way to free themselves from a process that is not part of their plans. When this time comes, it is critical to meet youth where they are and offer them possibilities that can maximize their potential in a way that appreciates their vision and goals. The alternative, in too many circumstances, becomes homelessness, prison, alienation, serious mental health issues, and lack of meaningful employment. Preparing for transition begins way before adolescence and young adulthood arrives. It is a mentality of empowerment that seeps through all phases of development. Youth's goals, priorities, and visions should always be at the forefront of what is done. A discussion with youth related to the possibilities of what can occur and what they want to occur in their lives should begin the assessment. As the youth builds a relationship with the practitioner, the areas of need should be addressed. This too can be done for a strength-based orientation and in a way that highlights the areas of success. The phase of transition offers youth the option to say "no." This chapter challenges practitioners to shoot for a "yes."

STRUCTURING THE TRANSITIONING YOUTH ASSESSMENT

The end result of any assessment should be the compilation of usable information to best inform a workable service plan. To support this process, engagement is essential to ensure that information is relevant and a true reflection of the youth's capacities, strengths, and needs. Transition-age youth are often poorly prepared to discuss their histories, as their caregivers have dominated this process or represented the youth as being at fault and behaviorally out of control. These types of experiences may have left youth feeling guilty, misunderstood, and confused about the origin and etiology of their behavioral and emotional challenges. To best engage a youth in these circumstances, an assessment that is strengths based, present and future oriented, and completed in partnership with the youth should be offered. Giving the youth control in as many ways as possible will also maximize the usefulness of results. Youth should be asked to choose the way in which discussions can best take place, the order and

Table 11.1
Interview Questions Related to Communication Skills

- Are there times when you believe that others do not understand what you are trying to say?
- If so, has this caused difficulties? Can you describe how?
- Are there times when it is challenging to understand what others are saying to you?
- Has this caused difficulties in any way?
- Can you think of anything that makes communicating with others more likely to go smoothly?
- Can you think of any reasons that communicating with others can be made more difficult?
- What situations do you feel the most success in communicating? With whom might it be easiest?

---

sequence of the interview, who should be included in the discussion, and the manner in which the information will be used.

DEVELOPMENTAL FUNCTIONING

Communication Abilities

Communication challenges are not limited to childhood, and quite often they continue into adulthood. Three to five percent of high school students have language disorders, and up to 80 percent of students with learning disabilities have communication challenges (Reed, 1986). The functions of language include receptive language function, expressive language function, and pragmatics of speech. Receptive language difficulties are present when there are challenges in understanding words, gestures, and written communication. Expressive language refers to the ability to communicate by speaking, writing, and gestural communication. The pragmatics of speech include interpreting, writing, and gesturing in socially appropriate ways. Challenges in these areas include difficulty combining words grammatically, difficulty attaching meaning to words, poor storytelling and conversation skills, and challenges modifying language to suit the listener. More specifically, apraxia, dysarthria, and stuttering are conditions that are identified as common communication challenges in older youth or adults. Apraxia is a motor speech disorder in which there is difficulty sequencing the sounds in syllables and words. Dysarthria is another motor speech disorder, which may be present as the result of medical conditions (e.g, a stroke). Stuttering is a disruption in the fluency of speech, which begins in childhood and can last throughout the lifespan. This includes repetitions of words or parts of words and prolongations of speech (Oates & Grayson, 2004).

Language disorders can complicate functioning in social and emotional development in a variety of ways. Social interaction with peers, employers, and others can be affected by difficulty responding appropriately to directions, poor ability following conversations, relating stories, telling jokes, or handling conflict. Additionally, emotional problems that manifest as poor self-esteem, problems forming friendships, poor motivation, and reluctance to participate with others may develop as the result of strained interactions (Patchell & Hand, 1993). Assessment should include a complete history and type of treatment/intervention that may have occurred. Table 11.1 identifies sample questions related to communication skills.

Table 11.2
Interview Questions Related to Cognitive Functioning

- Did you get special help in school at any time?
- If so, was there anything that made learning new things less of a challenge?
- Are there activities that are difficult to do or expectations that are difficult to meet?
- What areas of your life would you say you feel able to handle and do what is expected?

Cognitive Abilities

For transition-age youth, there continues to be fine-tuning and growth in a number of areas related to cognition. Abstract thinking becomes more complex, and this is manifested in the use of metaphors, analogies, and logical thinking. The ability to think through problems and the complexities of situations and issues is more firmly established. When identifying solutions, transition-age youth now have the ability to focus beyond what is in front of them and consider possibilities. The thought process is more multidimensional and much less concrete (Wadsworth, 2003). These abilities should be reflected in day-to-day interactions and behaviors. These skills are demonstrated primarily through observation and interactions between the practitioner and youth.

When intellectual disabilities are present in transition-age youth, there should typically be a history of special education involvement. When this is the case, there may be associated challenges in living skills that require the help of others. Transition-age youth with intellectual disabilities often present as difficult to manage behaviorally. Aggressive behavior is one of the most common reasons why youth and young adults with intellectual disabilities are referred for services. The underlying cause of this behavior may stem from the presence of a mood disorder. Because of challenges articulating concerns, there may be difficulty seeing behaviors as a reflection of a mood disorder. When medications are prescribed for mood disorders, noncompliance with dosage recommendations is also problematic. Social isolation, exclusion from services, and a higher likelihood of experiencing physical abuse also are concerns for transition-age youth with cognitive disabilities. (Atezaz Saeed, 2008). Table 11.2 identifies sample questions related to cognitive functioning.

Sensory Processing Abilities

Sensory processing challenges are not solely isolated to youth. They are experienced by all ages and manifest in multiple ways. Just as youth have specific patterns of behavior in response to sensory stimuli, young and older adults have common response patterns and coping strategies (Kinnealey, Oliver, & Wilbarger, 1995). In response to the various types of sensory input—taste, smell, movement, visual, touch, and auditory—the brain either has a high or low threshold for the stimuli that is being presented. When the brain has a high threshold for input, it takes a great deal of stimulation for the brain to recognize the activity. The behavioral response in this case is often sensory seeking. When a person demonstrates a low threshold for sensory input, there is high sensitivity in their reactions. The behavioral reaction in this case is sensory avoiding. Brown, Tollefson, Dunn, Cromwell, and Filion

Table 11.3
Interview Questions Related to Sensory Processing

- Many people feel overwhelmed or annoyed by sounds, sights, touch, or smells. Do you experience anything in any of these areas that annoys you? Do you have any preferences in any of these areas?
- If so, do these preferences or frustrations get in the way in any areas of your life?
- What strategies might you have found to deal with any frustrations?
- Do others around you understand how you feel and help or hurt the problem?

(2001) describe the Adult Sensory Profile as a tool in which these patterns can be determined. Statements that are endorsed by the examinee indicate typical patterns of sensory response.

Awareness of sensory patterns is valuable information. Sensory challenges may cause difficulty with focusing and attending to tasks, managing frustration, and persisting with tasks. Youth can use information about their sensory responses to predict challenges and develop appropriate coping strategies. In addition, giving this information to peers, coworkers, and family members can increase their level of awareness and understanding in reactions to behaviors. Table 11.3 identifies sample questions related to sensory processing.

Social and Emotional Development

Having skills in the area of social and emotional development has a significant impact on transition-age youth's overall sense of well-being. Managing interactions with others and monitoring emotions is an everyday task. During adolescence, five psychosocial tasks are primary. The tasks of adolescence include establishing identity, establishing autonomy, establishing intimacy, developing a level of comfort with sexuality, and achieving independence from caregivers. Through association with peer groups and a preferred set of friends, viewpoints related to life views, goals, and a vision begin to develop. A sense of self is born out of these relationships, and the youth develop perceptions related to who they are, their abilities, and their motivations. During adolescence and into early adulthood, conflict with family, depression, self-destructive, and risk-taking behavior are more likely to occur than in other stages. Emotional reactions are often intense and volatile in part due to challenges in seeing others' perspectives and believing that others do not understand their perspective (Morgan & Huebner, 2008).

There are many skills related to social and emotional functioning that reflect how transition-age youth interact with other people in small and large groups. The various types of relationships—family, peers, friends, authority figures, employers, and coworkers—require different skills and capacities. Socially, an adolescent or young adult must develop the capacity to recognize needed skills, make changes based on the situation, and execute the skill in order to function optimally. Skills related to understanding what is expected in a social situation, adjusting behavior to fit the situation, and interpreting others' reactions are all essential components to successful interactions. Emotionally, it is necessary to have an awareness of feelings, the ability to express feelings, interpret others' feelings, and cope with others' emotions. A sample of secondary-school youth in a study conducted by

Table 11.4
Interview Questions Related to Social and Emotional Development

- Do you enjoy spending time with people your age? Are there any times when you find this to be difficult?
- How do you find interacting with people in authority?
- Do you feel that you are accepted by people your age?
- Do you feel comfortable in social situations? Uncomfortable? Do others seem to feel comfortable with you? What have others told you about this?
- Is it challenging for you to express your feelings?
- In what situations is it easiest to express your feelings?
- Have you found strategies to help you cope with your feelings?
- Are there any people that help in this area?

Table 11.5
Interview Questions Related to Independent Living Skills

- Do you feel capable of taking care of your everyday needs?
- Are there chores or household activities that you do well with? Are there any you feel are difficult?
- How is budgeting and managing money for you?
- Is it challenging to make calls for appointments etc.?
- Are you living on your own now? Would you like to be?

Wagner, Kutash, Duchnowski, Espstein, and Sumi (2005) indicated that those with emotional disabilities demonstrated greater impairment overall in social skills as compared to peers with other types of disabilities. Of the subscales of social functioning— self-control, assertion, and cooperation—there was the greatest variance in functioning in the area of cooperation. Table 11.4 identifies sample questions related to social and emotional development.

Independent Living Skills

Transition-age youth with emotional challenges may have experienced setbacks and situations that prevented the development of adequate independent living skills. Youth who have been preoccupied with emotional or behavioral issues may not have been able to experiment with or practice these skills. Caregivers may have been reluctant to allow the development of independence, and conflict may develop around this area. It is also a concern when family relationships have been strained as the result of behavioral challenges, and therefore the primary teachers, the caregivers, of independent living skills have often been unable to support this situation. There are a number of areas to consider in the assessment of these capabilities. Exposure to skills, cognitive functioning, challenges or barriers in executing the skills, and the interaction between youth and their environment should all be considered. Table 11.5 identifies sample questions related to independent living skills.

Table 11.6
Interview Questions Related to Mood and Affective Disorders

- Are you happy with what your mood is most of the time?
- Do you feel able to control your temper?
- Does your mood change easily?
- Are there times when you feel on edge and worried?
- Do you have any sleep or appetite issues?
- If you have difficulties with your mood, what strategies do you have for coping?
- Are there people that help with this area?

MENTAL HEALTH FUNCTIONING

Mood and Affective Disorders

Mood and affective disorders are often identified in studies as being the most prevalent of the mental health conditions in transition-age youth (Manteuffel, Stephens, Sondheimer, & Fisher, 2008). Depression remains a highly misunderstood condition for consumers of mental health services as well as the general public. The notion that depression does not necessarily come about as a reaction to a stressor or negative event is not widely understood. Often, those who experience depression that does not seem linked to a cause identify themselves as weak or unappreciative. Social stigma and past negative experiences with treatment also contribute to a reluctance to discuss depression. It is difficult in these circumstances for young adults to admit or even identify feelings of depression.

Depression is often not expressed in words but rather in behaviors. Many adolescents and young adults do not verbalize sadness. They express negative feelings through irritability, oppositional behavior (see Chapters 9 and 10 in this volume), withdrawal, or negative comments. In addition to these symptoms of depression, adolescents and young adults have been identified as demonstrating anxiety as either a precursor or symptom of depression. Impulsivity was also identified as a common manifestation of depression (Smith & Blackwood, 2004; Parker et al., 1999). Other symptoms include poor psychosocial functioning, lower life and career satisfaction, interpersonal difficulties, greater need for social support, and suicidal ideation. Depression appears to be a biopsychosocial and multifactorial process that is influenced by temperament, genetic heritability, caregiving style, cognitive vulnerability, stressors, and interpersonal relations. Additionally, media exposure was associated with bringing awareness of depression, especially in males (Premack, Swanier, Georgiopoulos, Land, & Fine, 2009). When considering a youth's history in the assessment process, it is also important to identify past episodes of behavioral or emotional difficulties and family histories of depression. Depression in adolescence, as well as a diagnosis of oppositional defiant disorder, has been linked to young adult depression (Copeland, Shanahan, Costello, & Angold; Fergusson & Woodward, 2002). Other conditions (e.g., substance abuse) may also reflect an underlying issue of depression. Table 11.6 identifies sample questions related to mood and affective disorders.

Table 11.7
Interview Questions Related to Thought Disorders/Psychosis

- Some people experience symptoms that are related to the balance of hormones within their brain. Do you ever experience hearing, seeing, or feeling things that others say are not there? Have you in the past?
- Do you worry about things that may happen or what others are thinking?
- If this has been a problem for you, talk about what has helped?
- What strategies do you have for coping with these symptoms?

Thought Disorder/Psychosis

Psychotic symptoms (e.g., hallucinations, delusions, and thought disorders) are generally more prevalent in adolescence than in previous stages of development. Five percent of adults with schizophrenia report an onset of symptoms before the age of 15. Nonspecific psychotic symptoms include odd beliefs, mistrust of others, and magical thinking. These symptoms, along with poor academic and interpersonal functioning, may precede the first psychotic episode. When psychosis is present, the symptoms may be associated with affective disorders, schizophrenia, schizoaffective disorder, substance-induced psychosis, or brief psychotic disorder. Pervasive developmental disorder, organic conditions, and dissociative disorder should also be included in the differential diagnostic process (Imran & Clark, 2008). Adolescent schizophrenia has been associated with a history of motor and language delays, cognitive and social impairments, and family histories of schizophrenia. A careful history and information from multiple sources (e.g, caregivers, significant others, teachers, and community supports) and physical examination is needed to support diagnosis (Hollis, 2000). Table 11.7 identifies sample questions related to thought disorders/psychosis.

Trauma Reactions/Disorders

A high percentage of transition-age youth have been exposed to a variety of circumstances that can be considered traumatic. Trauma symptoms are often overlooked or identified as a behavioral disorder. Trauma reactions are varied and may include aggression, refusal to engage in specific activities or situations, depression, anxiety, behavioral and conduct problems, physiological reactions, or nonspecific medical or somatic complaints. Symptoms can be classified as intrusive, avoidance, or arousal. Intrusive symptoms are memories or images that suddenly occur in either day or night. Avoidance symptoms are behaviors in which situations, events, or people that remind the youth of the traumatic event are avoided. Arousal symptoms include hypervigilance or "on guard" and preoccupied behavior that is used to prevent further harm or reoccurrence of the trauma. Specific symptoms, according to the National Child Traumatic Stress Network (n.d.), may include the following:

- Generalized anxiety or fears;
- Loss of interest in activities;

Table 11.8
Interview Questions Related to Trauma

- Are there any situations or experiences that make you feel nervous, worried, or remember a difficult situation?
- Do you have times in which you have thoughts that you cannot get out of your mind?
- Do you ever feel jumpy or on guard?
- What ways do you cope with any of these symptoms?
- Are there people that help you?

- Guilt related to involvement in the trauma or not being able to stop trauma from occurring;

- Irritability or anger;

- Indifference or emotional numbing;

- Changes in academic or occupational functioning;

- Use of substances to cope with feelings; and

- Frequent discussion of the event.

It is important to remember that past traumatic experiences can cause long-term difficulties in a number of areas. The way that youth may relate to others and cope with changes or difficulties in relationships may be compromised. In addition, the way youth may understand and perceive situations may be altered based on their past experiences. They may easily feel victimized or perceive a threat in situations where others would not. Table 11.8 identifies sample questions related to trauma.

Personality Disorders

Personality disorders are psychiatric conditions that are characterized by chronic patterns of behavior that are inflexible and present in a broad range of settings. These patterns have significant impact on a transition-age youth's interpersonal relationships, social and occupational functioning, and overall sense of well-being. Legal difficulties and ongoing emotional issues may be present. Symptoms are considered to be the result of a combination of temperamental traits, environmental events, and developmental events. Recognizing the presence of personality disorders occurs in reaction to interactions, observations of behavior, and descriptions from significant others. The style of engagement of a youth with a personality disorder may indicate a pattern of behavior that is dysfunctional. The interpersonal behaviors may also be the cause of strong reactions in the practitioner. Demands on a practitioner's time, availability, and ability to help may seem overwhelming. Despite feedback, transition-age youth's insights related to their behaviors are often minimal or not present (Ward, 2004). Identifying patterns of behavior that may indicate a personality disorder occurs most often through discussions that describe ways of thinking, relationship patterns, and functioning in main areas. Specific lines of questioning do not usually occur in this area. Most of the time, these characteristics are not completely in a youth's awareness and do not become apparent to a practitioner through questioning. If needed, an assessment—the Adolescent to Adult Personality Functioning Assessment (ADADFA)—has been developed to assist in this area. The tool has six domains in the areas of education and employment, love relationships, negotiations, social contacts, friendship, and coping (Naughton, Oppenheim, & Hill, 1996).

Substance Use/Abuse

Alcohol and other drug use is a significant issue for transition-age youth in this country. The pattern of use is often different from adult patterns. Transition-age youth are more likely to abuse alcohol in combination with other drugs (Center for Substance Abuse Treatment, 1999). The progression of dependence may be more rapid in adolescents than adults (Martin, Kaczynski, Maisto, Bukstein, & Moss, 1995). Although this progression occurs more quickly in adolescents, there may be a great deal of difficulty recognizing or accepting problem behavior. Problem identification is in part due to common characteristics of adolescents (e.g., risk-taking behavior, rebellion of norms, and self-centeredness). The presence of withdrawal symptoms and medical problems are often not present in transition-age youth, demonstrating further the distinctions in the profile of an adult and adolescent with substance abuse issues (Langenbucher & Martin, 1996).

The assessment of substance abuse issues typically occurs in the context of an interview and formal screening/assessment tool. In the interview process, focusing on consequences related to drinking, rather than classifying behavior as abusive or dependent, may lead to meaningful information. Additional areas in the interview process to discuss include frequency of use, amount, history of problems in the family, previous problems or treatment, and efforts/thoughts of stopping use. A variety of screening and assessment tools are available. Tools that are available include the Drug Abuse Screening Test for Adolescents (Martino, Grilo, & Fehon, 2000) and the Adolescent Drinking Index (Harrell & Wirtz, 1989).

COMMUNITY FUNCTIONING

Recreation and Leisure Time

Enjoying recreation and leisure time can have a significant effect on a transition-age youth's mental health functioning. Multiple benefits in physiological, psychological, and sociocultural domains have been identified. According to Driver (1992), some of these benefits include the following:

- A sense of independence and autonomy;

- Enhanced self-competence;

- Improved self-worth;

- Self-reliance and self-confidence;

- Nurturance of desired self-identity;

Table 11.9
Interview Questions Related to Recreation and Leisure

- What types of activities do you find enjoyable?
- In your free time, do you enjoy being alone or with others?
- Do you feel that you have enough time for enjoyable activities?
- Are there things that you would like to do in your free time that you do not do now?
- Do you feel there is a balance between work/school and leisure activities in your life?

- Improved ability to relate to others;
- Improved ability to function as part of a team;
- Value clarification;
- Positive changes in mood;
- Stress management;
- Social integration;
- Strengthened family and peer bonds;
- Fostered sense of adaptability and resiliency;
- Decreased sense of alienation;
- Improved problem solving; and
- Enhanced ethnic and cultural identity.

In assessing the impact of recreation and leisure time on a youth's life, several areas should be to discussed. The number of activities, both presently and in the past, gives the practitioner a perspective for how this area of a youth's life has been developed. The type and range of activities is also telling regarding interests and preferences. If youth do not appear involved in activities, consideration should be given to the availability of different activities and the feasibility of involvement in those activities. Table 11.9 identifies sample questions related to recreation and leisure.

School/Employment

A transition-age youth spends a great deal of time at school or in school-related activities. This is a major part of youth's lives in which their desires, needs, and preferences should be made clear. The broad categories related to school include attendance, academic functioning, and behavioral functioning. Within these categories, it is valuable to focus on areas in which a youth feels competence, interest, and a desire to develop. This is especially relevant when considering secondary educational opportunities.

Employment is an activity that serves a number of purposes. Employment obviously improves a youth's financial situation, but being employed also serves to build self-competence, socialization, a sense of purpose and structure to a youth's life. Five

Table 11.10
Interview Questions Related to School/Employment

- Are you satisfied with your school or work experiences?
- Are there any areas in which school or work could better meet your needs?
- How is attendance for you at work or school?
- Are there any issues with peers, teachers, or employers?
- What are the areas you feel strongest about related to school or work?
- What have you been told by teachers or employers that you do well?

major areas of psychological benefits have been identified. These include structured time, social contact, collective purpose, personal identity, and activity (Jahoda, 1982). Table 11.10 identifies sample questions related to school/employment.

Participation Within the Community

Community involvement has been cited in several resiliency studies as serving as a protective factor (Werner & Smith, 1992). Feeling a part of a community reinforces a sense of connection with a larger group outside of the family. This evokes a shared understanding of a history, values, and cultural traits. This experience also supports a feeling of acceptance and communal trust. The sense of connectedness is identified as a coping strategy in dealing with adversity. Social support is also born out of community interaction. This support can be from the community as a whole, organizations, or community members. Volunteerism has many benefits as well. It promotes a sense of responsibility, self-efficacy, self-esteem, and meaning. On a practical level, job skills and job-related social skills are developed. Volunteers may be a part of a community process in which change, problems, or issues are being addressed (Atlantic Health Promotion Research Centre, 1999). The ability to feel a part of a change process is highly impactful. This develops problem-solving, coping, and socialization skills (Gottlieb, 1982). Transition-age youth with serious emotional difficulties benefit from interaction with others and reduced feelings of isolation, which often reduces emotional difficulties. As part of recovery from trauma, reestablishing and strengthening ties with others is a major goal (Lebowitz, Harvey, & Herman, 1993). Through continued and sustained interactions with others, empathy and a desire to support others is fostered and further developed (Herman, 1992).

Youth's level of involvement in the community may be related to a number of factors. Participation in community programs is sometimes prevented by several barriers. Lack of knowledge related to the programs, cost, transportation, and a lack of interesting programs have been cited as significant barriers (Scales & Leffert, 1999). In assessing how this area of a youth's life is progressing, it is helpful to get a history of experiences within the community. The way in which involvement came about and significant others' feelings about their involvement is important to assess. Information regarding the current level and type of involvement is also needed. This can be obtained through conversation and allowing youth to "tell their stories" in this area. Comments related to motivations, feelings, costs and benefits, and challenges are important to attend to. Table 11.11 identifies sample questions related to participation in the community.

Table 11.11
Interview Questions Related to Participation in the Community

- How would you describe your community?
- Do you feel a part of your community? Can you describe how or how not?
- Can you describe any activities you are involved in or, if not, are there any activities you would like to be involved in?
- Are there people in your community that you can turn to?
- Do you feel that your community has activities, people, and resources that are helpful to you and others? Can you give some examples?
- How would you change your community?
- What do you like about your community?

RISK BEHAVIORS

Suicidal/Homicidal Ideation

In screening for suicidal ideation, it is important to be conscious of the level of discomfort many individuals have in discussing this topic. It is helpful to precede the questioning with a statement such as "Next I will ask questions that are important to ask everyone so that, if help is needed, we can provide it." Practitioners should be aware of the best way to frame the questions. Making statements such as "I'm guessing you're not feeling like harming yourself are you?" is definitely not likely to get a truthful response if suicidal ideation is being considered. Practitioners should be aware of signs and symptoms of suicidal ideation. A study by Viñas, Canals, Gras, Ros, and Domènich-Llaberia (2002) identified several important findings related to suicidal ideation. These findings include the following:

- Suicidal ideation is not isolated to adolescents as often believed by lay people as well as professionals.

- In all ages, depressive symptoms, low self-esteem, hopelessness, and negative perceptions of the family environment are risk factors for suicidal ideation.

- Suicidal ideation may be present in the absence of depressive symptoms. An example of this situation may be learned behavior as a response to difficult circumstances.

Screening for homicidal ideation should not be overlooked, and it should be considered a possibility in children of all ages. Table 11.12 suggests questions that can help in the assessment of suicidal or homicidal ideation.

Legal Issues

Transition-age youth with serious emotional and behavioral challenges are at risk of experiencing legal difficulties. This risk is three times higher in youth with serious emotional challenges (Stoep, Davis, & Collins, 2000). A high number of transition-age youth in the criminal justice system experience mental health difficulties. Of a sample

Table 11.12
Interview Questions Related to Suicidal/Homicidal Ideation

- Are you currently feeling as if you may want to harm yourself in any way?
- Do you have any plans to do so?
- If so, can you describe what you are thinking about?
- Have you had these thoughts before?
- Have you felt as if you would want to harm anyone else?
- Do you have any plans for doing so?

Table 11.13
Interview Questions Related to Legal Issues

- Are you having any difficulties presently with legal concerns?
- If so, do you have the support you need?
- Is it challenging for you to stay out of trouble?
- Are there strategies or people that help you to avoid legal difficulties?

of 753 youth, approximately two thirds of the group had at least one contact with police, 43.3 percent had been arrested at least once, and 34.4 percent were considered delinquent or convicted of a crime (Greenbaum et al., 1996, pp.140-141).

A variety of issues are helpful to discuss with youth to best assist them in this area. Youths may have a history of legal difficulties for numerous reasons. Even though it is helpful to understand what these conditions may have been, a youth's perceptions and beliefs related to criminal activity are important to discuss. Many youth have made mistakes that may represent impulsive behavior and poor decision making. A youth who feels remorse and has attempted to prevent this from reoccurring is in a different place than a youth who has managed not to get arrested but feels no concern about this possibility. The consequences of actions and experiences with police and the court system should be explored. A comprehensive history related to type, frequency, and consequences of behaviors will assist in developing a plan for interaction and support. Table 11.13 identifies sample questions related to legal issues.

HEALTH AND WELLNESS NEEDS

General Health

How people feel physically is an important component to their overall well-being and emotional health. Often, transition-age youth who have struggled with pain or physical conditions have comorbid physical health conditions. Somatic complaints are common in such disorders as depression and anxiety. In considering general health, both chronic and acute conditions should be considered. Some youth describe an overall poor quality of health that is manifested by fatigue, low motivation for activity, poor sleep, and numerous somatic complaints. Attendance at work and school may be poor in youth with a history of poor overall health. Other youth may experience

Table 11.14
Interview Questions Related to Health and Wellness

- Are you happy with the way that you feel physically most of the time?
- Do you have a doctor that you feel meets your needs?
- Are there any physical conditions that interfere with your life?
- Do you fit exercise into your life?
- Do you feel good about your diet?
- In terms of taking care of yourself, what do you think you do particularly well?

chronic health conditions. Some chronic health conditions may be managed quite successfully and rarely cause a youth to feel poorly. Other situations may result in frequent hospitalizations or doctor visits. How a youth's functioning relates to his/her physical health should be explored. This demonstrates the impact general health may have in various domains.

Nutrition and Exercise

Nutrition and exercise are important concerns for the transition-age youth. The rate of growth that occurs in adolescence and young adulthood is phenomenal, second only to the first year of life. Nutrition during this time period is critical, as it affects energy level, adequate growth, and overall psychological well-being. Good eating behaviors related to the amount, frequency, and an appropriate range of foods are essential to good health. Poor habits related to an excess of fat, cholesterol, sodium, sugar, and low intakes of fruit, vegetables, and calcium-rich foods are common in both genders. Screening for eating disorders should occur as well. Physical activity has numerous benefits for the adolescent and young adult. These benefits include increased bone strength, developing lean muscle mass, reducing body fat, maintaining appropriate weight, and decreasing symptoms of anxiety and depression. Sixty minutes a day of exercise is of significant benefit to a transition-age youth (Hagan, Shaw, & Duncan, 2008). Assessment in this area should include frequency, type, level of enjoyment, amount of time spent, and how the youth prioritizes this activity. Table 11.14 identifies sample questions related to health and wellness.

STRENGTHS DISCOVERY

Unique Skills/Talents

Many transition-age youth are able to evidence a talent or interest in areas that can support them in a number of ways. Youth who find enjoyment in specific areas can rely upon this to provide them with enjoyment and entertainment to alleviate stress. Feeling competent in an area can also foster positive self-esteem and a sense of accomplishment. These skills are not only enjoyable but a base from which to build a core of employment-related competencies. Many youth with unique talents develop a vision of a career that will allow for the utilization of these skills. Youth with these types of talents may or may not be using the skill in their everyday life. Discussing with youth their preferences in their leisure time (see "Recreation and Leisure Time") and desires

Table 11.15
Interview Questions Related to Unique Skills and Talents

- What are some skills that you feel especially proud of?
- What are some things that others believe you do well?
- What are some activities that you find enjoyment in?
- What would be the things that your friends would say you are good at?
- What types of tasks come easy for you?

Table 11.16
Interview Questions Related to Resiliency

- Do you have automatic thoughts or behaviors that help you when a crisis or difficult situation occurs?
- Do you have people you can turn to when in need?
- Do you have people or activities in your life that make you feel valued or important?
- What strategies do you have for dealing with stress?
- Do you do better with coping short term or in the long term?

for further development in this area can shed light on talents that are present or under-utilized. Table 11.15 identifies sample questions related to unique skills and talents.

Resiliency Characteristics

Transition-age youth often are unable to describe the important characteristics related to resiliency that they may possess. These skills may be an attitude, natural inclination, or a way of interacting with others and their environment that serves them well. The identification of these traits as protective or helpful may not be present for the youth. Temperament and individual characteristics, family supports, and community supports are broad categories in which resiliency characteristics may be present.

The identification of these skills takes a combination of observation, speaking with the individual, and attending to comments and discussion from significant others. These are not typically skills or characteristics that youth easily identifies as helpful, in part due to the innate and "default" way that these characteristics show themselves. The Healthy Kids Resilience Assessment (Constantine & Benard, 2001), has identi-fied external and internal assets that reflect what has been learned from decades of resiliency research as important components. External assets include the general areas of school, home, community, and peers. Caring adult relationships, high expectations, and meaningful participation in each of these areas is assessed. Caring adult relation-ships are assessed by asking youth questions related to adults acknowledging their abilities, supporting them, and believing in them. Meaningful participation is assessed by determining if youth is involved in activities in the home, school, and community that are desirable and interesting to them. Internal assets are identified as cooperation and communication, empathy, problem solving, self-efficacy, self-awareness, and goals and aspirations. Additional consideration is also given to spiritual/religious con-nection, family behavioral monitoring, and appreciation of diversity (Constantine & Benard, 2001). Table 11.16 identifies sample questions related to resiliency.

Table 11.17
Interview Questions Related to Support Systems

- Are there people that you can turn to for socialization or help?
- Do you feel comfortable with the people that offer you support?
- Are there situations in which you are reluctant to ask for help?
- What makes it easier to ask for help? Accept help?
- Do you feel able to help others who help you?

Social Support System

Everyone benefits in numerous ways from having a social support system. A social support system is the most important element in a person's ability to cope with stressors and needs. Emotional concerns can be significantly reduced when others are available for social support. The support that one obtains from significant others may be the result of an arrangement that acknowledges the needs, or, in many cases, the relationships and interactions alone are enough to empower someone to keep persisting when times are difficult. Table 11.17 identifies sample questions related to support systems.

CONCLUSION

It is critical to engage transition-age youth in the service delivery system because of the numerous risk factors that are associated with unmet needs. Youth of this age may not be accustomed to discussing needs and strengths from their perspective, as their caregivers led this process when they were younger. Youth need time to feel comfortable with practitioners before needs or past histories are discussed. Establishing a relationship with youth that emphasizes their possibilities and strengths is needed prior to discussing needs. When needs are discussed, practitioners must find ways to understand the positive elements that are related in the discussion. As with any age, but perhaps more often with transition-age youth, the assessment process should be seen as a foundation for a relationship and ongoing discovery.

References

Atezaz Saeed, S. (2008). Working with individuals with mental illness and developmental disabilities: Synthesizing the best information for the practicing clinician. *Psychiatric Quarterly, 79*, 153-155.

Atlantic Health Promotion Research Centre (1999). *A study of resiliency in communities.* Ottawa: Health Canada.

Brown, C., Tollefson, N., Dunn, W., Cromwell, R., & Filion, D. (2001). The adult sensory profile: Measuring patterns of sensory processing. *American Journal of Occupational Therapy, 55*, 75-82.

Center for Substance Abuse Treatment (1999). *Screening and assessing adolescents for substance use disorders.* Treatment Improvement Protocol Series No. 31. Rockville, MD: Substance Abuse and Mental Health Services Administration.

Constantine, N. A., & Benard, B. (2001). California healthy kids survey resilience assessment module: Technical report. Berkeley, CA: Public Health Institute.

Copeland, W. E., Shanahan, L. Costello, J., & Angold, A. (2009). Childhood and adolescent psychiatric disorders as predictors of young adult disorders. *Archives of General Psychiatry 66*, 764-772.

Driver, B. L. (1992). The benefits of leisure. *Parks and Recreation 27*(11), 16-23.

Fergusson, D. M., & Woodward, L. J. (2002). Mental health, educational, and social role outcomes of adolescents with depression. *Archives of General Psychiatry 59*, 225-231.

Gottlieb, B. H. (1982). Mutual help groups: Members' views of the benefits and of roles for professionals. *Prevention in Human Services, 1*, 55-67.

Greenbaum, P. E., Dedrick, R. F., Friedman, R., Kutash, K., Brown, E., Lardieri, S., et al. (1996). National adolescent and child treatment study (NACTS): Outcomes for individuals with serious emotional and behavioral disturbance. *Journal of Emotional and Behavioral Disorders, 4*, 130-146.

Hagan, J. F., Shaw, J. S. & Duncan, P. M. (2008) *Bright futures: Guidelines for health supervision of infants, children, and adolescents* (3rd ed.). Elk Grove, IL: American Academy of Pediatricians.

Harrell, A. V., and Wirtz, P. W. (1989). Screening for adolescent problem drinking: Validation of a multidimensional instrument for case identification. *Psychological Assessment: A Journal of Consulting and Psychology, 1*, 61–63.

Herman, J. L. (1992). *Trauma and Recovery*. New York: Basic Books.

Hollis C. (2000). Adolescent schizophrenia. *Advanced Psychiatric Treatment, 6*, 83-92.

Imran, S., & Clark, A. (2008). Adolescent psychosis: A practical guide to assessment and management. *Psychiatric Times, 25*(11). Retrieved February 7, 2010, from http://www.psychiatrictimes.com/bipolar-disorder/content/article/10168/1336526?pageNumber=3

Jahoda, M. (1982). *Employment and unemployment: A social psychological analysis.* Cambridge, England: Cambridge University Press.

Kinnealey, M., Oliver, B., Wilbarger, P. (1995). A phenomenological study of sensory defensiveness in adults. *American Journal of Occupational Therapy, 49*, 444-451.

Langenbucher, J., & Martin, C. S. (1996). Alcohol abuse: Adding context to category. *Alcohol Clinical and Experimental Research, 20*(Suppl.), 270a–275a.

Lebowitz, L., Harvey, M. R., & Herman, J. L. (1993). A stage-by-dimension model of recovery from sexual trauma. *Journal of Interpersonal Violence, 8*, 378-391.

Manteuffel, B., Stephens, R. L., Sondheimer, D. L., & Fisher, S. K. (2008). Characteristics, service experiences, and outcomes of transition-aged youth in systems of care: Programmatic and policy implications. *Journal of Behavioral Health Services & Research, 35*, 469-487.

Martin, C. S., Kaczynski, N. A., Maisto, S. A., Bukstein, O. M., & Moss, H. B. (1995). Patterns of DSM–IV alcohol abuse and dependence symptoms in adolescent drinkers. *Journal of Studies on Alcohol, 56*, 672–680.

Martino, S., Grilo, C. M., & Fehon, D. C. (2000). Development of the Drug Abuse Screening Test for Adolescents (DAST–A). *Addict Behavior, 25*, 57–70.

Morgan, E., & Huebner, A. (2008). *Adolescent growth and development* (Publication No. 350-850). Retrieved June 24, 2010, from http://www.nvc.vt.edu/mft/Family_and_Child_Development_—_Adolescent_Growth_and_Development.mht

National Traumatic Stress Network. (n.d.). *Trauma in the lives of gang-involved youth: Tips for volunteers and community organizations*. Retrieved February 9, 2010, from http://www.nctsnet.org/nctsn_assets/pdfs/trauma_and_gang_involved_youth.pdf

Naughton, M., Oppenheim, A., & Hill, J. (1996). Assessment of personality functioning in the transition from adolescent to adult life: Preliminary findings. *British Journal of Psychiatry, 168,* 33-37.

Oates, J., & Grayson, A. (2004). *Cognitive and language development.* Malden, MA: Blackwell.

Parker, G., Wilheim, K., Mitchell, P., Austin, M. P., Roussos, J., & Gladstone, G. (1999) The influence of anxiety as a risk to early onset major depression. *Journal of Affective Disorders, 52,* 11–17.

Patchell, F., & Hand, L. (1993). An invisible disability: Language disorders in high school and the implications for classroom teachers. *Independent Education,* December, 31-36.

Premack, B. A., Swanier, B., Georgiopoulos, A. M., Land, S. R., & Fine, M. J. (2009). Association between media use in adolescence and depression in young adulthood: A longitudinal study. *Archives of General Psychiatry, 66,* 181-188.

Reed, V. (1986). Language disordered adolescents. In V. Reed (Ed.), *An introduction to children with language disorders.* New York: Macmillan.

Scales, P. C., & Leffert, N. (1999). *Developmental assets.* Minneapolis, MN: Search Institute.

Smith, D. J., & Blackwood, D. H. R. (2004). Depression in young adults. *Advances in Psychiatric Treatment, 10*(Part 1), 4-12.

Stoep, A. V., Davis, M., & Collins, D. (2000). Transition: A time of developmental and institutional clashes. In H. B. Clark & M. Davis (Eds.), *Transition to adulthood: A resource for assisting young people with emotional or behavioral difficulties* (pp. 3-28). Baltimore: Paul H. Brookes Publishing.

Viñas, F., Canals, J., Gras, E., Ros, C., & Domènich-Llaberia, E. (2002). Psychological and family factors associated with suicidal ideation in pre-adolescents. *Spanish Journal of Psychology, 5,* 20-28.

Wadsworth, B. J. (2003). *Piaget's theory of cognitive and affective development: Foundations of constructivism* (5th ed.). Upper Saddle River, NJ: Allyn & Bacon.

Wagner, M., Kutash, K., Duchnowski, A. J., Epstein, M. H., & Sumi, W. C. (2005). The children and youth we serve: A national picture of the characteristics of students with emotional disturbances receiving special education. *Journal of Emotional and Behavioral Disorders, 55,* 79-96.

Ward, R. K. (2004). Assessment and management of personality disorders. *American Family Physician, 70,* 1505-1512.

Werner, E. E., & Smith, R. S. (1992). *Overcoming the odds: High risk children from birth to adulthood.* Ithaca, NY: Cornell University Press.

Chapter 12

Assessing the Family

It is within the families themselves where peace can begin.
—Susan Partnow

The ritual of marriage is not simply a social event, it is a crossing of threads in the fabric of fate. Many strands bring the couple and their families together and spin their lives into a fabric that is woven on their children.
—Portuguese-Jewish Wedding Ceremony

INTRODUCTION

Society functions within the context of families. Families are the most basic form of all sociological institutions. Therefore, the influence and significance of families must always be appreciated and at the forefront of what practitioners who work with youth focus on. It is important to recognize the variety of families that practitioners work with. This includes households headed by the following:

- Biological parents;
- Single parents;
- Biological parents and stepparents;
- Biological parents and other caregivers;
- Grandparents; and
- Foster parents.

When one member of the family is struggling, the whole family is affected. This chapter, while it looks at the subgroups within a family, also encourages a view of the family as a system that is the sum of all of its parts. The focus of home- and community-based services fully appreciates this notion and strives to support the family as a unit. The goal of supporting the family must start with a focused effort in forming a relationship that supports an assessment process. The assessment, although comprehensive, strengths based, and culturally competent, will ultimately only offer a beginning and cursory understanding of dynamics. The stage must be set for further learning, as some dynamics will only be "allowed" to be shown once relationships are secure and the timing is right. Practitioners must appreciate the ongoing nature of assessment and the investment in engagement and relationship building to promote a mutual investment in supporting recovery.

RELATIONSHIPS WITHIN THE FAMILY

Caregiver Relationships

The impact of the caregiver relationship on a youth is monumental. When two caregivers are present in the home, their relationship with one another has an obvious impact on the youth. The tone for the household and overall level of safety and security is often intimately linked to the way in which the caregivers function. When caregivers function well, there are overall positive effects in the area of family stability, commitment to work performance, and improved caregiver-child relations. Youth are better able to cope with stress and have more successful school outcomes, including graduation from high school (Amato, 2007; Hair et al., 2009). In the assessment of this area, it is essential to discuss youth's perceptions related to their caregivers' functioning with them. Youth's perceptions, not necessarily what is perceived by others as reality, are what contribute to well-being or dysfunction (Erel & Kissil, 2003).

There are a number of dimensions within a caregiver relationship. The history of separations, or threatened separations, can offer a context for present functioning. The amount of time spent together, communication patterns, level of emotional satisfaction and connection, problem-solving abilities, strategies for handling conflict, and agreement in caregiving demands are important to discuss.

Caregivers may have distinct patterns of how they care for youth's needs within the family. There may be specific roles that are taken, and the way in which these roles have been determined may be a source of resentment for one of the caregivers. One caregiver may feel that he/she has sacrifices to make or challenges to overcome that the other caregiver does not. The caregiver who is not considered the main source of income in the family may be the one who must primarily care for the youth or attend meetings as needed. The satisfaction that each caregiver feels in his/her particular role must be determined, as this is relevant and meaningful to family interaction.

In general, couples that are in distress may demonstrate overt conflict or emotional distance, but the greater problem is considered to be the overt conflict. This may be manifested in numerous ways, including verbal and nonverbal interchanges. Criticism, disagreements, and lengthy chains of negative, as opposed to positive, interactions may be present (Herrington et al., 2008). Because these characteristics contribute to a negative environment and stress within youth in the family, the degree to which this occurs, whether it occurs in front of youth, and the length of time it has occurred

Table 12.1
Interview Questions Related to Caregiver Relationships

- How do you feel as a couple in your ability to work together to meet the needs of the children? How would you describe what goes well and what does not?
- When difficulties occur in your relationship, what ways work best to resolve them? What does not?
- Are there any concerns that the children are stressed by any relationship challenges between you?
- What helps you to work together and function at your best?

should be identified. Couples are often surprised by the degree youth are aware of tensions, despite the fact that they have tried to hide them. This information can be identified through conversations with the couple, the youth, and the family as a whole.

The quality of important relationships in single parents' lives should also be assessed, as this, too, has significant impact on youth. These relationships include the significant others involved in the single parents' lives as well as the extended family supports that are often very involved with the youth. Youth also are aware of the impact that these relationships have on their primary caregiver and often see these people as secondary caregivers for them as well. Single parents are often involved with the other parents of their children in some ongoing way in order to coordinate the care of their children. These relationships may become challenging, and the effects on the children should be assessed.

The best strategy for interviewing families may be to take their lead in the way in which the process occurs. This can begin by informing the couple of the needed components and working together to strategize on a method that takes into account their family culture. The components are often meeting with the couple together as well as individually and allowing the rest of the family to give input. Some caregivers may feel uncomfortable with the children offering their insight into the couple's functioning, and concerns and safeguards should be considered depending on the couple's openness and level of comfort. No strategy or intervention should take place unless the timing is correct and there is safety, both psychologically and physically, in family members speaking honestly and openly.

Observation as well as formal assessment tools should be considered. There is no better way to understand a system or subsystem than observation that occurs across multiple interactions. In addition, a formal assessment tool can contribute a great deal of insight. One such measure for assessing caregiver functioning is the Marital Satisfaction Inventory (MSI; Snyder, 1997). This tool is available through Western Psychological Services. In addition to focusing on marital or committed couples, practitioners must be assess the impact of the relationship between couples in which joint caregiving occurs. If there is tension between caregivers, this may be a difficult scenario for the youth to cope with. Table 12.1 identifies sample questions related to caregiver relationships.

Sibling Relationships

Siblings are youth's first playmates. This relationship presents many benefits for youth socially, emotionally, and cognitively. Socially, sibling relationships are the laboratory in which social learning first takes place. The skills of cooperation, sharing, and helping are modeled and developed within this relationship. This often is the basis of later development of social understanding and relating successfully with others. When sibling relationships are characterized as hostile and aggressive, this can later affect a youth's peer relationships. Youth with aggressive sibling relationships are more likely to provoke others and develop negative and often aggressive peer relationships. They also are less likely, in this instance, to demonstrate prosocial skills (Garcia, Shaw, Winslow, & Yaggi, 2000). The experience of conflict with siblings can also develop conflict resolution and negotiation skills that can assist in later peer relationships. This is especially true if the periods of conflict between siblings are coupled with an equal or greater amount of positive interactions. This balance in interactions tends to lead to the development of competence in conflict resolution as compared to greater episodes of aggression when interactions are primarily negative with siblings (Stormshak, Bellanti, & Bierman, 1996). Youth may first develop and practice an emotional language with their siblings. This gives them an awareness of the meaning and value of positive interactions with someone other than caregivers and other adults. The feelings of acceptance, connection, and enjoyment outside the caregiver relationship are meaningful and can encourage later development and desire for friendships. Cognitively, there have been studies to demonstrate how sibling relationships have a positive impact. Imitation of older siblings fosters learning and development of many skills. Younger siblings typically are the ones that benefit the greatest, although older siblings can develop their skills and learn from their siblings as well. In comparing sibling to peer interactions, siblings asked more questions of their siblings, requested more explanations, and challenged their siblings more frequently than they did peers in a laboratory situation. Additionally, the older siblings who took on the teaching role were more positive and provided a greater degree of guidance to the siblings than to their peers (Azmitia & Hesser, 1993). Youth who are in middle childhood demonstrate increased interaction with siblings in cooperative play and longer periods of time in which enjoyment and positive interactions occur as compared to other stages of development. It is also true that sibling relationships in middle childhood are also frequently negative, more so verbally than physically (Newman, 1994).

When assessing the nature and quality of sibling relationships, there are several dimensions and characteristics to observe and learn about. Within the sibling relationships what are the affective interchanges and how do these interchanges vary according to who is present? When the family has several children, it is important to determine the typical alliances, playmates, and roles that the siblings take with one another. Siblings may interact with one another differently based on age. Older siblings may rarely play with younger siblings but often nurture and support them. Some siblings play well together, for instance, and the addition of older or younger siblings changes this dynamic. In addition to the types of affective interchanges that are observed, how these experiences are received should also be recognized. Some siblings may be challenged in their ability to give as well as receive nurturance. The range of roles within the siblings should be apparent with observation. This may be either a source of support or a source conflict, depending on the situations. When older siblings are encouraged to discipline or oversee their younger siblings, this may cause resentment and behavioral disturbances. There may be resistance to taking on some roles as well as resistance to abandoning roles when no longer needed. When conflict is present, it is helpful to identify how it began, who initiated the actions, what behaviors ensued, and the duration of the conflict. If the conflict needed to be mediated or

Table 12.2
Interview Questions Related to Sibling Relationships

Input From Caregivers

- How would you describe the relationships between your children?
- Are you concerned about how well your children relate to each other?
- What areas related to how the children relate to one another are strong points? What areas are concerns?
- What do you think your children think about their relationships with each other? Do they have issues or concerns? Would they feel positive about certain aspects?

Input From Children

- What are some things that you like about how you and your siblings get along?
- What are some things that you do not like about how you get along?
- Do your siblings help you in any ways?
- Do your siblings do anything that makes things more difficult for you?
- Are there any activities that you enjoy doing with your siblings?

controlled by an adult, the manner in which this occurred and the consequences that were given contribute valuable information. How siblings interact in the home, the community, and the school may be different, and the interactions may be a source of support as well as conflict. As the assessment of sibling interactions develops, there are often nuances or specific patterns and issues to investigate further. Table 12.2 identifies sample questions related to sibling relationships.

Family Interaction Patterns

Although practitioners may identify healthy communication as a family characteristic that should be supported, modeled, and reinforced, the family's values, beliefs, and overall functioning in the area of communication must be explored and assessed before interventions are identified. The assessment process must appreciate the reality that some families may not be ready for candid conversations regarding family issues, and disclosing members' opinions in this area may be premature or even detrimental. Practitioners, despite wanting to talk with the family as a whole, may need to first meet with individual family members to get feedback regarding whether group communication is appropriate. This does not mean that the family cannot be assisted, later in services, in getting to a place where honest and respectful communication can be experienced. Prior to the assessment of family functioning, this issue can be discussed with caregivers in a supportive way. Caregivers can be encouraged to see feedback from their youth as a valuable thing, which can lead to true change. Caregivers should also acknowledge that it may be difficult or even contrary to family functioning or culture, and the practitioner will follow the family's lead in how to proceed in this area. Some caregivers may respond well to a plan to process feelings related to this issue first with the practitioner so that the children can experience being heard without consequences.

Every family is unique, and no assumptions should be made related to dynamics or interactions. Every family displays a hierarchy that is understood and honored by

Table 12.3
Interview Questions Related to Family Functioning

- Can you describe some situations in which your family works together to solve problems that affect the family?
- Can you describe special routines or activities that your family engages in?
- Can you describe how your family communicates with one another?
- Can you describe how your family celebrates birthdays, accomplishments, or successes?
- How does your family make decisions?
- How would you describe what you like most about your family? What do you like least?

all members. This may be manifested in who takes major responsibility for making decisions or communicating on behalf of the family. Often, the hierarchy is generational, and both caregivers are seen as having a higher level of authority and power in the family. There also are families who demonstrate a matriarchal or patriarchal hierarchal structure in which the mother or the father is the primary authority figure. The strength of this structure may vary, and situational variables may play a factor in this as well. Communication patterns are also unique to each family. Every family has a set of unspoken rules related to who can initiate conversation in given circumstances, what are appropriate responses, what are appropriate topics, and is there safety in expressing emotions. The way in which fathers and mothers communicate with their children is often different and related to the way in which men and women are socialized. Fathers tend to demonstrate a focus on resolving problems with less time spent listening to youth's concerns and attempting to understand their perspectives (Dino, Barnett, & Howard, 1995). Mothers demonstrate less emphasis on problem solving and are more likely to recognize and accept their youth's opinions (Fitzpatrick & Vangelisti, 1995). Table 12.3 identifies sample questions related to family functioning.

DETERMINING CAREGIVERS' NEEDS

Mental Health Needs

Caregivers with mental illnesses can be effective and nurturing caregivers to their children. Although it may be a challenge to be in a dual role, a consumer of mental health services and a caregiver, with appropriate supports, the challenges can be overcome (Ostler, 2008). It is important to establish if the caregiver has a good understanding of how the symptoms of the mental illness manifest, strategies to monitor functioning, and awareness of signs that additional support is needed. The practitioner should be familiar with the various mental health conditions (e.g., schizophrenia, bipolar disorder, depression, anxiety disorders, posttraumatic stress disorders, and personality disorders) so that adequate supports can be ensured based on an understanding of likely challenges. It is also beneficial to see each individual as having unique needs and strengths related to the management of his/ her condition, as no individual experiences it in the same way. If caregivers are receiving services, it should be a part of their treatment to adequately plan for a crisis situation. This should include the management and supervision of the youth.

If hospitalization should become necessary, a plan for care of the youth should have been discussed prior to the hospitalization and updated as part of the crisis plan. Coordination of care will be needed if the caregivers are receiving services in addition to the home- and community-based services. It is important that the two service providers/programs communicate the same philosophy of care and orientation to recovery. Interventions and caregiving feedback must be coordinated so that conflicting or confusing supports are not provided. When the assessment process identifies mental health concerns that are not being addressed adequately, an appropriate referral to services is warranted.

Substance Abuse Needs

Substance abuse among caregivers can obviously make caring for youth more challenging. Certainly, when youth have special needs, the complications can be even more apparent. Substance abuse includes the use of alcohol, illegal substances, as well prescription medications. Practitioners and caregivers may have different viewpoints about what constitutes a "problem" in this area. When assessing substance abuse, it is helpful to focus on what happens when caregivers use substances. The assessment is valuable when it leads the caregivers to identify areas that need to be addressed, despite the cause of these issues. The caregivers must decide if and when the want to address the substance abuse issue. When there are consequences that can be identified, and the caregivers are not ready to accept the presence of a substance abuse issue, time may be better spent solving other problems. Even if the cause of problems is related to substance abuse, success is achieved if the consequences of this use are addressed. Linking caregivers to supports or treatment in this area is ideal but must happen in a way that appreciates the caregivers' willingness to change.

Life Skills

Identifying caregivers' capacities to organize and support the family is imperative. Basic life skills (e.g., hygiene skills, cleaning and maintenance of the home, financial management, management of appointments, interacting with practitioners and school staff, and supervision and care of youth) may be poorly performed for many reasons. The assumption that there may be intellectual functioning issues on the part of the caregivers is often inaccurate. Poorly performed life skills may be a challenge for some caregivers because they feel overwhelmed, lack knowledge to perform the skills, or have too many other responsibilities. An assessment of what issues are impacting the caregivers' functioning is necessary from a perspective that is nonblaming and supportive. Concern in this area may come from observation or the referral source. It may be necessary to develop a relationship before these issues can be addressed, although a supportive and engaging stance should be able to support recognition of this issue. The caregivers may have unmet goals in this area, and they can join with the practitioner to eliminate concern that others may have.

Other life skills issues may be relevant to particular families based on their unique situations. Some caregivers may have difficulty organizing appointments. In determining what system has been used in the past and present, the problems may be broader than organization, as the systems that support youth with serious emotional

Table 12.4
Interview Questions Related to Caregivers' Needs

- Are there any areas in which support or resources would be helpful to you?
- Are there any stressors in your life that you feel challenged in managing?
- In managing your household, what areas do you feel you do well? Not so well?
- What are your ways of coping with stressors that you feel are the most helpful?
- Do you have people that are especially helpful?

disturbances may create difficult or conflicting expectations. There are a number of reasons why the life skills issue is of concern. The assessment process must appreciate both the identification of the problem as well as the contributing issues. This involves the caregivers' perspectives being sought, as the answer is not complete without this.

Barriers to Support of Youth

When considering the many areas that caregivers must attend to in managing a household, there is a plethora of issues that may cause difficulties. Meeting basic needs will typically be of primary concern. When caregivers are in situations where the needs for food, clothing, shelter, and safety are not being met, there is little else they can attend to. When caregivers need to meet their own needs for support and emotional well-being, it is challenging to focus on the needs of their youth. Identifying, strengthening, and building a support network should always be a priority. Last, viewpoints related to mental health issues (see "Mental Health Needs"), which prevent caregivers from understanding their youth's needs, can be a barrier to promoting long-term success and effective coping skills. Table 12.4 identifies sample questions related to caregivers' needs.

DETERMINING SIBLINGS' NEEDS

While interviewing the caregivers regarding the high-risk youth, discussion should include an assessment of other children's unmet needs. This is especially relevant when their needs are negatively affecting their functioning or impacting the family. The needs may be related to school or community activities but should not be excluded because of their nature. Youth have a broad range of needs that, if unmet, can cause significant stressors. Often, the siblings in the family have been unable to have some experiences within the community due to caregivers' inabilities to adequately support themselves, the high-risk youth, and the siblings. This can be an impactful intervention that aides the entire family, if opportunities are created or barriers broken down to participation.

Sibling Challenges

When siblings are not functioning well within the family system, this must be addressed. Although the family may be focused on the high-risk youth, it is necessary to support all members on behalf of the high-risk youth. No member of the family can have needs without those needs affecting other members of the family. Caregivers may, out of need, focus on the youth who is most symptomatic and inadvertently ignore a need in another youth. When this occurs, it is unlikely that the issue will just "go away." It is of more benefit to the family to mutually support all of the members. The sibling in need may be temporarily struggling with needs that may have surfaced due to adjustment or life transition issues. In this case, interventions may be minimal but meaningful. If a sibling is indeed having significant issues that are affecting his/her functioning, strong consideration of evaluating those needs further should take place. The high-risk youth may be in need of specialized and focused interventions that are specific to him/her.

There has been research to substantiate that siblings of youth with disabilities experience both negative and positive effects related to being in this role. Nixon and Cummings (1999) conducted a study in which siblings of youth with disabilities were exposed to videotaped segments in which conflicts between family members were displayed at various levels of intensity. Siblings of youth with disabilities displayed a greater level of emotional distress and reactivity to family conflict as compared to youth without a sibling with a disability. Siblings of youth with disabilities demonstrated a greater likelihood of taking responsibility for others' behaviors and felt compelled to assist in the resolution of conflict. These siblings were also identified as having greater adjustment problems and challenges in adequately processing social cues when conflict was involved. These findings suggest the need to screen for difficulties in these areas. On the positive side, siblings of youth with disabilities exhibited higher levels of sensitivity toward others and greater ability to interact with those in need. Finding appropriate and fulfilling ways in which these characteristics can be utilized and rewarded may support youth with these characteristics.

Mental Health Education

While the caregivers and high-risk youth may be educated on mental health issues, practitioners must not forget to educate the entire family. Often, siblings are exposed to inaccurate messages from a number of sources. Family dynamics may have inappropriately focused on a youth being "bad" or inadvertently labeled the youth in a manner that is not a true reflection of his/her needs. Additionally, the comments of others in the community may not have been rooted in a true understanding of the youth's needs. The way in which this occurs can take several formats. The practitioner can meet with the siblings individually or as part of a family discussion. When issues or resentments seem to be present, a specialized group or meeting for the siblings may be quite beneficial. Some programs have developed specialized groups for siblings, which attempt to reduce stigma and provide needed support. Table 12.5 identifies sample questions related to sibling needs.

CONCLUSION

The focus on the family as a whole is vital to the end result of empowering the family to fully support the youth in need in the best way possible. Careful attention to all members of the family is the way in which this can be accomplished. All

Table 12.5
Interview Questions Related to Siblings' Needs

Input From Caregivers

- Are there any areas related to the other children in your family who you would like to better attend to?
- Are there any activities or opportunities that you would like for your other children to be involved in?
- When your child is having challenges in his/her behavior or coping, how do you feel it affects the other children?
- What strategies do you feel have worked in meeting the needs of the other children?
- Is there anything that could make it easier to meet the needs of the other children?

Input From Children

- Can you describe how it is to have a brother/sister with special needs?
- What happens when your brother/sister needs help that you like or do not like?
- Are there any activities that you would like to take part in?

members of the family have importance in the youth's life and can inadvertently hurt or significantly help the identified youth in the family as needing intervention. As with any other assessment, this is an ongoing process that is continually occurring as the practitioner interacts with the family.

References

Azmitia, M., & Hesser, J. (1993). Why siblings are important agents of cognitive development: A comparison of siblings and peers. *Child Development, 64*, 430-444.

Amato, P. R. (2007). Strengthening marriage is an appropriate social policy goal. *Journal of Policy Analysis and Management, 26*, 952-955.

Dino, G. A., Barnett, M. A., Howard, J. A. (1984). Children's expectations of sex differences in parent' responses to sons and daughters encountering interpersonal problems. *Sex Roles, 11*, 709-717.

Erel, O., & Kissil, K. (2003). The linkage between multiple perspectives of the marital relationship and preschoolers' adjustment. *Journal of Child & Family Studies, 12*, 411-423.

Fitzpatrick, M. A., & Vangelisti, A. L. (1995). *Explaining family interactions*. Thousand Oaks, CA: Sage Publications.

Garcia, M. M., Shaw, D. S., Winslow, E. B., & Yaggi, K. E. (2000). Destructive sibling conflict and the development of conduct problems in young boys. *Developmental Psychology, 36*, 44-53.

Hair, E. C., Moore, K. A., Hadley, A. M., Kaye, K., Day, R. D., & Orthner, D. K. (2009). Parental marital quality and the parent-adolescent relationship: Effects on adolescent and young adult health outcomes. *Marriage and Family Review, 45*, 189-217.

Herrington, R., Mitchell, A., Castellani, A., Joseph, J., Snyder, D., & Gleaves, D. (2008). Assessing disharmony and disaffection in intimate relationships: Revision of the Marital Satisfaction Inventory factor scales. *Psychological Assessment, 20*, 341-350.

Newman, J. (1994). Conflict and friendship in sibling relationships: A review. *Child Study Journal, 24*, 119-152.

Nixon, C. L., & Cummings, E. M. (1999). Sibling disability and children's reactivity to conflicts involving family members. *Journal of Family Psychology, 13*, 274-285.

Ostler, T. (2008). *Assessment of parenting competency in mothers with mental illness.* Baltimore: Paul H. Brookes Publishing.

Stormshak, E., Bellanti, C., & Bierman, K. (1996). The quality of sibling relationships and the development of social competence and behavioral control in aggressive children. *Developmental Psychology, 32*, 79-89.

Synder, D. K. (1997). *Marital Satisfaction Inventory-Revised (MSI-R) manual.* Los Angeles: Western Psychological Services.

Part 4

Service Planning and Implementation of Therapeutic Interventions

Chapter 13

Designing an Effective Service Plan

Aim at nothing and you'll succeed.

—Anonymous

To tend, unfailingly, unflinchingly, towards a goal, is the secret of success.
—Anna Pavlova

INTRODUCTION

What youth and families want most when they request services is for their lives to get better in some way. An assessment is only as good as its ability to inform the service planning process. Planning is an investment and, if done correctly, can have a major impact on whether success occurs. The development of a plan is perhaps the most important activity in the service delivery process. This process includes several steps and considerations that are identified and discussed within this chapter. It is important that there is careful attention to the process and the interrelated components, as planning will either support or undermine the service delivery process depending on the quality and attention it is given.

GOALS OF SERVICE PLANNING

The wraparound approach (see Chapter 3 in this volume) is described as "a definable planning process that results in a unique set of community services and natural supports that are individualized for a child and family to achieve a positive set of outcomes" (Burns & Goldman, 1999, p.69, cited in Burchard, Bruns, & Burchard, 2002). Whether home-based services are a part of a well-defined wraparound process or not, service planning has the same overall goal. When considering what would be hoped for in experiencing this process, it can be further clarified in two additional goal statements. First, the service delivery process should ensure that the needs and strengths of the youth and families are effectively addressed. The foundation for this is a comprehensive strengths and needs assessment. The information obtained from this discovery process must drive the development of the plan. Second, the service plan should serve as a guide to service delivery in which the agreed-upon interventions occur and are continually assessed for effectiveness. This speaks to the notion of accountability for the implementation of interventions as well as the commitment to keeping the plan relevant and useful to the family.

COMPILING NEEDS AND STRENGTHS

Sharing Assessment Results

An assessment process that is completed in collaboration with the youth and family will ultimately end in the practitioner determining, from all sources of information, the areas that appear to be strengths and needs. The process of listing the identified needs and strengths has many benefits for the family and youth. Although it may be somewhat awkward at times to acknowledge areas that families and youth may not deem problematic, the process of transparency is supportive of overall engagement and investment in the planning. The family and youth should be reminded, prior to review of the list, how information was used and the practitioner's role in determining areas of need. The emphasis on their choices of priority needs and types of interventions should be part of this discussion. This may be discussed as part of the process, but there are times when additional information is obtained through discussions with other practitioners or information sources after the meeting with the family. Reviewing the list prior to planning also ensures that the service plan is relevant to the needs of the family and reflects a use of strengths. The listing of what was determined from the assessment keeps the planning process focused and related to the assessment. If a list is produced for all Child and Family Team (CFT) members, this empowers the CFT to work from a common focus. This significantly focuses the discussion and keeps the family feeling in control of the planning process.

Determining Issues and Concerns Related to Needs

Once a compilation of needs and strengths is given to all CFT members, the work of clearly stating the actual needs begins. A major area of concern (e.g., "anger control") may be identified, and it is important to answer the question "what needs to happen to make this area better?" Once the CFT gives input into this answer, the result may be a statement such as "Johnnie needs to develop strategies to control anger." In this scenario, it becomes clear that the needs are the circumstances underlying the problem area. The needs describes the area in which services are intended to help. With this focus, needs are identified and addressed rather than services being "thrown" at the family, without consideration for what truly is needed. This also allows for creative thinking and exploring multiple options within the community, natural supports, formal supports, or informal supports. It is important that an appropriate amount of time is spent clarifying needs to ensure that the supports are indeed helpful (Child & Family Support Services, 2007).

Prioritizing Needs

Most families have an idea prior to the assessment process of what they see as their priorities. These issues are often the ones that are causing the most disruption and immediate effects on the welfare and safety of family members. The family, as it moves through the assessment process, may begin to reprioritize or see issues differently as a result of the process. In either case, it is important that the family members and youth are able to consider and determine what areas are of greatest concern. This may be assisted with input of the CFT members but is definitely a decision that is made by the family. When youth and caregivers disagree on the priority or even presence of needs, the facilitator of the planning process should focus on bringing them to consensus, as this will greatly improve the likelihood of success. If youth are forced to work on issues they do not agree on, success is more unlikely.

In the process of prioritization, it can be helpful to request the CFT to rate areas of need that must be addressed (e.g., safety issues), areas that are significant and warrant immediate attention, and areas that can wait or are minimally impactful on the family's functioning. Starting with the highest priorities and moving down the list ensures that a plan is developed that is not too overwhelming or unmanageable. (See Exhibits 13.1, 13.2, and 13.3 for tools that can be of assistance in this area.)

Identifying Strengths to Use in Planning

The needs and strengths assessment process identifies strengths that should be listed and clarified further for the planning process. Strengths are determined during the assessment process in a conversational manner in which discussion is encouraged regarding insight into how the youth and family have coped thus far, what has worked for them, and what they want for their lives. The strengths can and should reflect psychological, physiological, or environmental strengths (Early & GlenMaye, 2000). Strengths are considered qualities that assist the youth or family in facing challenges and improving overall functioning. Strengths describe the family's unique attributes including skills, values, and abilities (Rotto, McIntyre, & Serkin, 2008). Asking questions such as "How does this strength show itself?" or "How does Johnny use this skill/strength on regular basis?" gives a more informed position from which to build on and utilize the strengths. This helps to take the focus away from what has not worked and areas that may seem overwhelming to change. Both the strengths of the youth as well as family members should be considered in this process. While attempting to mitigate the effects of the needs that are present, there should be a focus on building strengths in all areas of a youth's life such as school, community, family, extended family, natural supports, and community supports.

DISCUSSING POSSIBLE SERVICE DELIVERY OPTIONS

The ultimate goal related to supporting youth and families is to strengthen or develop the capacity to function optimally without dependence on formal or paid supports. In considering what can be built into a service plan, it is in keeping with the model to first consider the natural and community supports that are available to families and youth. These supports should be utilized as available as well as considered to work alongside paid professionals to strengthen their capacity to support the family beyond formal service provision. Families and youth may need some degree of services for an extended period of time, although what is strived for is to leave the family feeling fully capable of managing its needs. Families need to understand the types of services that can be provided through home-based services in order to make decisions regarding what can occur. The following sections describe typical services in a family-centered home-based services program.

Education of Youth, Family, Teachers, and Other Practitioners

Youth with mental health challenges are often misunderstood by family members, teachers, and community members. This is an area in which home-based practitioners can have an impact. The President's New Freedom Commission on Mental Health (2003) recognized the importance of educators being better informed regarding mental health conditions in the following statement:

> Schools are where children spend most of each day. While schools are primarily concerned with education, mental health is essential to learning as well as to social and emotional development. Because of this important interplay between emotional health and school success, schools must be active partners in the mental health care of our children. (p. 58)

Because of the importance of reducing the stigma and inaccurate information that may be present in the minds of the many people who support youth, this must be considered an important service delivery component when recognized as a need. Spending time listening to family members' perceptions and looking for opportunities to support alternate ways of thinking and understanding their youth should be infused into the services. This same need is present for the other people in youth's lives who are important to them.

Table 13.1
Skills Training Topics

Social Skills: Interpreting social cues, making new friends, keeping friends, dealing with conflict, apologizing, negotiating, responding to teasing, keeping out of fights, dealing with peer pressure, respecting differences, sharing, listening, learning to avoid tattling, learning to cooperate with others, learning to take turns, recognizing differences in relationships, developing tolerance of others, giving and receiving compliments, handling making mistakes, handling rejection.

Expression of Feelings: Defining various feelings, linking feelings to behaviors, developing a feeling vocabulary, distinguishing between emotional and physical pain, recognizing differences in the way people feel, recognizing various levels of intensity in feelings, learning that others do not control one's feelings, linking feelings to thoughts.

Anger Management: Developing an understanding of how one views anger, making an anger log, coping with anger towards self, defining various levels of anger, trigger thoughts, managing anger outbursts, communicating anger appropriately, using self-control steps, recognizing other's anger.

Impulse Control: Defining impulse control, developing strategies to wait, developing strategies to control frustrations, thinking before acting, recognizing situations in which challenges are likely.

Rule Compliance: Defining rules for oneself, recognizing the need for rules, accepting discipline, discussing feelings related to discipline, avoiding negative behavior, accepting consequences, making wise choices.

Attending to Task: Ignoring distractions, determining level of distractibility, strategies for remaining on task, time management, organization.

Self-Esteem: Defining self-esteem, expressing positive things about oneself, identifying strengths and weaknesses in balanced way, focusing on areas to build from.

Value Clarification/Life Skills: Journal writing, developing a life book, managing stress, resolving conflict, self-awareness, relaxation, staying calm, communication, forgiveness, empathy training, interdependence, coping skills, problem solving.

Skills for Caregivers Related to Discipline: Strategies for establishing rules, maintaining consistency, setting limits, balancing nurture and limit setting, managing frustration, using discipline to teach skills, managing needs of multiple youth, disciplining each youth differently according to needs, seeing behavior as unmet needs.

Skills for Siblings: Coping with caregivers attending to sibling, managing anger, accepting differences, role in crisis intervention, behaviors that promote successful interactions, replacing instigating behaviors, getting needs met, coping with stigma.

Practicing Skills

The development of skills in a number of areas is often a primary focus of home- and community-based services. In line with empowerment theory (see Chapter 1 in this volume), teaching families actual skills that they can use to make a real difference in their functioning is what can make a significant difference. Table 13.1 provides skills training topics that can be promoted with families.

Linkage to Resources

Frequently, families are in need of supports in a number of areas. Families may need links to organizations that can help with basic needs related to food, shelter, and safety. There may be financial issues, respite care issues, advocacy needs, day care, or recreational/social needs. Families who are able to feel that the practitioner is assisting in meeting their needs may develop trust and an overall level of comfort in the service delivery process. This may be a first step in forming a relationship.

Coordination of Care

An important service delivery need is the coordination of care. This includes strategies to ensure that all interventions are working in a way that moves the family forward and does not conflict in any manner. The practitioner will work to see that services fit together in a way that does not cause conflict with other appointments or types of services. The various service practitioners or organizations should also be unified in their approach and understanding of the families' strengths and needs. This can ideally occur through the support of a wraparound facilitator or practitioner who prioritizes this role. The coordination of care also refers to the monitoring and management of the service plan to ensure that services remain relevant and in the best interests of the family. The practitioner may convene meetings, make phone calls, and coordinate the sharing of relevant information as guided by the family.

Counseling

Counseling is a service that may be offered individually, with the family as a whole, or with individual family members depending on the needs and situations. Although there is a focus in improving overall family functioning, this does not mean that meeting with individuals alone sabotages this process. The counseling of individuals may be needed to optimize the likelihood that family sessions will be as effective as possible. At times, caregivers may not be able to work effectively with their youth on some issues without previous consultation or individual support from a practitioner.

Crisis Planning

Crisis planning may very well be one of the most important services that can be offered to a family. Crisis planning give the family a chance to gain an overall sense of preparedness and the experience of planning to cope with crisis situations. If crisis situations can be prevented or minimized, families may feel a huge sense of relief and feel empowered to meet their youth's needs in the best way possible. Many times, families enter services believing that this is not possible.

Crisis planning as a service takes many forms. There are preventative plans and strategies; reactive plans, which advise on the needed steps that should occur once crisis happens; and ongoing strategies to minimize the frequency and intensity of problem situations.

Table 13.2
Sample Wraparound Facilitator Job Duties

I. CFT meetings:
   A. Preparation for meeting
      1. Review chart and past CFT meeting minutes.
      2. Create an agenda
         i. Call CFT for input
         ii. Typ agenda
         iii. Make copies for CFT members.
      3. Arrange for location of meeting.
      4. Review of wellness binder to make sure it is up to date.
      5. Make copies of crisis plan and treatment plan for CFT discussion/review.
      6. Send reminders a week prior to meeting to CFT members.
      7. Research and coordinate possible natural supports for CFT.
      8. Coordinate celebration items if need be (food, etc.).
   B. Facilitate CFT meeting
      1. Guide CFT on meeting discussion
         i. Review agenda for additions
         ii. Discuss strengths, needs/concerns, interventions
         iii. Review crisis plan for updates/changes
         iv. Review treatment plan for updates/changes
         v. Discuss service hours and needs.
      2. Provide resource options when needed.
      3. Take notes of meeting.
   C. Follow up after CFT meeting
      1. Collaborate with CFT on any assigned tasks from meeting.
      2. Provide CFT members with updates from other CFT members.
      3. Link and research appropriate resources discussed in meeting.
      4. Complete CFT meeting minutes
         i. Create CFT meeting minutes
         ii. Make copies for wellness binder, file, and CFT members
         iii. Forward to CFT members.
II. Review monthly practitioner's reports and CFT reports.
III. Update flex funds
   A. Research alternative resources prior to using flex funds.
   B. Keep running report on flex funds used on each client.
   C. Make sure purchase is related to treatment plan.
   D. Obtain permission from supervisor and CFT before using flex funds.
IV. Wellness binders
   A. Make copies of everything for binder.
   B. Keep updated with paperwork in regards to client in binder.
   C. Research resources to put in binder.
V. Social marketing
   A. Provide CFT and community with ongoing education about systems of careand wrap
      around process.
VI. Surveys
   A. Wraparound and Fidelity Index (WFI) surveys
      1. Set interview up.

(Continued)

Table 13.2 *(Continued)*

---

      2. Provide information to WFI surveyor.
      3. Assist surveyor in getting a hold of family and CFT members.
   B. CFT meeting surveys
      1. Get releases.
      2. Give CFT members copies of survey to complete.
      3. Provide CFT members envelopes/stamps for survey.
VII. Other paperwork requirements
   A. Complete service plan updates.
   B. Reassessments (e.g., Comprehensive Child and Adolescent Needs and Strengths (CANS)).
   C. Update releases.
   D. Update CFT members contact sheet.

Prepared by Bobbi Jo Short, BA. Adapted with permission.

COORDINATION WITH THE WRAPAROUND FACILITATOR

Role of Direct Support Service Practitioner Supporting Wraparound Process

The wraparound facilitator (see Chapter 3 in this volume) serves the role of monitoring progress, communicating with the family and practitioners, coordinating the plan development, monitoring the plan, and coordinating transition and crisis planning. Table 13.2 identifies sample job duties of a wraparound facilitator.

If there is no formal wraparound process in place, a home- and community-based program can identify a practitioner to coordinate the planning process in a manner consistent with wraparound principles. Home-based practitioners involved with a CFT recommend a range of appropriate services and interventions and only initiate such with the agreement of the CFT. The practitioner is accountable to the CFT and must report progress and recommend changes to the facilitator. Most CFTs support practitioners in making minor changes to interventions prior to monthly meetings as long as the facilitator is notified as soon as possible. The role of the facilitator is to ensure accountability to the plan and that changes are driven by the youth and family. Practitioners must be flexible and prepared to make needed adjustments as directed by the CFT. Prior to monthly meetings, the practitioner must discuss his/her report with the family and ensure that there is agreement on the assessment of progress. This may take many formats, which could include a written or verbal report presented to the facilitator prior to the CFT meeting or the same types of reports submitted at the time of the meeting. These decisions are agreed to at the initial CFT meetings (Penrod, 2008). Table 13.3 identifies key concepts that practitioners must remember in working with the CFT.

Activities Within Wraparound Phases

As practitioners agree to be part of a CFT process, they must understand the importance of aligning their services with the phase of service delivery that the CFT identifies as the current phase for the family. The interventions in the various phases

Table 13.3
Concepts Related to Working With a Child and Family Team

- All practitioners agree to adhere to wraparound principles.
- Practitioners understand need to account to CFT on adherence.
- Practitioners agree to report to CFT any recommendations or modifications to the plan.
- Practitioners are a part of a CFT unified to work on families' behalves.
- Families and youth make decisions and are fully supported by CFT in doing so.
- Attendance at meetings and communication with wraparound facilitator is required.

must reflect the needed tasks and strategies that are identified as critical in each phase. In the phases of service delivery, the family is expected to be in need of support in making changes, while in the transition phases, the focus is more on consolidating gains and supporting recovery. Practitioners need to come to meetings with details related to what exactly is occurring within their service delivery in a manner that can put the CFT in the position to evaluate appropriateness.

DESIGNING INTERVENTIONS IN A FAMILY-DRIVEN/ YOUTH-GUIDED MANNER

Supporting the Youth and Family Together

Davies and Wright (2008) conducted a literature review examining youth perspectives on mental health services. A common theme was youth's request to give input related to how they may best be served and be treated respectfully in this process. This finding emphasizes how critical it is to establish mutual agreement between the youth and family related to services so that youth can feel the same sense of involvement as their caregivers. If service plans are designed without the youth agreeing on the emphasis and way in which interventions are delivered, they are destined to be less effective. In addition to the input related to interventions, balancing family versus individual interventions is important in order to engage both youth and families in designing service plans.

Determining When, What Level of Intensity, and Where Interventions Occur

The family and youth should always direct the decisions that are made regarding how interventions take place. Practitioners must always allow family members to make choices that will best suit the needs of their families. Families know in what ways they will best receive information, in what locations, and at what level of intensity. Taking into account a family's culture in this process must take place. The practitioner's role is to give guidance related to the choices and to ensure that a clinically appropriate plan is put in place. If the family makes choices that appear contraindicated, there should be discussion regarding the reasons why choices are of concern. Most of the time, practitioners who truly listen to the needs and wishes of the family are able to work through this situation successfully, in a way that is satisfying to the family.

Table 13.4
Questions to Support the Service Planning Process

- What is the family's vision for how it should function?
- In a perfect world how would you describe your family and the way you would help one another?
- What are the baby steps it will take to get there?
- How will we know things are getting better?
- What will the siblings do to show things are better?
- What will the caregivers and youth do to show things are better?
- Who can be responsible for providing supports in the process?
- What does the family as a whole need to accomplish?
- What do the children need to accomplish?
- What do the caregivers need to accomplish?

Considering How Needs Manifest in Different Environments

In order to understand what underlies behavior, an appreciation for the differences in environments is recognized as critical to consider. Behavior reflects an individual's ability to get needs, emotional or otherwise, met by either him-/herself or those around him/her. Behavior therefore can look different in different environments depending on the ways in which the environment and people within it affect the youth. It is common for youth with issues related to activity level and attention, for instance, to present differently in the school versus home environments. When planning interventions, this should be taken into consideration. Table 13.4 identifies questions that can help in the service planning process.

DEVELOPING A MEASURABLE PLAN TO DETERMINE SUCCESS

One of the important wraparound principles is related to developing outcome measures (Burchard et al., 2002). The family and CFT must agree on ways to determine if the plan is effective and working toward goals. There must be an objective way to measure this, which is agreed upon by all. The family and youth must educate the CFT on ways that will fit with their unique family structure and culture. One family may be oriented to tracking progress in a chart-like format and has experienced success in using such a method. Another family may determine that this would not be useful in its home. The practitioner or facilitator can guide the family and CFT with questions that develop measures for objectives in a way that works best for all.

USING SERVICE PLAN AS A GUIDE

In the past, many programs developed plans that ended up being filed away in charts and only seen at the next review period. When this occurs the likelihood that services are most effective and in tune to family needs is poor. Youth and family development is dynamic and ever changing. It is unlikely that, if services are being provided in the way they should, the need to amend interventions will only occur at scheduled reviews. There is a constant effort to better understand family functioning, and this may lead to a need to refocus objectives or interventions. The plan is a valuable document that holds the practitioner accountable and continually reminds him/her, as well as the family, of the work that needs to be done. Practitioners should ensure that all family members are given a copy of the plan and that it is reviewed on a regular basis if not at the end of every visit. It is best for practitioners to carry the plans with them so that it is available for review at visits.

CONCLUSION

Service planning is a process that is directly linked to the assessment of needs and strengths. There should be no disconnect in these two activities. The principles of wraparound, empowerment, and recovery must all be represented in this process so that the service provision truly reflects these important concepts. When emphasis and adequate time is given to this vital element, practitioners are more likely to facilitate meeting the needs of families and ushering in recovery.

References

Burchard, J. D., Bruns, E. J., & Burchard, S. N. (2002). The wraparound approach. In B. Burns & K. Hoagwood (Eds.), *Community treatment for youth: Evidence-based interventions for severe emotional and behavioral disorders* (pp. 69-90). New York: Oxford University Press.

Burns, B. J., & Goldman, S. K. (Eds.). (1999). *Systems of care: Promising practices in children's mental health, 1998 series: Volume IV. Promising practices in wraparound for children with severe emotional disorders and their families*. Washington, DC: Center for Effective Collaboration and Practice, American Institutes for Research.

Child & Family Support Services. (2007). *Module 4: Assessing, coordinating, and monitoring support services through the CFT.* Retrieved September 20, 2009, from http://mmwia.com/download-confirmation/?k=d9f5a6522dba4e3b71beb550d0fbc959

Davies, J., & Wright, J. (2008). Children's voices: A review of the literature pertinent to looked-after children's views of mental health services. *Children and Adolescent Mental Health, 13,* 26-31.

Early, T. J., & GlenMaye, L. F. (2000). Valuing families: Social work practice with families from a strengths perspective. *Social Work, 45,* 118-130.

Penrod, T. (2008). Direct support services in wraparound. In E. J. Bruns & J. S. Walker (Eds.), *The resource guide to wraparound.* Portland, OR: National Wraparound Initiative, Research and Training Center for Family Support and Child Mental Health.

President's New Freedom Commission on Mental Health (2003). *Achieving the promise: Transforming mental health care in America. Final report for the President's New Freedom Commission on Mental Health.* (SMS Publication No. 03-3832). Rockville, MD: Author.

Rotto, K., McIntyre, J. S., & Serkin, C. (2008). Strengths-based, individualized services in systems of care. In B. Stroul & G. Blau (Eds.), *The system of care handbook: Transforming mental health services for children, youth, and families* (pp. 401-435). Baltimore: Paul H. Brookes Publishing.

Exhibit 13.1
Individualized Service Planning Worksheet

CANS 5-18

Who are some of the important people in _____'s life who you'd like to be involved in
treatment planning and support? _____

_____

_____

_____

Needs/Strengths Identified from the CANS

Life Domain Functioning	Acculturation
1.	1.
2.	2.
3.	3.
4.	4.
5	
6.	**Child's Needs**
7.	1.
8.	2.
9.	3.
10.	4.
11.	5.
12.	6.
13.	7.
14.	8.
	9.
Child's Strengths	10.
1.	**Child's Risk Behaviors**
2.	1,
3.	2.
4.	3.
5.	4.
6.	5.
7.	6.
8.	7.
9.	8.
10.	9.
11.	10.
Caregivers' Needs/Strengths	
1.	
2.	
3.	
4.	
5.	
6.	

(Continued)

Exhibit 13.1 *(Continued)*

7.
8.
9.
10.

Prioritization of Needs

- Asterisk needs that must be addressed.
- After giving options for meeting needs, determine if all areas or some will be addressed

Discuss Roles of CFT Members in Meeting Needs

For Every Identified Need

Goal: How would I like things to be in this area?

Objective(s): Steps in making progress. What needs to happen in order to show I'm on my way to meeting my goal?

Interventions: Strategies that youth, caregivers, mental health practitioners, natural supports, and others can use to help us in meeting goals and objectives. Use strengths in interventions.

Exhibit 13.2
Description of How Needs May Manifest

Anger: Tense posture, loud and demanding tone of voice, pacing, frequent arguments, noncompliance, verbal or physical aggression, defiance, attempts to undermine authority, or threatening behavior.

Depression: Indifference to praise or rewards, crying, whining, negative statements, poor eye contact, slowed speech, slowed movements, distracted appearance, blank stare, unsmiling face, little inflection in voice, sighs, lowered energy, fatigue, physical complaints, decreased concentration, poor memory, lack of interaction with others, lack of interest in playing.

Anxiety: Statements of worry or fear, inability to sit still, pacing, flashes of smiles, rigid posture, avoidance of people or activities, nervous habits such as scratching, fidgeting, repetitive movements, coughing, darting eyes, shaky voice, disconnected sentences or statements, startling easily, jumpiness, over sensitivity to stimuli, lessened concentration, poor eye contact, and withdrawn behavior.

Interaction With Peers: (Positive) Mutual enjoyment, laughter, initiating contact in appropriate ways, responding appropriately to social cues, sharing, reciprocal communication, ability to compromise. (Negative) Frequent arguments, aggression, intrusiveness, poor ability to negotiate with others, excessive dependence on adults for negotiating peer relationships, lack of understanding of social cues, provoking others.

Interaction With Adults: (Positive) Ability to accept direction, compliance with directives, sharing stories or information openly, seeking attention in positive ways, responding to questions. (Negative) Lack of cooperation, arguing, sarcastic comments, inappropriate comments, aggression, inability to accept direction, guarded or withdrawn behavior.

Exhibit 13.3
Example of Individualized Service Plan

The CFT consists of Annie, Mother, Aunt, Guidance Counselor, Probation Officer, Therapist, and Case Manager.

LIFE DOMAIN FUNCTIONING:

Social Functioning

Goal: Annie will feel comfortable around peers.

Strengths to Be Utilized in Meeting This Goal: Annie has awareness of this need and is motivated to work in this area. She has interest in school activities, such as Students Against Drunk Driving, and can use this social opportunity to practice socialization.

Objective: Annie will respond verbally to peers who initiate conversation at least once daily.

Interventions:

1. Annie and Mother will discuss school day daily and review social interactions.
2. Annie will process social experiences at school with Guidance Counselor as needed.
3. Therapist and Case Manager will practice conversational skills.
4. Therapist and Case Manager will practice eye contact and develop steps to ensure such.
5. Therapist and Case Manager will ensure referral to psychiatrist.
6. Therapist and Case Manager will monitor progress of interventions.
7. Therapist and Case Manager will coordinate care and ongoing CFT meetings.
8. Therapist and Case Manager will develop and monitor an appropriate crisis intervention plan.
9. Therapist will provide individual therapy to assist Annie in processing feelings and behaviors.

Measurement of Objective: Annie will report to Mother, Therapist, and Case Manager success or lack of success in responding to peers. Documentation of this will occur in Annie's journal.

Frequency: Intervention 1 will occur daily. Intervention 2 will occur as needed. Interventions 3, 4, and 9 will occur two times weekly. Intervention 5 will occur once or as needed. Interventions 6, 7, and 8 will occur one time weekly.

School

Goal: Annie will improve school performance.

Strengths to Be Utilized in Meeting This Goal: Annie is motivated and has the support of her school counselor. Annie has a history of good school performance. Annie's Mother is in support of good attendance and homework compliance and will reinforce importance and strategies for improvement.

Objective: Annie will increase school attendance by reducing absences from once a week to once a month.

Interventions:

1. Mother will transport Annie to school daily and, if Annie presents as ill, the school nurse will assess appropriateness for medical intervention.

(Continued)

Exhibit 13.3 *(Continued)*

2. Therapist will monitor appropriateness of crisis plan and report to CFT monthly.
3. Therapist will assist Annie in processing feelings underlying issues related to poor school attendance.
4. Therapist and Case Manager will monitor progress and report to CFT members.
5. Probation Officer will monitor absences and process with Annie monthly.

Measurement of Objective: Guidance Counselor will report attendance to Therapist and Case Manager monthly.

Frequency: Intervention 1 will occur daily. Interventions 2 and 4 will occur weekly. Intervention 3 will occur weekly. Intervention 5 will occur monthly.

Judgment/Anger Control/Impulsivity

Goal: Annie will demonstrate ability to exercise good judgment.

Strengths to Be Utilized in Meeting This Goal: Annie has supports identified in school as well as home to assist her in processing feelings. Annie wants to be successful in getting off of probation.

Objective: Annie will utilize one of three coping strategies when angry.

Interventions:

1. Annie will process strategies with Therapist for improving judgment.
2. Annie will utilize Mother and Aunt to process struggles with peers.
3. Therapist and Case Manager will monitor appropriateness of crisis plan and report to CFT members.
4. Annie will attend psychiatric appointments
5. Annie will comply with medication recommendations.

Measurement of Objective: Annie will report use of coping strategies to Therapist and Case Manager. Guidance Counselor and Mother will monitor use of strategies as well.

Frequency: Interventions 1 and 3 will occur weekly. Intervention 2 will occur as needed. Intervention 4 will occur monthly. Intervention 5 will occur daily.

Sleep

Goal: Annie will sleep six hours per night.

Strengths to Be Utilized in Meeting This Goal: Annie has a regular routine and support of Mother in maintaining good sleep habits.

Objective: Annie will utilize at least one relaxation technique prior to bedtime daily.

Interventions:

1. Annie will process with Mother, Therapist and Case Manager sleep issues.
2. Annie will discuss sleep issues with Therapist.
3. Therapist and Case Manager will monitor progress and appropriateness of interventions.

Measurement: Annie will report technique used daily to Therapist.

Frequency: Intervention 1 will occur at least weekly or as needed. Intervention 2 will occur monthly. Intervention 3 will occur weekly.

(Continued)

Exhibit 13.3 *(Continued)*

Legal/Delinquency

Goal: Annie will "get off probation."

Strengths to Be Utilized in Meeting This Goal: Annie has the support of Aunt and Probation Officer who is willing to coordinate with CFT. Annie is highly motivated and has a good history of rule compliance.

Objective: Annie will remain compliant with probation requirements.

Interventions:

1. Annie will report to probation monthly.
2. Therapist and Probation Officer will monitor progress.
3. Aunt will assist Annie in community service project with her church.

Measurement: Probation officer will report compliance.

Frequency: Intervention 1 will occur monthly. Intervention 2 will occur weekly. Intervention 3 will occur weekly.

ACCULTURATION: No areas of need identified.

CAREGIVERS' NEEDS:

Knowledge

Goal: Annie's Mother will develop understanding of Annie's mental health needs.

Strengths to Be Utilized in Meeting This Goal: Annie and Mother have a loving relationship and Mother is hopeful and willing to receive support in this area.

Objective: Mother will be able to express understanding of typical trauma reactions.

Interventions:

1. Therapist and Case Manager will provide information to Mother.
2. Therapist and Case Manager will assist Mother in determining Annie's specific reactions to trauma.
3. Annie will discuss feelings with Mother in family sessions regarding mental health needs.

Measurement: Mother will report to Therapist and Case Manager understanding of trauma reactions.

Frequency: Interventions 1, 2, and 3 will occur weekly.

Chapter 14

Developing Interventions to Support Caregivers and Family Within the Home and Community

Never tell people how to do things. Tell them what to do and they will surprise you with their ingenuity.

—General George S. Patton

We must not, in trying to think about how we can make a big difference, ignore the small daily differences we can make which, over time, add up to big differences that we often cannot foresee.

—Marian Wright Edelman

INTRODUCTION

The vehicle for change within the family is always the relationship between the practitioner and the family. This relationship nurtures a shared understanding of needs and strengths, and the ability to mutually develop the interventions that can promote change. The presence and caring attitude of the home-based practitioner facilitates this relationship. Further, the experience of being understood and having needs addressed strengthens the relationship. The commitment to recognizing the family's uniqueness, routines, and traditions in its own environment sends a powerful message. It emphasizes the importance of guiding the family toward change at the time the family needs it the most, in the place that is most relevant to it, and in a way that will translate more easily to continued strategies. The discussion of strategies in an office setting simply does not fully support these things. The practitioner sends the message that "You can teach me about your family" rather than "I'm going to tell you what to do," when providing services in the home. In an office setting, the family may be poorly able or unable to articulate the challenges it is experiencing. The most important elements in the therapeutic process are the development and maintenance of the relationship. The feeling that a positive relationship is present brings hope and optimism for the future. Interventions born out of this relationship will continually be tested, changed, and ultimately be facilitators of true recovery and the development of resiliency.

COLLABORATING WITH CAREGIVERS REGARDING ASSESSMENT OF NEEDS

In the process of completing a needs and strengths assessment, the determination of needs may have required a judgment on the part of the practitioner that caregivers do not agree with. This does not mean that the assessment is not valid or disregards the voices of the caregivers. The more important variable is the way in which this information is shared and how a conversation related to the caregivers' priorities and desired interventions occurs. Sharing the results of the assessment is an important part of the process that, in some traditional models, does not always occur. Many caregivers were not apprised of the important issues identified through the assessment process and were merely given a plan for how the practitioner would intervene. Empowerment as a paradigm embraces the notion that caregivers are partners with practitioners in all aspects. This is demonstrated by relationships that are reciprocal, honest, and open in their communication as well as sharing responsibility and cooperation (Dunst, Trivette, & LaPointe, 1994). If caregivers are not given the same information that practitioners have, this prevents these characteristics from occurring. Openly discussing differences in opinions regarding the identification of a problem is highly valuable. It first manifests the practitioner's role of offering guidance. Recognizing a difference of opinion does not mean forcing a service or focus that caregivers do not want. If caregivers' wishes are allowed to be heard and reflected, the recognition of a problem on the part of the practitioner does not have to be experienced as alienating. Conversely, honest feedback may be experienced as a safety net in that caregivers can take comfort that the practitioner is committed to providing an accurate assessment. The practitioner demonstrates respect for the caregivers' opinions by a commitment to bringing knowledge and experience to the table for the caregivers' consideration. The choices of which areas to focus on, the order of needs, and the types of interventions must be made with the results of the assessment in mind. Caregivers can best put this information into perspective and make the relevant determinations that will mark the plan as potentially successful.

UTILIZING THE STRENGTHS OF THE CAREGIVERS AND FAMILY

The development of interventions should always value using the competencies and strengths that are present and have been used in the past. These strengths should be fostered, and ways to utilize them in the mitigation of needs is a primary focus. Practitioners should not communicate or allow their services to somehow supplant the natural tendencies and abilities that are already developed in the family. The focus should rather be to uncover and nurture these areas. Even when the strengths are inconsistent or rarely used, they should be acknowledged and fostered.

In considering the ways in which strengths can be used, several strategies are possible. In addressing the needs that the family chooses to focus on, past attempts to correct the problems should be explored. Even when the attempts were not successful, there were likely some components that may have been working well. Building on these components can be a good place to start. Additionally, finding strategies to preserve skills that highlight the family rather than attempting to replace them with new or unnatural ones is more likely to develop change. For example, if a caregiver finds that one of her greatest strengths with her child is to predict disruptions, but her

Table 14.1
Ways to Utilize Strengths in Interventions

- Use strengths of *all* family members and supports in planning.
- Build capacities through involvement in activities that reflect interests, talents, and abilities.
- Focus on the building of relationships that are meaningful and supportive to youth.
- Identify ways to strengthen caregiver-youth relationships in the areas they feel most competent rather than beginning with most challenging interactions.
- Identify the component of an interaction that reflects the greatest skill level and work to enhance this rather than starting with the area that does not work well. (For example, if a child does well remaining calm and expressing his opinion unless he is ignored, rather than focusing on the calming skills when he is ignored, work with caregivers to intervene differently at the point in which the child is calm.)
- Allow the youth to participate in activities that are desirable and enjoyable to him/her to cope with distress.
- Identify and support the naturally occurring interventions and activities within the family rather than starting over with "what the professional knows is best."

weakness remains staying calm once it occurs, interventions should revolve around her ability to monitor her child's mood. Caregivers can also be assisted in finding alternative ways to address their weaknesses, which may include the use of friends or extended family to assist when needed. Table 14.1 assists in the identification of ways to use strengths in interventions.

MUTUALLY DETERMINING WAYS TO INTERVENE

Families know best what will work for them. If interventions are imposed or not invested in, the chances of success are minimal. To best make this determination, the family must be given a rationale for why different options may be desirable and others may not. They must be given the information they need to make this decision. The type of interventions (e.g., counseling, skill building, and coaching) should be described and differentiated. Not only the type of intervention but the timing, intensity, style in which it is administered, and how it is used should be decided upon by the family. Caregivers or family members know when the most difficult times of the day are for the family and can suggest the best time for the practitioner to arrive. The other aspect of timing involves deciding the point in treatment at which new skills or issues should be addressed. Practitioners can make suggestions regarding the sequence of activities, but families may have good reasons why this course of action may not work for them. The intensity of services is also something that families often have preferences about. Sometimes a family may feel that too many practitioners are coming into the home, and these efforts must be streamlined and coordinated. There may have been a long history of this occurring, and the family may best be engaged with less frequent contact. Throughout the intervention phase, the family must be continually engaged in discussion about remaining flexible in altering interventions to reflect the needs and changing environments. Families and youth must be invited to give input about interventions that may or may not work for them.

There are a number of factors to consider when designing interventions with families. The traditions that are a part of any given family's life are important to understand, respect, and preserve. Routines are also reflective of who the family is, and altering such, unless it is determined to be problematic, is not usually accepted well by the family. Families gravitate toward traditions and routines as a way of feeling secure as well as establishing a family identity. The values that a family holds must be considered in the interventions as well. Religious beliefs, caregiving beliefs, and family members' roles may reflect these values and should be maintained and supported. The feelings that the youth and caregivers have with regard to the services may have a strong impact on the role of the practitioner. Some families need a great deal of time to build a relationship and feel comfortable with the process. Caregivers may have strong opinions about how the practitioner interacts with them in the home, especially in front of the children. Caregivers can help the practitioner by explaining the children's various temperaments and past experiences with practitioners. This can be an invaluable part of the planning, as it can optimize the likelihood for engagement and relationship building. Caregivers should be asked about trauma experiences or associations with counseling that may have been negative. Some youth may associate counseling with removal from the home, punishment, or blame. Most importantly, family members emphasizing the areas in which they feel comfortable, competent, and the most family unified is a good place to strengthen and mitigate needs.

Naturalistic Opportunities in Supporting Interaction

Caregivers, if given an understanding of the benefits of addressing issues "in the here and now," will be able to engage in the planning of the interventions. They should be asked questions that will help to predict potential issues or considerations for the implementation of the intervention strategy. Some youth are extremely worried about being judged by the practitioner as "bad," and this means that carefully attending to the way in which issues are addressed is especially important. Youth also may be easily embarrassed, and caregivers may want to invite the youth to reinforce that the practitioner sees the good as well as the difficult circumstances that occur within the home; all family members must understand that issues will remain confidential. Most families have not allowed everyone who comes into their home to see how challenges are handled, and it may be disconcerting for a youth to discuss issues with the practitioner within the home. Preparing family members for the way in which the intervention typically unfolds is helpful, and family members' input about feelings and concerns should be sought. Caregivers may have the same feelings that youth do, and inviting them to process this with the practitioner is important. The experience of being in therapy and what is discussed in therapy may cause a number of reactions and emotions that may be difficult to deal with. Practitioners should always keep this conversation alive, as it is often the most relevant topic that keeps a family engaged.

Addressing Caregivers' Barriers to Change

A conversation must take place with caregivers about what may be preventing change from occurring or keeping certain unhealthy situations in place. This is often a difficult but critical discussion. Any behavior or circumstance has meaning that may not be understood clearly. Along with this, the secondary gain or latent functions of that behavior should be considered and possibly replaced with other ways of getting the needs met. At times, there are concrete barriers to change that, if understood, can be met and no longer prevent what is needed.

Empowering Caregivers Without Taking Over Caregivers' Roles

Caregivers form attachments, maintain attachments, and strengthen attachments by being available and able to meet youth's needs. This role should always remain the primary function of the caregivers. Within the home-based services environment, the practitioner does not want to take over this role at all costs. Discussion with the caregivers related to how important this concept is should occur, as there are times when caregivers are so overwhelmed that they want the practitioner to be in this role. The practitioner should appreciate where caregivers are, in terms of their stress level, and find ways to work with caregivers in ways they can tolerate. The practitioner may use nonverbal communication and develop plans for discussions away from the youth to coach the caregivers. Coaching can be carefully executed and worded to not insult or disrespect the caregivers. The practitioner should also use reflective supervision to assist caregivers in monitoring their motives and interactions related to this.

CHANGING INTERVENTIONS AS FAMILIES MOVE THROUGH SERVICE DELIVERY PHASES

Initiating Intervention

When interventions are initiated, there is a need to support the rationale and motivations of the family that underlie the need for the intervention. To support an environment of change, the family needs to be supported in remaining invested and hopeful for the future. Sometimes, it is difficult to think that an alternate way of functioning will be better and later be able to be sustained. Other times, there may be reasons why change will bring about additional issues or upset the family dynamics. The practitioner should be mindful of these possibilities and be looking for opportunities to support the family with challenges and dynamics. The practitioner should reinforce the previously stated reasons for the interventions and point out progress to fuel continued efforts. When a lack of progress is present, this should be attended to promptly, and modifications to the intervention may be needed. The practitioner must be careful to maintain a positive working environment that does not leave the family feeling that the tasks are too daunting. Interjecting fun, humor, and positive interactions should always balance difficult and strained interactions. During some sessions, the family may benefit solely from having enjoyable and positive interactions, especially when there has been a great deal of negativity.

Skill-Building Phase

During the skill-building phase, interventions are often supported primarily by the practitioner. The initiation and guidance for executing the skill is supported by the practitioner much of the time. The practitioner may be modeling and later reinforcing the skills that were worked on. When the practitioner is not present, the family may or may not use the same interventions. Often, the family may practice components or steps in the skill when the practitioner is not present and practice the entire task when the practitioner is present. As this phase progresses, the practitioner takes less and less responsibility for leading the interventions, and the family continues to work on the entire skill or task without the practitioner. When the family feels comfortable and successes have been reported, it is time to shift into the next phases of support.

Sustaining Skills and Facilitating a Recovery Environment

When the family has experienced success and seen the results of changing a pattern of interaction or developing a skill, it is now invested in maintaining this experience and often communicates good feelings about what the change has brought about (see Figure 14.1). The family works with the practitioner to develop routines and strategies to ensure that progress is maintained. When routines are developed, the family is more likely to maintain the practice. In addition, the development of a way to monitor progress and regression should be developed (see Chapter 13 in this volume).

BUILDING CAREGIVERS' CAPACITIES IN PROVIDING FOR BASIC NEEDS AND SAFETY

Linking to Resources

Not having the resources to meet basic needs for food, shelter, and safety is a crisis situation. Families are not able to focus on other tasks until this situation is addressed. This situation may occur at the beginning of services as well as throughout treatment. At the beginning of services, the family needs food, shelter, and safety to be fully assessed and addressed. When a family is unfamiliar with the practitioner, there are some additional tasks related to linkage that should be discussed. Simply offering a phone number to a resource may not be sufficient. Since the relationship between the practitioner and the family is new, it is likely that there are factors that may be difficult to discuss related to this situation, which may have a great deal of relevance in how it is handled. The practitioner may not know yet that a family has exhausted resources in a certain area, has history with an agency, feels uncomfortable asking for help, or needs the practitioner to help with follow through.

Linkage to resources should always be followed up with a plan for how to maintain the resource and prevent the same need from happening again. A discussion regarding past strategies, changes in life circumstances, strengths that the family has, and natural supports that can help are all relevant areas that can contribute information needed to build a plan.

Crisis Planning

The development and use of a crisis plan can offer the family some additional assurances that it did not have prior to services. Although the development of a plan is an essential element to include in services, it is not enough in and of itself to address

Figure 14.1
Stages of Intervention

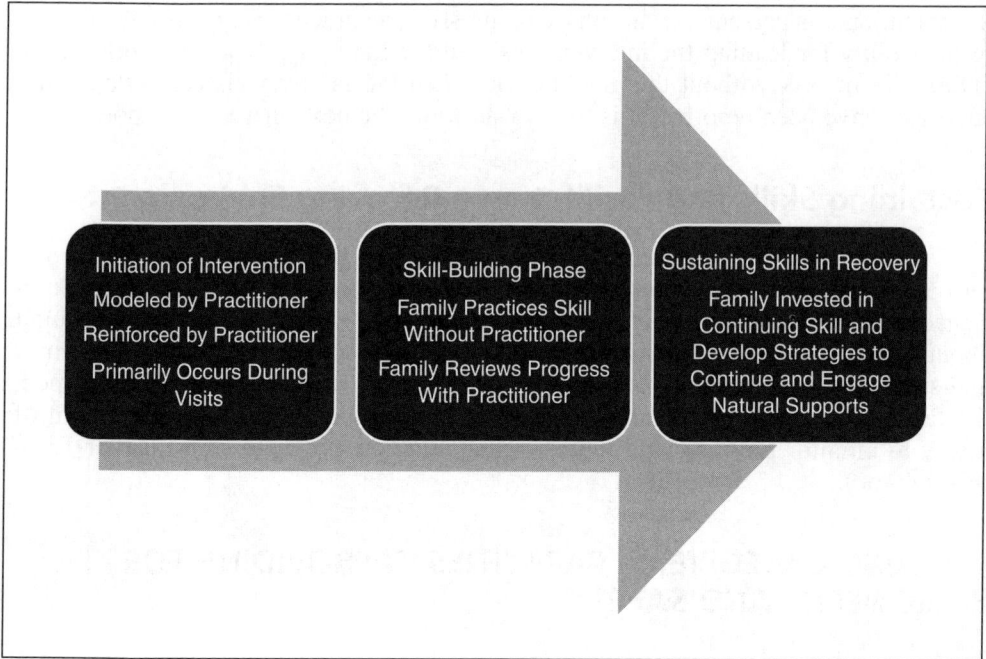

Initiation of Intervention

Modeled by Practitioner

Reinforced by Practitioner

Primarily Occurs During
Visits

Skill-Building Phase

Family Practices Skill
Without Practitioner

Family Reviews Progress
With Practitioner

Sustaining Skills in Recovery

Family Invested in
Continuing Skill and
Develop Strategies to
Continue and Engage
Natural Supports

safety issues. Many families can accept the notion of a plan, but due to ongoing chaos in the house, they have great difficulty activating the plan or even finding the plan when needed. Other families may not completely agree to the activities identified in the plan, and this will only be revealed through keeping the communication open related to the plan, strategies, and perceptions about issues related to safety and crisis. This occurs through active listening, processing situations in which violence could have erupted, and fostering a mindset with the family that alternatives to violence can be developed. The practitioner should strive to develop preventative strategies in the family that include identification of stressors at an early stage; putting strategies in place to diffuse violence, stress, or potentially at-risk situations; and everyday interactions that promote positive interactions. Families should be advised that if potentially difficult situations arise, the practitioner or Child and Family Team (CFT) providing services should be contacted. Programs may develop policies for assisting families in crisis such as supervisor support or attendance at visits, two CFT members attending sessions, or phone contact with a supervisor at the visit (Tracy, 2001).

Removing Barriers

The coordination and planning of interventions should always be a part of the process, especially when a CFT is working with a family. In the case of safety and basic needs being met, understanding the many factors that may be contributing to the issue may be the basis of new interventions. For this reason, it is important that all involved are on the same page, and planning occurs to address needs. If the underlying cause of the issue or contributing factor is not also addressed, there will be continued issues. Underlying issues may relate to a lack of concrete resources, emotional issues or concerns, or lack of natural or community supports.

Enlisting Natural Supports

Practitioners must always be careful not to disable the use of the natural and community supports. Some families may feel that they must first seek professional help rather than the people they have always turned to first. In other cases, natural supports may be overwhelmed or frustrated with their attempts to help. Always considering the way in which the family can best be supported after the services are ended is a good practice. If natural supports are not available or are being used in a manner that is not working, development and support is needed from the practitioner to correct or repair this situation. Practitioners can also assist in the development of relationships or connect families to community resources that can further expose them to others from whom helping relationships may develop.

BUILDING CAREGIVERS' CAPACITIES TO SET LIMITS AND DISCIPLINE

Providing Educational Opportunities

Practitioners can surely benefit from listening more than talking when providing services to families. Before giving guidance in the area of discipline and limit setting, it is essential to understand the viewpoints, values, routines, traditions, and past and present strategies. Caregivers' beliefs related to discipline and limit setting are related to a number of factors. Some of the factors include how they were disciplined as children, their cultures, levels of education, socioeconomic status, religious beliefs, and influence from extended family (Landy & Menna, 2006). It may be difficult for caregivers to ask for help, as they may feel judged and incompetent. Giving information can happen in a way that either leaves caregivers feeling understood and assisted or lectured at and disrespected. This evolves by forming a relationship with the caregivers and an understanding of how they can best receive information. Limit setting and discipline issues may be highly charged topics and are linked to the caregivers' own senses of self.

Coaching When Challenges Occur

Limit setting is often not seen as an activity that meets a youth's needs. The need to feel that caregivers will assist youth when they are out of control is vital to their functioning. Reframing for caregivers that acting out of control is distressing for youth and usually not a situation that they would choose helps support caregivers in this task. Skills in this area are many. Caregivers should be supported in clearly communicating expectations, monitoring the environment and conditions that are part of the child's ability to comply, setting the limit, and reestablishing a connection. Most of the time, there are some skills in this area that are more difficult than others for caregivers.

Caregivers can develop insight into why they are having challenges in limit setting through processing these experiences.

Caregivers and practitioners should work collaboratively to design an intervention plan for limit setting that meets the needs of the family and is comfortable to the caregivers. Caregivers may be more comfortable discussing limit setting without the youth present or by allowing the practitioner to make sure the youth understands that practitioners' roles are different from caregivers' roles. The practitioner demonstrating the role of collaborator and coach is perceived differently than one who takes over during a discipline action or criticizes the caregivers. Families who use practitioners to support them during actual difficulties can benefit more than recounting an incident to the practitioners. Practitioners help caregivers the most by observing the reactions of the youth being disciplined, the other siblings, as well as the caregivers, and coaching on how to maintain focus in spite of the reactions. The most difficult task for caregivers may be to remain empathetic to the youth's needs while simultaneously setting a limit. Processing the incident afterward with the youth to reestablish the connection is also challenging for some caregivers. Practitioners will want to coach caregivers to communicate empathy while not apologizing for their concerns or actions unless something inappropriate has occurred. Caregivers may feel so uncomfortable with their youth being angry that the teaching moment becomes replaced with a statement such as "It's ok, Mom was just mad." This type of statement is confusing and leaves the youth feeling that his/her caregivers are not in control.

In this area, discipline should reflect the needs of youth as well as an understanding of their mental health challenges. This is often difficult for caregivers, as some mental health issues related to trauma and attachment require unique styles of interaction that may be different than what it typical. Youth with attachment and trauma issues often need to know that their caregivers are not deserting them when their behavior requires disciplinary action. These youth are best disciplined not by "time out" types of procedures, but rather remaining with their caregivers throughout the interaction and punishment. Other times, caregivers may need assistance understanding how discipline strategies may need to be adapted when youth have certain types of mental health conditions.

Arranging Respite Care

When families experience ongoing stress and tension within the home, there may be a need for respite care. The purpose of the respite care is to refuel the caregivers psychologically, physically, and emotionally in order to improve and maintain their ability to parent effectively. Respite care occurs when the child is cared for by another adult in an effort to give the caregivers a needed break. Most frequently, the child is cared for in another home for a given period of time. When caregivers have been interviewed to discuss their feelings related to respite, a number of themes emerged in various studies. Ashworth and Baker (2000) reported that caregivers identified the benefits to respite as including obtaining sleep and combating exhaustion. Feelings of losing control and desperation were a part of the emotional exhaustion that they were experiencing. There was also a great benefit in attending to other household tasks that were often neglected. This created a feeling of "normalcy" that was in part due to their ability to interact with the outside world. In a similar study by Olsen and

Maslin-Prothero (2001), caregivers were thankful for the time to interact and focus on their other children as well as their spouses.

In seeking to help caregivers with respite needs, there are a number of ways in which this can be done. A conversation with caregivers related to their feelings, needs, and the needs of the youth may be the best option. MacDonald and Callery (2004) identified options that caregivers typically chose. These included short breaks provided by family or friends, short breaks provided by an agency, and overnight respite. In-home respite is another option that can be offered, especially if the youth has been traumatized, and separation is overwhelming. An important insight that was also gained from the MacDonald and Callery study was the fact that caregivers were more likely to ask assistance of other caregivers when their children played together, and there was an ability to "repay" the favor. This may be an important element to consider when assisting caregivers in identifying and using others for support.

When families demonstrate a sense of being overwhelmed, respite may be a strategy to include in a manner that is planned and not tied to crisis situations. Depending on the nature of the youth's emotional difficulties, it may be much easier to cope with separation when it is not linked to crisis. In the same vein, it is best if "bad" behavior is not linked to respite, especially with youth who struggle with the child-caregiver relationship. Caregivers will need to be coached to present respite in a positive manner. Upon return from respite, practitioners can coach caregivers on assisting youth in transitioning back to their normal routines and giving time to acknowledge the changes in the respite and home environments. Caregivers may feel frustrated with reports that the youth was "no problem," as it contributes to feelings of inadequacy in them. Practitioners should acknowledge the normalcy in these feelings and the frequency of youth behaving differently in these situations.

Caregivers may have significant concerns about who cares for their youth and the manner in which the care occurs. Several related concerns may result from exploring this area. Caregivers do not want to feel sabotaged in their attempts to manage behavior or emotional needs. Caregivers also may need to feel that the substitute caregivers can handle the youth and that the strategies that they choose do not cause harm. In these cases, it is important for the practitioner to arrange for the potential respite practitioners to be interviewed by the caregivers. Practitioners can also assist in giving pertinent information related to the youth, their needs, and appropriate strategies to manage and care for them.

Exploring Natural Supports

The support system that the caregivers identify can significantly help in areas related to discipline and limit setting. Exploring the caregivers' needs in this area and helping them to communicate these needs can be a first step. Often, what well-meaning friends and family may assume that caregivers need is not necessarily what they actually need. Caregivers who are not able to discuss this clearly with others may inadvertently alienate those offering help or discourage ongoing help. Practitioners may misinterpret the caregivers' reactions as not wanting or needing help. Many caregivers would appreciate someone to vent to, but they do not want anyone to comment or attempt to intervene during interactions with their youth. It is important for caregivers to discuss with natural supports their needs related to conversations between the youth and the natural supports before, during, or after a difficult interaction. Caregivers may become upset by natural supports making statements that are construed as sabotaging or emphasizing the wrong message. Practitioners can serve caregivers well by exploring these and similar issues to best make use and preserve the natural supports that are available in a family's life.

Reviewing Successes and Setbacks

The work of being a caregiver never ends. Caregivers may lose sight of the progress that is made in the numerous areas they may be working on. Small successes may seem meaningless or get lost in the chaos. Pointing these gains out to caregivers and keeping hope and optimism alive is important. Continually listening for the strengths that have been displayed or developed in situations is also crucial in keeping the momentum moving in the right direction. Caregivers may also need help with the concept that setbacks do not mean that all gains have been eliminated. The normalcy of ups and downs should be discussed. Learning from all situations should be framed as the goal. Recognizing the difficulty that some caregivers may have in acknowledging what they perceive as failure is also needed as well as pointing this out to them.

BUILDING CAREGIVERS' CAPACITIES TO PROVIDE STRUCTURE

Assisting in the Development of Routines

Some individuals are more in need of routines than others. Caregivers vary greatly in their recognition of this and their capacity to provide a sense of predictability related to activities within their homes. This becomes recognized as an issue especially when youth's and caregivers' needs are different. Caregivers who do not feel inclined to schedule events or activities in a similar or predictable fashion may not have insight into the sense of anxiety that this may cause their youth. The issue may also be the opposite when caregivers are excessively rigid and not able to vary routines to meet the needs of the youth. Building awareness that youth benefit from structure and routine, despite the lack of ability to express or demonstrate this, is often needed. Some youth may appear to not need or want this despite the well-established fact that this is typically needed and helpful.

Home-based practitioners can best assist families in this task by looking for times in the past as well as the present in which some degree of structure and routine has occurred. These are often the times when youth need the most structure such as morning routine, mealtimes, homework time, and bedtime. Especially when families can describe a previous history of success in this area, it becomes a helpful place from which to build. Caregivers may need help with the actual activities that will contribute to and result in a more predictable routine. It is helpful to encourage caregivers to get youth's input so that they can mutually invest in the plan. Both caregivers and youth can discuss areas in which increased structure and the tasks that need to be accomplished are most important. Once there is an understanding of particular routines and the tasks that could improve the situation, a plan can be made. This can be developed by both observing routines and listening to families' concerns. It may be helpful to go through the day from morning to evening and develop a plan to make transitions and expectations more predictable. Table 14.2 indicates typical times in which routines are needed and possible interventions.

Table 14.2
Developing Family Routines

Morning Routine

- Determining strategies for waking on time and expectations for children upon waking up.
- Determining roles in preparing breakfast.
- Developing special traditions that have meaning for family and supporting positive interactions

After-School Routine

- Assisting in developing clear expectations and roles.
- Identifying schedule for after-school activities that respect family culture.
- Identifying places to put school materials.
- Assisting in balancing "down time" with chores, homework time, etc.

Mealtime

- Determining roles in meal preparation.
- Identifying family chores.
- Establishing alternative schedules or planning when routine changes.
- Assisting in the establishment of special family traditions.
- Assisting in identifying chores and activities related to individual members' strengths and skills.

Bedtime

- Identifying what goes well and what does not from all family members' perspectives.
- Developing roles and expectations with family.
- Creating special routines.
- Establishing a problem-solving plan for meeting all youth's needs.

Reducing Challenges and Barriers

Changing patterns of behavior and interactions may not be an easy task. It is helpful to know if there have been times when the attempted changes that families are trying to make have been in place. If the family has experienced previous success, learning from both the challenges as well as the successes can bring about better-informed strategies. Insight can be developed through discussions in which families share their views related to what did and did not work. Caregivers can be supported by meeting with practitioners individually to process their feelings related to reinforcing the changes. Sometimes feelings of guilt, being overwhelmed, or fear of rejection can underlie caregivers' difficulties in enforcing rules within the household. If caregivers describe being tired, stressed, or unable to cope with caregiving expectations, linking to resources or problem solving to build capacity is needed. If practitioners are present during times in which changes are being attempted, observing the interactions can lead to coaching both youth and caregivers. Caregivers may need help in the ways they approach their youth. Preparing youth for changes and communicating empathy may be areas in which caregivers need support. Caregivers also need assistance in framing consequences for behavior and allowing for some flexibility, as appropriate. Routines can still be in place and a strong part of the family schedule, while still allowing for flexibility, as appropriate, to appreciate the youth's input. Youth can also be assisted in coping with routines by appreciating their perspectives. The most important intervention can be assisting caregivers to appreciate youth's perspectives and developing ways to positively support youth in complying or completing tasks they do not enjoy. Strategies to assist with this often revolve around finding opportunities to make the interactions enjoyable and less burdensome. The relationship between youth and caregivers may be strengthened through these types of activities.

Determining Support Needs

As practitioners and caregivers work collaboratively to process progress, they may identify ways in which friends or extended family may be able to assist. Families may need another adult present during difficult times, someone to talk to, or respite care. When sleep is needed, others can assist in this area by taking children so that caregivers can get some rest. Other stressors that can be eliminated through education or support may include poor organization or financial management. When issues are present, the specifics related to who will help, how it will occur, and how progress and needed changes to the plan will be determined must be decided. The practitioner must be careful to provide support in a way that is comfortable to the caregivers and does not leave them feeling undermined.

BUILDING CAREGIVERS' CAPACITIES TO PROVIDE NURTURING INTERACTIONS

The nurturing of a child takes many forms and is manifested differently as the child develops. A child will feel nurtured if his/her physical and psychological needs are met in a caring manner. When youth are cared for in a nurturing way, they experience warmth, sensitivity, and contingent responses to their cues (the signals that they give usually through facial expressions and behaviors that indicate a need for interaction or attention of some kind). This lays a foundation for the development of trust in others and the ability to interact positively with others (Baumrind, 1989). Children's cues are often difficult to understand. This misunderstanding can leave them feeling frustrated and uncared for. Caregivers may misunderstand youth's capacity to control emotional reactions and their intentions when distressed. Mental health issues can also have an impact on ability to nurture. Mothers who neglected their children have been shown to be more depressed and have lower self-esteem than mothers who did not neglect their children (Culp, Culp, Soulis, & Letts, 1989). Interventions to build caregivers' capacities in coping with stress and managing child behavior can have significant benefits in the area of nurturing, as these issues often leave caregivers overwhelmed. Role playing has been shown to assist the development of these skills as well as improving the quality of interactions. When caregivers are able to interact in a positive manner with their youth, it is more likely that youth will respond in a similar manner (Egan, 1983).

Pointing Out Youth's Needs and Opportunities

Caregivers can always benefit from the reinforcement of how important their interactions are to their children. The knowledge of warm and nurturing interactions being linked to secure attachment, improving overall development, and protecting against the development of many emotional and behavioral disorders can be powerful (Sanders, 2008). Although hearing the tremendous benefits of caring interactions for youth is helpful, there is nothing more impactful than experiencing the power these caring interactions have on youth. Practitioners should look for opportunities to point out to caregivers how youth react positively to nurturing interactions. This can take the form of words, positive gestures, touch, or providing for needs. Practitioners can also support youth by encouraging them to tell their caregivers how they felt about the positive interactions. At times when youth are distressed or challenged in their behavior, practitioners can support empathic communication through modeling or reframing. Modeling empathic communication coupled with limit setting can be beneficial, as this is often a new skill. At the end of a discipline interaction, there may be a huge benefit to emotional support. Many caregivers need assistance in how this can be communicated while maintaining the reason for the limit or consequence. Especially with youth who have struggled with attachment-related issues, the process of reconnecting and maintaining a sense of being cared for is essential. Caregivers can be coached to find ways to improve the quality of their interactions in small and frequent ways, and to continually communicate love and affection despite a hectic or chaotic schedule. Leaving notes in lunchboxes, spending a few minutes praising or acknowledging a child, or a gentle touch are all ways that this can occur.

Building an Understanding Alliance

Practitioners should be sensitive to caregivers' feelings when assisting them in providing nurturing interactions with their children. Coaching in this area should occur in a way that will allow them to continue their efforts. Feelings of being inadequate can result, especially if caregivers are frustrated and feel unable to express affection. It may be difficult for some caregivers to make progress in this area, and therefore close attention to small successes and efforts should happen and be communicated. There is a high level of anger and frustration, and positive interactions may need to occur slowly over time. Practitioners should guide the way in making it comfortable for caregivers to process challenges in nurturing their children and work at a pace that is in line with caregivers' needs.

Developing Recognition of Youth's Cues and Caregivers' Reactions

Some youth may give confusing or conflicting cues related to their needs or responses to nurturance. Practitioners who empower caregivers to value their unique positions in being the experts on the youth can best align with the caregivers to determine the meaning of these cues. Even when cues are unfamiliar or confusing to caregivers, if a mutual working relationship is present, there is more chance for reflection and guidance. Statements such as "I wonder if Johnny is trying to ask for . . . or tell us . . .?" can allow for caregivers to consider the possible meaning of the cues. Youth should be supported in clarifying their preferences and intentions whenever possible, as this shows the importance of understanding their needs. When cues are recognized and caregivers feel unable to respond, one-on-one interventions with caregivers can be valuable. Recognizing and accepting feelings and developing strategies to cope with feelings are needed skills in this case. This can also occur in the moment, if discussed in a way that does not embarrass or alienate the family members.

Supporting Humor, Play, and Connectedness

No matter what the age of the youth is, there is always value in infusing positive interactions that reflect fun and humor. These times build a base for the more difficult tasks of coping with limit setting or consequences. For every negative interaction, there should be many more positive ones to strengthen the relationship. Finding times throughout the day to interact in a way that is enjoyable to the youth and led by the youth is helpful to both the youth and the relationship. Practitioners should coach caregivers to use these times to listen to their youth and gain insight into who their youth is. Practitioners often use home-based services to model the importance of these interactions by organizing family activities, games, or projects that serve to build connections. Sessions can begin or end with these types of activities to keep their importance primary in everyone's minds. Practitioners can also model and support the development of playful interactions when driving, waiting in lines, or down times are present.

BUILDING REFLECTIVE FUNCTIONING AND COMMUNICATING EMPATHY

Reflective functioning refers to the uniquely human capacity to understand behavior by considering an individual's mental state and intentions. It supports the formation of relationships, connectedness to others, and affects regulation. The youth's experience of being "considered" and understood in these terms not only is essential to healthy attachment but allows for this capacity to be developed in the youth. This capacity is not only essential to the development of relationships but without it, psychopathology often occurs (Slade, Grienenberger, Bernbach, Levy, & Locker, 2005). Fonagy, Gergely, Jurist, and Target (1995) relate a direct link in an individual experiencing trauma to the increased likelihood of developing borderline personality disorder when low reflective functioning is present. The capacity to have awareness and process difficult experiences protects against the development of mental health conditions and facilitates resilience.

Practitioners can find great benefit in describing their thought processes with caregivers to model the skills related to reflective functioning. Taking for granted that these skills or experiences may be understood can be a mistake that prevents progress in reflective functioning from occurring. Pointing out to caregivers the recognition that there are differences in their thinking and yours teaches a needed skill that aids caregiving. This can happen with a statement such as "I noticed that my thoughts about why Johnny acted aggressively seem to be different than yours." The statement reinforces the notion that the same situation can be interpreted in different ways. This assists in the ability to view another's perspective. By pointing out differences in thinking, it models the benefit in clarifying what others may be thinking and, through this process, accepting their thoughts. Related to this is the awareness that emotional expressions can mask what someone is truly thinking and can change over time. When caregivers demonstrate behaviors, it is meaningful to think aloud with caregivers about the underlying meaning in these behaviors. This is a critical skill that caregivers must continually practice with their youth. It is often difficult not to make assumptions or judgments regarding the meaning of behavior. The ability to think deeper can lead to interventions that have much greater meaning and ability to impact change.

Providing a Parallel Process

Reflective functioning is a skill that must be experienced before it can be fully developed (Slade et al., 2005). A practitioner who provides this experience for the caregivers supports this capacity in them. It allows for the development of these experiences between the caregivers and youth. The concept of a parallel process appreciates this dynamic and utilizes the concept of reflective supervision of practitioners to facilitate the process. Supervisors meet with practitioners to support their abilities to be in the helping role by providing a safe environment to process feelings and feel supported. Practitioners can then transfer these feelings to the caregivers who, in turn, allow the youth to feel the same (Parlakian, 2001). Continually remembering that the focus of intervention is the relationship between caregivers and youth guides this practice.

Pointing Out Youth's Needs and Intentions

Determining the underlying need related to a youth's behavior is a special skill. Considering the meaning of the behavior rather than making assumptions is an important first step. As practitioners promote this understanding of behavior to all family members, it opens up the ability to develop this skill and a methodology in which to do so. Practitioners can lead the way in modeling this to family members and youth alike. When issues arise, the skill of questioning the motives and simultaneously promoting the youth in articulating his/her true concerns can be modeled in a way that family members can later replicate. It is sometimes difficult for caregivers to consider the meaning of the behavior in a collaborative manner with their youth, if an overall sense of structure or safety is not present. Practitioners should address how this can occur while containing the potential negative effects of the behavior. Table 14.3 illustrates potential strategies for exploring the meaning of behaviors.

BUILDING CAPACITY TO ADVOCATE FOR YOUTH AND FAMILY

Caregivers of youth with special needs present with a wide range of skills related to advocacy. Caregivers may not define their past efforts to meet their youth's needs as advocacy, but it has undoubtedly occurred. Caregivers often need to explain their youth's needs or intentions to other caregivers, other youth, or teachers. Depending on how these experiences have gone for caregivers, there may be some degree of hesitancy in interacting with practitioners. Caregivers may expect practitioners to take on this role. In this case, it is important to support caregivers in sharing their insights,

Table 14.3
Strategies for Exploring Meaning of Behavior

- Setting the stage for containment of inappropriate and unsafe behavior.
- Assessing the best way in which youth and family members can communicate.
- Posing the questions "What could happen that would make this less of an issue?" and "What triggered this behavior or happened prior to the behavior?"
- Teaching the youth to express feelings, worries, and concerns, and identify patterns in behavior.
- Teaching caregivers to identify patterns in behavior.
- Building a safe way for caregivers and youth to explore meanings of behavior.

strategies, and predictions of their youth's needs in appropriate ways and settings. When small steps take place for families in this realm, they can reinforce the strong value in working collaboratively with practitioners. Caregivers who advocate for their children improve their own self-confidence and their overall beliefs in their abilities. These feelings can be developed when the practitioner guides the way and gradually transfers the skills over to the caregivers.

Developing and Supporting Skills in Advocating for Youth

Following an assessment of what areas caregivers would benefit from in gaining skills, teaching advocacy skills should occur in stages. The first step in this process is supporting the notion that caregivers along with their youth are the experts in what may work for them. In preparation for communication with teachers or other practitioners, practitioners can work with caregivers to develop the needed confidence and skills. Assisting caregivers in identifying and listing their ideas and concerns in the presence of the practitioner allows for skill building in communicating thoughts and feeling valued. This skill can then be furthered by practitioners assisting caregivers in role playing to practice clear and assertive communication. Practitioners should be aware of caregivers' worries and develop a plan to assist them if needed. Practitioners should facilitate a meeting at which support of the caregivers' needs and response to others' ideas takes place. The practitioner will want to manage the tone of the meeting by attending to the dynamics and working toward a positive outcome. As caregivers become more comfortable with interactions, the practitioner will want to encourage the family to take the lead in communication efforts and eventually develop ongoing meetings and discussions. The skill of evaluating a plan, either during or after its development, is a part of advocacy that will also need practice. The development of advocacy skills for caregivers of youth with special needs, in many circumstances, has been seen as the most powerful intervention that practitioners can employ (Mattaini, 1999).

Linking to Resources

A number of resources, organizations as well as individuals, are available to support families in their advocacy efforts. Practitioners should seek out possible links to resources that benefit families. There are organizations that specialize in information related to specialized issues such as special education laws or related matters. These organizations can be vital to families so that they know what their rights are in given areas. Many schools, programs, or communities have caregiver groups with advocacy as a main part of their mission. Often, what is needed is ongoing support once services are discontinued. Caregivers who have the opportunity to meet on a regular basis with others who share a similar vision can continue to maintain this skill and be exposed to new opportunities.

Compiling Resources

As practitioners move through the service delivery process with families, it is useful to compile resources that can be used in the future to meet youth needs. This information can empower families to feel prepared for possible future needs. As part of this process, practitioners can assist in compiling past service plans, reports, assessments, etc., in case future services or planning is needed. Practitioners and families can collect resources that may be needed as youth make transitions. With a better understanding of how behavior reflects youth's needs and how mental health conditions present, families can anticipate what may be needed in the future. It is useful in supporting families to predict what will be needed to maintain recovery. Table 14.4 provides an example of the possible contents that can be compiled into a resource binder for families to use throughout services as well as upon discharge from services.

Teaching Skills in Leading Coordination and Advocacy Efforts

Toward the end of service provision, and as families transition out of services, many opportunities can present in which families can advocate for their youth's needs without the practitioner; this can also further establish their sense of competency. Some families may need or want to process these experiences to obtain feedback and share their successes. Practitioners should transfer as many of the coordination efforts to the family as they feel comfortable with and serve to support them afterwards as needed. Some families may choose to prepare the agenda and planning related to the CFT process while the practitioner continues in the role of facilitator. Other caregivers may want to lead this process as a way to practice what they may continue in the future.

Supporting Family Dynamics and Patterns of Interaction

Research regarding family resiliency can guide the work of home- and community-based practitioners. Family members display resiliency when they support one another, have clear roles and boundaries, have harmonious environments, hold strong beliefs, describe rituals and traditions, celebrate members' accomplishments and milestones, are cohesive, are adaptable, and communicate well (McCubbin & McCubbin, 1988; Olsen, Russell, & Sprenkle, 1989). Practitioners should look for opportunities to create these conditions within the home environment wherever possible, in unique and engaging ways.

Despite the fact that services often are initiated due to the challenges of one youth, the interventions in an empowerment model should be family focused. The family holds tremendous power in improving the quality of life for the youth and promoting a recovery environment. Additionally, problems that are experienced by one family member are felt by all family members in some manner. Being educated about how mental health conditions affect individuals as well as families assists in developing a common understanding. The common understanding may correct misconceptions and false assumptions regarding motives and intentions, and it may build empathy. This

Table 14.4
Sample Table of Contents for Resource Binder for Families

School

- Coping with Bullies
- Behavior Plan
- Peer Relationships
- Understanding the IEP
- Guidelines for Teachers

Home

- Privileges
- Allowance
- Chores
- Behavior Chart
- Home triggers
- Resources
- Family meetings
- Crisis plan
- Short term goals
- Activities

Mental Health

- Understanding Your Diagnosis
- Medications, resources
- Treatment Plan
- Transition Plan
- Discharge Plan

Physical Health

- Sleep
- Eating
- Exercise
- Dental Health
- County Health Nurse

Developed by Amy Deaton, B.A. Reprinted with permission.

also prepares the family for situations that may be problematic and allows for the development of strategies to appreciate these circumstances. When strategies are in place to minimize the occurrence of difficulties for the family as a whole, the overall level of stress may go down.

Supporting Siblings' Needs

Siblings of youth with special needs are often struggling with their own stressors or issues. It is difficult for overwhelmed caregivers to attend to siblings' needs consistently, especially when caregivers have developed strategies to meet their own needs or keep worries to themselves. Practitioners should be looking for opportunities to gain awareness of what occurs in siblings' lives and ways in which they may be helpful. The strategies for practitioners include linkage to resources, emotional support to siblings, and building ways in which caregivers can spend time with all of their children. Practitioners can spend time with caregivers discussing individual children in the family and devise plans for spending one-on-one time with all children. Awareness of the needs of the siblings can also develop through these conversations. Siblings may significantly benefit from their own form of respite. Arguing, tension, or chaos is difficult to cope with, even when the focus is someone other than the siblings. Caregivers may not be able to find the energy or ability to make logistics work so that siblings can be involved in activities. Practitioners can problem solve ways in which these activities can occur and seek to develop resources to support their continuance. Practitioners can support siblings through group activities or support groups as needed. Many programs have developed curricula to meet the needs of siblings. One such model is described in *Sibshops: Workshops for Siblings of Children With Special Needs* (Meyer & Vadasy, 2007).

CONCLUSION

Interventions that are determined to be of benefit to the family must be designed with family input as well as the guidance of the practitioner. It becomes challenging to blend together the wishes of the youth, family members, and the input of the practitioner. It can be difficult for a practitioner to allow a family to take the lead in prioritizing tasks and goals when its focus appears to be vastly different than the practitioner's opinions. This skill should be promoted and supported by supervisors in the supervisory process. Only when someone in the family is at risk of harm should priorities be reassessed. The skill of providing information for families to consider yet allowing their voice to be heard is high level and one that takes continual support. This chapter emphasizes promoting the needs of the entire family, with the strong recognition that youth do not operate within a vacuum. The family who is supported as a whole is more likely to see success in its individual members.

References

Ashworth, M., & Baker, A. (2000). 'Time and space': Carers' views about respite care. *Health & Social Care in the Community*, 8, 50-56.

Baumrind, D. (1989). Rearing competent children. In W. Damon (Ed.), *Child development today and tomorrow* (pp. 349-378). San Francisco, CA: Jossey-Bass.

Culp, R. E., Culp, A. M., Soulis, J., & Letts, D. (1989). Self-esteem and depression in abusive, neglecting, and non-maltreating mothers. *Infant Mental Health Journal, 10,* 243-251.

Dunst, C. J., Trivette, C. M., LaPointe, N. (1994). Meaning and key characteristics of empowerment. In C. J. Dunst, C. M. Trivette, & A. Deal (Eds.), *Supporting and strengthening families: Methods, strategies and practices.* Cambridge, MA: Brookline Books.

Egan, K. (1983). Stress management and child management with abusive parents. *Journal of Clinical Child Psychology, 12,* 292-299.

Fonagy, P., Gergely, G., Jurist, E., & Target, M. (2002). *Affect regulation, mentalization, and the development of self.* New York: Other Press.

Landy, S., & Menna, R. (2006). *Early intervention with multi-risk families: An integrative approach.* Baltimore: Paul H. Brookes Publishing.

MacDonald, H., & Callery, P. (2004). Different meanings of respite: a study of parents, nurses and social practitioners caring for children with complex needs. *Child: Care, Health and Development, 30*, 279-288.

Mattaini, M. A. (1999). *Clinical intervention with families.* Washington, DC: NASW Press.

McCubbin, H. I., & McCubbin, M. A. (1988). Typologies of resilient families: emerging roles of social class and ethnicity. *Family Relations, 37*, 247-254.

Meyer, D. J., & Vadasy, P. F. (2007). *Sibshops: Workshops for siblings of children with special needs* (Rev. ed.). Baltimore: Paul H. Brookes Publishing.

Olsen, D. H., Russell, C. S., & Sprenkle, D. H. (Eds.). (1989). Circumplex model: Systematic assessment and treatment of families. New York: Haworth Press.

Olsen, R., & Maslin-Prothero, P. (2001). Dilemmas in the provision of own-home respite support for parents of young children with complex health care needs: evidence from an evaluation. *Journal of Advanced Nursing, 34*, 603-610.

Parlakian, R. (2001). *Look, listen, and learn: Reflective supervision and relationship-based work.* Washington, DC: Zero to Three.

Sanders, M. (2008). Triple P-Positive Parenting Program as a public health approach to strengthening parenting. *Journal of Family Psychology, 22*, 506-517.

Slade, A., Grienenberger, J., Bernbach, E., Levy, D., & Locker, A. (2005). Maternal reflective functioning and attachment: Considering the transmission gap. *Attachment & Human Development, 7*, 283-298.

Tracy, E. M. (2001). Interventions: Hard and soft services. In E. Walton, P. Sandau-Beckler, & M. Mannes (Eds.), *Balancing family-centered services and child well-being: Exploring issues in policy, practice, theory, and research* (pp. 155-178). New York: Columbia University Press.

Chapter 15

Designing Interventions to Support Youth With Mental Health Challenges

There is a fountain of youth: It is your mind, your talents, the creativity you bring in your life and the lives of people you love.

—Sophia Loren

It takes a village to raise a child.

—African Proverb

INTRODUCTION

Determining interventions that reflect youth's needs should be given careful consideration. Several issues are of concern. The interventions must be in line with both the family's and the youth's priorities and beliefs about what will work for them. Interventions that may seem likely to work for one family may be completely inappropriate for another. There may be tension between the adult's focus and the youth's focus on the causes and issues related to a problem area. Attempting to bring these two views together and, as a result, build mutual investment may be challenging. A youth will not invest in a plan that does not have meaning to him/her. Balancing family and individual or community-based interventions is also an important consideration. This chapter reviews the ways in which youth are supported in understanding how empowerment principles (see Chapter 1 in this volume) are demonstrated in the types of interventions that are offered as well as their value. The range of interventions is then discussed, primarily from the viewpoint of meeting needs specifically manifested in the youth.

COMPILING NEEDS AND STRENGTHS

Youth may have experienced minimal participation in an assessment and planning process. They may have felt that their caregivers answered questions for them or that their ideas were not solicited. Youth may have spent very little time with the practitioner alone, or even with their caregivers, so that they could offer their inputs. Caregivers typically initiate the request for assessment and services, and, at times, they may have difficulty seeing the needs from a family perspective. Youth involvement in assessment, planning, and service delivery must be demonstrated by truly requesting and utilizing their feedback in a meaningful way. This gives them the empowering experience of having their voices heard and utilized. The result can be a strengthened sense of confidence, pride, and identity (Matarese, McGinnis, & Mora, 2005). Through involvement in care, youth are able to see themselves as potential change agents by receiving the continual message that their ideas are valued and that they have the tools, if supported, to make changes. This message is first delivered and more importantly demonstrated to the youth through their full involvement in the assessment and planning process. The three objectives related to strengths and needs assessment, according to Dêschenes, Clark, Herrygers, Blasé, and Wagner (2009, p. 7), are as follows:

1. Learn about the strengths and resources of the youth and their families.

2. Demonstrate interest in the youth and perspectives of people important to him/her.

3. Encourage the youth and key players to see him/her in a positive light.

The end result of the assessment process becomes a compilation of what was determined as areas of strengths and needs from the inputs of the youth, caregivers, and relevant others. The unique experience from this perspective is the viewing of needs from a strength-based orientation. Needs are not seen as negative, but they may be seen as manifestations of why the youth is not receiving the type of support that will result in the ability to meet his/her potential. This activity that is completed, depending on age, with input from both youth and caregivers, allows for the prioritization of what is to be addressed and the ways in which this will occur. This critical activity gives the youth and family the opportunity to develop the plan from their perspectives in a way that will optimize investment. Youth who do not see the rationale in or agree with the goals are not likely to improve in those areas. When caregivers feel strongly that certain issues need to be addressed despite youth resistance, serious efforts should be made to come to consensus and start where the youth is ready to begin. This may mean later addressing issues in a more focused manner. The benefits of strength-based treatment, addressing areas that are weaknesses by building competency, can be emphasized when caregivers are need focused. Explaining that problem areas will be lessened when other outlets and opportunities are developed for the youth can bring about a level of comfort in taking the youth's lead.

BUILDING ON STRENGTHS

Practitioners may be unaware that what are common terms to them may not have the same meanings for others and may need explanation. Even though the concept of building on strengths may seem clear, giving youth examples is often needed so that they can fully grasp this concept. Rapp and Goscha (2006) describe this concept well in the following statement:

> The strengths model does not suggest that problems be ignored. . . . At the same time, recovery is not fueled merely by overcoming problems, distress, and challenges in their lives. People tend to grow and develop based on their individual interests, aspirations, and strengths. We tend to spend time doing the things that we do well, that we enjoy, and that have meaning. We tend to avoid things we do poorly or that we think we will do poorly. At best, solving problems returns us to equilibrium, but exploiting strengths and opportunities promotes growth. (p. 57)

Providing examples of how youth have already tended to gravitate toward areas in which they feel competency can help illustrate this concept. Examples of how the family chooses to spend its time, and the meaning and enjoyment surrounding these activities, can demonstrate the value in positive experiences. When discussing youth's responses to difficult situations or feelings, an illustration of a skill or strategy that can be developed is often illustrated. Despite the fact that the end result may be poor, there is a point in time in which the youth demonstrated some skill in coping that, if fostered, may have resulted in a better outcome. A youth may describe a positive intention, a wish to cope more effectively, or a strategy that will only continue to work with proper support. A youth, for example, may do very well asking for some time alone when upset, but when the youth is not given this opportunity or is pushed to talk about the issue, he/she may then begin to yell and even hit. Focusing on anger management strategies or deescalation is not the place to

Table 15.1
Opportunities for Building Adult/Community Supports

- Linking youth to Big Brother or Big Sister.
- Identifying mentoring opportunities at workplace.
- Supporting time spent with adults teaching areas of interest (e.g., family friend teaches youth auto mechanics).
- Participating in church volunteer activities.
- Becoming involved in youth groups or clubs.
- Introducing youth to policeman, fireman, etc., to explain job roles and interactions in community.
- Engaging and supporting youth in developing youth organizations.

begin; rather, fostering the youth's recognition of a need to be alone can be further supported and developed. If caregivers find this particular situation difficult, using problem solving, once the youth has the requested alone time, may be a way to meet both youth's and caregivers' needs.

DEVELOPING STRENGTHS AND RESILIENCY

Youth who have experienced adverse life events have an opportunity to develop or strengthen coping skills. Adults or supportive peers who help youth process difficulties can support the development of resiliency or ability to cope in the future in a new and enhanced way. Youth benefit from processing situations in a way that promotes self-understanding and the ability to engage in cognitive appraisal of their actions. Practitioners and caregivers who promote independence, autonomy, and self-mastery maximize the likelihood of future positive coping and overall resilience (Manicavasagar, 2008). Practitioners can use their understanding of protective factors and characteristics of resiliency to expose youth to the conditions that can later serve to insulate them from the effects of stress. Identifying and supporting the development of positive adults role models in the school, community, and home environments is one such strategy. Youth may need encouragement to develop these relationships and skills in maintaining them. Promoting with caregivers the strong benefit in positive adult relationships outside of the family can support this opportunity. Caregivers may feel uncomfortable or feel that they are abandoning the caregiving role when other adults step into a significant role with their youth. Understanding and supporting their perspectives can open up possibilities for mentoring relationships that can appreciate the caregivers' beliefs, values, and traditions. Nurturing the development of meaningful activities, talents, or interests are also important ways to build strengths. Practitioners can be creative in finding opportunities for exposure to people, activities, or resources that can develop interests. Table 15.1 provides possible opportunities for building adult and community supports.

USE OF NONTRADITIONAL STRATEGIES

Youth with emotional and behavioral challenges can and do benefit from a wide variety of strategies and supports. In the past, a youth with a mental health diagnosis was immediately assumed to need the help of a psychologist and/or psychiatrist. Empowerment theory (see Chapter 1 in this volume) and the wraparound principles (see Chapter 3 in this volume) appreciate that this is not necessarily the only or even best way to help all youth and families. Paid supports that are related yet not the traditional clinic-setting professionals are frequently what is needed and support the most effective changes. In a publication by Pires (2002), this concept was illustrated by highlighting several federal project sites that deemphasized formal supports and emphasized nontraditional, community, and natural supports in their service provision to youth with serious emotional difficulties. The Frontiers Project in Utah was pointed out because of its extreme lack of formal services and the conscious efforts to utilize alternatives. This region of the country is described as frontier by nature, and the cultural influences include strong values related to self-reliance, conservatism, distrust of outsiders, religion, work orientation, and individualism. These values made formal services less desirable even if they were more accessible and available. These values are similar and overlap with the way people from rural areas often evaluate formal services. Nontraditional services include the use of peer-to-peer mentors; youth advocates; respite care; tutors; paraprofessionals visiting the home, school, or community settings; crisis intervention services; family-to-family support; and treatment foster care. Other services (e.g., equine therapy) have great value for certain types of needs. Youth may be open to alternate types of supports, and the practitioner's job is to offer a rationale for the benefits of the alternative supports and make these choices available whenever possible. These services may supplement the work that occurs in the family home or community setting. The individual youth may need some assistance to focus more heavily on individual skill development and coping strategies.

DEVELOPING A RECOVERY ORIENTATION

Youth who experience mental health challenges may give themselves a number of negative labels. They may not understand the true nature of their challenges, or they may have been exposed to stigmatizing comments. When a practitioner engages with a youth, it is critical to assume that negative feelings may have occurred, and the practitioner should relate the key principles of recovery orientation. Without an understanding of the key principles, youth will not be able to fully engage in the process, as they will not understand its importance. Additionally, youth who are armed with accurate information related to their capabilities and challenges will be more likely to assist in designing plans that are relevant to them.

Youth must first realize that mental health challenges do not mean that they are destined to a life of despair; they must understand that recovery is attainable and probable with the right supports. The assumptions that youth make in this area can be quite alarming. Table 15.2 provides a list of assumptions youth make regarding mental health challenges.

Youth must have an understanding of the key components that are part of the recovery process. The key components have been identified as instilling hope, healing, empowerment, and developing a support system. Youth should be assisted in understanding how specific strategies and attitudes of the practitioner support this process. The practitioner will assist the youth by serving as a "guide" to recovery. Steps that will need to take place include identifying needs, committing to change, focusing on

Table 15.2
Youth Assumptions Regarding Mental Health Challenges

- I am a bad person; something is wrong with me.
- I will not be able to live or work on my own.
- I cannot be a part of teams or clubs because of my issues.
- I am going to be like this the rest of my life.
- I will never graduate from high school.
- I will be placed in an institution.

strengths, looking toward the future, celebrating small steps, and fostering a sense of optimism. All of these concepts and attitudes must be explained and modeled, as youth may find these to be foreign concepts (Jacobson & Greenley, 2001).

Another concept related to recovery that youth will need support in understanding is the interpretation of behavioral issues. Youth typically believe that challenging behavior reflects the notion that they are "bad" people. They may believe that since many others do not act in the way that they do, there is something wrong with them. To reframe and emphasize the point that behavioral issues represent unmet needs can be powerful. This statement does not imply that the behavior is acceptable or that the youth is free of responsibility, but rather it emphasizes the underlying unmet need that is driving the behavior. When a youth who has been indoctrinated into a recovery orientation is later asked about the outcomes of services, his/her response should be something like "myself and my family now know the best ways to help me when I'm in need." It should not be a statement such as "I quit acting bad."

When youth enter into services, they also need to understand the power of their inputs. It may be a new concept to think that their insights are important and many times the key to change. Youth may see practitioners as the keepers of this knowledge and potential, and this mentality must be challenged. The youth and family should be empowered to see themselves as "professionals" on their own family and what is likely to help or not help. Related to this, it is important to validate that decisions that are made related to services may need to be changed and modified to better meet needs. Youth should be supported in understanding that a lack of progress or need to change interventions does not mean that their inputs were not important or valuable. Practitioners should create an environment in which a lack of progress does not mean failure in the youth and family but an alarm that the plan is failing. A common statement is "families don't fail, plans fail."

FOSTERING SUPPORTS OF SIBLINGS, CAREGIVERS, SIGNIFICANT OTHERS, AND COMMUNITY

Family members, extended family, friends, and community members may attempt to help a youth who has challenges. Youth may not consider the need to offer feedback to these people about what helps as well as what may hurt them. Youth may identify siblings, for example, as instigating trouble while also being a true support to them when others are mean to them. The practitioner can be valuable in helping the youth to communicate the areas that need to be addressed as well as the areas that

Table 15.3
Questions to Identify Helping Behaviors

- What are some activities that you would like to do with your siblings, caregivers, or others?
- What are some things others can do that would be helpful when you are upset?
- What are some things others can do that would not be helpful when you are upset?
- When is it easiest for you to accept help?
- When is it hardest?

should be continued or strengthened. Additionally, the practitioner who is looking for examples of this serves the youth well, as the youth may be unable to articulate what occurs for them.

Youth should be supported in expressing the details of how and when others can support them as well as what others can do to help. Siblings can be a great help to youth as well as a source of additional stressors. Siblings often spend a great deal of time with one another, and supporting a positive relationship is an obvious opportunity for improving family functioning. Siblings can be engaged in the process of supporting youth in difficult situations in a number of ways. The practitioner and caregivers will need to assess what the relationship between siblings will support. The strategies could range from determining inappropriate behaviors that worsen situations to promoting interactions that calm or distract the youth in need. Youth may have strong opinions related to feeling respected in the process and worry about later being talked about or made fun of. Siblings often must be encouraged to support youth in a way that does not reveal unnecessary information about the youth and family or embarrass the youth. Siblings can be supported through role playing the ways in which they can support the youth. The youth and siblings must also have a plan for discussing failures in their plan or frustrations in the process, as it is likely that this process will always be seen as positive by the youth.

In regard to caregivers, there are valuable lessons that can be learned through discussing past crisis situations or escalations from the youth's perspective. Recognizing the importance of the caregiving role and ultimate decision-making power of the caregivers, there still are valuable perceptions, feedback, and suggestions that the youth can offer to give caregivers additional ideas on how to help.

When mentors, community members, or other adults are involved, family members can be supported in processing these experiences with their youth. Table 15.3 identifies questions that practitioners can use to identify helping behaviors that reflect the youth's preferences.

INTERVENING WITH MENTAL HEALTH/ BEHAVIORAL CONCERNS

Supporting Needs for Education

Youth should have accurate information related to mental health challenges. Perceptions related to course, cause, and the likelihood of recovery may be distorted, and if this is corrected, it can dramatically change a youth's attitude and ability to cope. This occurs best within the context of a conversation that ideally lends itself to important clarifications. Youth typically respond better to this type of intervention than a lecture-type format. An important consideration when issues related to mental illness need clarification is the use of a peer support specialist. Peer support specialists are consumers of mental health services who can offer the unique perspective of what it feels like to be a consumer, and peer support specialists can offer insights into both mental health issues and coping strategies. Many peer support specialists have developed excellent advocacy skills as well. The significant value of peer support specialists in improving mental health services has been documented and promoted for several decades (Delaney, 2010). The peer support specialist (whether adult or youth) can quite possibly make the strongest impact in this area.

Promoting Youth Involvement in Care

Youth of all ages can significantly benefit from developing a sense of self-determination. The experience of determining goals and actions to reach those goals is impactful for youth (Johnson, Brown, & Edgar, 2000). The sense of being in control of the planning process develops a stronger likelihood that investment and motivation to succeed will result. As practitioners seek to gain insight and guidance from youth in the service delivery process, they must do this in a way that understands the youth's comfort and ability to provide insight and guidance. Some youth may need individual support, questioning that expands their thinking, or frequent prompts to facilitate their ability to express their thoughts. Youth should be engaged in a discussion related to how the practitioner can best obtain their feedback. Some youth may indicate that discussing their preferences within a Child and Family Team (CFT) meeting may be overwhelming or that it is too difficult to answer questions without time to process the options. It is important to show the youth that whatever needs to be done to accommodate the youth having a voice in the process will be done.

Developing Measures of Progress and Regression

How the youth, family, and CFT identify success or need for modifications is an essential element. These measures must be developed through the input of the youth and family, and be reachable and written in the language of the youth and family. It may be challenging for practitioners to find ways to measure improvement in a way that reflects the wishes and ideas of the family. Table 15.4 identifies useful questions that can support this process.

The service plan that identifies the goals, objectives, and measures should always be considered a working document that will be modified as needed. Modifications should be supported as necessary to keep services relevant and not a problem or inconvenience.

Supporting Strategies to Ask/Accept Assistance

Youth with mental health challenges, depending upon their ages and experiences, may or may not have well-developed skills in the area of asking for or accepting help. This may also be related to difficulty understanding their emotional reactions or needs.

Table 15.4
Designing Measures for Success

- What will it look like when you no longer need services?
- What is the vision that you have for your family?
- What areas do you want to focus on first?
- How will we know we are making progress?
- What will the steps be in getting to our goals?
- How can we keep track of our successes?
- How will we insure that everyone giving input rates progress in the same way?

An assessment of youth's abilities to recognize their feelings, anticipate behaviors related to their feelings, and accept or ask for help should be an ongoing process. A key factor to recovery is the ability of youth and their support systems to manage difficulties when they arise. Youth's abilities to allow for this process to happen should be a priority in the service delivery process. When practitioners are present in the home during times of distress, coaching in this process can be beneficial. Breaking the skill into components and developing mastery in steps can promote youth feeling more in control of this situation. Possible skill steps in this area should begin at the youth's level of competency. If a youth has not yet demonstrated the ability to acknowledge distress prior to an outburst, processing the event afterwards may be the place to begin. Youth can be assisted in discussing what they feel triggered the incident and clarifying their emotional reactions and distress. If issues are present for the youth related to accepting help, the underlying feelings or past experiences should be discussed to gain insight into the youth's perspectives.

Teaching Coping Skills

The development of coping skills should begin with an assessment of what already takes place and what may have worked in the past. Understanding the youth's temperament, preferences, and support systems can inform both the youth and practitioner in developing a strategy that is likely to be successful. Sensory processing issues also need to be taken into consideration. The way in which a youth experiences sensations, such as sound, sight, touch, taste, smell, movement, and balance, will guide the types of interventions that are chosen. A youth who has strong reactions to any sensory modality will be less able to tolerate this when stressed. This knowledge should inform the environmental modifications that may need to be made when a youth is stressed. Youth should be taught to identify these preferences and express ways in which supports can help or hurt them.

As coping skills are identified and promoted by the practitioner, an ongoing assessment and evaluation of their effectiveness should continually occur. Some youth may actively take part in the practicing of using skills for calming. Other youth will find this embarrassing, and the support may need to take place in other ways or when a youth is in crisis. Youth should be encouraged to develop multiple layers of coping skills that can be used preventatively as well as in reaction to a crisis. As the practitioner continues to form a relationship with the youth, the practitioner will be in

Table 15.5
Coping Strategies

- Self-affirmations.
- Reframing thoughts and concerns.
- Reappraisal of events.
- Checking in with trusted adults.
- Balancing time with and without others.
- Accepting feelings as neither right nor wrong.
- Relaxation exercises: deep breathing, muscle relaxation, and meditation.
- Distracting activities.
- Good overall health and wellness behaviors: diet, exercise, sleep, and checkups.

a better position to understand how individual, family, and situational and contextual factors influence the types of coping strategies the youth prefers. In a study by Ebata and Moos (1994), coping strategies commonly used by adolescents were identified as approach-oriented strategies and avoidance strategies. Approach-oriented strategies included attempts to understand or change ways of thinking and actively attempting to resolve the stressor. Avoidance strategies included denial, withdrawal, or avoidance of the stressor. Approach-oriented strategies were associated with older adolescents, more active adolescents, adolescents with social resources, and when the stressor was perceived as a challenge. Avoidance strategies were associated with youth who were easily distressed, had experienced more negative life events, and chronic stress (Ebata & Moos, 1994). This research can be utilized to consider possible preferences of youth who may fit in either category. It is important to promote skills that are most likely to be utilized as well as exposing youth to additional strategies. Table 15.5 provides possible strategies that can be introduced to youth.

INTERVENTIONS WHEN SCHOOL/VOCATIONAL PROBLEMS EXIST

Collaborating With School Staff

The various school staff that a practitioner may come in contact with include teachers, special education teachers, principals, guidance counselors, bus drivers, cafeteria workers, and support staff. All of the above can be impactful in improving as well as hindering a youth's level of functioning within the school. If school staff are identified by the family as either expressing concerns or supporting the youth, collaboration can be impactful in supporting youth's school experiences. Table 15.6 identifies potential roles of the practitioner in supporting a youth at school.

Communication with school staff must occur in a way that promotes collaboration. School staff may feel that the goals of what they are attempting to achieve, the limitations of their roles, or the confines of the school setting may not be fully understood. Practitioners must work to understand the focus and language of the school staff so that unrealistic expectations are not placed on the staff. If school staff feel reluctant to make accommodations, it is important to make use of a positive

Table 15.6
Potential Roles of the Home- and Community-Based Worker
in School Environments

- Develop a crisis plan related to potential school crises.
- Develop an intervention plan that is accepted and understood by all.
- Establish weekly reviews of academic and behavioral concerns.
- Facilitate progress reports sent to caregivers.
- Attend case conferences.
- Provide crisis debriefing and intervention.
- Provide skills coaching.

Table 15.7
Discussion Points With School Staff

- What do you view as this child's strongest points?
- What are some challenges this child may be having academically?
- Are there indications that these problems are related to factors other than ability such as poor organization, poor follow through with homework, or distractibility?
- Are there problems with attendance or ability to learn once here?
- How would you describe this child's interactions with peers?
- Are there certain conditions that help the child to work better?
- Are there behavioral challenges? If so, what seems to trigger the behavior?
- Have there been discussions or communications with caregivers about this?
- Does the child seem to have good relationships with other adults in the building?
- How is the child's behavior on the bus? At recess? In the lunchroom?
- Who are the people that the child has responded to the best?

relationship to support the possibility of these changes if and when they are accepted. Table 15.7 suggests ways in which conversations can occur with school staff regarding school issues.

Coaching and Teaching Skills

Just as a practitioner would work with caregivers to design interventions that are sensitive to their authority within the home, the practitioner should do the same when considering coaching skills either within the school environment or for use at school. Teachers may identify the need for crisis intervention in which a practitioner comes to the school to assist the youth in calming. Additionally, meeting with youth during school time to prevent difficulties may be requested. For example, a practitioner may meet with a youth at the end of recess due to a history of issues related to recess that interfere with classroom expectations in the afternoon. If the school supports it, a practitioner may even observe or be available for support during recess. The skills that are needed should be developed through input from the teachers or school staff, caregivers, and youth. The identification of which skills are needed to focus on must ultimately be directed by the caregivers, although the ways in which these skills will

Table 15.8
Possible School Interventions

- Developing organizational strategies with youth.
- Promoting teachers' communications with caregivers regarding assignments and progress.
- Assisting youth in organizing lockers and desks.
- Engaging teachers in prompts related to needed materials for classes.
- Coaching youth in appropriate interactions with teachers and peers.
- Engaging teachers in identifying and using child strengths.

be developed must be guided by the input of the youth. The skill steps should always include introducing the skill, practicing the skill, and reinforcing the steps. Table 15.8 identifies possible school interventions.

Collaborating With Employers

When youth are employed, there are strategies that can be put in place to support the youth in maintaining appropriate work behaviors and actions that will maintain employment. If youth determine this intervention is a needed service, the practitioner can collaborate with the employer to support continued employment. Teaching and supporting the youth in areas such as time management, organization, prioritizing tasks, arriving to work on time, and working well with coworkers and supervisors can be influential.

INTERVENING WITH COMMUNITY CHALLENGES

Promoting Positive Community Relationships

Relationships with caring and supportive adults have long been identified as contributing to the development of resiliency in youth (Werner & Smith, 2001). Specific positive findings have been the increase in school attendance and academic success when youth have positive adult relationships within their community (Israel, Beaulieu, & Hartless, 2001; Rhodes, Grossman, & Resch, 2000). There are many activities and opportunities for interaction within the community available to youth. These activities include after-school programs, school activities, sports teams, clubs, mentoring programs, church groups, or programs (e.g., the YMCA).

Home-based practitioners can meet with youth to promote positive behaviors, review expectations for behaviors and interactions, and process these experiences to improve the likelihood that community interaction is successful. Adults supporting the youth in the community can also be supported in their interactions with youth. At times, assumptions about youth with mental health challenges can interfere with how adults interact with youth. Some organizations falsely believe that all youth with mental health challenges are going to be inappropriate for their programs. If the staff of these programs are presented in a supportive way with the inaccuracies of this thinking and given an opportunity for support if issues do arise, they are more likely to allow participation and have it be meaningful to the youth.

Table 15.9
Teaching Appropriate Interactions

- Social boundaries.
- Social behaviors.
- Appropriate comments.
- Ways to assess safety of situations and ability to remove self from difficult situations.
- How to introduce self and engage with a group.

Modeling and Practicing Appropriate Interactions

When youth interact with the community, there are many opportunities for growth and development. This type of learning must take place as difficulties arise. It will not be as effective when the issues have to be explained after the fact by the youth. The subtle cues or interactions may not be understood by the youth to accurately reflect what even occurred. More importantly, practitioners who engage with youth in the community find numerous opportunities to point out their strengths and positive interactions. This promotes continued focus and a desire to continue interacting with others even when difficulties arise. Table 15.9 identifies areas of development that can assist in community interaction.

CONCLUSION

Youth with special needs may be supported in a variety of ways. The primary interventions typically occur within the home environment, although supports within school and community are often needed. The balancing of interventions is necessary for supporting both the youth and the family. When youth are further supported in making progress in areas outside the home, their abilities to function improve within the home as well. As youth and families are able to identify the small steps that need to occur to meet the goals they have outlined for themselves, there are many opportunities for feeling success and motivation for continued efforts.

References

Delaney, K. (2010). The Peer Specialist Movement: An interview with Gayle Bluebird, RN. *Issues in Mental Health Nursing, 31*, 232-234.

Deschênes, N., Clark, H. B., Herrygers, J., Blasé, K., & Wagner, R. (2009). *Strength discovery and needs assessment: A process for working with transition-age youth and young adults.* Tampa, FL: National Network on Youth Transition for Behavioral Health.

Ebata, A., & Moos, R. (1994). Personal, situational, and contextual correlates of coping in adolescence. *Journal of Research on Adolescence, 4*, 99-125.

Israel, G. D., Beaulieu, L. J., & Hartless, G. (2001). The influence of family and community social capital on educational achievement. *Rural Sociology, 66*, 43-68.

Jacobson, N., & Greenley, D. (2001). What is recovery? A conceptual model and explication. *Psychiatric Services, 52*, 482-485.

Johnson, C., Brown, P., & Edgar, G. (2000). *Transition guide for Washington State*. Seattle, WA: Center for Change in Transition Services, University of Washington. Retrieved March 20, 2010, from http://www.seattleu.edu/ccts/Default.aspx?id=34096

Manicavasagar, V. (2008). *Psychological resilience*. Retrieved March 1, 2010, from http:// ezinearticles.com/?Psychological-Resilience&id=1688230

Matarese, M., McGinnis, L., & Mora, M. (2005). *Youth involvement in systems of care: A guide to empowerment*. Washington, DC: Technical Assistance Partnerships Publications.

Pires, S. A. (2002). *Building systems of care: A primer.* Washington DC: National Technical Assistance Center for Children's Mental Health.

Rapp, C. A., & Goscha, R. (2006). *The strengths model: Case management with people with psychiatric disabilities* (2nd ed.). New York: Oxford University Press.

Rhodes, J. E., Grossman, J. B., & Resch, N. L. (2000). Agents of change: Pathways through which mentoring relationships influence adolescents' academic adjustment. *Child Development, 71*, 1662-1671.

Werner, E. E., & Smith, R. S. (2001). *Journeys from childhood to midlife: Risk, resilience, and recovery.* New York: Cornell University Press.

Chapter 16

Crisis Plan Development and Monitoring

The difficulties which I meet with in order to realize my existence are precisely what awaken and mobilize my activities, my capacities.
—Jose Ortega Y Gasset

INTRODUCTION

Crisis planning may be overlooked in the service delivery process. Families, at the time of referral, may be desperate for stabilization and a sense of hope. With supports being designed to specifically meet the needs of families, the reality that crisis is likely to occur despite services may be minimized. The focus of crisis planning is to uncover the family's capacities and limitations as described in their stories and explanations of past crises. This information is carefully attended to so that the who, what, when, where, and how of what may help in the next crisis situation can be determined.

This chapter offers a philosophy regarding crisis management and planning that will fully appreciate the families' needs to feel prepared and fully supported. The critical elements to consider and include in the process are discussed. Strategies to ensure that the appropriate monitoring occurs as families move through the stages of service delivery are discussed and described in greater detail.

GOALS FOR CRISIS MANAGEMENT AND PLANNING

The goals for crisis management include (1) ensuring safety for the youth and family within the home and community and (2) promoting the youth's and family's abilities to predict, plan for, and cope with crisis situations.

The first goal is critical in the sense that it becomes the "bottom line" for whether a youth can remain in the community. Acute hospitalization or residential placement should only occur when all other alternatives have been exhausted. Keeping the youth in the community is of utmost importance to the well-being of the youth and family. This decreases the disruption to the youth in being removed from everyday routines and close relationships, and optimizes the influence of the key figures in the youth's life (Meyers, Kaufman, & Goldman, 1999). This is often the driving force for the funding and philosophy of programs and is reflected in the value base of the wrap-around principles (see Chapter 3 in this volume). At times, the referral for services has been made because there is an immediate threat that the youth will be removed from the home. The family may be at the point where it is unsure of its youth's safety, and it is unsure if there are alternatives to placement. In these circumstances, the youth may be concerned with the notion of placement, and this additional stressor may compound the issues. The introduction of a crisis plan can alleviate anxiety and create an environment in which change can begin to occur. Nothing takes more precedence over safety, and the need is strong to facilitate a crisis plan. Crisis plan development should serve to assist in preventing a crisis from occurring and provide an action plan if a crisis does occur.

The second goal has many implications. First, a family who is under chronic stress is typically functioning poorly and perhaps in a manner that impedes progress for a youth with special needs. Family members, who do not feel that they have an adequate plan for crisis, are often extremely stressed. When caregivers are under stress, this may result in negative attitudes toward caregiving, decreased levels of family cohesion, and increased levels of conflict (Peterson & Hawley, 1998). It is of greater concern when multiple stressors exist, as the accumulative effect is significant. When several stressors are present and the complication of unresolved past issues exists as well, the family may see the next stress from a more heightened state of concern. Developmental transitions, the ongoing effects of coping attempts, and the end result of past incidents are critical to consider in understanding the impact of crisis (McCubbin & McCubbin, 1993). How a family deals with stressors appears to be a combination of what the stressors are, the family's perception of the stressors, and the resources that are available to the family (Hill, 1958).

With a home-based practitioner assisting the family in crisis planning, the family's ability to predict crisis and adapt to youth's needs becomes more developed. This in itself serves to alleviate the family from some degree of stress because situations are better understood and prepared for. When caregivers can give the youth an experience

Table 16.1
Benefits of Crisis Planning

Benefit	Rationale to Youth and Caregivers
• Keep youth and family safe	• "A crisis plan is a way to prevent issues from getting to the point that safety becomes a concern."
• Maintain youth in community	• "Being prepared for challenges keeps Johnny with the people that know and can support him best."
• Build sense of competence for family	• "When families feel prepared, it reminds them that they can handle anything that needs to be handled with the right supports."
• Develop internal resources	• "By developing a plan and practicing how to handle challenges, all members of the family will uncover lots of hidden skills and talents that can be of great help in crisis situations."
• Build and uncover strengths in youth and family	• "By developing and using a crisis plan, it will help us to see what areas your family is especially good at and use these strengths to improve successes."

of being understood, this typically results in a stronger relationship. The crisis planning process often reveals strategies to prevent crisis from occurring, as strategies are uncovered that are preventative and reflective of unique needs of the youth and family. Table 16.1 details the benefits of crisis planning.

IMPORTANT CONSIDERATIONS IN THE PROCESS OF CRISIS PLANNING

While moving through the steps of crisis planning, it is important to remember the nature of crisis management in the service delivery process. As the family experiences a sense of security in the development of a plan, it should also be reminded that experiencing crisis does not mean failure. The crisis plan will give the family a guide for how to intervene and hopefully keep the situation from becoming unmanageable. The following principles assist the practitioner in ensuring that plan development and monitoring takes into consideration key points and concerns.

Defining a Crisis Situation

Many theorists have attempted to define "crisis." Roberts (1995) identifies five components of a crisis:

1. The presence of a stressful or traumatic event;
2. A vulnerable or unbalanced state;
3. Precipitating factors;
4. An active crisis state as identified by the individual; and
5. Resolution.

Dass-Brailsford (2007) contributes to this understanding of crisis by identifying five characteristics:

Table 16.2
Potential Precipitating Factors

Youth Factors
• Experiencing restrictions or discipline.
• Peer issues.
• Difficulty within school environment.
• Feeling poorly.
• Attempting to master new tasks, challenges, or experiences.
• Experiencing trauma triggers (situational triggers, sensory triggers).
Family Factors
• Individual family members feeling overwhelmed and less connected to others.
• Unorganized or chaotic home environment.
• Stress caused by transitions or changes.
• New stressors for family to cope with resulting in less support of members.

1. The event precipitating the crisis is perceived as threatening.

2. There is an apparent inability to impact or reduce the impact of stressful events.

3. There is an increased fear, tension, and/or confusion.

4. There is a high level of subjective discomfort.

5. A state of disequilibrium is followed by rapid transition to an active state of crisis. (p. 94)

The youth and family's assessment of a stressful or traumatic event is what identifies it as such. Although, one family's assessment may be different from another's assessment, it is important to listen and respond to the youth and family. It may be that the family's "bar" for when a crisis is occurring is much lower or higher than the home-based practitioner's assessment. The current family and youth situation must be assessed, with the goal of improving the family's ability to prevent and cope with crisis.

When considering what constitutes a "vulnerable" state, there are several factors to consider. The emotional and physical state of youth may be fragile due to illness, chronic stress, medication issues, or the presence of unmanaged symptoms. The family as a whole may be coping with transitions, changes in constitution, or challenges, and it may have difficulty coping. Any of these factors, in combination with a new situation or trauma, taxes youth and families in a heightened manner.

Any crisis situation has events that can be considered precipitants. Precipitants may be events or situations that result in an emotional or behavioral reaction, which later contributes to the development of a crisis (see Table 16.2). When families and youth look back, they often recall that some precipitants were bothersome but not enough to result in a crisis. Some precipitants may seem harmless, although they trigger memories that are difficult to cope with. It may be the accumulation of numerous precipitants that result in the crisis. Others are enough to provoke a crisis in and of itself.

An active phase of crisis is best defined as when both the adults and youth are unable to determine a plan for how to intervene when either one is behaviorally or emotionally in need of stabilization. Typically, most consider a crisis to be manifested when a youth is behaviorally unstable and not able to be contained. The youth may be threatening harm to others, yelling, or damaging property. Some youth may be in dire need of intervention due to depression, although their behaviors are not what others may consider "out of control." They may appear compliant yet extremely withdrawn and disconnected. It also may be that the adult is in need of assistance while the youth, although the source of stress, may not be in need. Regardless of who is in need, what affects one family member affects the entire family. Reactions are often states of confusion, fear, or agitation (Dass-Brailsford, 2007). Intervention is needed due to overwhelming feelings or behaviors that cannot be ignored.

Engaging the Youth and Family in Crisis Planning

By the time many families reach the point of assessment, they may have experienced numerous crisis situations and may feel desperate to keep this from reoccurring. Conversely, some families may be describing serious issues while not recognizing or prioritizing a need to intervene. Despite which position the family takes, it is the job of the practitioner to help anticipate possible crises and plan for them. While practitioners may be processing what is said to them in terms of what needs to change, they must recognize and respect the current family situation. It is critical to remember that the goal in crisis planning is to assist the family in devising a plan that is workable and will prevent a challenging situation from becoming "out of control."

During the first meeting with families, it is important to give them an experience of being heard as well as something concrete and tangible that decreases their anxieties—a functional crisis plan. What families expect during the first assessment session, despite best efforts to inform them of what usually occurs, varies drastically from family to family. Factors such as past experiences with counseling, what others have told them, and the urgency of their current situation may all contribute to the families' expectations. Allowing a family to discuss its reasons for requesting an assessment, as well as priority concerns, leads nicely into the topic of developing a crisis plan. Some families and youth may be intimidated for a variety of reasons if a practitioner introduces the topic of a crisis plan without allowing this to occur first. Some families and youth may interpret "crisis plan" as reflective of the practitioner's intention to push for hospitalization or placement prematurely, especially when this has occurred previously. Without appropriate timing and initial rapport building, youth and families may also be hesitant to discuss their challenges for fear of being judged or misunderstood. Practitioners need to remember that what seems to be standard procedures or even valued components of the service delivery may be new concepts to youth and families. It may take some time and conversation to assist the family and youth in their understanding of crisis planning. Families may have experienced little or no services at the time of referral except for crisis intervention. This may have meant spending hours in an emergency room. When a home-based practitioner comes to the home to begin an assessment, the family is often hopeful that services will replace the need for crisis intervention, and they may have difficulty accepting the notion of a crisis plan. It may be the hope that crisis will not reoccur once services begin. Additionally, youth may beleive that a crisis plan means that hospitalization is imminent. Framing the concept of crisis in a way that normalizes this experience is important. Families and youth can benefit from understanding that crisis experiences do not represent failure, but rather opportunities to learn and develop. Although, crisis experiences may never be eliminated, it is a reasonable goal to expect that they become less frequent and more manageable.

Use of Child and Family Team for Crisis Planning

Families who are supported by the wraparound process (see Chapter 3 in this volume) and home-based services may have experienced extreme frustration with past crisis intervention services. A well-thought-out crisis plan may not be in place. When a crisis situation occurs, the family may have phoned a hospital or crisis intervention line only to speak with someone who was not familiar with the particular family. When in a crisis, it is probably the worst time to clearly communicate needs, preferences, and nuances of a family culture to ensure that an appropriate intervention or option is arrived at. Due to the lack of history, the practitioner may be significantly challenged in making decisions that fit the family well, and services may even be counterproductive. The recommendations may have been more in support of a system and its working hours, policies, and procedures than the family. All of these possibilities have been a reality— thus the strong emphasis wraparound principles place on effective crisis planning.

A Child and Family Team (CFT) serves many functions in a crisis situation. First and foremost, the emphasis is placed on following the wraparound principles. When this occurs, the family's and youth's voices in crisis planning are heard, and strategies are strengths based and congruent with the culture of the family. The benefits to this are impactful and longlasting. When families experience multiple system partners or practitioners, the CFT can oversee the development of a coordinated and clearly articulated plan. This will eliminate the possibility of being advised in conflicting manners when in crisis.

Multiple Sources of Support. CFTs bring together a group of people all invested in the well-being of the individual youth and family. This opens up doors for additional ideas, sources of support, and connections to community. The CFT offers additional resources to a family in the development of interventions and assists in developing additional natural and community supports. When families need system navigation and support in crisis, members who are representative of various systems on the CFT may be able to play a role in this. This does not mean that practitioners take the responsibility for activating or managing the plan. Their involvement, if necessary, is determined by the family, and their assistance is sought by the family. Involvement of system partners may be needed if hospitalization or legal issues occur as a result of the crisis. All members of the CFT should be aware of the plan, and if a potential role for a member exists, the plan should be accessible to them when needed.

Planning for Crisis in School/Other Environments. The CFT has the unique advantage of offering insight from members who interact with youth in various environments. This advantage can drastically change the family's understanding of what occurs in other environments (e.g., the school or the community). It also reminds the individual family of the importance of considering emotional distress or behavior issues in various settings. This CFT advantage reinforces the viability of the wraparound planning process in the community because it meets needs for community and school safety. Table 16.3 provides some proactive strategies that can be used in school environments.

Table 16.3
Proactive Strategies to Utilize in School Environments

- Teachers and administrators can identify warning signs that reflect distress in youth.
- Teachers and administrators can work with family, youth, and providers to develop unique responses to warning signs: supporting youth one on one, allowing youth to assist teacher, or allowing youth to wear headphones when overstimulated.
- Adults that work well with youth are identified and utilized in creative ways: bus driver, janitors, lunch room workers, etc.
- Peer "buddies" are utilized to support youth in challenging situations such as recess, lunch, and transitions.

Reliance on Natural and Community Supports

When asked "who would you call for help if you were stranded on the side of the road with a flat tire?" many individuals have an immediate response. The answer usually is a spouse, extended family member, or friend. When the family as a whole is in crisis, the immediacy of its response may be not be as automatic, although there are definite advantages when an immediate response exists. Many families have utilized friends, extended family, or community members for support, and, after a period of time, the family may no longer feel that these supports are available. In crisis, it is the natural and community supports that can be the most impactful, available, and supportive to the family. The field of child mental health is now embracing the benefit of strengthening a family's social relationships and community connections to build resiliency and promote development (Walker & Sage, 2006). The wraparound process (see Chapter 3 in this volume) seeks to develop this scenario when it is not in place and preserve the use of natural supports when established. One goal in crisis planning is to establish natural and community supports being the first and final point of intervention as often as possible. Paid supports should not be the main implementers of a plan nor be relied upon to oversee the process. The most successful plans consider this as a last alternative. Even when practitioners are consulted, it is helpful to enlist natural supports to remain available to consult with and support the family. Watching an individual struggle emotionally and having to make decisions that may be challenging are difficult.

The natural supports that are identified and available to assist in a crisis plan need support and nurturing to remain in place and useful to the family. The presence of natural supports is often based on a relationship, and it is helpful to consider with the family how to preserve and monitor these vital relationships. When a family is in crisis, especially when things do not go well, the family may inadvertently alienate or upset those they have enlisted to help. Paid practitioners typically have ways to process a challenging situation with the family, and consideration should be given to how this needs to occur with nonpaid assistance. This consideration can help sustain the ultimate goal of families using natural and community supports throughout the wraparound process as well as after transition has occurred.

When facilitators and home-based practitioners become involved in crisis planning, it is important to understand the role of natural supports and not inadvertently sabotage or disrespect their significance. This can occur if paid practitioners "take over" the roles of natural supports or override their contributions in the planning process. Many natural supports may feel devalued or no longer necessary to the family if this occurs. Nonverbal as well as verbal interaction should always reflect the true value of the benefit and need for supports chosen by the family. Feedback from the youth and family can also assist in understanding this dynamic and how the supports are responding to the process.

Youth, their caregivers, and other family members all experience crisis in unique ways. They do not necessarily benefit from the same social supports. Adults may focus on supportive social networks as providing advice and emotional support, while youth find support in the experiences and interactions that they have with their peers and extended family as a significant value (Kernan & Morilus-Black, 2008). Youth may determine that their friends and important adults in their lives are those they should turn to. An adult family member, despite his/her hierarchy in the family, will benefit from appreciating this concept and endorsing the supports identified by the youth to help.

Development and Initiation of a Back-Up Plan

Despite the best planning, a crisis plan may fail. This should be routine thinking in the planning process. Additionally, all situations cannot be anticipated. Plans that contain both proactive and immediate strategies for intervention are ideal but not always enough. A back-up plan that typically is used when safety is threatened should always be considered. This plan should only be initiated after the determination that the crisis plan is not effectively managing the situation. How this occurs should be thought out prior to its occurrence. A back-up plan may be removal of the child from the family to defuse the situation or using paid supports to intervene. It is critical to take the lead from the caregivers and youth in making these determinations.

Cultural Relevance of Plan

Crisis planning as well as all phases of service delivery must reflect cultural competency. Cultural competence must take into account the significance of culture and social influences on health care beliefs and practices. This is especially important to consider when a family is in crisis, as this usually brings people back to what they are used to and what has been engrained in the fabric of their beings. Although current theories devalue classifying ethnic and cultural groups into categories with a "pick list" of attributes, there is value in understanding broad concepts related to ethnicity. Some examples include understanding folk remedies, incidence of conditions, prevalence, and outcomes. What has been emphasized and is more instructive to practitioners is developing an appreciation for social and cultural beliefs related to health care that crosses the boundaries of all cultures. This includes behaviors related to communication, family roles, decision-making preferences, sexual and gender roles, and issues related to trust and prejudice. These influences must be considered when designing interventions to ensure quality crisis plans (Betancourt, Green, Carrillo, & Ananeh-Firempong, 2003). In addition, cultural beliefs regarding the cause of child behavior problems, concerns regarding stigma, help-seeking behavior, severity appraisal of child behavior problems, and affective response to behavior problems must be determined (Lou & Takeuchi, 2001). In applying a cultural discovery to crisis situations, there are several factors that, if understood and reflected in the planning, will either augment or handicap the plan's effectiveness.

There is a difference between awareness of another's culture and acceptance of another's culture. Additionally, how the acceptance of another's culture occurs and how this is reflected in the service delivery process needs to be understood. Theorists have determined that in the process of acculturation, the core task is the negotiation of a relationship between two distinct cultural groups. There are differences in acculturation theorists in the interpretation of whether this occurs by cultures taking on the characteristics of the dominant culture or the development of mutual respect for both and a preservation of each culture. Understanding how families have negotiated this task is part of the crisis planning process. Interestingly, it has been postulated and demonstrated in research that lower levels of family cohesion and adaptability would occur, and higher levels of adolescent-caregiver conflict would occur, when families experience higher levels of adolescent assimilation into the dominant culture than their caregivers. This process has been described as an acculturation conflict (Smokowski, Rose, and Bacallao, 2008). Table 16.4 identifies characteristics in crisis planning that demonstrate attention to the principles of family driven, youth guided, culturally competent and community based.

Regular Review of Plan

A crisis plan is intended to be a document that is usable and consumer friendly. Caregivers and the youth must feel that it has meaning and can be helpful when needed. In order for this to occur, the plan must be relevant to the current situation and reflect an ongoing understanding of the family. As rapports and relationships are fostered, new information, insights, and strategies should become apparent and be reflected in the plan.

Certainly, if crisis has occurred, it is critical to analyze the plan and determine what was effective and what needs revising. A plan should be in place for how the CFT will be notified that a crisis has occurred. The youth, caregivers, and other identified helpers on the plan should all have input and be a part of review and updating. The incident should be reviewed and "taken apart" on a step-by-step basis to determine effectiveness. All perspectives should be considered and strongly valued in this process. It is also helpful to the youth and family to consider five areas: regret, risk, rehabilitation, restoration, and reconnection. Regret refers to the feelings that members of the family may be having related to the incident. Strategies can be identified to allow family members to not have regrets interfere with further growth and development in their ability to cope with crisis. Risk focuses on identifying the areas that are concerning and identifying what strategies may need to be developed to prevent further issues. An understanding of how risks affect the family is needed as well. Rehabilitation identifies the skills and capacities that can be built upon. Planning for safety drills may be included in this area. Restoration seeks to repair any damages to the community or family in an effort to regain trust. Finally, reconnection supports the importance of communities and families communicating an ongoing commitment to meeting the needs of the youth (Miles, 2009). The timing of processing the event may need to be strongly considered, as too far out from the crisis diminishes the relevance of the processing, yet too close to the crisis may be problematic as well.

As families move through the service delivery process, it is hoped as well as expected that progress is made and strengths are developed. A crisis plan that has not been reviewed due to the lack of crisis occurring may miss opportunities for improvement and relevance

Table 16.4
Incorporating System of Care Values Into Crisis Planning:
Family Driven, Youth Guided, Culturally and Linguistically
Competent, and Community Based

Family Driven • Practitioner gives the family time to express its concerns, priorities, and stories related to past and present challenges. • The family identifies the nature of the crisis. • The family identifies the priorities and order in which issues will be addressed. • Interventions are described by the family with the practitioner supporting the development of the plan.
Youth Guided • Youth are supported in expressing concerns and potential challenges even when different from caregivers' perspectives. • Youth are encouraged to express what helps or hurts in difficult situations. • Youth are allowed to choose natural supports/peers that are valued by them. • Youth have clear roles and strategies to utilize when in crisis.
Culturally Competent • Plan reflects values, beliefs, and traditions of family. • Relevant people to the family are included in the planning process as well as the plan. • Development of plan and roles of family members reflect unique family dynamics and culture. • Assumptions are not made about cultural influences so that the uniqueness of each family is respected.
Community Based • Interventions occur in the youth's environments. • Interventions do not automatically include bringing youth to an office or hospital setting unless all else has failed. • Interventions do not rely upon practitioners. • Interventions include the people, places, and resources of the family's support network and community.

to the family's current state. As skills and capacities are evidenced, it is helpful to embed them into the crisis planning process. Again, use of strengths in the service delivery process is always the goal and more helpful to the family.

REACTIVE AND PROACTIVE CRISIS PLANNING

In regard to crisis, families must know what to do to prevent a crisis as well as how to respond when it does occur. Reactive crisis plans are utilized when a crisis has developed, and action is needed to stabilize a situation that is potentially harmful to an individual. It may be that an individual family member is distressed to the point that intervention needs to occur immediately. It also could mean that a situation has occurred that is potentially threatening to a family or community member and needs immediate attention. Stabilizing crisis is a critical task in the first phase of the wraparound process (see Chapter 3 in this volume) to ensure safety and support the youth and family in attending to the team-building process (Walker, Bruns, & National Wraparound Initiative Advisory Group, 2008). This is often referred to in the engagement phase as a stabilization plan, as it provides enough support for the family to then move on to more proactive planning. This concept supports Maslow's hierarchy of needs, which indicates that basic needs must be secured before more sophisticated and high-level needs can be considered. Physiological needs such as food, water, sleep, and homeostasis and safety, which include security of body, employment, resources, family, and health, are fundamental to a family (Maslow, 1943). A stabilization plan may not be needed, although a reactive crisis plan is always needed. Although the assessment should take longer than one session, the initial session should not be ended until a basic crisis plan is initiated. The youth and family should have a plan that they feel comfortable with, which addresses safety and crisis issues with specific interventions. The reactive crisis/safety plan will continue to be developed beyond the first visit as needed, and once an initial CFT meeting is completed, a proactive plan will also be developed. A reactive crisis plan is also needed throughout the wraparound process to ensure that action can be taken when needed.

Proactive crisis planning is a process that seeks to prevent a crisis from occurring. This process supports the entire CFT, anticipating strategies that can augment the existing service plan's attempts to diminish needs in the youth and family. When this occurs, it is more likely that crisis will be avoided. The entire CFT working together to develop prevention strategies occurs in the second phase of the wraparound process, initial plan development (Walker et al., 2008).

Important Components of Reactive and Proactive Crisis Plans

It is critical from the beginning of services to initiate assistance in developing a plan for maintaining safety or coping with a crisis as identified by the family. Reactive crisis plans value the input of the family and youth in determining what safety and crisis issues may occur. Although the family and youth are the driving force in designing the plan, they may need some assistance in defining these situations. Safety must be considered at all times, and families may need to be supported in accepting the reality of this issue possibly occurring and needing to plan for it.

Reactive crisis plans must fully support the family in taking action. In order to accomplish this task, there must be clear and concrete action steps. Simple and to the point steps that will move the family toward stability must be determined. It is critical that there are not too many steps so that the plan breaks down. The person responsible for initiating the action step must also be clearly identified. The plan must include, in simple language, clearly defined roles, responsibilities, and required actions for all implementers of the plan (Vandenberg, 2003). In considering the effect of crisis on all members of the family, there should be planned actions for all members that may include removing some members from the situation. The most successful plans are easily executed with little room for breakdowns.

The effective plan must include a method to activate the plan. The threshold for determining that the plan needs to be activated must be agreed upon as part of the planning process. The process of activating the plan should be the responsibility of the adult monitoring the situation. This decision may be made either through input of the youth in crisis or by behavioral observations that have been predetermined to signal the need to implement the plan. These decisions may be based on findings from past crisis situations. Finding ways to gauge reactions and supports is necessary while neither underreacting nor overreacting.

Components of an effective reactive crisis plan have been outlined by Patricia Miles (2009, pp. 4, 10). The components include the following:

- Preserves and respects the right of the family to live in crisis;
- Assures that interventions are timed appropriately;
- Addresses the needs of all family members;
- Determines next steps; and
- Reassures the family that crisis can be managed.

When safety of a family member is threatened the plan must include the following:

- Promotes skills and capacities to avoid harm;
- Assures family voice;
- Binds all parties (system and family);
- Defines when activation occurs;
- Can be implemented without professionals;
- Identifies individualized and clearly stated roles;
- Clarifies when crisis is over; and
- Makes immediate decisions.

Proactive crisis plans serve to prevent crisis from occurring and are built on the interventions that are determined through the CFT process. Although the assessment should take longer than one session, the initial session should not be ended until a basic crisis plan is initiated. The youth and family should have a plan that they feel comfortable with, which addresses safety and crisis issues with specific interventions. The reactive crisis/safety plan will continue to be developed beyond the first visit as needed, and once an initial CFT meeting is completed, a proactive plan will also be developed. (See Exhibits 16.1 to 16.5 for sample forms to be used in crisis planning.)

Learning From Past Crises to Develop Reactive Crisis Plans

The ideal way to develop a reactive crisis plan is to learn from past situations. It is likely that these situations will repeat themselves, and identifying what went right as well as wrong in past situations can assist in planning for the future. The family and youth at the beginning of the assessment process are usually able to identify past situations that they would label crises. As the family begins to tell its story, it is quite likely that prioritized needs will be identified. Home-based practitioners can begin by asking families and youth to describe a past situation that was problematic. Information that will assist in developing an understanding includes the following:

- How did the situation develop? How did it become apparent to the youth and family members that the individual was distressed? Can the family identify precipitants? Did the youth and other family members see the precipitants in the same way?

Table 16.5
Considerations in Developing Calming Strategies

- Youth preferences for certain individuals.
- Balance between alone time and support from others.
- Sensitivities to sound, touch, lights, visual stimuli, clothing, fabrics, etc.
- Ability to process language when upset.
- Needs of caregivers or adults when youth is upset.
- Needs of other family members during crises.

- What exactly occurred in the situation? What family members were involved?

- What happened in the situation to make things better? What may have happened to make things worse? Who helped or made things worse? Were there other helpers (e.g., extended family members, neighbors, or friends) who were called upon?

- Were there specific strategies that the individual used to feel some relief?

- How did the other family members in the situation react?

- If practitioners were consulted, how did they help or hinder the situation?

- How was the situation resolved?

- How did the family function after the crisis?

- Are there any ongoing concerns, issues, or worries regarding the past crisis situation?

The primary focus in this exercise with the family and youth is to gain insight into the innate strengths and skills that the family can make use of in the future. There may be effective strategies that the youth has for calming that, if allowed to be used, can deescalate the situation. The youth must have input in determining these strategies, as if they are imposed upon him/her, it will not be valued by the youth. The youth also should be allowed to verbalize what others can do that helps or worsens the situation.

Youth and Family Identifying Calming Strategies

All individuals have preferences for certain types of sensory input and the way in which this sensory input is received. Although some are less tolerant of certain types of sensory experiences at all times, most individuals are more reactive and in a heightened sense of awareness when under emotional distress. It is helpful to assist both the youth and family in considering these preferences when identifying crisis interventions. Table 16.5 identifies areas to consider in developing calming strategies.

Cultural Relevance of the Plan

Ultimately, the development of a crisis plan that reflects an appreciation of the culture, informal supports, and strengths of the family is the primary goal. A crisis intervention plan is only as valuable as it is relevant to the family. No plan should be "canned" or more reflective of the program and staffing needs than the needs of the

Table 16.6
Crisis Plan Example

1. Billy or adult in charge will suggest Billy has time alone to try calming activity (e.g., video game, drawing, or jumping on indoor trampoline).
2. Mom will call Uncle Bob to advise he may be needed. Reverend Dave will be used if Uncle Bob unavailable.
3. Mom will call her friend Dorie to come to take other children.
4. Mom will check in fifteen minutes or sooner if needed. Billy will stay in room unless he needs help.
5. If Billy does not report feeling better, Mom or adult in charge will call Uncle Bob to come over.
6. Uncle Bob will talk alone with Billy and take Billy to his house if needed. Billy will be allowed to do activities previously agreed upon to calm him.
7. Mom will be on standby, and Uncle Bob will call if Billy becomes unsafe. 911 will be used only if Uncle Bob unable to keep Billy safe.
8. Crisis number called if Billy is safe but unable to return to a calm state.

Phone Numbers Needed: Uncle Bob_____, Reverend
Dave_____, Crisis Line_____

family. A plan that truly meets the needs of the family is born out of conversations and an understanding of what truly occurs. Understanding the antecedents and results of crisis within the family is instructive in the development of a plan. Listening carefully to what families tell practitioners will naturally guide this process. The plan therefore should capture each family's unique needs in the time of crisis. It should definitely be seen by the family as usable and supportive. Cultural relevance is critical for families. A plan will not be used if it does not reflect the beliefs, values, and practices of individual families. All individuals and families resort to what they know and what has been their "default" way of functioning.

A reactive crisis plan should be simplistic and easy for the family members to execute. Each step should clearly state who the implementer is and when movement to the next step is indicated. Emergency numbers and needed information regarding implementers should be identified as well. Table 16.6 provides an example of a reactive crisis plan.

CONCLUSION

Crisis planning is by far one of the most critical and empowering ways in which practitioners support families. The act of preparing for crisis best occurs in the absence of crisis when family members can be guided to reflect on what works best for their individual family. Families often have many of the needed skills and supports that, if built upon and planned ahead of time, will work to leave families feeling more competent and capable. Youth should play at least an equal part if not more in the determination of what can work. Crisis planning is an activity that should not be forgotten about as service provision takes place. The discussion of crisis planning should be ongoing and continually monitored. The activities of this task should gradually be turned over entirely to the family to prepare it for recovery.

References

Betancourt, J. R., Green, A. R., Carrillo, J. E., & Ananeh-Firempong, O. (2003). Defining cultural competence: A practical framework for addressing racial/ethnic disparities in health and health care. *Public Health Reports, 118*, 293-302.

Dass-Brailsford, P. (2007). A *practical approach to trauma: Empowering interventions*. Thousand Oaks, CA: Sage Publications.

Hill, R. (1958). Generic features of families under stress. *Social Casework, 49*, 139-150.

Kernan, J., & Morilus-Black, M. (2008). Social supports for youth and families. In C. Newman, C. Lieberton, K. Kutash, & R. M. Friedman (Eds.), *The 20th annual research conference proceedings: A system of care for children's mental health: expanding the research base* (pp. 275-276). Tampa: University of South Florida, Louis de la Parte Florida Mental Health Institute, Research and Training Center for Children's Mental Health.

Lau, A., & Takeuchi, D. (2001). Cultural factors in help-seeking for child behavior problems: Value orientation, affective responding, and severity appraisals among Chinese-American parents. *Journal of Community Psychology, 29*, 675-692.

MacPhee, D., Fritz, J., & Miller-Hey, J. (1996). Ethnic variations in personal social networks and parenting. *Child Development, 67*, 3278-3295.

Maslow, A. H. (1943). A theory of human motivation. *Psychological Review, 50*, 370-396.

McCubbin, M. A., & McCubbin, H. I. (1993). Family coping with health crises: The resiliency model of family stress, adjustment, and adaptation. In C. Danielson, B. Hamel-Bissell, & P. Winstead-Fry (Eds.), *Families, health, and illness* (pp. 21-64). New York: Mosby.

Meyers, J., Kaufman, M., & Goldman, S. (1999). Promising practices: Training strategies for serving children with serious emotional disturbance and their families in a system of care. *Systems of care: Promising practices in children's mental health, 1998 series* (vol. 5). Washington, DC. Center for Effective Collaboration and Practice, American Institute for Research.

Miles, P. (2009). *Crisis and safety planning: Building the right balance.* Presentation made at The Child Welfare Issues Conference held in East Lansing, Michigan.

Peterson, J. & Hawley, D. R. (1998). Effects of stressors on parenting attitudes and family functioning in a primary prevention program. *Family Relations, 47*, 221-227.

Roberts, A. R. (Ed.). (1995). *Crisis intervention and time-limited cognitive treatment.* Thousand Oaks, CA: Sage.

Smokowski, P. R., Rose, R., & Bacallao, M. L. (2008). Acculturation and Latino family processes: How cultural involvement, biculturalism, and acculturation gaps influence family dynamics. *Family Relations, 57*, 295-308.

Vandenberg, J. (2003). The professional child and family team process facilitator: The basics of the child and family team practice model. Retrieved July 16, 2009, from http://www.azdhs.gov/bhs/contracts/gaz/rfd/tm/cf/pdf/cftday1.pdf

Walker, J. S., Bruns, E. J., & National Wraparound Initiative Advisory Group. (2008). Phases and activities of the wraparound process. In E. J. Bruns and J. S. Walker (Eds.), *The resource guide to wraparound*. Portland, OR: National Wraparound Initiative, Research and Training Center for Family Support and Children's Mental Health.

Walker, J. S., & Sage, M. (2006). Strengthening social support: Research implications for interventions in children's mental health. *Focal Point: A National Bulletin on Family Support and Children's Mental Health, 20*(1), 3-9.

Exhibit 16.1
Crisis Plan Review Checklist

Date Reviewed On_____

1. If the plan was used: What went well?

2. If the plan was used: Did anything not go well?

3. Did the people identified in the plan know what to do?

4. Are there any new strengths or natural supports that we would like to include? YES or NO

    If yes, please describe and modify plan accordingly:

5. Are there any interventions that are no longer applicable? YES or NO

    If yes, please describe and modify plan accordingly:

6. Are there any supports listed that are no longer available? YES or NO

    If yes, please describe and modify plan accordingly:

7. Do you have a current copy of your crisis plan and do you know how to access it? YES or NO

    If no, please provide a new copy of the plan and provide a note on the plan of where to keep it for easy access.

Form written by Tracy Mock, LMHC. Reprinted with permission.

Exhibit 16.2
Crisis Plan Information Sheet

Client: _____ **Age:** _____ **ID:** _____

Parent/Guardian: _____ **Living Situation**: _____

Date Plan Developed:	Date of most recent update:
Team Members who helped create the plan:	
Copies of the plan were provided to:	

Diagnosis

Axis I	
Axis II	
Axis III	
Axis IV	
Axis V	Current GAF:

Current Medications

Medication	Dosage	Frequency	Rationale
Allergies:			
Medical conditions:			

(Continued)

Exhibit 16.2 *(Continued)*

History of Hospitalizations

Hospital	Dates	Reason
Youth and family preference regarding hospitalization:		

Past Interventions and Responses/Other Pertinent Information

Form written by Tracy Mock, LMHC. Reprinted with permission.

Exhibit 16.3
Crisis Prevention Plan: Youth

Crisis:

If I feel _____ I can help myself by:

My _____ can help me when I feel this way by:

Parent/Guardian

My family, especially _____, can help me when I feel this way by:

Siblings/Relatives in the home

My friend/relative/natural support _____ can help me when I feel this way by:

Form written by Tracy Mock, LMHC. Reprinted with permission.

Exhibit 16.4
Crisis Prevention Plan: Parent/Guardian/Teacher

Crisis:

When _____ is feeling _____ I can help myself by:

When _____ is feeling this way I can help them by:

When _____ is feeling this way our family/class can help by:

_____ can help _____ by:

Friend/Relative/Natural Support/School Personnel

Phone number:

Form written by Tracy Mock, LMHC. Reprinted with permission.

Exhibit 16.5
Commonly Needed Information

	Name	Address	Phone Number
Poison Control			1-800-382-9097
Primary Care Physician			
Dentist			
Pharmacy			
School			
On Call #			
Case Manager			

Form written by Tracy Mock, LMHC. Reprinted with permission.

Chapter 17

Developing Effective Strategies for Transition

Nobody can go back and start a new beginning, but anyone can start today and make a new ending.

—Maria Robinson

Dream as if you'll live forever, live as if you'll die today.

—James Dean

INTRODUCTION

Families are all too familiar with the challenges that take place at certain junctures. Families may even begin services due to the difficulties that are present related to a life change. The concept of preparing for these changes is typically easily grasped as an important strategy for maximizing outcomes. Families can relate to the need to prepare for life changes; therefore, transitioning from services should be presented in the same fashion. This chapter begins with an overview of the concepts of recovery and resiliency in order to build an understanding of what needs to occur for successful transition out of services. The important elements of transition activities that begin from engagement throughout service delivery and the development of a plan are discussed relative to the current status of the families. Barriers and concerns that families may have regarding transition are addressed in a way that can serve to optimize success.

DEVELOPING A VISION FOR RECOVERY AND RESILIENCY

The President's New Freedom Commission on Mental Health (2003) recommends that the concepts of recovery and resiliency be a part of a transformed system that delivers behavioral health care to children, adolescents, and adults. The report states, "care must focus on increasing consumers' ability to successfully cope with life's challenges, on facilitating recovery, and on building resilience" (p. 7).

On May 10, 1995, Patricia Deegan, a consumer of mental health services presented at a conference cosponsored by the Alliance for the Mentally Ill of Massachusetts and the Department of Mental Health of Massachusetts Curriculum and Training Committee (Deegan, 1996). She stated as follows in her presentation:

> Recovery does not mean cure. Rather recovery is an attitude, a stance, and a way of approaching the day's challenges. It is not a perfectly linear journey. There are times of rapid gains and disappointing relapses. There are times of just living, just staying quiet, resting and regrouping. Each person's journey of recovery is unique. Each person must find what works for them. This means that we must have the opportunity to try and to fail and to try again. In order to support the recovery process mental health professionals must not rob us of the opportunity to fail. Professionals must embrace the concept of the dignity of risk and the right to failure if they are to be supportive of us. (pp. 96-97)

The principles of recovery should be introduced at the beginning of services as well as throughout services. These principles have been discussed and described by Davidson, O'Connell, Sells, and Staeheli (2003) as follows:

- Renewing hope and commitment;
- Redefining self;
- Incorporating illness;
- Being involved in meaningful activities;
- Overcoming effects of discrimination;
- Assuming control;
- Becoming empowered and more involved in the community and citizenship activities;
- Managing symptoms; and
- Being supported by others.

In promoting these principles, Davidson et al. (2003) further describe a recovery oriented environment as follows:

- Encouraging individuality;
- Promoting accurate and positive portrayals of psychiatric disability;
- Focusing on strengths;

- Using language of hope and possibility;

- Offering a variety of options for treatment, rehabilitation, and support;

- Supporting risk taking;

- Actively involving service users, family members, and natural supports;

- Encouraging user participation in advocacy activities;

- Helping develop connections with communities; and

- Helping people develop valued social roles, interests, and hobbies.

While there are many parallels between the two paradigms, there are also a few differentiations. Resiliency as a construct is less focused on the identification of conditions such as bipolar disorder or schizophrenia; rather it emphasizes developmental and life challenges that may underlie mental health challenges. Research in resiliency has identified individual, family, and community characteristics that promote ability to cope with adversity. Resiliency traits for individuals include easy-going temperaments, high self-esteem, talents, faith, and many more. Family resiliency characteristics include a close relationship with caring caregivers, authoritative caregiving, and extended family networks. Community traits include the presence of good role models, connection to community organizations, and effective schools (Masten & Coatsworth, 1988; Friesen, 2005). Transitions are emphasized in literature (Clark & Davis, 2000) as presenting potential challenges to individuals. Transitions may include movement between developmental stages, schools, or systems. Therefore, planning and promoting the use of strengths is strongly needed.

Friesen (2005) discusses the benefits of focusing on the contributions from both frameworks resulting in an integrated framework, resiliency, and recovery. This would have many positive implications for service delivery and transition planning. A first implication would be including lessons from research in individual planning, which focus on the principles of recovery and resiliency. This reinforces building protective factors and supporting recovery rather than measuring success by eliminating symptoms. This common mentality only further stigmatizes youth and families. Second, with this orientation, transition planning should reflect strengths or the development of strengths in the individual, community, and family. Last, as part of transition planning, consideration for stigma reduction activities should be incorporated (Friesen, 2005).

GOALS OF TRANSITION PLANNING

From the time that a youth and his/her family begin treatment, the discussion of ending services should begin. Transition planning first acknowledges the all-important concept that services will have a beginning and an end that should be carefully planned. It should be explained from an empowerment and recovery perspective that formal services may serve as a means to establishing recovery but are not necessarily always needed. Transition planning should appreciate the importance of preparing for needed transitions from levels of care, discharge from services, or even phases of life. These transitions should be anticipated and supported in a manner that reflects readiness of the youth and family, preparedness, and the development of needed supports to maintain success. Transition planning (see Exhibit 17.1) should allow for an active process of developing what is needed to maximize the benefit of formal services and transferring this support to natural and community supports. Additionally, developing a mindset in the youth and family that recovery is possible and that the family can be prepared to know what to do in a future crisis is the goal. Some families may not believe that this is possible, and skills throughout the service delivery process that can be promoted to allow this to happen should be incorporated into the planning. The overall goals for transition planning have been identified and described by Vandenberg & Rast (2004) and Bruns, Burchard, Suter, Leverentz-Brady, and Force (2004) as follows:

- Identify needs, services, and supports that will continue to need attention past the formal wraparound process (see Chapter 3 in this volume);

- Plan for the development of skills and enlist supports to end the need for the formal wraparound process;

- Develop a posttransition crisis management plan;

- Create a document that highlights the strengths of the youth and family, and documents the progress and strategies that were used; and

- Develop a plan for follow-up or checking-in with the youth and family.

Although all youth are in need of a plan for transition, the needs of transition-age youth are often significant. Transition-age youth may be in need of assistance in reaching independence, pursuing employment or secondary education, enlisting support of peers and adults, and accessing adult services. The youth who are in foster care and experience emotional and behavioral challenges have been identified as being particularly at risk for a poor transition to adulthood or needed services in an adult system. According to a national study, youth who had left the foster care system two and one-half to four years prior demonstrated significantly lower high school graduation rates and a higher likelihood of involvement in illicit drug use, illegal activities, and homelessness (Cook, 1991). Transition plans, if developed appropriately, can maximize the likelihood that youth meet their potentials. Geenen and Powers (2006) conducted a study investigating the educational and transition experiences of foster care youth with disabilities. The transition plans of youth in foster care with special education needs that were reviewed demonstrated significant flaws, which should serve to instruct future transition planning. The plans of those in foster care, as opposed to those who were not, demonstrated the following:

- Fewer goals for secondary education;
- Fewer goals to develop independent living skills;
- Fewer goals overall;
- Frequent lack of action steps related to goals;
- Less advocate and caseworker involvement;
- Frequent listing of student as solely responsible for working on goals with no support from others;
- Lack of specific timeline for goal completion;

- Frequent failure to focus on career development; and

- Little understanding of foster care issues.

Further research in this area emphasized that youth in foster care with disabilities may lack a sense of self-determination. The mentality of being able to influence change in one's life can be enhanced through careful planning. Plans must seek to develop decision-making skills, support self-direction, and enlist support from others (Geenen, Powers, Hogansen, & Pittman, 2007).

INFUSING TRANSITION PLANNING IN ALL PHASES OF SERVICE DELIVERY

Engagement and Assessment

When youth and families enter services in which empowerment, recovery and resiliency, and the wraparound principles (see Chapter 3 in this volume) are guiding factors, practitioners must not make assumptions regarding their understanding of such. Many families assume that practitioners know best and that other supports are "second best." Families may not consider the notion that they can manage their youth without formal supports. As part of engagement and assessment, these concepts and related principles need to be explained and given time to be understood. Some families may not agree with some concepts, and this too must be accepted. The assessment process appreciates the need to begin transition planning from the beginning of services. Through conversations, the youth's and family's beliefs, values, and traditions will shine through to guide the work of devising a transition plan that can reflect their uniqueness.

Transition planning begins from the first contact with statements such as "What will things look like when we know we're ready to discontinue services?" or "What do we need to overcome in order to no longer need services?" Although transition-related activities and planning are initiated from the start of services, as relationships develop and the needs, strengths, and culture of the family become clearer, the plan evolves and is revisited on a regular basis (Grealish, 2000). Activities that lay the foundation for successful transition must be intentional and begin with engagement. Such activities include the following:

- Assisting the youth and family in understanding the assessment, service planning, and Child and Family Team (CFT) process;

- Determining the family's and the youth's understandings and investments in empowerment, recovery and resiliency, and the wraparound principles;

- Assisting the youth and the family in identifying how services could best suit their needs;

- Explaining and reinforcing the types of interventions and how these interventions can transition from formal supports to family and natural and community supports;

- Determining how the family will know when services are no longer needed and how family, community, and natural supports will be better able to meet family needs;

- Assisting in identifying barriers to success;

- Educating the family and the youth on components of resiliency that can be built upon or developed;

- Developing a strategy for coordinating information (e.g., service plans, school records, etc.) from the onset of treatment;

- Assisting the family in identifying all areas that require coordination and planning (e.g., school, activities, and visits with other family members); and

- Identifying what is needed for the family to feel that its youth is best served and supported.

Transition Interventions During the Service Planning and Implementation Process

Throughout the process, skills must be developed so that the youth and the family feel that they will no longer need formal services at some point. The services and skills that the practitioner is utilizing to provide supports should be taught to the caregivers and youth. The process of service planning will become an ongoing task of families to organize youth's needs. The process of developing a service plan to guide the service provision will later be replicated by a plan to unite family and natural supports in the goal of maintaining recovery.

Activities that are relevant during the implementation phase must be related to the wishes, values, and beliefs of the family. Assuming families want to learn new ways of advocating for and meeting their needs, skills can be modeled, reinforced, practiced, and reviewed to ensure that the role of the practitioner can be transferred to the families, youth, and support systems. Transition activities that may be relevant in this phase include the following:

- Modeling and reinforcing ways to determine if services are meeting needs;

- Developing ways to communicate to others the uniqueness of the youth and family in terms of culture, strengths, and needs;

- Developing strategies to advocate for youth and family;

- Developing strategies to monitor and coordinate care;

- Developing an understanding of youth's needs and mental health challenges;

- Fostering and developing natural and community supports;

- Developing skills in maintaining relationships with natural and community supports;

- Developing a strategy for maintaining needed information and records;

- Continually assessing and evaluating crisis needs and plans;

- Helping the family and youth to gain confidence in new skills and in natural and informal supports;

- Transferring use of these skills and supports into other plans (e.g., school, probation, etc.);

- Practicing crisis responses;

- Assisting in advocating for community awareness and change, and facilitating family involvement in advocacy; and

- Working with the CFT to develop mutual investment and plan for when the stage of transition should begin.

Transition

Once the youth and family determine that progress reflects the need to more intensely focus on transition, the phase of transition begins. At this point, it is beneficial to "step back" and review the progression of services and determine how needs and strengths may have taken a different focus (Vandenberg & Rast, 2004). The transition plan should be reviewed, and significant revisions may be needed as transition is closer. The activities and tasks of the transition phase that have been identified by Walker et al. (2004) include the following:

- Planning for ending the formal wraparound process (see Chapter 3 in this volume) (links to alternative supports or adult services should be established);

- Creating a posttransition crisis management plan;

- Modifying the wraparound process to reflect transition (new members representing posttransition supports can be added to team to practice discussing supports and potential response to crisis);

- Producing a document that describes the journey through the wraparound process highlighting successes, strengths, developed skills, successful interventions, and met goals;

- Celebrating success; and

- Developing a follow-up plan.

PREPARING FOR TRANSITION

Reducing Frequency and Focus of Services

The frequency and intensity of service should be related to need. An overwhelmed family benefits greatly from experiences of reduced chaos and positive interactions. As the practitioner appreciates the need for intense support initially, the reduction of intensity and frequency is equally as impactful. The overall goal for services is to empower families to meet their needs in a way that is effective and appreciative of their unique family and cultural influences.

Reducing the frequency of services is a process that should be planned carefully and occur as part of a process. The service planning process is a process and discussion that should be a part of ongoing visits. It is not an event that happens only at scheduled reviews. The practitioner should request feedback from the youth and family at each session regarding their perceptions of the progress. Youth and families should

Table 17.1
Crisis Drill Review

- Was the plan accessible?
- Did the youth know how to activate the plan?
- Were there any unseen circumstances?
- Was it clear to family members their roles in the plan?
- Did the family know when to move to next steps?
- Did members follow through with interventions as planned?
- Did the plan meet the needed objectives?
- Did the plan address all family members' needs?

be asked to discuss the preestablished measures of success, which they should have developed and agreed upon. The practitioner typically leads the skill management, teaches the skill, allows the family to practice the skill, and assists in coaching strengths and weaknesses related to the skill.

Practicing for Crisis

The concept that youth with behavioral and emotional challenges will never have issues in the future should never be communicated. The notion that a crisis is present only when caregivers or the youth do *not* know what to do is the better message. After the family experiences a crisis, there should always be a review of what worked and what did not work. This information should then inform the development of a new plan. As transition becomes closer, practicing the response to a crisis should be incorporated into the service provision. The family and youth can assist the practitioner in developing a crisis drill so that they can benefit and learn from it. Practitioners may agree to surprise drills or planned practices. The goal of learning from the drill should be primary. Table 17.1 identifies areas that can be evaluated in the family's response to a crisis drill.

Preparing Youth and Family for Change

When families receive services within the home and community environments, a strong bond may develop between the family and the practitioner. The dynamic of being a part of the family's environment on a frequent basis may foster a strong relationship. Families as well as practitioners may have strong feelings about ending this relationship. Practitioners must first take stock of their own feelings related to transition in order to best support the family members in coping with their feelings. Supervisory support is often critical in working through this transition in the most professional and beneficial manner. Finding ways to continually communicate belief in the family's and youth's accomplishments and abilities assists with the fears that they may be experiencing regarding the loss of services. Youth and caregivers may need individual support to identify their fears so that the family can best discuss them as a whole. Recognizing the "ups and downs" in this process as often reflective of ambivalence is a helpful stance as well.

Components of Transition Planning

As with all activities related to home- and community-based services, the transition plan should be completed with the family and youth. The concept of transition should include any type of upcoming change (e.g., educational level, day care arrangements, moving to new area, or transitioning out of care or to another level of care). The transition plan should begin with the youth's and family's visions of what success in this area would "look" like to them. This is how they would describe the ideal, and this discussion should evolve further into a determination of what markers of success would be related to their visions. If the transition plan is related to discharge from services, this discussion should already have taken place and is guiding the work. The markers of success definitely include the family as a whole. Within the plan, there should be careful and thorough descriptions of what the youth and family do well, and these areas should be reflected in the interventions. The interventions should include all types of supports, strategies, and individuals who will assist the youth and family in successfully mastering transition or maintaining recovery. Crisis management should always be included, as this is a critical and needed skill to cope with any change. The crisis management plan should always be something that the family and youth have devised for themselves and can be implemented without dependence on a practitioner or services. The way in which the plan will be evaluated by the family as well as followed up on by the practitioner should be identified as well. If the family is ending services, the transition plan should include a summary of treatment. This should be thought of as a document that tells the story of the family's journey through services. This, as with all other documents that are written for and about the family, must be completed collaboratively with the youth and family. Families may even choose to "tell" their stories in unique and creative manners (e.g., through video-taped presentations or artwork). A summary of care can be developed in combination with one of the above creative methods. The summary of care can be a celebration of successes as well as a guide to support the development of future services as needed. Family members will want to compose the document by imagining everything they would want a new practitioner to know about their family to avoid the unnecessary stress of rehashing difficult information without the benefit of a relationship and making mistakes that have occurred previously with regard to treatment interventions. The relevant history can be written from the perspective of the family and youth and only relate information that is necessary and comfortable to the family. Emphasizing a future orientation and not focusing unnecessarily on past history is important. The strengths that have been developed and the supports that are now a part of the family's life should be emphasized. The way in which interventions unfolded and how the family felt with regard to its abilities to help or hurt its situation can be articulated in a helpful manner. The history of doctor appointments, medication usage, and diagnosis should be clearly listed as well. See Exhibit 17.2 for an example of a format for the plan and summary of care.

CONCLUSION

The tasks and activities related to transition should not be overlooked or discounted in their importance. These tasks are carefully woven into the treatment process in a way that reflects the needed pace and types of interventions required by the family. The timing of these interventions is important, and the interventions build on one another. The hope for transition planning is the development of a skill set that can be utilized to cope successfully with the numerous transitions that all family members will make as part of the journeys in their lives. Practitioners must discuss transition activities within a supervisory process, as it may be difficult for the practitioner as well as the family to cope with feelings related to the transition. The act of modifying or decreasing the intensity of services to reflect family progress is a part of this skill set for practitioners, which can become challenging. As with any other process related to home- and community-based services, there must always remain room for flexibility and change based on what is the best interests of the family. Learning from these experiences is always the goal; and transition gives both the family and the practitioner a wealth of opportunities to develop competencies.

References

Bruns, E. J., Burchard, J. D., Suter, J. C., Leverentz-Brady, K., & Force, M. M. (2004). Assessing fidelity to a community-based treatment for youth: The Wraparound Fidelity Index. *Journal of Emotional and Behavioral Disorders, 12*, 79-89.

Clark, H. B., & Davis, M. (2000). *Transition to adulthood: A resource for assisting young people with emotional or behavioral difficulties.* Baltimore: Paul H. Brookes Publishing.

Cook, R., Fleishman, E., & Grimes, V. (1991). *A national evaluation of the title IV-E foster care independent living programs for youth: Phase 2.* (Final Report, Vol. 1.). Rockville, MD: Westat.

Davidson, L., O'Connell, M., Sells, D., & Staeheli, M. (2003). Is there an outside to mental illness? In L. Davidson, *Living outside mental illness: Qualitative studies of recovery in schizophrenia* (pp. 31-60). New York: New York University Press.

Deegan, P. (1996). Recovery as a journey of the heart. *Psychosocial Rehabilitation Journal, 19*, 91-97.

Friesen, B. J. (2005). The concept of recovery: "Value added" for the children's mental health field? *Focal Point Research, Policy, and Practice in Children's Mental Health, 19*(1), 5-8.

Geenen, S. J., & Powers, L. E. (2006). Transition planning for foster youth with disabilities: Are we falling short? *Journal for Vocational Special Needs Education, 28*(2), 4-15.

Geenen, S. J., Powers, L. E., Hogansen, J. M., & Pittman, J. O. E. (2007). Youth with disabilities in foster care: Developing self-determination within a context of struggle and disempowerment. *Exceptionality, 15*, 17-30.

Grealish, M. (2000). *The wraparound process curriculum.* McMurray, PA: Community Partners.

Masten, A. S., & Coatsworth, J. D. (1998). The development of competence in favorable and unfavorable environments: Lessons from research on successful children. *American Psychologist, 53*, 205-220.

President's New Freedom Commission on Mental Health. (2003). *Achieving the promise: Tranforming mental health care in America. Executive summary* (DHHS Publication No. SMA-03-3831). Rockville, MD: Author.

Vandenberg, J. E., & Rast, J. (2004). *Wraparound coaching and supervision toolkit.* Englewood, CO: Vroon Vandenberg.

Walker, J. S., Bruns, E. J., Vandenberg, J. D., Rast, J., Osher, T. W., Miles, P., et al. (2004). *Phases and activities of the wraparound process.* Portland, OR: National Wraparound Initiative, Research and Training Center on Family Support and Children's Mental Health, Portland State University.

Exhibit 17.1
Transition Plan

Family Vision

Family Markers of Success

Youth Strengths and Accomplishments

Family Strengths and Accomplishments

Plan for Meeting Youth Needs Throughout Transition and Recovery (include types of activities, supports and individuals that will assist youth and indicators that problems may be reoccurring or changes need to be made)

Plan for Meeting Family Needs Throughout Transition and Recovery (include needs of all family members and plan for identify when family is in need of supports or changes in the plan for recovery)

Crisis Management Plan

Follow-Up Plan

Needed Numbers and Resources

Exhibit 17.2
Summary of Care

Relevant History (needs and problem areas that resulted in referral, past attempts at help, past hospitalizations or residential treatment, perceptions of the youth and family regarding needs and strengths)

Strengths of Youth and Family Upon Referral

Needs of Youth and Family Upon Referral

Identification of Needs Following Assessment and Prioritization

Interventions That Were Successful (include crisis intervention strategies)

Interventions That Were Not Successful (include crisis intervention strategies)

Medication History and Psychiatric Services

Diagnosis

Developed Strengths in Youth and Family

Natural and Community Supports for Youth and Family

Concerns About Formal Services or Lessons Learned Regarding Meeting Family Needs

Appendix A
Case Study in Early Childhood Intervention

Tracy remembered feeling physically sick the moment she learned that her sister had died in a car accident. The shock and confusion she felt at this moment were quickly overshadowed by an overriding sense of panic about the status of her two nieces, one of whom she had never met. She struggled to remember "the little one's" name and wondered how old she would be. Tracy's sister, Ashley, had been a constant source of worry for Tracy. Tracy and Ashley had been so close when they were younger. Being only two years apart, they spent a lot of time together and had many of the same friends. Everything changed when Ashley met Derek. He had introduced her to drugs, and before long Ashley was only a shadow of the person Tracy had often called her best friend. Before long, drug addiction became such an issue that Tracy's parents put Ashley in rehabilitation. The hospital stay seemed to help but not for long. After numerous issues, including stealing from and threatening her parents, Ashley moved two states away with her boyfriend Derek. Tracy met Ashley's oldest child, Haley, shortly after she was born, but after a long lecture that ended in disaster, Tracy was "dead" to Ashley. Tracy has spent the last four years worrying about the sister she lost and the nieces she was never to know.

Four-year-old Haley woke up confused. Where was she and, more importantly, where was her 2-year-old sister, Anna? Anna always slept with her, and it felt strange to not know where she was. She remembered the lady telling her she was going to some "nice people's" house for a while. Haley jumped out of bed and went looking for her sister. The house was so big and so quiet. She heard no sounds coming out of any rooms and started to panic that they took her sister away. She didn't cry, she didn't yell, she knew those kinds of behaviors would never work. If Anna was there, she was going to find her.

Anna sat smiling as the lady fed her the best breakfast she had ever had. As Haley came down the hallway into the kitchen, Anna quickly lit up and reached for her sister. Haley quickly went to her sister's side and wondered what this lady was doing feeding *her* sister. Haley found it hard to look at the lady and turned her back to the lady, as she watched her sister's every move. The lady was talking, but Haley did not even consider that she was talking to her. When the lady touched her and tried to get her to turn to look at her, Haley stiffened and felt an overall sense of discomfort. What did this lady want?

It did not take more than a moment for Tracy to decide the answer to the question that the woman on the other end of the phone was asking. The woman explained that she had been called by the hospital and talked to Ashley before she died. Tracy jotted down the address of where she needed to go and agreed to meet the woman at her office as soon as she could get a flight. Tracy knew this was going to be an adjustment, but the reality of how life changing this would actually be had not yet hit her. Ashley had requested that Tracy take responsibility for her two daughters. Tracy had been up all night worrying about the well-being of her nieces. She briefly considered her parents' reactions to Tracy taking the girls, and, no doubt, it would be hard for them to hear what Ashley had requested prior to her death.

Tracy fought back tears as her parents sat motionless in a state of shock and deep despair. They had prayed every day for Ashley and hoped that her drug addiction would somehow get under control. The support group they attended had backed them 100 percent in their decision not to help Ashley to keep using drugs. When they pulled the purse strings, Ashley became so infuriated that she moved and never spoke to them again. They each remembered the special times they had with Ashley when she was little. Both of their girls had been their lives, and they often wondered how this could happen. Now there was nothing to hope for; fate had intervened and their worst nightmares had come true.

Tracy boarded the plane so preoccupied that she barely was aware of her surroundings. When the man sitting in the seat next to her made small talk and asked her if she was "coming or going," she didn't even respond. She apologized when she realized she had ignored his comment and continued to think about the litany of questions, worries, and fears that flooded her thoughts. The plane landed before Tracy had a chance to collect her thoughts in any fashion, and she struggled to orient herself to what she was about to do. She had hoped for this moment for four years, but she never imagined it would be under these circumstances.

The Ford Taurus that the practitioner from Family Services drove slowed down in front of a large white house in a nice neighborhood. Tracy stared at the doorway and tried to gather her thoughts about what was about to happen and how she should handle it. She felt helpless to determine what to say and do. The practitioner from Family Services tried to alleviate her concerns but seemed somewhat rushed to move things along. Tracy felt little confidence that this was going to go well.

Haley heard that lady talking to her sister again. She tried to ignore her most of the time, but when she talked to Anna, Haley paid close attention. Something was said about her aunt coming. Haley wondered what that meant. She didn't think she or Anna had an aunt. She really wasn't sure what that meant but thought it was something like a grandma. She knew she had a grandma but hadn't seen her in a long time. After her daddy left, the visits with her grandma went away too. Haley knew they said her mother was dead and wasn't coming back but still couldn't understand what that meant. Her mommy stayed away sometimes but also always came back. The lady was just confused; she didn't know about her mommy like Haley did.

Everyone wanted Haley to look at her aunt who reminded her of her mommy. Haley didn't like looking at her and didn't want her to hug her again. She didn't know why Anna was letting her aunt hold her, and it was making Haley mad. She wanted to tell Anna to get down and let her hold her. She was the one who knew Anna, not those other people. She couldn't talk, she couldn't look at them, she just wanted to take Anna and run. Haley wanted to know where they were taking her, but she couldn't ask. She really didn't listen when they told her the first time. She was busy wondering where their stuff was. Anna was going to need her Teddy, and no one said anything about where it was.

Tracy lay in bed staring at the ceiling. She knew this was hard for Haley but couldn't understand her aloofness. Nothing she said or did seemed to please her or bring a smile to her face. She didn't want anyone to care for Anna, and Tracy was perplexed about how she should handle this. If Ashley had been raising the kids on her own like the practitioner from Family Services reported, there must have been little time for Haley. She was way too concerned about her sister, and Tracy felt that Haley had been caring for Anna in the ways that Ashley couldn't.

The moment that Tracy made the call to the program that the practitioner had given her, she almost hung up. How could she not handle this herself? What would the program staff think of her? Was she an idiot? Haley was quiet and didn't cause any behavior problems. She just didn't seem to be adjusting. She didn't seem to even expect Tracy to take care of her, and she did a better job with Anna than Tracy did. Tracy wondered how she would even articulate what she needed help with. Should she say "My niece doesn't like me"? Thankfully, the secretary made her feel comfortable, and she simply said, "I just know we need help."

The practitioner who came out to see Tracy had called her and tried to tell her what was going to happen at the "assessment," but she had really not even processed anything that was said. Tracy was still worried about being seen as incapable of caring for her nieces. The day that the woman came to see her, Tracy remembers being shocked at her appearance. She didn't expect this woman to look so casual and be loaded down with toys. Tracy had forgotten that she was supposed to tell the kids that the practitioner was coming. See, she was already messing this up! The woman reminded Tracy that her name was Amy and that she had some toys that the kids could play with while they talked. Amy didn't make a big deal when Tracy said that she had forgotten to tell the kids that Amy was coming. Tracy introduced the kids to Amy and before too long the kids were playing with the toys in the living room while Tracy and Amy sat at the kitchen table. Amy started out by saying that she wanted to give Tracy some information so she could determine if the program would be a good fit for them. She also said several times that if Tracy wanted to have an assessment that she would really like her ideas on how this would best work for her. Amy was going to give Tracy some information about what an assessment was and the things that normally would be done, but she really wanted Tracy to help her decide how it would happen. Tracy didn't expect this and thought that this process was feeling much different than she expected. Amy really seemed to listen as Tracy told her all of her worries and fears about both Haley and herself. She found herself saying that she was afraid she wasn't going to be able to do this and that she was overwhelmed. Tracy shared that her parents were willing to help, but she didn't want them to feel like she couldn't do this. She felt bad enough that her sister had asked her to take the kids in the first place. She knew she needed her parents' help, but wanted to try it on her own for a while. At the end of the visit, Amy asked Tracy to call her and let her know if she would like her to come back again. She reminded her that this was her decision and that if the program wasn't what she wanted, she would link her with something that she did want. Tracy found herself saying "Just come back, I know I need your help."

Tracy was nervous the day that Amy was scheduled to come back. Amy had called to remind her that she was coming, and it made her think again how Amy made her feel comfortable. The assessment was mostly a conversation. It wasn't prying or negative in the way that Tracy expected. She kept hearing Amy say positive things and talk about possibilities for how things could be. Tracy started to imagine that everything could be OK.

Haley looked like she was playing with the toys, but she was so preoccupied with that lady being in the kitchen that she couldn't really play. She didn't want to go back to the other lady, and she didn't want them to take away Anna. She still hadn't figured out why this lady was coming, even though Tracy had told her "she's here to help us." Haley didn't know what she was going to help them with, and she really didn't know if she could believe Tracy anyway. When the lady came over to talk to her and Anna she just wanted to run, but she just sat there looking away and watching over Anna. The lady didn't pinch her cheeks and make her look at her like all those other people always did. She hated that. Didn't they know that was mean? The lady just played with them and really didn't make her talk too much. She didn't ask her a million questions either. Maybe this was gonna be OK.

Amy found herself thinking about Tracy, Haley, and Anna quite a bit after the assessment. She left a message for her supervisor that she wanted to process the feelings she was having about serving this family. Tracy seemed so unsure of herself, and she knew she had to work hard to build her feelings of competence. Tracy needed some time with her to understand how Haley may be feeling and to develop the plan. There didn't seem to be any time for Tracy to meet with her without Haley, and she wondered how to proceed. It was time to begin the planning process, and she was feeling overwhelmed with the way in which she could best do this. On top of it all, Haley actually smiled at her during their last visit and made eye contact. When she was leaving, Tracy said to her in a meek voice "that's more than she's given me."

Amy sat nervously in her supervisor's office and finally started the conversation with "I don't know why this family is feeling so hard for me, I know I've been doing this a long time, but I just don't know what to do." The supervisor, who had known her for quite some time, looked at her and said, "I can tell you feel really worried and even nervous about this situation. I can remind you that years of experience don't take away your status as a person with feelings, but let's spend some time talking this through."

Feeling more balanced, Amy pulled up at Tracy's house and knocked on the door. It was so quiet and strange to be in the house without the girls. Tracy mentioned that she was somewhat relieved that she had some time away from the girls. Her mom had been so excited when she asked her to watch them. Amy acknowledged how hard it had been for Tracy and how good it can feel to have people to help when you need them. Amy picked her words carefully and said, "I see how much you want to be there for the girls, and I can almost feel for myself how bad it makes you feel when Haley doesn't seem to respond. The other day I heard the sadness in your voice when you told me that Haley hasn't yet smiled at you. I'm wondering what you are thinking about this." Tracy looked at Amy and spent the next several minutes wiping away tears as she explained how scared she was of failure, how worried she was about Haley, and sad about her sister being gone for good. As Amy listened to Tracy, she considered the timing of giving her some information about what appeared to be important explanations of Haley's behavior but she reconsidered. She knew the strong importance of Tracy feeling competent in this situation and knew that Tracy had the capacity and knowledge to get there with Amy as her guide. Amy probably only made a few comments like "I bet you've been thinking a lot about what Haley has been through. Have you thought about Haley's preoccupation with caring for her sister as being something she needed to do when she was living with your sister?" Before long, Amy noticed a much calmer and composed woman who seemed fully capable of empathy, reflection, and a strong sense of determination. As Tracy and Amy continued to discuss the family as a whole, they continually came back to the same two needs, which led them to the decision to build the service plan around these two needs. Tracy didn't want to forget about Anna and what she needed from her, and she wanted both the girls to feel cared for. Amy heard Tracy talking about how different Anna and Haley were and how challenging it was to relate to them in such different ways. Anna seemed happy and easy to care for, while Haley just wanted Tracy to "back off" and let her handle everything. Every effort she made to show Haley she cared for her just left her frustrated. Tracy was surprised when Amy pointed out to her at the end of the conversation how much she had already shown her that she knew about both the girls. Amy repeated the many comments that really showed Tracy that she wasn't nearly as bad at this as she believed. Amy helped Tracy to find ways to use these insights to begin the work that they were about to engage in. Amy reminded Tracy about how helpful it was to have this time alone and how maybe asking her parents to be a part of this process might be helpful. Tracy took a long time to answer, and after a deep breath, she said, "I think you're right. I'm gonna ask them tonight when I go to get the girls if they'll be a part of this." Amy knew how hard it was for Tracy to ask for help and reflected this to her saying "you'll probably go back and forth with this one." It's OK to let me know as we go." They agreed to invite the grandparents to the planning meeting.

Tracy found it much easier than she expected to plan the work ahead after meeting with Amy. Amy's questions and observations made it obvious the place in which they should begin. Tracy perked up when Amy pointed out the comments that she had made about Haley's interests, and they decided together that playing her favorite games and activities together was a great place to start. Instead of seeing her caretaking of Anna as a problem, they were going to join with Haley and allow her to "teach" Tracy what Haley knew so much about. Tracy was going to allow Haley to feel the control she needed by supporting this, and gradually Amy was going to help Tracy find ways to help Haley to feel safe enough to let Tracy begin to care for her. Tracy and her parents had a part in the plan, and Tracy really felt listened to and good about the decisions she had made. They were going to work together to do just what Tracy had said she and the girls needed. She found herself surprised and maybe even a little worried that Amy was talking about how Tracy would manage without her and when they would know it was time to stop. She had to remember to talk to Amy about that the next time they talked.

Tracy had been thinking for days about the questions she was going to ask and the ideas she had been having when Amy arrived. She knew they had a plan, but she had started to worry that the girls were going to see Amy as more important than her. She remembered Amy telling her to let her know about any worries she might have, so she vowed to find a way to tell Amy her thoughts. Amy left the box of toys in the car, and at first Tracy wondered where the toys were. Amy noticed the strange look Tracy was giving her and said, "Kids, Tracy had the best idea ever, she knows just what you guys like to play with and she thought we'd all play together." Anna followed Haley's lead and helped her sister as she pulled the baby dolls and dishes out of their new toy box. Tracy was startled when Amy whispered in her ear "Turn around and say baby dolls." Amy exclaimed in an exaggerated fashion, "Tracy, close your eyes and guess what Haley is getting." Tracy did what Amy said and yelled "baby dolls." Haley looked up and smiled. Tracy thought she heard Amy saying something about smiling and turned around to see her first big smile. She knew at that moment that she could do this.

The next week when Amy came to visit, Tracy had so much to tell her. She had seen some progress but also had some big worries. Amy helped her to prioritize, and they decided to change their plan a little bit. Tracy had some great ideas about how to interact with Haley when Anna needed something, but she needed some new ideas to help Haley know she was thinking about her too. They decided that the relationship between the two sisters might be the place to begin having Haley talk about what she wanted and needed. Before long, they had a plan. As Amy and Tracy got out the ingredients from the refrigerator for a snack, they asked Haley for help deciding how Anna liked her ice cream. Haley eagerly told them. Tracy turned to Amy and said, "Amy, Haley knows just how Anna likes her sprinkles so I bet Anna knows just how Haley likes her sprinkles." Amy laughed and said, "Tracy, you're silly, Anna can't talk that good yet!" Tracy said, "Well, Amy, I think Haley can tell us what she would say. Haley can you tell us what Anna would say about how *you* like your sprinkles. Haley looked confused and said, "Anna knows I like mine in a cup so I can pour them on myself." Tracy said, "Well, I'm so happy to know that, let me do that for you."

Tracy lay in bed nearly six months later with a slight smile on her face. She had just put both the girls to bed after watching Scooby Doo with one girl cuddled up on either side of her. This had been a long six months with a lot of ups and downs, but things had definitely started to change. She was surer of herself as a caregiver. She knew that these were *her* girls, and she was going to be there for them no matter what. She also knew that she needed help and that it was OK to get that break every once in a while. When Amy came back, she was gonna tell her she was ready. She knew they were planning for this, but the time felt right. She was ready. It was time to say goodbye. Tracy looked at the picture on her dresser of Ashley and her when they were little and smiled. She knew Ashley was smiling too.

Appendix B

Table of Abbreviations and Acronyms

ACLU-EM	American Civil Liberties Union of Eastern Missouri
ADADFA	Adolescent to Adult Personality Functioning Assessment
ADAMHA Reorganization Act	Alcohol, Drug Abuse, and Mental Health Administration Reorganization Act
ADHD	attention deficit hyperactivity disorder
BERS	Behavioral and Emotional Rating Scale
CANS	Child and Adolescent Needs and Strengths Assessment
CASSP	Child and Adolescent Service System Program
CFT	Child and Family Team
CJC/MSI	St. Louis Justice Center and the Medium Security Institute
CMHS	Center for Mental Health Services
DC 0-3 R	*Diagnostic Classification: 0-3 R (Revised)*
DSM-IV-TR	*Diagnostic and Statistical Manual of Mental Disorders,* fourth edition, text revision
IAITMH	Indiana Association of Infant and Toddler Mental Health
IEP	individualized education plan
MCTQ	Middle Childhood Temperament Questionnaire
MSI	Marital Satisfaction Inventory
ODD	oppositional defiant disorder
SAMHSA	Substance Abuse and Mental Health Services Administration
SATI	School-Age Temperament Inventory
SET	Starting Early Together program
TIP	Transition to Independence Process
TOM	Team Observation Measure
WFI-4	Wraparound Fidelity Index 4.0

Appendix C
Bibliography

Addams, J. (1910). *Twenty years at Hull House*. New York: Macmillan.

Aguilar, B., O'Brien, K. M., August G. J., Aoun, S. L., & Hektner, J. M. (2001). Relationship quality of aggressive children and their siblings: A multiinformant, multimeasure investigation. *Journal of Abnormal Child Psychology, 29*, 479-489.

Allen, S. F., & Tracy, E. M. (2008). Developing student knowledge and skills for home-based social work practice. *Journal of Social Work Education, 44*, 125-143.

Amato, P. R. (2007). Strengthening marriage is an appropriate social policy goal. *Journal of Policy Analysis and Management, 26*, 952-955.

American Academy of Child and Adolescent Psychiatry. (2009). Facts for families: Children with oppositional defiant disorder. No. 72. Retrieved June 16, 2010, from http://www.aacap.org/es/root/facts_for_families/children_with_oppositional_defiant_disorder

American Civil Liberties Union. (1996). *ACLU fact sheet on the juvenile justice system*. Retrieved on November 9, 2009, from http://aclu.org/racial-justice_drug-law-reform _immigrants-rights_womens-rights/aclu-fact-sheet-juvenile-justice-syst

American Psychiatric Association. (2000). *Diagnostic and satistical manual of mental disorders* (4th ed., text rev.). Washington, DC: Author.

American Psychiatric Association. (2000). *Diagnostic and statistical manual of mental disorders* (4th ed., text rev.). Washington, DC: Author.

Antonovsky, A. (1991). The structural sources of salutogenic strengths. In C. L. Cooper & R. Payne (Eds.), *Personality and stress: Individual differences in the stress process* (pp. 67-104). New York: Wiley.

Apple, K., Bernstein, S., Fogg, K., Fogg, L., Haapala, D., Johnson, E., et al. (1997). Walking our talk in the neighborhoods. Building professional/natural helper partnerships. *Social Policy, 27*(4), 54-63.

Aron, E. N. (2002). *The highly sensitive child: Helping our children thrive when the world overwhelms them*. New York: Broadway Books.

Asarnow, J. R., Jaycox, L. H., & Tompson, M. C. (2001). Dep*ression in* Youth: Psychosocial interventions. Journal of Clinical Child Psychology, 30, 33-47.

Ashworth, M., & Baker, A. (2000). 'Time and space': Carers' views about respite care. *Health & Social Care in the Community, 8*, 50-56

Atezaz Saeed, S. (2008). Working with individuals with mental illness and developmental disabilities: Synthesizing the best information for the practicing clinician. *Psychiatric Quarterly, 79*, 153-155.

Atlantic Health Promotion Research Centre (1999). *A study of resiliency in communities*. Ottawa: Health Canada.

Ayoub, C., & Jacewitz, M. M. (1982). Families at risk of poor parenting: A model of service delivery, assessment, and intervention. *Child Abuse and Neglect, 6*, 351-358.

Ayres, J. (2005). *Sensory integration and the child: 25th Anniversary edition*. Los Angeles: Western Psychological Services.

Azmitia, M., & Hesser, J. (1993). Why siblings are important agents of cognitive development: A comparison of siblings and peers. *Child Development, 64*, 430-444.

Bailey, D. B. (1991). Issues and perspectives on family assessment. *Infants and Young Children, 4*(1), 26-34.

Barker, R. L. (1995). *The Social Work Dictionary* (3rd ed.). Washington, DC: NASW Press.

Baumrind, D. (1989). Rearing competent children. In W. Damon (Ed.), *Child development today and tomorrow* (pp. 349-378). San Francisco, CA: Jossey-Bass.

Baumrind, D. (1991). The influence of parenting style on adolescent competence and substance use. *Journal of Early Adolescence, 11*, 56-95.

Beckman, P. J., & Bristol, M. M. (1991). Issues in developing the IFSP: A framework for establishing family outcomes. *Topics in Early Childhood Special Education, 11*(3), 19-31.

Beder, J. (1998). The home visit, revisited. Families in society. *Journal of Contemporary Human Services, 79*, 514-522.

Behar, L. B. (1986). A state model for child mental health services: The North Carolina experience. *Children Today, 15,* 16-22.

Beitchman, J. H., Wilson, B., Brownlie, E. B., Walters, H., & Lancee, W. (1996). Long term consistency in speech/language profiles: I. Developmental and academic outcomes. *Journal of American Academy of Child and Adolescent Psychiatry, 35,* 804-814.

Benard, B., & Educational Resources Information Center (U.S.). (1991). *Fostering resiliency in kids: Protective factors in the family, school, and community*. Portland, OR: Western Center for Drug-Free Schools and Communities, Far West Laboratory.

Bernard, J. M., & Goodyear, R. K. (2004). *Fundamentals of clinical supervision* (3rd ed.) Boston: Allyn & Bacon.

Bertacchi, J. (1996). Relationship-based organizations. *Zero to Three, 17*(2), 1, 3-7.

Bertalanffy, L. von (1968). *General system theory.* New York: Braziller.

Betancourt, J. R., Green, A. R., Carrillo, J. E., & Ananeh-Firempong, O. (2003). Defining cultural competence: A practical framework for addressing racial/ethnic disparities in health and health care. *Public Health Reports, 118*, 293-302.

Bhavnagri, N. P., & Krolikowski, S. (2000). Home-community visits during an era of reform (1870-1920). *Early Childhood Research and Practice, 2*(1), 1-39. Retrieved May 26, 2009, from http://ecrp.uiuc.edu/v2n1/bhavnagri.html

Booth, P. B., & Jernberg, A. M. (1999). *Theraplay: Helping parents and children build better relationships through attachment based play* (2nd ed.). San Francisco, CA: Jossey-Bass.

Brauner, C. B., & Stephens, B. C. (2006). Estimating the prevalence of early childhood serious emotional/behavioral disorders: Challenges and recommendations. *Public Health Reports, 121*, 303-310.

Brazelton, T. B., & Greenspan, S. I. (2000). *The irreducible needs of children: What every child must have to grow, learn, and flourish*. Cambridge, MA: Perseus Publishing.

Brenner, V., & Fox, R. A. (1998). Parental discipline and behavior problems in young children. *Journal of Genetic Psychology, 159*, 251-256.

Bronfenbrenner, U. (1979). *The ecology of human development: Experiments by nature and design*. Cambridge, MA: Harvard University Press.

Bronfenbrenner, U. (1995). Developmental ecology through space and time: A future perspective. In P. Moen, G. H. Elder, Jr., & K. Luscher (Eds.), *Examining lives in context: Perspectives on the ecology of human development.* (pp. 619-647). Washington, DC: American Psychological Association.

Brookman-Frazee, L., Haine, R. A., Gabayan, E. N., & Garland, A. F. (2008). Predicting frequency of treatment visits in community-based youth psychotherapy. *Psychological Services, 5*, 126-138.

Brooks, R. B. (1994). Children at risk: Fostering resilience and hope. *American Journal of Orthopsychiatry, 64*, 545-553.

Brown, C., Tollefson, N., Dunn, W., Cromwell, R., & Filion, D. (2001). The adult sensory profile: Measuring patterns of sensory processing. *American Journal of Occupational Therapy, 55*, 75-82.

Bruder, M. B. (1996). Interdisciplinary collaboration in service delivery. In R. A. McWilliam (Ed.), *Rethinking pull-out services in early intervention* (pp. 27-48). Baltimore: Paul H. Brookes Publishing.

Bruno, F. J. (1957). *Trends in social work practice: 1874-1956.* New York: Columbia University Press.

Bruns, E. J., Burchard, J. D., Suter, J. C., Leverentz-Brady, K., & Force, M. M. (2004). Assessing fidelity to a community-based treatment for youth: The Wraparound Fidelity Index. *Journal of Emotional and Behavioral Disorders, 12*, 79-89.

Bruns, E. J., Walker, J. S., & National Wraparound Intitiative Advisory Group. (2008). Ten principles of the wraparound process. In E. J. Bruns & J. S. Walker (Eds.), *The resource guide to wraparound.* Portland, OR: National Wraparound Initiative, Research and Training Center for Family Support and Children's Mental Health, Portland State University.

Bruns, E. J., Walker, J. S., Adams, J., Miles, P., Osher, T. W., Rast, J., et al. (2004). *Ten principles of the wraparound process.* Portland, OR: National Wraparound Initiative, Research and Training Center for Family Support and Children's Mental Health, Portland State University.

Burchard, J. D., Bruns, E. J., & Burchard, S. N. (2002). The wraparound approach. In B. Burns & K. Hoagwood (Eds.), *Community treatment for youth: Evidence-based interventions for severe emotional and behavioral disorders* (pp. 69-90). New York: Oxford University Press.

Burns, B. J., & Goldman, S. K. (Eds.). (1999). *Systems of care: Promising practices in children's mental health, 1998 series: Volume IV. Promising practices in wraparound for children with severe emotional disorders and their families.* Washington, DC: Center for Effective Collaboration and Practice, American Institutes for Research.

Caplan, E., Blankenship., K., & McManus, M. (1998). Family participation in policymaking. *Focal Point: A National Bulletin on Family Support & Children's Mental Health, 12*(1), 1-32.

Carrilio, T. E. (2007). *Home-visiting strategies: A case-management guide for caregivers.* Columbia: University of South Carolina Press.

Carrilio, T. E., Cohen, R. G., & Goldman, A. R. (1980). The team method of delivering services to the elderly: An interim report. *Journal of Jewish Communal Service 52*, 56-62.

Carter, A. S., Briggs-Gowan, M., & Davis, N. (2004). Assessment of young children's social-emotional development and psychopathology: Recent advances and recommendations for practice. *Journal of child Psychology and Psychiatry, 45,*109-134.

Carter, J. W., Enyedy, K. C., Goodyear, R. K., Arcinue, F., & Puri, N. N. (2009). Concept mapping of the events supervisees find helpful in group supervision. *Training and Education in Professional Psychology, 3*(1), 1-9.

Catalano, R. F., Loeber, R., & McKinney, K. C. (1999). School and community interventions to prevent serious and violent offending. *Juvenile Justice Bulletin.* Washington, DC: Office of Juvenile Justice & Delinquency Prevention.

Center for Mental Health in Schools at UCLA. (2008). *Conduct and behavior problems related to school age youth.* Los Angeles: Author.

Center for Substance Abuse Treatment (1999). *Screening and assessing adolescents for substance use disorders.* Treatment Improvement Protocol Series No. 31. Rockville, MD: Substance Abuse and Mental Health Services Administration.

Centers for Disease Control and Prevention. (2007). *Suicide trends among youths and young adults aged 10-24 Years—United States, 1990-2004.* Retrieved June 15, 2010, from http://www.cdc.gov/mmwr/preview/mmwrhtml/mm5635a2.htm

Chamberlain, P., & Patterson, G. R. (1995). Discipline and child compliance in parenting. In M. H. Bornstien (Ed.), *Handbook of parenting: Vol. 4. Applied and practical parenting* (pp. 205-225). Hillsdale, NJ: Lawrence Erlbaum Associates.

Cheney, D., & Osher, T. (1997). Collaborate with families. *Journal of Emotional & Behavioral Disorders, 5,* 36-40.

Cheon, J. W. (2008). Convergence of a strengths perspective and youth development: Toward youth promotion practice. *Advances in Social Work 9,* 176-190.

Child & Family Support Services. (2007). *Module 4: Assessing, coordinating, and monitoring support services through the CFT.* Retrieved September 20, 2009, from http://mmwia.com/download-confirmation/?k=d9f5a6522dba4e3b71beb550d0fbc959

Choi, J. (2000). Valuing the voice of our young people. *Focal Point: A National Bulletin on Family Support and Children's Mental Health, 14*(2), 9-10.

Clark, H. B., & Davis, M. (2000). *Transition to adulthood: A resource for assisting young people with emotional or behavioral difficulties.* Baltimore: Paul H. Brookes Publishing.

Clark, H. B., Deschenes, N., & Jones, J. (2000). A framework for the development and operation of a transition system. In Hewitt B. Clark & Maryann Davis (Eds.), *Transition to adulthood: A resource for assisting young people with emotional or behavioral difficulties* (pp.29-51). Baltimore: Paul H. Brookes Publishing.

Clausen, J., Landsverk, J., Ganger, W., Chadwick, D., & Litrownik, A. (1998). Mental health problems of children in foster care. *Journal of Child & Family Studies, 7,* 283-296.

Cohen, M. S., Jacobs, J. P., Quintessenza, J. A., Chai, P.J., Lindberg, H. L., Dickey, J., et al. (2007). Mentorship, learning curves and balance. *Cardiology in the Young, 17*(Suppl.2), 164-174.

Cohen, P., Cohen, J., Kasen, S., Velez, C., Hartmark, C., Johnson, J., et al. (1993). An epidemiological study of disorders in late childhod and adolescence-I. Age- and gender-specific prevalence. *Journal of Child Psychology and Psychiatry and Allied Disciplines, 34,* 851-867.

Collins, P. M. (1994). Does mentorship among social workers made a difference? An empirical investigation of career outcomes. *Social Work, 39,* 413-419.

Collins, W. A. (Ed.). (1984). *Development during middle childhood: The years from six to twelve.* Washington, DC: National Academy Press.

Constantine, N. A., & Benard, B. (2001). California healthy kids survey resilience assessment module: Technical report. Berkeley, CA: Public Health Institute.

Constantine, N. A., Benard, B., & Diaz, M. D. (1999, June). *A new survey instrument for measuring protective factors in youth: The healthy kids resilience assessment.* Paper presented at the Society for Prevention Research National Conference, New Orleans.

Cook, R., Fleishman, E., & Grimes, V. (1991). *A national evaluation of the title IV-E foster care independent living programs for youth: Phase 2.* (Final Report, Vol. 1.). Rockville, MD: Westat.

Copa, A., Lucinski, L., Olsen, E., & Wollenburg, K. (1999). Promoting professional and organizational development: A reflective practice model. *Zero to Three, 20,* 3-9.

Copeland, W. E., Shanahan, L. Costello, J., & Angold, A. (2009). Childhood and adolescent psychiatric disorders as predictors of young adult disorders. *Archives of General Psychiatry 66,* 764-772.

Cornett, S. (2009). *The impact of culture: Early childhood mental health continuing studies guidelines*. Retrieved January, 9, 2010, from http://www.iaitmh.org/cmhc/csg/5-ImpactCulture.pdf

Costello, E. J., Messer, S. C., Bird, H. R., Cohen, P., & Reinherz, H. (1998). The prevalence of serious emotional disturbance: A re-analysis of community studies. *Journal of Child & Family Studies, 7*, 411-432.

Cox, C. (1992). Expanding social work's role in home care: An ecological perspective. *Social Work 37*, 179-183.

Cox, K. F. (2006). Investigating the impact of strength-based assessment on youth with behavioral or emotional disorders. *Journal of Child and Family Studies, 15*, 287-301.

Crittenden, P. M., Lang, C., Claussen, A. H., & Partridge, M. F. (2000). Relations among mothers' dispositional representations of parenting. In P. M. Crittenden & A. H. Claussen (Eds.), *The organization of attachment relationships: Maturation, culture and context* (pp. 214-233). New York: Cambridge University Press.

Culp, R. E., Culp, A. M., Soulis, J., & Letts, D. (1989). Self-esteem and depression in abusive, neglecting, and non-maltreating mothers. *Infant Mental Health Journal, 10,* 243-251.

Dass-Brailsford, P. (2007). *A practical approach to trauma: Empowering interventions.* Thousand Oaks, CA: Sage Publications.

Davidson, L., O'Connell, M., Sells, D., & Staeheli, M. (2003). Is there an outside to mental illness? In L. Davidson, *Living outside mental illness: Qualitative studies of recovery in schizophrenia* (pp. 31-60). New York: New York University Press.

Davies, D. (2004). *Child development: A practitioner's guide* (2nd ed.). New York: Guilford Press.

Davies, J., & Wright, J. (2008). Children's voices: A review of the literature pertinent to looked-after children's views of mental health services. *Children and Adolescent Mental Health, 13*, 26-31.

Davis, M., & Sondheimer, D. (2005). Child mental health systems' efforts to support youth in transition to adulthood. *Journal of Behavioral Health Services and Research, 32,* 27-42.

Davis, M., & Vander Stoep, A. (1997). The transition to adulthood for youth who have serious emotional disturbance: Developmental transition and young adult outcomes. *Journal of Mental Health Administration, 24*, 400-427.

De Civita, M. (2006, Winter). Strength-based efforts for promoting recovery from psychological harm. *Reclaiming Children & Youth, 14*, 241-244.

DeBellis, M. (2001). Developmental traumatology: The psychobiological development of maltreated children and its implications for research, treatment, and policy. *Development and Psychopathology, 13*, 539-564.

Deegan, P. (1996). Recovery as a journey of the heart. *Psychosocial Rehabilitation Journal, 19*, 91-97.

Delaney, K. (2010). The Peer Specialist Movement: An interview with Gayle Bluebird, RN. *Issues in Mental Health Nursing, 31*, 232-234.

Deschênes, N., Clark, H. B., Herrygers, J., Blasé, K., & Wagner, R. (2009). *Strength discovery and needs assessment: A process for working with transition-age youth and young adults.* Tampa, FL: National Network on Youth Transition for Behavioral Health.

Dino, G. A., Barnett, M. A., Howard, J. A. (1984). Children's expectations of sex differences in parent' responses to sons and daughters encountering interpersonal problems. *Sex Roles, 11,* 709-717.

Donahue, M. P. (1985). *Nursing, the finest art: An illustrated history.* St. Louis, MO: CV Mosby.

Doxsee, D. J., & Kivlighan, D. M. (1994). Hindering events in interpersonal relations groups for counselor trainees. *Journal of Counseling & Development, 72*, 621-626.

Dreyer, B. (1976). The mental hygiene movement: Institutional response to individual concern. The early years of the Philadelphia Child Guidance Clinic. *American Journal of Public Health, 66*, 85-91.

Driver, B. L. (1992). The benefits of leisure. *Parks and Recreation 27*(11), 16-23, 25, 76.

Duchnowski, A. J., & Kutash, K. (2007). *Family-driven care.* Tampa: University of South Florida, The Louis de la Parte Florida Mental Health Institute, Department of Child and Family Studies.

Dunst, C. J. & Trivette, C. M., & Deal, A. G. (1994). *Supporting & strengthening families: Methods, strategies and practices.* Cambridge, MA: Brookline Books.

Dunst, C. J., Trivette, C. M., LaPointe, N. (1994). Meaning and key characteristics of empowerment. In C. J. Dunst, C. M. Trivette, & A. Deal (Eds.), *Supporting and strengthening families: Methods, strategies and practices.* Cambridge, MA: Brookline Books.

Dunst, C., Trivette, C. M., Davis, M., & Cornwell, J. C. (1994). Characteristics of effective help-giving practices. In C. J. Dunst, C. M. Trivette, & A. C. Deal (Eds.), *Supporting and strengthening families: Methods, strategies and practices.* Cambridge, MA: Brookline Books.

Durlak, J. (1979). Comparative effectiveness of paraprofessional and professional helpers. *Psychological Bulletin, 86*, 80-92.

Earls, F. (1981). Temperament characteristics and behavior problems in three-year-old children. *Journal of Nervous and Mental Disease, 169*, 367-373.

Early, T. J., & GlenMaye, L. F. (2000). Valuing families: Social work practice with families from a strengths perspective. *Social Work, 45,* 118-130.

Early, T. J., & GlenMaye, L. F. (2000). Valuing families: Social work practice with families from a strengths perspective. *Social Work, 45*, 118-130.

Early, T. J., & Poertner, J. (1995). Examining current approaches to case management for families with children who have serious emotional disorders. In B. J. Friesen & J. Poertner (Eds.), *From case management to service coordination for children with emotional, behavioral, or mental disorders: Building on family strengths* (pp. 37-59). Baltimore: Paul H. Brookes Publishing.

Ebata, A., & Moos, R. (1994). Personal, situational, and contextual correlates of coping in adolescence. *Journal of Research on Adolescence, 4*, 99-125.

Eby, L. T. (1997). Alternative forms of mentoring in changing organizational environments: A conceptual extension of the mentoring literature. *Journal of Vocational Behavior, 51*, 125-144.

Egan, K. (1983). Stress management and child management with abusive parents. *Journal of Clinical Child Psychology, 12*, 292-299.

Embry, L. E., Vander Stoep, A., Evens, C., Ryan, K. D., & Pollack, A. (2000). Risk factors for homelessness in adolescents released from psychiatric residential treatment. *Journal of the American Academy of Child and Adolescent Psychiatry, 39*, 1293-1299.

Enns, R., Reddon, J., & McDonald, L. (1999). Indications of resilience among family members of people admitted to a psychiatric facility. *Psychiatric Rehabilitation Journal, 23*, 127-135.

Ensher, E. A., Thomas, C., & Murphy, S. E. (2001). Comparison of traditional, step-ahead, and peer mentoring on protégés' support, satisfaction, and perceptions of career success: A social exchange perspective. *Journal of Business and Psychology, 15,* 419-438.

Epstein, M. (1999). The development and validation of a scale to assess the emotional and behavioral strengths of children and adolescents. *Remedial & Special Education, 20*, 258-262.

Epstein, M. H., & Sharma, J. (1998). *Behavioral and Emotional Rating Scale: A strength-based approach to assessment.* Austin, TX: PRO-ED.

Epstein, M. H., Harniss, M. K., Robbins, V., Wheeler, L., Cyrulik, S., Kriz, M., et al. (2003). Strength-based approaches to assessment in school. In M. D.Weist, S. W. Evans, & N. A. Lever (Eds.), *Handbook of school mental health: Advancing practice and research* (pp. 285-300). New York: Kluwer Academic/Plenum Publishers.

Epstein, M. H., Harniss, M. K., Pearson, N., & Ryser, G. (1999). The Behavioral and Emotional Rating Scale: Test-retest and inter-rater reliability. *Journal of Child & Family Studies, 8*, 319-327.

Erel, O., & Kissil, K. (2003). The linkage between multiple perspectives of the marital relationship and preschoolers' adjustment. *Journal of Child & Family Studies, 12*, 411-423.

Erickson, M., & Egeland, B. (2002). Child Neglect. In J. Myers, L. Berliner, J. Briere, C. Hendrix, C. Jenny, & T. Reid (Eds.), *The APSAC handbook on child maltreatment* (2nd ed., pp.3-20). Thousand Oaks, CA: Sage Publications.

Evangelista, N., & McLellan, M. J. (2004). The Zero to Three diagnostic system: A framework for considering emotional and behavioral problems in young children. *School Psychology Review, 33*, 159-173.

Family resiliency: Building strengths to meet life's challenges. (n.d.). Retrieved June 8, 2009, from http://www.extension.iastate.edu/Publications/EDC53.pdf

Fergusson, D. M., & Woodward, L. J. (2002). Mental health, educational, and social role outcomes of adolescents with depression. *Archives of General Psychiatry 59*, 225-231.

Fink, A. (1942). *The field of social work.* New York: Henry Holt.

Fink, A. (1955). *The field of social work* (3rd ed.). New York: Henry Holt.

Fitzpatrick, M. A., & Vangelisti, A. L. (1995). *Explaining family interactions.* Thousand Oaks, CA: Sage Publications.

Fonagy, P., Gergely, G., Jurist, E., & Target, M. (2002). *Affect regulation, mentalization, and the development of the self.* New York: Other Press.

Foster, E. M., & Jones, D. E. (2005). The high costs of aggression: Public expenditures resulting from conduct disorder. *American Journal of Public Health, 95*, 1767-1772.

Fraser, M. W., Kirby, L. D., & Smokowski, P. R. (2004). Risk and resilience in childhood. In Mark W. Fraser (Ed.), *Risk and resilience in childhood: An ecological perspective.* Washington DC: NASW Press.

Freud, A., & Burlingham, D. (1944). *Infants without families.* New York: International Universities Press.

Friedman, R. M., Katash, K., & Duchnowski, A. J. (1996). The population of concern: Defining the issues. In B. A. Stroul (Ed.), Children's mental health: Creating systems of care in a changing society (pp. 69-96). Baltimore: Paul H. Brookes Publishing.

Friesen, B. J. (2005). The concept of recovery: "Value added" for the children's mental health field? *Focal Point Research, Policy, and Practice in Children's Mental Health, 19*(1), 5-8.

Garcia, M. M., Shaw, D. S., Winslow, E. B., & Yaggi, K. E. (2000). Destructive sibling conflict and the development of conduct problems in young boys. *Developmental Psychology, 36*, 44-53.

Gard, G. C., & Berry, K. K. (1986). Oppositional children: Taming tyrants. *Journal of Clinical Child Psychology, 15*, 148-158.

Gardner, H. (1983). *Frames of mind: The theory of multiple intelligences.* New York: Basic Books.

Garmezy, N. (1994). Reflections and commentary on risk, resilience, and development. In R. J. Haggerty, L. R. Sherrod, N. Garmezy, & M. Rutter (Eds.), *Stress, risk, and resilience, in children and adolescents: Processes, mechanisms, and interventions* (pp. 1-18). Cambridge, England: Cambridge University Press.

Geenen, S. J., & Powers, L. E. (2006) Transition planning for foster youth with disabilities: Are we falling short? *Journal for Vocational Special Needs Education, 28*(2), 4-15.

Geenen, S. J., Powers, L. E., Hogansen, J. M., & Pittman, J. O. E. (2007). Youth with disabilities in foster care: Developing self-determination within a context of struggle and disempowerment. *Exceptionality, 15*, 17-30.

Germain, C. B. (1973). An ecological perspective in casework practice. *Social Casework, 54*, 323-330.

Germain, C. B. (1979). Ecology and social work. In C. B. Germain (Ed.), *Social work practice: People and environments: An ecological perspective* (pp. 1-22). New York: Columbia University Press.

Giler, J. Z. (2000). *Socially ADDept: A manual for parents of children with ADHD or learning disabilities.* Santa Barbara, CA: CES Publications.

Gilkerson, L., & Ritzler, T. (2005). The role of reflective process in infusing relationship-based practice into an early intervention system. In K. Finello (Ed.), *The handbook of training and practice in infant, preschool mental health* (pp. 427-452). San Francisco: Josey-Bass.

Ginsburg, K. R., & Jablow, M. M. (2006). *A parent's guide to building resilience in children and teens: Giving your child roots and wings.* Elk Grove Village, IL: American Academy of Pediatrics.

Goldman, S. K. (1999). The conceptual framework for wraparound: Definition, values, essential elements, and requirements for practice. In B. J. Burns & S. K. Goldman (Eds.), *Systems of care: Promising practices in children's mental health, 1998 series, vol. IV. Practices in wraparound for children with severe emotional disorders and their families* (pp. 27-34). Washington, DC: Center for Effective Collaboration and Practice, American Institutes for Research.

Goldstein, H. (1973). *Social work practice: A unitary approach.* Columbia: University of South Carolina Press.

Gomby, D., Larson, C. S., Lewit, E. M., & Behrman, R. E. (1993). Home visiting: Analysis and recommendations. *Future of Children, 3*, 6-22.

Gottlieb, B. H. (1982). Mutual help groups: Members' views of the benefits and of roles for professionals. *Prevention in Human Services, 1*, 55-67.

Gowan, L. K., & Walker, J. S. (2009). Stigmatization. *Focal Point: Research, Policy, & Practice in Children's Mental Health, 23*(1), 3-6.

Grealish, M. (2000). *The wraparound process curriculum.* McMurray, PA: Community Partners.

Greeff, A. P., Vansteenwegen, A., & Ide, M. (2006). Resiliency in families with a member with a psychological disorder. *American Journal of Family Therapy, 34*, 285-300.

Green, B., Johnson, S., & Rodgers, A. (1999). Understanding patterns of service delivery and participation in community-based family support programs. *Children's Services: Social Policy, Research & Practice, 2*, 1-22.

Greenbaum, P. E., Dedrick, R. F., Friedman, R., Kutash, K., Brown, E., Lardieri, S., et al. (1996). National adolescent and child treatment study (NACTS): Outcomes for individuals with serious emotional and behavioral disturbance. *Journal of Emotional and Behavioral Disorders, 4*, 130-146.

Greenberg, M. T., Cicchetti, D., & Cummings, E. M. (1990). *Attachment in the preschool years: theory, research and intervention.* Chicago: University of Chicago Press.

Greenspan, S. I., & Meisels, S. J. (1996). Toward a new vision for the dvelopmental asessment of infants and young children. In S. J. Meisels & E. Fenichel (Eds.), *New visions for the developmental assessment of infants and young children* (pp. 11-26). Washington DC: Zero to Three Press.

Grizenko, N., & Pawliuk, N. (1994). Risk and protective factors for disruptive behavior disorders in children. *American Journal of Orthopsychiatry, 64*, 534-544.

Gudykunst, W. B., Lee, C. M., Nishida, T., & Ogawa, N. (2004). Theorizing about intercultural communication: An introduction. In W. B. Gudykunst (Ed.), *Theorizing about intercultural communication* (pp. 3-33). Thousand Oaks, CA: Sage Publications.

Guerney, L. F., & Gavigan, M. A. (1981). Parental acceptance and foster parents. *Journal of Clinical Child Psychology, 10*, 27-32.

Haber, R. (1996). *Dimensions of psychotherapy supervision: Maps and means.* New York: Norton.

Hagan, J. F., Shaw, J. S. & Duncan, P. M. (2008) *Bright futures: Guidelines for health supervision of infants, children, and adolescents* (3rd ed.). Elk Grove, IL: American Academy of Pediatricians.

Hair, E. C., Moore, K. A., Hadley, A. M., Kaye, K., Day, R. D., & Orthner, D. K. (2009). Parental marital quality and the parent-adolescent relationship: Effects on adolescent and young adult health outcomes. *Marriage and Family Review, 45*, 189-217.

Hancock, B. L., & Pelton, L. H. (1989). Home visits: History and functions. *Social Casework, 70*, 21-27.

Harrell, A. V., and Wirtz, P. W. (1989). Screening for adolescent problem drinking: Validation of a multidimensional instrument for case identification. *Psychological Assessment: A Journal of Consulting and Clinical Psychology, 1*, 61–63.

Hattie, J. A., Sharpley, C. F., & Rogers, H. J. (1984). Comparative effectiveness of professional and paraprofessional helpers. *Psychological Bulletin, 95*, 534-541.

Haynes, D. T., & White, B. W. (1999). Will the "real" social work please stand up? A call to stand for professional unity. *Social Work, 44*, 385-391.

Heffron, M. (2005). Reflective supervision in infant, toddler, and preschool work. In K. Finello (Ed.), *The handbook of training and practice in infant, preschool mental health* (pp. 114-136). San Francisco: Josey-Bass.

Hegvik, R. L., McDevitt, S. C., & Carey, W. B. (1982). Middle childhood temperament questionnaire. *Developmental and Behavioral Pediatrics, 3*, 197-200.

Herman, J. L. (1992). *Trauma and Recovery.* New York: Basic Books.

Herrington, R., Mitchell, A., Castellani, A., Joseph, J., Snyder, D., & Gleaves, D. (2008). Assessing disharmony and disaffection in intimate relationships: Revision of the Marital Satisfaction Inventory factor scales. *Psychological Assessment, 20*, 341-350.

Hiatt, S., Sampson, D., & Baird, D. (1997). Paraprofessional home visitation: Conceptual and pragmatic considerations. *Journal of Community Psychology, 25*, 77-93.

Hill, R. (1958). Generic features of families under stress. *Social Casework, 49*, 139-150.

Hoagwood, K., Burns, B., Kiser, L., Ringeisen, H., & Schoenwald, S. K. (2001). Evidence-based practices in child and adolescent mental health services. *Psychiatric Services, 52*, 1179-1189.

Hoegl, M., & Gemuenden, H. (2001). Teamwork quality and the success of innovative projects: A theoretical concept and empirical evidence. *Organization Science, 12*, 435-449.

Hoese, J. (1987). An exploratory investigation of group supervision: Trainees, supervisors and structure. *Dissertation Abstracts International, 48*, 2285.

Hollis C. (2000). Adolescent schizophrenia. *Advanced Psychiatric Treatment, 6*, 83-92.

Horowitz, L. J., & Rost, C. (2007). Helping hyperactive kids: A sensory integration approach. Alameda, CA: Hunter House Publishers.

Houchens, C. (2008). *A children's guidebook to intensive youth services.* Unpublished manuscript.

Houck, G. M. (1999). The measurement of child characteristics from infancy to toddlerhood: Temperament, developmental competence, self-concept, and social competence. *Issues in Comprehensive Pediatric Nursing, 22,* 101-127.

Houck, G. M., & LeCuyer-Maus, E. A. (2002). Maternal limit-setting patterns and toddler development of self-concept and social competence. *Issues in Comprehensive Pediatric Nursing, 25,* 21-41.

Hudson, R. (2009). *Suffering in silence: Human rights abuses in St. Louis correctional centers.* Retrieved September 17, 2009, from http://www.acluem.org/downloads/ACLUSufferingSummary.pdf

Hughes, D. (1997). *Facilitating developmental attachment: The road to emotional recovery and behavioral change in foster and adoptive children.* Northvale, NJ: Jason Aronson.

Imran, S., & Clark, A. (2008). Adolescent psychosis: A practical guide to assessment and management. *Psychiatric Times, 25*(11). Retrieved February 7, 2010, from http://www.psychiatrictimes.com/bipolar-disorder/content/article/10168/1336526?pageNumber=3

Irwin, J. R., Carter, A. S., & Briggs-Gowan, M. J. (2002). The social-emotional development of "late-talking" toddlers. *Journal of American Academy of Child and Adolescent Psychiatry, 41,* 1324-1332.

Israel, G. D., Beaulieu, L. J., & Hartless, G. (2001). The influence of family and community social capital on educational achievement. *Rural Sociology, 66,* 43-68.

Jacobson, N., & Greenley, D. (2001). What is recovery? A conceptual model and explication. *Psychiatric Services, 52,* 482-485.

Jahoda, M. (1982). *Employment and unemployment: A social psychological analysis.* Cambridge, England: Cambridge University Press.

Janus, M., & Goldberg, S. (1995). Sibling empathy and behavioral adjustment of children with chronic illness. *Child: Care, Health and Development, 21,* 321-331.

Jellinek, M., Patel, B. P., & Froehle, M. C. (2002). *Bright futures in practice: Practice guide, mental health* (Vol. 1). Arlington, VA: National Center for Education in Maternal and Child Health.

Jenkins, S., Bax, M., & Hart, H. (1980). Behavior problems in preschool children. *Journal of Child Psychology and Psychiatry, 21,* 5-17.

Johnson, C., Brown, P., & Edgar, G. (2000). *Transition guide for Washington State.* Seattle, WA: Center for Change in Transition Services, University of Washington. Retrieved March 20, 2010, from http://www.seattleu.edu/ccts/Default.aspx?id=34096

Johnson, M. K., & Freidman, R. M. (1991). Strength-based assessment. *Program Update, 7,* 10-11.

Johnston, L. D., O'Mallery, P. M., & Bachman, J. G. (2001). *The monitoring the future national results on adolescent drug use: Overview of key findings, 2000.* Bethesda, MD: National Institute on Drug Abuse.

Kagan, J., Snidman, N., Arcus, D., & Reznick, J. S. (1994). *Galen's prophecy: Temperament in human nature.* New York: Basic Books.

Kalmanson, B., Pekarsky, J. H. (1987). Infant-parent psychotherapy with an autistic toddler. *Zero to Three, 7*(3), 1-6.

Keck, G., & Kupecky, R. (1995). *Adopting the hurt child: Hope for families with special needs kids.* Colorado Springs, CO: Piñon Press.

Kemp, S., Whittaker, J, & Tracy, E. (1997). Person-environment practice: The social ecology of interpersonal helping. New York: Aldine De Gruyter.

Kernan, J., & Morilus-Black, M. (2008). Social supports for youth and families. In C. Newman, C. Lieberton, K. Kutash, & R. M. Friedman (Eds.), *The 20th annual research conference proceedings: A system of care for children's mental health: expanding the research base* (pp. 275-276). Tampa: University of South Florida, Louis de la Parte Florida Mental Health Institute, Research and Training Center for Children's Mental Health.

Kilmer, R., Cook, J., Taylor, C., Kane, S., & Clark, L. (2008). Siblings of children with severe emotional disturbances: Risks, resources, and adaptation. *American Journal of Orthopsychiatry, 78*(1), 1-10.

King, N. J., & Sharpley, C. F. (1990). Headache activity in children and adolescents. *Journal of Paediatrics and Child Health 26*: 50-54.

Kinnealey, M., Oliver, B., Wilbarger, P. (1995). A phenomenological study of sensory defensiveness in adults. *American Journal of Occupational Therapy, 49,* 444-451.

Klass, C. S. (2008). *The home visitor's guidebook: Promoting optimal parent and child development* (3rd ed.). Baltimore: Paul H. Brookes Publishing.

Knitzer, J. (1982). *Unclaimed children: The failure of public responsibility to children and adolescents in need of mental health services*. Washington, DC: Children's Defense Fund.

Kolvin, I., Nicol, A. R., Garside, R. F., Day, K. A., & Tweedle, E. G. (1982). Temperamental patterns in aggressive boys. In R. Porter & G. M. Collins (Eds.), *Temperamental difficulties in infants and young children* (pp. 252-268). London: Pitman.

Kopp, C. B. (1982). Antecedents of self-regulation: A developmental perspective. *Developmental Psychology, 18,* 199-214.

Koppelman, J., George Washington University, & National Health Policy Forum. (2004). *Children with mental disorders: Making sense of their needs and the systems that help them.* Washington, DC: National Health Policy Forum.

Koren, P. E., DeChillo, N., & Friesen, B. J. (1992). Measuring empowerment in families whose children have emotional disabilities: A brief questionnaire. *Rehabilitation Psychology, 37,* 305-321.

Kram, K. E. (1983). Phases of the mentoring relationship. *Academy of Management Journal, 28,* 608-625.

Kram, K. E. (1985). *Mentoring at work: Developmental relationships in organizational life.* Glenview, IL: Scott, Foresman.

Kram, K. E., & Isabella, L. A. (1985). Mentoring alternatives: The role of peer relationships in career development. *Academy of Management Journal, 28,* 110-132.

Kranowitz, C. S. (1998). *The out-of-sync child : Recognizing and coping with sensory integration dysfunction*. New York: Perigee.

Kristal, J. (2005). *The temperament perspective: Working with children's behavioral styles.* Baltimore: Paul H. Brookes Publishing.

Landy, S. (2002). *Pathways to competence: Encouraging healthy social and emotional development in young children*. Baltimore: Paul H. Brookes Publishing.

Landy, S., & Menna, R. (2006). *Early Intervention with multi-risk families: An integrative approach,* Baltimore: Paul H. Brookes Publishing.

Langenbucher, J., & Martin, C. S. (1996). Alcohol abuse: Adding context to category. *Alcohol Clinical and Experimental Research, 20*(Suppl.), 270a–275a.

Lau, A., & Takeuchi, D. (2001). Cultural factors in help-seeking for child behavior problems: Value orientation, affective responding, and severity appraisals among Chinese-American parents. *Journal of Community Psychology, 29,* 675-692.

Laursen, E. K. (2000). Strength-based practice with children in trouble. *Reclaiming Children and Youth: Journal of Strength-Based Interventions, 9,* 70-75.

Laursen, E. K. (2004). Creating a change-oriented, strength-based milieu. *Reclaiming Children and Youth, 13,* 16-21.

Lavigne, J. V., Gibbons, R. D., Christoffel, K. K., Arend, R., Rosenbaum, D., Binns, H., et al. (1996). Prevalence rates and correlates of psychiatric disorders among preschool children. *Journal of American Academy of Child and Adolescent Psychiatry, 35*, 204-214.

Lavigne, J. V., LeBailly, S. A., Hopkins, J., Gouze, K. R., & Binns, H. J. (2009). The prevalence of ADHD, ODD, depression, and anxiety in a community sample of 4-year-olds. *Journal of Clinical Child and Adolescent Psychology, 38*, 315-328.

Lebowitz, L., Harvey,M. R., & Herman, J. L. (1993). A stage-by-dimension model of recovery from sexual trauma. *Journal of Interpersonal Violence, 8*, 378-391.

Lee, J. A. B. (1996). The empowerment approach to social work practice. In F. J. Turner (Ed.), *Social work treatment: Interlocking theoretical approaches* (4th ed., pp. 218-249). New York: Free Press.

Lempers, J. D., & Clark-Lempers, D. S. (1997). Economic hardship, family relationships and adolescent distress: An evaluation of a stress-distress mediation model in mother-daughter and mother-son dyads. *Adolescence, 32*(126), 339-357.

Levy, T., & Orlans, M. (1998). *Attachment, trauma, and healing: Understanding and treating attachment disorder in children and families.* Washington, DC: Child Welfare League of America Press.

Li, F., Li, Y., & Wang, E. (2009). Task characteristics and team performance: The mediating effect of team member satisfaction. *Social Behavior and Personality, 37*, 1373-1382.

Lindblad-Goldberg, M., Dore, M. M., & Stern, L. (1998). *Creating competence from chaos: A comprehensive guide to home-based services.* New York: W. W. Norton.

Linetsky, M. (2000). Youth development: Putting theory into practice. *Focal Point: A National Bulletin on Family Support and Children's Mental Health, 14*(2), 11-14.

Loney, B., Frick, P., Clements, C., Ellis, M., & Kerlin, K. (2003). Callous-unemotional traits, impulsivity, and emotional processing in adolescents with antisocial behavior problems. *Journal of Clinical Child & Adolescent Psychology, 32*, 66.

Lourie, I. S., Katz-Levy, J., DeCarolis, G. & Quilan, W. A. (1996). The Role of federal government. In B. Stroul (Ed.), *Children's mental health: Creating systems of care in a changing society* (pp. 99-114). Baltimore: Paul H. Brookes Publishing.

Lyons, J. S. (2004). *Redressing the emperor: Improving our children's public mental health service system.* Westport, CT: Praeger.

Lyons, J. S., Cornett, S., & Walton, B. (2009). *Child and adolescent needs and strengths: Comprehensive multisystem assessment (birth to 5).* Winnetka, IL: Praed Foundation.

Lyons, J. S., & Bell, S. (2003). Young adults' needs and strengths assessment: An information tool for young adults with mental health challenges. Winnetka, IL: Praed Foundation.

Lyons, J. S., Ryan (Cornett), S., & Duran, F. (2007). *Child and adolescent needs and strengths, (early childhood): An information integration tool for young children ages birth to eight.* Winnetka, IL: Buddin Praed Foundation.

MacDonald, H., & Callery, P. (2004). Different meanings of respite: a study of parents, nurses and social practitioners caring for children with complex needs. *Child: Care, Health and Development, 30*, 279-288.

MacPhee, D., Fritz, J., & Miller-Hey, J. (1996). Ethnic variations in personal social networks and parenting. *Child Development, 67*, 3278-3295.

Mahler, M. S., Pine, F., & Bergman, A. (1975). *The psychological birth of the human infant.* New York: Basic Books.

Malysiak, R. (1997). Exploring the theory and paradigm base for wraparound. *Journal of Child & Family Studies, 6*, 399-408.

Manicavasagar, V. (2008). *Psychological resilience.* Retrieved March 1, 2010, from http://ezinearticles.com/?Psychological-Resilience&id=1688230

Manteuffel, B., Stephens, R. L., Sondheimer, D. L., & Fisher, S. K. (2008). Characteristics, service experiences, and outcomes of transition-aged youth in systems of care: Programmatic and policy implications. *Journal of Behavioral Health Services & Research, 35*, 469-487.

Martin, C. S., Kaczynski, N. A., Maisto, S. A., Bukstein, O. M., & Moss, H. B. (1995). Patterns of DSM–IV alcohol abuse and dependence symptoms in adolescent drinkers. *Journal of Studies on Alcohol, 56*, 672–680.

Martino, S., Grilo, C. M., & Fehon, D. C. (2000). Development of the Drug Abuse Screening Test for Adolescents (DAST–A). *Addict Behavior, 25*, 57–70.

Mashinot, B. (2008). *The changing face of the United States: The influence of culture on child development*. Washington, DC: Zero to Three.

Maslow, A. H. (1943). A theory of human motivation. *Psychological Review, 50*, 370-396.

Masten, A. S., & Coatsworth, J. D. (1998). The development of competence in favorable and unfavorable environments: Lessons from research on successful children. *American Psychologist, 53*, 205-220.

Matarese, M., McGinnis, L., & Mora, M. (2005). *Youth involvement in systems of care: A guide to empowerment*. Washington, DC: Technical Assistance Partnerships Publications.

Mathiesen, K. S., & Sanson, A. (2000). Dimensions of early childhood behavior problems: Stability and predictors of change from 18-30 months. *Journal of Abnormal Child Psychology, 28*, 15-31.

Mattaini, M. A. (1999). *Clinical intervention with families*. Washington, DC: NASW Press.

Matthews, W., & Johnson, C. (1997). Strengthening diverse and dysfunctional families via family resiliency education. Presentation at the annual meeting of the American Association of Family and Consumer Sciences, Washington, DC.

McClowry, S. G. (1995). The influence of temperament on development during middle childhood. *Journal of Pediatric Nursing, 10*, 160-165.

McCubbin, H. I., & McCubbin, M. A. (1988). Typologies of resilient families: emerging roles of social class and ethnicity. *Family Relations, 37*, 247-254.

McCubbin, H. I., McCubbin, M. A., & Thompson, A. I. (1993). Resiliency in families: The role of family schema and appraisal in family adaptation to crisis. In T. H. Brubaker (Ed.), *Family relations: Challenges for the future* (pp. 153-177). Beverly Hills, CA: Sage.

McCubbin, M. A., & McCubbin, H. I. (1993). Family coping with health crises: The resiliency model of family stress, adjustment, and adaptation. In C. Danielson, B. Hamel-Bissell, & P. Winstead-Fry (Eds.), *Families, health, and illness* (pp. 21-64). New York: Mosby.

McDonald, T. (2005). Building an effective team. *Health Care Registration: The Newsletter for Health Care Registration Professionals, 15*(2), 3-4.

McEvoy, A., & Welker, R. (2000). Antisocial behavior, academic failure, and school climate: A critical review. *Journal of Emotional and Behavioral Disorders, 8*, 130-140.

McKay, M. (2009). *Messages: The communication skills book*. Oakland, CA: New Harbinger Publications.

McMillan, D. (1996). Sense of community. *Journal of Community Psychology, 24*, 315-325.

Meehan, B., Hughes, J., & Cavell, T. (2003). Teacher-student relationships as compensatory resources for aggressive children. *Child Development, 74*, 1145-1157.

Meisels, S. J., & Provence, S. (1989). *Screening and assessment: Guidelines for identifying young disabled and developmentally vulnerable children and their families*. (A Report of the National Early Childhood Technical Assistance System). Washington, DC: Zero to Three/ National Center for Clinical Infant Programs.

Mendenhall, J. (1990). *Family-centered assessment: Six central elements*. Eagan, MN: Project Dakota Outreach.

Meyer, D. J., & Vadasy, P. F. (2007). *Sibshops: Workshops for siblings of children with special needs* (Rev. ed.). Baltimore: Paul H. Brookes Publishing.

Meyers, J., Kaufman, M., & Goldman, S. (1999). Promising practices: Training strategies for serving children with serious emotional disturbance and their families in a system of care. *Systems of care: Promising practices in children's mental health, 1998 series* (vol. 5). Washington, DC. Center for Effective Collaboration and Practice, American Institute for Research.

Michigan Association of Infant Mental Health. (2005). *Guidelines for comprehensive assessment of infants and their parents in the child welfare system* (2nd ed.). Ann Arbor, MI: Author.

Miles, P. (2009). *Crisis and safety planning: Building the right balance.* Presentation made at The Child Welfare Issues Conference held in East Lansing, Michigan.

Miles, P., Bruns, E. J., Osher, T. W., Walker, J. S., & National Wraparound Initiative Advisory Group. (2006). *The wraparound process user's guide: A handbook for families.* Portland, OR: National Wraparound Initiative, Research and Training Center on Family Support and Children's Mental Health, Portland State University.

Minuchin, P. (1985). Families and individual development. Provocation from the field of family therapy. *Child Development, 56,* 289-302.

Morgan, E., & Huebner, A. (2008). *Adolescent growth and development* (Publication No. 350-850). Retrieved June 24, 2010, from http://www.nvc.vt.edu/mft/Family_and_Child_Development_—_Adolescent_Growth_and_Development.mht

Morrison, J., & Anders, T. F. (1999). *Interviewing children and adolescents: Skills and strategies for effective DSM-IV diagnosis.* New York: Guilford Press.

Mosier, J., Burlingame, G. M., Wells, M. G., Ferre, R., Latkowski, M., Johansen, J., et al. (2001). In-home, family-centered psychiatric treatment for high-risk children and youth. *Children's Services: Social Policy, Research, and Practice, 4,* 51-68.

Moss-Torres, C., & Lazear, K. J. (2004). *Successmakers: The story of a natural helper team— An EQUIPO approach to supporting and strengthening families in our communities.* Tampa, FL: University of South Florida, Louis de la Parte Florida Mental Health Institute.

Murdach, A. D. (2007). Situational approaches to direct practice: Origin, decline and re-emergence. *Social Work, 52,* 211-218.

National Center for Injury Prevention and Control, Division of Violence Prevention (2008). *Suicide prevention: Youth suicide.* Retrieved January 23, 2010, from http://www.cdc.gov/ncipc/dvp/suicide/youthsuicide.htm

National Child Traumatic Stress Network. (2001). *Understanding child traumatic stress.* Retrieved November 9, 2009, from http://www.nctsn.org

National Traumatic Stress Network. (n.d.). *Trauma in the lives of gang-involved youth: Tips for volunteers and community organizations.* Retrieved February 9, 2010, fromhttp://www.nctsnet.org/nctsn_assets/pdfs/trauma_and_gang_involved_youth.pdf

Naughton, M., Oppenheim, A., & Hill, J. (1996). Assessment of personality functioning in the transition from adolescent to adult life: Preliminary findings. *British Journal of Psychiatry, 168,* 33-37.

Nelson, J. R., Roberts, M., & Smith, D. J. (1998). *Conducting functional behavioral assessments.* Longmont, CO: Sopris West Educational Services.

Newman, J. (1994). Conflict and friendship in sibling relationships: A review. *Child Study Journal, 24,* 119-152.

Newschaffer, C. J., Croen, L. A., Daniels, J., Giarelli, E., Grether, J. K., Levy, S. E., et al. (2007). The epidemiology of autistic spectrum disorders. *Annual Review of Public Health, 28,* 235-258.

Nixon, C. L., & Cummings, E. M. (1999). Sibling disability and children's reactivity to conflicts involving family members. *Journal of Family Psychology, 13*, 274-285.

Oates, J., & Grayson, A. (2004). *Cognitive and language development.* Malden, MA: Blackwell.

Olsen, D. H., Russell, C. S., & Sprenkle, D. H. (Eds.). (1989). Circumplex model: Systematic assessment and treatment of families. New York: Haworth Press.

Olsen, R., & Maslin-Prothero, P. (2001). Dilemmas in the provision of own-home respite support for parents of young children with complex health care needs: evidence from an evaluation. *Journal of Advanced Nursing, 34*, 603-610.

Olson, P. P., & Hains, A. H. (1992). Birth to three time line. In S. Robbins (Ed.), *Toward parent and professional partnership: Guidelines for Wisconsin's individualized family service plan* (p. 7). Madison, WI: Division of Community Services.

Osher, T. W., Osher, D., & Blau, G. (2006). *Shifting gears to family-driven care: Ambassadors tool kit.* Rockville, MD: Federation of Families for Children's Mental Health.

Osher, T., Penn, M., & Spencer, S. A. (2008.) Partnerships with families for family-driven systems of care. In B. A. Stroul & G. Blau (Eds.), *The system of care handbook: Transforming mental health services for children, youth and families* (pp. 249-273). Baltimore: Paul H. Brookes Publishing.

Ostler, T. (2008). *Assessment of parenting competency in mothers with mental illness.* Baltimore: Paul H. Brookes Publishing.

Parker, G., Wilheim, K., Mitchell, P., Austin, M. P., Roussos, J., & Gladstone, G. (1999) The influence of anxiety as a risk to early onset major depression. *Journal of Affective Disorders, 52*, 11–17.

Parlakian, R. (2001). *Look, listen, and learn: Reflective supervision and relationship-based work.* Washington, DC: Zero to Three.

Parlakian, R., & Seibel, N. L. (2001). *Being in charge: Reflective leadership in infant/family programs.* Washington, DC: Zero to Three.

Patchell, F., & Hand, L. (1993). An invisible disability: Language disorders in high school and the implications for classroom teachers. *Independent Education,* December, 31-36.

Patrick, K., Spear, B., Holt, K., & Sofka, D. (Eds.). (2001). *Bright futures in practice: Physical activity.* Arlington, VA: National Center for Education in Maternal and Child Health.

Paxson, C., & Waldfogel, J. (2002). Work, welfare, and child maltreatment. *Journal of Labor Economics 3,* 435-440.

Pecora, P. J., Reed-Ashcraft, K., & Kirk, R. S. (2001). Family-centered services: A typology, brief history, and overview of current program implementation and evaluation challenges. In E. Walton, P. Sandau-Beckler, & M. Mannes (Eds.), *Balancing family-centered services Child well-being: Exploring issues in policy, practice, theory, and research* (pp. 1-33). New York: Columbia University Press.

Pecora, P. J., Jensen, P. S., Romanelli, L. H., Jackson, L. J., & Ortiz, A. (2009). Mental health services for children placed in foster care: An overview of current challenges. *Child Welfare, 88*, 5-26.

Pennsylvania Child Welfare Training Program, University of Pittsburgh: School of Social Work Online Curricula. (2009). *Effects of abuse and neglect on child development: Handout #4.* Retrieved June 7, 2010, from http://www.pacwcbt.pitt.edu/Curriculum/ Core%20103/Handouts/HO%204%20Effects%20of%20Abuse%20and%20Neglect%20 on%20Development.pdf

Penrod, T. (2008). Direct support services in wraparound. In E. J. Bruns & J. S. Walker (Eds.), *The resource guide to wraparound.* Portland, OR: National Wraparound Initiative, Research and Training Center for Family Support and Children's Mental Health.

Perkins, D. D., & Zimmerman, M. A. (1995). Empowerment theory, research, and application. *American Journal of Community Psychology, 23*, 569-579.

Perry, B. D. (1996). *Violence and childhood trauma: Understanding and responding to the effects of violence on young children.* Cleveland, OH: Gund Foundation.

Perry, B. D. (2001). Violence and childhood: How persisting fear can alter the child's developing brain. In D. Schetky & E. Benedek (Eds.), *Textbook of child and adolescent forensic psychiatry* (pp. 221-238). Washington, DC: American Psychiatric Press.

Peterson, B., West, J., Tanielian T., & Pincus, H. (1998). Mental health practitioners and trainees. In R. W. Manderscheid & M. J. Henderson (Eds.), *Mental health: United States 1998* (pp. 214-246). Rockville, MD: Center for Mental Health Services.

Peterson, J. & Hawley, D. R. (1998). Effects of stressors on parenting attitudes and family functioning in a primary prevention program. *Family Relations, 47*, 221-227.

Pires, S. A. (2002). *Building systems of care: A primer.* Washington DC: National Technical Assistance Center for Children's Mental Health.

Porterfield, S. L. (2002). Work choices of mothers in families with disabilities. *Journal of Marriage and Family, 64,* 972-981.

Powers, E. T. (2001). New estimates of the impact of child disability on maternal employment. *American Economic Review, 91*, 135-139.

Powers, E. T. (2003). Children's health and maternal work activity: Estimates under alternative disability definitions. *Journal of Human Resources, 38*, 522-556.

Premack, B. A., Swanier, B., Georgiopoulos, A. M., Land, S. R., & Fine, M. J. (2009). Association between media use in adolescence and depression in young adulthood: A longitudinal study. *Archives of General Psychiatry, 66*, 181-188.

President's New Freedom Commission on Mental Health. (2003). *Achieving the promise: Tranforming mental health care in America. Final report* (DHHS Publication No. SMA-03-3832). Rockville, MD: Author.

President's New Freedom Commission on Mental Health. (2003). *Achieving the promise: Tranforming mental health care in America. Executive summary* (DHHS Publication No. SMA-03-3831). Rockville, MD: Author.

Prieto, L. R. (1996). Group supervision: Still widely practiced but poorly understood. *Counselor Education and Supervision, 35,* 295-307.

Pumariega, A. J. (2003). Cultural competence in a systems of care for children's mental health. In A. J. Pumariega & N. C. Winters (Eds.), *The handbook of child and adolescent systems of care: The new community psychiatry* (pp. 82-107). New York: Jossey-Bass.

Ranson, K., & Urichuk, L. (2008). The effect of parent-child attachment relationships on child biopsychosocial outcomes: A review. *Early Child Development & Care, 178*, 129-152.

Rapp, C. A. & Goscha, R. J. (2006). *The strengths model: Case management with people with psychiatric disabilities* (2nd ed.). New York: Oxford University Press.

Ravets, P. (1993). Group supervision: A multiple case study. *Dissertation Abstracts International, 54,* 2768.

Reed, V. (1986). Language disordered adolescents. In V. Reed (Ed.), *An introduction to children with language disorders.* New York: Macmillan.

Rhodes, J. E., Grossman, J. B., & Resch, N. L. (2000). Agents of change: Pathways through which mentoring relationships influence adolescents' academic adjustment. *Child Development, 71*, 1662-1671.

Rice, C. (2009). Prevalence of autism spectrum disorders—Autism and Developmental Disabilities Monitoring Network, United States, 2006. *MMWR Surveillance Summaries, 58*(SS-10), 1-24.

Richman, J. M., Bowen, G. L., & Woolley, M. E. (2004). School failure: An eco-international developmental perspective. In Mark W. Fraser (Ed.), *Risk and resilience in childhood: An ecological perspective* (2nd ed.) (pp. 133-160). Washington, DC: NASW Press.

Richmond, M. (1922). *What is social casework? An introductory description.* New York: Russell Sage Foundation.

Richmond, M. E. (1899). *Friendly visiting among the poor: A handbook for charity workers.* New York: Macmillan.

Ridgway, P. (2001). Re-storying psychiatric disability: Learning from first person narrative accounts of recovery. *Psychiatric Rehabilitation Journal, 24,* 335-343.

Roberts, A. R. (Ed.). (1995). *Crisis intervention and time-limited cognitive treatment.* Thousand Oaks, CA: Sage.

Roberts, R. N., Wasik, B. H., Casto, G., & Ramey, C. T. (1991). Family support in the home: Programs, policy, and social change. *American Psychologist, 46,* 131-137.

Rosenzweig, J. M., & Huffstutter, K. J. (2004). Disclosure and reciprocity: On the job strategies for taking care of business . . . and family. *Focal Point: A National Bulletin on Family Support and Children's Mental Health, 18*(1), 4-7.

Rosenzweig, J. M., Brennan, E. M., & Malasch, A. M. (2009). Breaking the silence: Parents' experiences of courtesy stigmatization in the workplace. *Focal Point: Research, Policy, & Practice in Children's Mental Health, 23*(1), 29-31.

Rosin, P., Jesien, G. S., Whitehead, A. D., & Begun, A. L. (1996). *Partnerships in family-centered care: A guide to collaborative early intervention.* Baltimore: Paul H. Brookes Publishing.

Rotto, K., McIntyre, J. S., & Serkin, C. (2008). Strengths-based, individualized services in systems of care. In B. Stroul & G. Blau (Eds.), *The system of care handbook: Transforming mental health services for children, youth and families* (pp. 401-435). Baltimore: Paul H. Brookes Publishing.

Rotto, K., McIntyre, J. S., & Serkin, C. (2008). Strenth-based, individualized services in systems of care. In B. A. Stroul & G. Blau (Eds.), *The system of care handbook: Transforming mental health services for children, youth and families* (pp. 401-435). Baltimore: Paul H. Brookes Publishing.

Saleebey, D. (1992). *The strengths perspective in social work practice* (2nd ed.). New York: Longman.

Saleebey, D. (1996). The strengths perspective in social work practice: Extensions and cautions. *Social Work 41,* 296-305.

Sandau-Beckler, P. (2001). Family-centered assessment and goal setting. In E. Walton, P. Sandau-Beckler, & M. Mannes (Eds.), *Balancing family-centered services and child well-being: Exploring issues in policy, practice, theory, and research* (pp. 93-127). New York: Columbia University Press.

Sanders, M. (2008). Triple P-Positive Parenting Program as a public health approach to strengthening parenting. *Journal of Family Psychology, 22,* 506-517.

Santrock, J. W. (1993). *Children* (3rd ed.) . Dubuque, IA: Wm. C. Brown Communications.

Sargent, J. R., Sahler, O. J., Roghmann, K. J., Mulhern, R. K., Barbarian, O. A., Carpenter, P. J., et al. (1995). Sibling adaptation to childhood cancer collaborative study: Siblings' perceptions of the cancer experience. *Journal of Pediatric Psychology, 20,* 151-164.

Scales, P. C., & Leffert, N. (1999). *Developmental assets.* Minneapolis, MN: Search Institute.

Scheeringa, M., & Gaensbauer, T. (2000). Posttraumatic stress disorder. In C. H. Zeanah (Ed.), *Handbook of infant mental health* (2nd ed.) (pp. 369-381). New York: Guilford Press.

Schore, A. N. (2001). Effects of a secure attachment relationship on right brain development, affect regulation, and infant mental health. *Infant Mental Health Journal, 22,* 7-66.

Seifter, H. & Economy, P. (2001). *Leadership ensemble: Lessons in collaborative leadership from the world's only conductorless orchestra.* New York: Times Books, Henry Holt.

Shapiro, D., & Koocher, G. (1996). Goals and practical considerations in outpatient medical crisis. *Professional Psychology: Research and Practice, 122,* 109-120.

Sharlin, S. A., & Shamai, M. (1995). Intervention with families in extreme distress (FED). *Marriage and Family Review, 21,* 92-122.

Sharlin, S. A., & Shamai, M. (2000). *Therapeutic intervention with poor, unorganized familes: From distress to hope.* New York: Haworth Clinical Practice Press.

Sharlin, S. A., & Shamai, M. (2000). *Therapeutic intervention with poor, unorganized familes: From distress to hope.* New York: Haworth Clinical Practice Press.

Shonkoff, J. P., Phillips, D., & Board on Children, Youth, and Families (États-Unis), Committee on Integrating the Science of Early Childhood Development (Eds.). (2000). *From neurons to neighborhoods: The science of early childhood development.* Washington, DC: National Academy Press.

Slade, A. (2002). Keeping the baby in mind: A critical factor in perinatal mental health. *Zero to Three, 22,* 10-16.

Slade, A., Grienenberger, J., Bernbach, E., Levy, D., & Locker, A. (2005). Maternal reflective functioning and attachment: Considering the transmission gap. *Attachment & Human Development, 7,* 283-298.

Smith, D. J., & Blackwood, D. H. R. (2004). Depression in young adults. *Advances in Psychiatric Treatment, 10*(Part 1), 4-12.

Smokowski, P. R., Rose, R., & Bacallao, M. L. (2008). Acculturation and Latino family processes: How cultural involvement, biculturalism, and acculturation gaps influence family dynamics. *Family Relations, 57,* 295-308.

Spector, B. (2007). *Implementing organizational change: Theory & practice.* Upper Saddle River, NJ: Prentice Hall.

Staples, L. H. (1990). Powerful idea about empowerment. *Administration in Social Work, 14,* 29-42.

Stoep, A. V., Davis, M., & Collins, D. (2000). Transition: A time of developmental and institutional clashes. In H. B. Clark & M. Davis (Eds.), *Transition to adulthood: A resource for assisting young people with emotional or behavioral difficulties* (pp. 3-28). Baltimore: Paul H. Brookes Publishing.

Stormshak, E., Bellanti, C., & Bierman, K. (1996). The quality of sibling relationships and the development of social competence and behavioral control in aggressive children. *Developmental Psychology, 32,* 79-89.

Stroul, B. A. (1988). *Home-based services. Volume I. Series on community-based services for children and adolescents who are severely emotionally disturbed.* Washington, DC: Georgetown University Child Development Center.

Stroul, B. A., & Friedman, R. M. (1986). A system of care for children and youth with severe emotional disturbances. (Rev. ed.). Washington, DC: Georgetown University Child Development Center, CASSP Technical Assistance Center.

Substance Abuse and Mental Health Service Administration, 58 Fed. Reg. 29,422 (May 20, 1993).

Summers, C. R., White, K. R., & Summers, M. (1994). Siblings of children with a disability: A review and analysis of the empirical literature. *Journal of Social Behavior and Personality, 9,* 169-184.

Synder, D. K. (1997). *Marital Satisfaction Inventory-Revised (MSI-R) manual.* Los Angeles: Western Psychological Services.

Taylor, E. (1998). Advances in the diagnosis and treatment of children with serious mental illness. *Child Welfare, 77*, 311-332.

Teplin, L. A., Abram, K. M., McClelland, G. M., Dulcan, M. K., & Mericle, A. A. (2002). Psychiatric disorders in youth in juvenile detention. *Archives of General Psychiatry, 59*, 1113-1143.

Thomas, A., & Chess, S. (1977). *Temperament and development.* New York: Brunner/Mazel.

Thomas, A., Chess, S., & Birch, H. (1968). *Temperament and behavior disorders in children.* New York: New York University Press.

Thomlison, B. (2004). Child maltreatment: A risk and protective factor perspective. In Mark. W. Fraser (Ed.), *Risk and resilience in childhood: An ecological perspective* (2nd ed., pp. 89-131). Washington, DC: NASW Press.

Torrey, E., Bowler, A. E., Taylor, E. H., & Gottesman, I. I. (1994). *Schizophrenia and manic depressive disorder: The biological roots of mental illness as revealed by the landmark study of identical twins.* New York: Basic Books.

Tracy, E. M. (2001). Interventions: Hard and soft services. In E. Walton, P. Sandau-Beckler, & M. Mannes (Eds.), *Balancing family-centered services and child well-being: Exploring issues in policy, practice, theory, and research* (pp. 155-178). New York: Columbia University Press.

Trautman, S. (1999). *Technical peer mentoring handbook: The art of sharing what you know with the person working next to you.* Seattle, WA: Solution Strategies.

U.S. Bureau of the Census. (2000). *Census data reports and profiles.* Retrieved June 3, 2010, from http://www.census.gov/main/www/cen2000.html

U.S. Census Bureau. (2001, May). *Profiles of general demographic characteristics: 2000 census of population and housing.* Retrieved February 1, 2009, from http://www.census.gov/prod/cen2000/dp1/2kh00.pdf

U.S. Department of Health and Human Services, Substance Abuse and Mental Health Services Administration, Center for Mental Health Services. (2006). *EvalBrief: Systems of care: Transition-age youth receiving services in systems of care, 7*(6), 1-4.

U.S. Department of Health and Human Services, Substance Abuse and Mental Health Services Administration, Center for Mental Health Services. (2007). *EvalBrief: Systems of care: Characteristics of children in systems of care who have experienced trauma, 8*(7), 1-4.

U.S. Department of Health and Human Services. (1999). *Mental health: A report of the surgeon general.* Rockville, MD: U.S. Department of Health and Human Services, Substance Abuse and Mental Health Services Administration, Center for Mental Health Services, National Institute of Health, National Institute of Mental Health.

U.S. General Accounting Office (2003). *Child welfare and juvenile justice: Federal agencies could play a stronger role in helping states reduce the number of children placed solely to obtain mental health services.* Retrieved November 9, 2009, from http://www.gao.gov/new .items/d03397.pdf

Vandenberg, J. E., & Rast, J. (2004). *Wraparound coaching and supervision toolkit.* Englewood, CO: Vroon Vandenberg.

Vandenberg, J., Bruns, E. J., & Burchard, J. (2008). History of the wraparound process. In E. J. Bruns & J. S. Walker (Eds.), *The resource guide to wraparound.* Portland, OR: National Wraparound Initiative, Research and Training Center for Family Support and Children's Mental Health, Portland State University.

Vandenberg, J., Bruns, E., & Burchard, J. (2003). History of the wrap-around process. *Focal point: A National Bulletin on Family Support and Children's Mental Health: Quality and Fidelity in Wraparound, 17*(2), 4-7.

Vandenberg, J. (2003). The professional child and family team process facilitator: The basics of the child and family team practice model. Retrieved July 16, 2009, from http://www.azdhs .gov/bhs/contracts/gaz/rfd/tm/cf/pdf/cftday1.pdf

Viñas, F., Canals, J., Gras, E., Ros, C., & Domènich-Llaberia, E. (2002). Psychological and family factors associated with suicidal ideation in pre-adolescents. *Spanish Journal of Psychology, 5,* 20-28.

Wadsworth, B. J. (2003). *Piaget's theory of cognitive and affective development: Foundations of constructivism* (5th ed.). Upper Saddle River, NJ: Allyn & Bacon.

Wagner, M., Kutash, K., Duchnowski, A. J., Epstein, M. H., & Sumi, W. C. (2005). The children and youth we serve: A national picture of the characteristics of students with emotional disturbances receiving special education. *Journal of Emotional and Behavioral Disorders, 55,* 79-96.

Walker, J. S. (2008). *How and why does wraparound work: A theory of change.* Portland, OR: National Wraparound Initiative, Portland State University.

Walker, J. S. (2008). Workforce: Staffing the transformation of children's mental healthcare systems. *Focal Point: A National Bulletin on Family Support and Children's Mental Health, 22*(1), 3-4.

Walker, J. S., & Child, B. (2008). *Involving youth in planning for their education, treatment, and services: Research tells us we should be doing better.* Portland, OR: Research and Training Center on Family Support and Children's Mental Health, Portland State University.

Walker, J. S., & Sage, M. (2006). Strengthening social support: Research implications for interventions in children's mental health. *Focal Point: A National Bulletin on Family Support and Children's Mental Health, 20*(1), 3-9.

Walker, J. S., Bruns, E. J., & National Wraparound Initiative Advisory Group. (2008). Phases and activities of the wraparound process. In E. J. Bruns and J. S. Walker (Eds.), *The resource guide to wraparound.* Portland, OR: National Wraparound Initiative, Research and Training Center for Family Support and Children's Mental Health.

Walker, J. S., Bruns, E. J., & Penn, M. (2008). Individualized services in systems of care: The wraparound process. In. B. A. Stroul & G. Blau (Eds.), *The system of care handbook: Transforming mental health services for children, youth and families* (pp. 127-153). Baltimore: Paul H. Brookes Publishing.

Walker, J. S., Bruns, E. J., Vandenberg, J. D., Rast, J., Osher, T. W., Miles, P., et al. (2004). *Phases and activities of the wraparound process.* Portland, OR: National Wraparound Initiative, Research and Training Center on Family Support and Children's Mental Health, Portland State University.

Walker, J. S., & Schutte, K. (2004). Practice and process in wraparound teamwork. *Journal of Emotional & Behavioral Disorders, 12,* 182-192.

Walker, J. S., & Schutte, K. (2005). Quality and individualization in wraparound team planning. *Journal of Child & Family Studies, 14,* 251-267.

Walsh, F. (1998). *Strengthening family resilience.* New York: Guilford.

Ward, M. J., Lee, S. S., & Lipper, E. G. (2000). Failure-to-thrive is associated with disorganized infant-mother attachment and unresolved maternal attachment. *Infant Mental Health Journal, 21,* 428-442.

Ward, R. K. (2004). Assessment and management of personality disorders. *American Family Physician, 70,* 1505-1512.

Wasik, B. H., & Bryant, D. M. (2001). *Home visiting: Procedures for helping families* (2nd ed.). Newbury Park, CA: Sage.

Wasik, B. H., & Roberts, R. N. (1994). Home visitor characteristics, training, and supervision: Results of a national survey. *Family Relations, 43,* 336-341.

Weick, A., Rapp, C., Sullivan, W. P., & Kisthardt, W. (1989). A strengths perspective for social work practice. *Social Work, 34,* 350-354.

Weiner, J. M. (1997). Oppositional defiant disorder. In J. M. Weiner (Ed.), *Textbook of child and adolescent psychiatry* (2nd ed., pp. 459-463). Washington, DC: American Psychiatric Press.

Weiss, H. B. (1993). Home visits: Necessary but not sufficient. *Future of Children, 3*, 113-128.

Wells, K. (1995). Family preservation services in context: Origins, practices, and current issues. In I. M. Schwartz & P. AuClaire (Eds.), *Home-Based services for troubled children.* (pp. 1-28). Lincoln: University of Nebraska Press.

Werner, E. E. (1990). Protective factors and individual resilience. In S. J. Meisels & J. P. Shonkoff (Eds.), *Handbook of early childhood intervention* (pp. 97-116). New York: Cambridge University Press.

Werner, E. E. (1993). Risk, resilience, and recovery: Perspectives from the Kauai longitudinal study. *Development and Psychopathology, 5*, 503-515.

Werner, E. E. (2000). Protective factors and individual resilience. In J. P. Shonkoff & S. J. Meisels (Eds.), *Handbook of early intervention* (2nd ed.) (pp. 115-132). New York: Cambridge University Press.

Werner, E. E., & Smith, R. S. (1989). *Vulnerable but invincible: A longitudinal study of resilient children and youth.* New York: Adams, Bannister, Cox.

Werner, E. E., & Smith, R. S. (1992). *Overcoming the odds: High risk children from birth to adulthood.* Ithaca, NY: Cornell University Press.

Werner, E. E., & Smith, R. S. (2001). *Journeys from childhood to midlife: Risk, resilience, and recovery.* Ithaca, NY: Cornell University Press.

Werner, E. E., Randolph, S. M., & Masten, A. S. (1996). *Fostering resiliency in kids: Overcoming adversity.* Proceedings of the Consortium of Social Sciences Associations, Washington, DC.

Wieder, B. & Boyle, P. (2007). Staff selection as a core component of evidence based practices implementation: Findings from Ohio's study of integrated dual disorders treatment (IDDT) program development. In C. Newman, C. Liberton, K. Kutash, & R. M. Friedman (Eds.), *The 19th annual research conference proceedings: A system of care for children's mental health: Expanding the research base* (pp. 71-74). Tampa: University of South Florida, Louis de la Parte Florida Mental Health Institute, Research and Training Center for Children's Mental Health.

Wise, J. B. (2005). *Empowerment practice with families in distress.* New York: Columbia University Press.

Wolin, S. J., & Wolin, S. (1993). *The resilient self: How survivors of troubled families rise above adversity.* New York: Villard Books.

Wolraich, M., Felice, M. E., & Drotar, D. (1996). *The classification of child and adolescent mental diagnoses in primary care: Diagnostic and statistical manual for primary care (DSM-PC) child and adolescent version.* Elk Grove Village, IL: American Academy of Pediatrics.

Yoe, J. T., Santarcangelo, S., Atkins, M., & Burchard, J. D. (1996). Wraparound care in Vermont: Program development, implementation, and evaluation of a statewide system of individualized services. *Journal of Child and Family Studies, 5*, 23-39.

Young, A. M., & Perrewe, P. L. (2004). The role of expectations in the mentoring exchange: An analysis of mentor and protégé expectations in relation to perceived support. *Journal of Managerial Issues, 16*, 103-126.

Zeanah, C. H., Mammen, O. K., & Lieberman, A. F. (1993). Disorders of attachment. In C. H. Zeanah (Ed.), *Handbook of infant mental health* (pp. 332-349). New York: Guilford.

Zembar, M. J., & Blume, L. B. (2009). *Middle childhood development: A contextual approach.* Upper Saddle River, NJ: Prentice Hall.

Zero to Three (1994). *Diagnostic classification of mental health and developmental disorders in infancy and early childhood*. Washington, DC: Author.

Zero to Three. (2005). *Diagnostic classification of mental health and developmental disorders of infancy and early childhood* (Rev. ed.). Washington, DC: Author.

Index

[References are to pages.]

A

Abuse and neglect, on youth, 8-4, 8-5

Academic functioning, 10-18–10-19

Activity level, 9-28

ADADFA. *See* Adolescent to Adult Personality Functioning Assessment (ADADFA)

Addams, Jane, 1-4, 1-5–1-6

ADHD. *See* Attention deficit hyperactivity disorder (ADHD)

Adjustment disorders, 2-8, 2-24

Administrative supervision, 5-6

Adolescent Drinking Index, 11-10

Adolescent to Adult Personality Functioning Assessment (ADADFA), 11-10

Adolescents
  with mental health issues, 2-14
  tasks of, 11-5

Adoption Assistance and Child Welfare Act of 1980 (Public Law No. 96-272), 1-7

Adult Sensory Profile, 11-5

Adults, interaction with, 13-14

Aggression/anger control issues, 9-21–9-22, 10-13, 11-4

Alcohol, Drug Abuse, and Mental Health Administration Reorganization Act (ADAMHA Reorganization Act; Public Law No. 102-321), 1992, 2-2

Alcohol/drug use. *See* Substance use/abuse

American Social Science Association, 1-3

Anger, 13-14
  control issues, 10-13
  management, 13-5

Anxiety, 2-3, 9-17–9-18, 13-14
  clinical manifestations of, 9-18
  of infancy and early childhood, 2-8, 2-9, 2-23

Approach/withdrawal, 9-28

Assessment
  components of
    assessing caregiver strengths and needs, 7-18
    assessing individual strengths and needs, 7-18
    determining family strengths and needs, 7-18
  engaging youth and family, 7-16
  function of, 1-23
  goals of
    comprehensive and individualized plan, committing to, 7-5

crisis stabilization, planning for, 7-2–7-3
    developing perspective of youth and family, 7-2
    practitioner questions to assisting family in identifying CFT members, 7-5
    youth and family team formation and functions, 7-3–7-5
  guiding principles of
    comprehensive nature of assessment, appreciating, 7-10
    culture impacts, appreciating, 7-9–7-10
    family-driven assessment, achieving, 7-6–7-8
    strength-based assessment, building, 7-12–7-14
    as tool for change, using assessment, 7-14–7-15
    youth-guided assessment, supporting, 7-8–7-9
  ongoing nature of, 1-23–1-24, 1-25
  orienting youth and family for, 7-15–7-16
    sample information, 7-17
  principles and components, 7-2–7-18, 7-22–7-30
  service delivery and, 1-23–1-24

Attachment relationship, 9-20–9-21
  signs in young children, 9-21

Attendance, relating to school functioning, 10-19–10-20

Attention, 9-23–9-24

Attention deficit hyperactivity disorder (ADHD), 2-3, 2-4, 2-13, 9-22

Atypical behaviors/autism spectrum disorders, 10-9–10-10

Authoritative caregiving, 8-14

Autism spectrum disorders, 10-9–10-10

B

Basic needs of youth, caregiver assessment and, 8-4–8-7

Behavioral and Emotional Rating Scale (BERS), 7-14

Behavioral concerns. *See also specific behaviors*
  within home environment, 10-21
  interventions with, 15-7–15-10
  within school environment, 10-11–10-13, 10-20–10-21

I-1